T0327018

THE
OLD TESTAMENT
AS LITERATURE

APPROACHING THE OLD TESTAMENT

◆ ◆ ◆

The Old Testament as Literature

THE

OLD TESTAMENT

AS LITERATURE

Foundations for Christian Interpretation

TREMPER LONGMAN III

Baker Academic
a division of Baker Publishing Group
Grand Rapids, Michigan

© 2024 by Tremper Longman III

Published by Baker Academic
a division of Baker Publishing Group
Grand Rapids, Michigan
BakerAcademic.com

Printed in the United States of America

Library of Congress Cataloging-in-Publication Data
Title: The Old Testament as literature : foundations for Christian interpretation / Tremper
    Longman, III.
Description: Grand Rapids, Michigan : Baker Academic, a division of Baker Publishing Group,
    [2024] | Series: Approaching the Old Testament | Includes bibliographical references and index.
Identifiers: LCCN 2023038259 | ISBN 9781540961310 (cloth) | ISBN 9781493444373 (ebook) | ISBN
    9781493444380 (pdf)
Subjects: LCSH: Bible as literature. | Bible. Old Testament—Criticism, interpretation, etc. | Bible.
    Old Testament—Language, style.
Classification: LCC BS535 .L585 2024 | DDC 220.6/6—dc23/eng/20231017
LC record available at https://lccn.loc.gov/2023038259

Baker Publishing Group publications use paper produced from sustainable forestry practices and postconsumer waste whenever possible.

24 25 26 27 28 29 30   7 6 5 4 3 2 1

To our two new grandchildren

Theodore James Longman (February 18, 2022)
Adelyn Jane Longman (June 14, 2022)

CONTENTS

Preface   ix

Abbreviations   xi

Introduction: Scope and Procedure   1

PART ONE: LITERARY THEORY AND THE CONVENTIONS OF BIBLICAL NARRATIVE AND POETRY   5

1. The Location of Meaning   7
2. History of the Study of the Old Testament as Literature   19
3. Genre Triggers Reading Strategy   47
4. Narrative Prose as Genre   61
5. Poetry as Genre   107
6. Intertextuality   157

PART TWO: THE ANALYSIS OF ILLUSTRATIVE PROSE-NARRATIVE TEXTS   177

7. Literary Readings of Prose Narratives from the Torah   179
   Genesis 3 • Genesis 6–9 • Genesis 22 • Exodus 1
8. Literary Readings of Prose Narratives from the Historical Books   199
   1 Samuel 17 • Nehemiah 13

PART THREE: THE ANALYSIS OF ILLUSTRATIVE POETIC TEXTS   209

9. Literary Readings of Poetic Texts from the Psalms   211
   Psalm 46 • Psalm 77 • Psalm 67 • Psalm 23

10. Literary Readings of Poetic Texts from Wisdom Literature   231
    Proverbs 9:1–6, 13–18 • Proverbs 14:1–7 • Ecclesiastes 9:11–12 • Job 38:2–7

11. Literary Readings of Poetic Texts from the Prophets and Epic Poetry   253
    Nahum 1:2–8 • Judges 5:19–27

Postlude: The Old Testament as Literature   265

Bibliography   267

Scripture Index   281

Author Index   287

Subject Index   291

PREFACE

I want to start by thanking Baker Academic and in particular Jim Kinney for inviting me to write a three-volume series of books titled Approaching the Old Testament. This book is the first contribution to the series and focuses on the literary quality of the Old Testament. I have already begun work on the second volume, about the Old Testament and history, and have started thinking about the third, on the theology of the Old Testament.

I have had the privilege of studying the Old Testament professionally for over forty years, having started teaching in 1980 and completing my doctorate in 1983. I have taught and written about the literary, historical, and theological dimensions of the Old Testament during this time, and this series affords me the opportunity to offer my best thinking at the twilight of my career. Jim assures me that he is not thinking of this as my end-of-life project. Indeed, some of my colleagues in the field are still making wonderful contributions in their eighties and nineties (I am 70 at the time of writing). Nonetheless, I approach this project with the awareness that these books may be my last opportunity to pass along my thinking on these three different but interlocking perspectives on the study of the Old Testament.

I thank Jim, who has been an encouragement to me throughout my career, for reading through the manuscript and offering suggestions. I also want to thank John Goldingay, a brilliant Old Testament scholar in his own right, for also giving me editorial guidance. Of course, especially since I did not always follow their advice, they bear no responsibility for any remaining errors or missteps in the book. In addition, I deeply appreciate the work of Wells Turner (senior editor) and his team for improving the manuscript and guiding the final steps of its production.

I have enjoyed returning to the topic of a literary approach to the Old Testament. My very first book was *Literary Approaches to Biblical Interpretation*. I have always been mindful of the importance of interpreting the Bible in light of the narrative and poetic conventions that Hebrew storytellers and poets used in their writing. Writing the present book has given me the opportunity to revisit the topic in a deeper way than I have since the 1980s and also to reconnect with the wider discipline of literary studies outside biblical scholarship. As I explain in more detail later in the book, literary study is quite different today from what it was in the 1980s. Back then, the recurrent mantra was that the author was dead, which signaled the belief that interpreters should give up talking about authorial intention in any sense. Today such skepticism is seen as an overreaction. I found it refreshing to discover that literary theory now spends less time seeking to question the possibility of textual meaning and more time providing the necessary terminology and tools to actually interpret the text.

My wife, Alice, and I celebrated our fiftieth wedding anniversary in June 2023. We have been blessed with three wonderful sons (Tremper IV, Timothy, and Andrew) and now eight beautiful grandchildren. This book is dedicated to the two newest members of our immediate family, Theodore (Rory) and Adelyn (Addie). Rory is our first grandson, and Addie is our seventh granddaughter. Rory and Addie, we welcome you into the world and love you dearly.

ABBREVIATIONS

General and Bibliographic

AD	*anno Domini* (in the year of our Lord)
BC	before Christ
BHS	*Biblia Hebraica Stuttgartensia*. Edited by Karl Ellinger and Wilhelm Rudolph. Stuttgart: Deutsche Bibelgesellschaft, 1987.
ca.	*circa*, about
CEB	Common English Bible
cent.	century
chap(s).	chapter(s)
DH	Documentary Hypothesis
e.g.	*exempli gratia*, for example
esp.	especially
ESV	English Standard Version
et al.	*et alii*, and others
HALOT	*The Hebrew and Aramaic Lexicon of the Old Testament*. Ludwig Koehler, Walter Baumgartner, and Johann J. Stamm. Translated and edited under the supervision of Mervyn E. J. Richardson. 4 vols. Leiden: Brill, 1994–99.
HB	Hebrew Bible
Heb.	Hebrew (language)
i.e.	*id est*, that is
JB	Jerusalem Bible
KJV	King James Version
NASB	New American Standard Bible
NIV	New International Version
NIVUK	New International Version—UK (Anglicized NIV)
NKJV	New King James Version
NLT	New Living Translation
n.p.	no page
NRSVue	New Revised Standard Version Updated Edition
NT	New Testament

OT   Old Testament
PL   Patrologia Latina [= *Patrologiae Cursus Completus*. Series Latina]. Edited
          by Jacques-Paul Migne. 217 vols. Paris, 1844–55.
trans.   translation
v(v).   verse(s)

Old Testament / Hebrew Bible

Gen.	Genesis	Eccles.	Ecclesiastes
Exod.	Exodus	Song	Song of Songs
Lev.	Leviticus	Isa.	Isaiah
Num.	Numbers	Jer.	Jeremiah
Deut.	Deuteronomy	Lam.	Lamentations
Josh.	Joshua	Ezek.	Ezekiel
Judg.	Judges	Dan.	Daniel
Ruth	Ruth	Hosea	Hosea
1 Sam.	1 Samuel	Joel	Joel
2 Sam.	2 Samuel	Amos	Amos
1 Kings	1 Kings	Obad.	Obadiah
2 Kings	2 Kings	Jon.	Jonah
1 Chron.	1 Chronicles	Mic.	Micah
2 Chron.	2 Chronicles	Nah.	Nahum
Ezra	Ezra	Hab.	Habakkuk
Neh.	Nehemiah	Zeph.	Zephaniah
Esther	Esther	Hag.	Haggai
Job	Job	Zech.	Zechariah
Ps(s).	Psalm(s)	Mal.	Malachi
Prov.	Proverbs		

New Testament

Matt.	Matthew	1 Tim.	1 Timothy
Mark	Mark	2 Tim.	2 Timothy
Luke	Luke	Titus	Titus
John	John	Philem.	Philemon
Acts	Acts	Heb.	Hebrews
Rom.	Romans	James	James
1 Cor.	1 Corinthians	1 Pet.	1 Peter
2 Cor.	2 Corinthians	2 Pet.	2 Peter
Gal.	Galatians	1 John	1 John
Eph.	Ephesians	2 John	2 John
Phil.	Philippians	3 John	3 John
Col.	Colossians	Jude	Jude
1 Thess.	1 Thessalonians	Rev.	Revelation
2 Thess.	2 Thessalonians		

INTRODUCTION

Scope and Procedure

The Hebrew Bible (HB) / Old Testament (OT), as recognized by Protestant Christians, is a collection of thirty-nine books. These thirty-nine books were written over a long period of time, between the second half of the second millennium BC and approximately 300 BC. The books also represent a variety of different types of literature, including history, law, wisdom, prophecy, and apocalyptic.

Jews and Christians have recognized all these books, in spite of their diversity, as canonical, the standard of faith and practice. This recognition implies confidence, at some fundamental level, in these thirty-nine books. The present three-volume project (Approaching the Old Testament) is intended to explore the OT from three perspectives (literary, historical, and theological) in order to discern its message.

The OT was written by multiple contributors. Studying the composition history of the biblical books is interesting and important, especially the issue of authorship, as is evident in the following chapters. For the most part, the authors of the HB are anonymous. The OT itself names some individuals as writing books or portions of books: among them are Moses (Exod. 24:4; 34:27; Num. 33:2; Deut. 31:22), David (Ps. 51:1), Solomon (Prov. 1:1), Isaiah (Isa. 1:1), and Jeremiah (Jer. 1:1). Of course, much debate surrounds the reliability of these authorship claims. For now, it is enough to note that the OT records lots of different human voices, even many anonymous ones. Sometimes these human voices explicitly claim to be speaking the Word of God, and the church has received these books, along with the books of the New Testament (NT), with that understanding. These books have been the object of intense scholarly and devotional study not just because of their antiquity but because many Jews and Christians regard them as ultimately God's words to his human creatures. This claim is further explored in the third volume of this trilogy, which focuses on theology. Here in the present volume, I assume the validity of this claim and assert that the ultimate goal of interpretation is to hear not just the voices of the human authors but ultimately the voice of the divine author.

Although the literature, history, and theology of the OT will be examined in three separate volumes, these three features deeply intertwine with one another. What the books of the OT teach about God and his relationship with humanity (theology) includes God's acts in space and time (history), such as the exodus. Recognizing how the book of Exodus claims that the rescue from Egypt happened in history is a consequence of understanding the genre of the book (literature). The literary shape of the stories and poems as presented in the HB not only informs readers of whether the author intends them to be regarded as accounts of what happened in history but also communicates a theological message.

Put another way, the books feature God and his relationship with his people and therefore are theological. Their authors spoke out of and about concrete historical situations and to specific actual audiences and are therefore historical. Yet the focus of the present volume is neither theological nor historical but literary, for the books of the OT are appropriately the subject of literary analysis. Because the books of the OT are literature, it is appropriate to use literary tools to interpret them. As we will see, the authors of the OT were not only conscious of their message (what they said) but intentional about how they said it.

Despite the intertwining of these three aspects, I believe it is possible to focus on one aspect of the OT—here the literary aspect—and momentarily bracket out the other two. A literary approach to the OT books explores how their authors present their narratives and poems. Since the OT/HB is a collection of books produced over many centuries, most, if not all, of the books have histories of composition resulting in the final forms we know today. But the books of the OT are not all of one type or genre. On the broadest level, the books contain prose narrative and poetry, but many different types of narratives and poems are included.

In this book, I discuss both literary theory and literary practice. Theory asks how texts construct meaning. Literary practice analyzes the strategies that authors use to express their message to their audience. Part 1 (chaps. 1–6) discusses theory and develops a strategy for performing literary analysis (with examples from the biblical text). Parts 2 and 3 (chaps. 7–11) present the literary analysis of several representative texts from different genres.

In chapter 1, I turn to the question of literary theory to present my perspective on how texts generate meaning or, to put it differently, to ask where meaning is located in a literary text. The discussion revolves around the act of literary communication as an author writes a text to an audience.

Until the middle decades of the twentieth century, literary scholars believed that interpretation involves recovering the author's intended meaning. This goal often means reading a text in the light of what can be known of the author's biography as a way of getting into the writer's mind. With the rise of Russian Formalism and New Criticism, the locus of meaning shifted from author to text, marked most notably by W. K. Wimsatt and M. Beardsley's highly influential work in questioning authorial intention.[1] Classical structuralists in the 1960s and 1970s furthered the strategy of simply focusing on the text and not appealing to anything outside the text itself. Reader-response theories, including the ideological approaches derived from them, shifted once again, this time to the reader. Some reader-response approaches argue that the text constrains the reader's interpretation; others argue against this limitation. Deconstruction simply denies that there is any determinate meaning to be discovered in a text. Interestingly, prominent secular theorists today are returning to a modified recognition of the importance of the author's intention, but this intention can only be discovered from the text itself. I conclude the chapter by surveying the landscape of literary study of the OT today and describing my own approach to literary theory.

In chapter 2, I summarize the past relationship between biblical and literary studies. Although pre-Enlightenment interpreters appreciated the literary quality of the biblical text, the modern period abandoned a literary approach in favor of a strictly historical study. From around 1800 to the 1980s, scholars pursued questions of the prehistory of the final forms of the biblical texts and asked questions about referentiality, such as How did Israel come to occupy the land? The last two decades of the twentieth century saw a literary turn that many describe as a paradigm shift. This literary turn means that scholars have bracketed historical questions, excising them from the discussion.

The literary turn was not a simple or univocal one. As biblical scholars turned to secular literary theory, they discovered diverse ideas and approaches: Russian Formalism, New Criticism, structuralism, deconstruction, and interpretive methods such as reader-response, feminist, Marxist, queer, postcolonial, and New Historicist. Though triggered by the insightful analysis of a close reader like Robert Alter, the literary study of the OT soon devolved into battles over theory.

By the early twenty-first century, the field's intense focus on literary theory and even literary practice seemed to taper, and there was a move back to issues

---

1. Wimsatt and Beardsley, "Intentional Fallacy."

of history. In chapter 2, I take a closer look at the ups and downs of literary approaches to biblical interpretation, ask about the present state of the issues, and look into the future.

In chapter 3, I develop a theory of genre for the purpose of applying it to the interpretation of texts. Genre theory asks questions like the following: What is a genre? How do genres help authors construct meaning and make that meaning accessible to readers? How do individual texts relate to genre(s)? My most important conclusion is that authors send genre signals to their readers to convey how to take their words and thus trigger a reading strategy. While texts can participate in multiple genres, this does not mean that they participate in all genres. Misidentifying the genre can lead to misreading a text. In the process of describing genre, I contrast what I consider to be the proper approach with the extremely influential but misguided approach developed by Hermann Gunkel over a century ago.

In terms of the broad conception of genre, the HB contains two types: narrative prose and poetry. Chapter 4 treats biblical narrative, and chapter 5 examines biblical poetry. As Alter points out regarding narrative, "Every culture, even every era in a particular culture, develops distinctive and sometimes intricate codes for telling its stories."[2] The same holds true for poetry. In chapter 4, I explore the conventions of narrative, utilizing categories and insights from contemporary narratology. I look at how authors use narrators to present the story, how characters are presented, settings are described, time is manipulated, and events are selected. Being aware of Hebrew storytelling conventions yields a richer and more accurate interpretation of the text. In chapter 5, I look at the conventions employed by ancient Hebrew poets: parallelism, voice, figurative language, and more, which enables us to gain greater interpretive depth and clarity. The final chapter in part 1 examines the phenomenon of intertextuality as it is employed today in the study of the OT.

Of course, the proof of the pudding is in the eating. Thus, after gaining a strategy for literary analysis in part 1, I put that strategy into practice in parts 2 and 3. Although several representative examples of prose and poetic texts are considered in part 1, parts 2 and 3 offer a more robust and well-rounded presentation, with a focus on the literary quality of the texts. In chapters 7 and 8, a variety of prose texts from Genesis, Exodus, Samuel, and Nehemiah are examined. Chapters 9 through 11 focus on poetic texts from several different biblical books, including lyric poetry, didactic poetry, prophetic poetry, and epic poetry.

2. Alter, "How Convention Helps Us Read," 115.

PART ONE

...

LITERARY THEORY
and the CONVENTIONS
of BIBLICAL NARRATIVE
and POETRY

We begin by exploring literary theory, in particular probing the question of how texts generate meaning. Authors write texts for readers, but where is meaning to be found in the process? Some look to the text apart from the author, while others believe that readers create meaning. We will defend the view that the goal of interpretation is to discover, through analysis of the text, the meaning intended by the author, while remaining mindful that readers interpret through lenses that are shaped by their gender, ethnicity, social position, and more. Even so, by reading in community, our individual interpretation can be deepened, corrected, or affirmed. Chapters 1 and 2 examine these issues and provide a historical orientation to the various interpretive approaches used by those in biblical and literary circles.

Since readers encounter an author's meaning in and through the text, we must become better informed about the type of writing we are reading. Thus, genre becomes key to interpretation, aided by an awareness of the conventions of narrative and poetry. Genre is discussed in chapter 3, and in chapters 4 and 5 we look at the conventions of biblical narrative and poetry.

ONE

The Location of Meaning

The books of the OT are products of literary communication. In the act of literary communication, authors write texts to readers. The purpose of the various books of the Bible, like that of all acts of writing, is to communicate a message to an audience. In oral communication, speakers intend to convey a message to whomever they are speaking. This communicative intention is true even if one is communicating with oneself, as when giving an oral soliloquy or writing in a personal journal. The act of literary communication may be represented by a simple diagram:

Author → Text → Reader

Because an author writes a text to communicate a message to the reader, it seems reasonable to locate a literary text's meaning in the intention of the author. If this understanding is correct, then the goal of interpretation is to discover the intention of the author. The interpreter reverses the direction of communication by reading the text to hear the voice of the author.

Such an understanding of writing and reading also applies to biblical literature. The author writes the text to communicate to readers, and readers then read biblical texts to hear the voice of the author. Although I defend what I consider to be a nuanced authorial-intention approach to interpretation, complications arise at every stage of the process. It is therefore worthwhile to look at each aspect more closely.

Author → Text → Reader

The Text

The text of the OT that most readers interpret is typically what appears in an English translation of the Bible, whether modern (e.g., NIV, NLT, ESV, NRSVue, JB, NAB) or traditional (e.g., KJV, NKJV). These versions are primarily based on medieval Hebrew manuscripts, especially Codex Leningradensis, as presented in *Biblia Hebraica Stuttgartensia* (*BHS*), along with notes identifying significant variants.

One complication that arises when reading an OT book to discover the author's meaning is that the vast majority of OT books were not written by one person at one time. For instance, virtually no one thinks that Moses wrote every word of the Pentateuch. At a minimum, someone other than Moses had to write the account of his death (Deut. 34). This does not require one to accept the so-called Documentary Hypothesis, which claims that the present form of the Pentateuch is a fusion of four main sources over a period of hundreds of years, but everyone must acknowledge that more than one hand in more than one time period has produced the Pentateuch as we now know it.

So one decision readers must make concerns what text they will interpret. Should they use the tools of historical criticism to determine the "original text" and free it from later additions? My answer is no. The object of interpretation is not some speculative earlier form but rather the final form of the biblical book, the form recognized as canonical by the church.

The book of Job offers a convenient example of this issue. Several questions arise when examining the compositional history of the book of Job.[1] Is the version of Job found in modern English translations, based on Codex Leningradensis, the original form of this biblical book? Many scholars claim that certain sections were added later, after the book's initial composition, and different theories are put forward to explain this. One theory is that the prose story was the original tale, which was later expanded by the poetic disputation between Job and his three friends.[2] Then later the Elihu monologue was added, followed even later by the poem on wisdom in Job 28. There are variations on this basic theory, but the scholarly consensus is that the book of Job in its present form is the product of a lengthy history of composition.

While such historical reconstruction may be a true account of the book's composition, it remains speculative, and more important, it does not in the final analysis affect the interpretive goal. Readers should primarily be inter-

1. For a more detailed description of my approach here, see Longman, *Job*, 24–27.
2. Fisher, *Many Voices of Job*.

ested in the final, canonical form of the biblical book. Even if a passage such as Elihu's speech was added later, we must ask how it functions within the book as it is now.

So the focus of my study is the final form of the text, regardless of the process of composition. Although some interpreters may claim to be uncertain about what is the precise final form of the text, in my view the biblical text preserved in Codex Leningradensis is an adequate representation of the final form of the Hebrew Bible.

Author

If, with few exceptions, the OT books are the products of lengthy composition histories, then they have no single identifiable author. The book of Proverbs illustrates this point. Proverbs explicitly mentions more than one contributor to the final form of the book as we have it.[3] The book begins: "The proverbs of Solomon son of David, king of Israel" (1:1). Although this might give the impression that Solomon wrote the entire book during his lifetime, other verses undermine this idea. First, two additional headings mention Solomon. The material in Prov. 10 is referred to as "the proverbs of Solomon" (10:1), which raises the possibility that Solomon is not the author of the content extending from 1:8 to 9:18. Then again at the opening of Prov. 25 we read: "These are more proverbs of Solomon, compiled by the men of Hezekiah king of Judah" (25:1). Although these proverbs are said to be Solomonic, they were compiled by the men of Hezekiah, a king of Judah who lived more than two hundred years after Solomon. This suggests that an earlier form of the book of Proverbs did not include chapters 25–29, which were added some two hundred years later.

Also intriguing is the reference to an anonymous group of sages simply labeled "the wise" in 22:17 (see also 24:23). In addition, at the very end of the book are enigmatic references to "the sayings of Agur son of Jakeh" (30:1) and "the sayings of King Lemuel—an inspired utterance his mother taught him" (31:1). Although such references within the book of Proverbs don't allow us to develop a detailed chronology of the growth of the book of Proverbs, they do show that the book grew over time as wisdom sayings from multiple individuals were collected to form the book of Proverbs as we know it.

Who then is the author of the book of Proverbs? In one sense, there is no one author, since many authors were involved. But the author of the final form of the book is the anonymous person who took the writings of all the contributors and shaped the book into its final form.

3. For more detail, see Longman, *Proverbs*, 23–26.

Although these observations may seem to eviscerate the idea of authorial intention, I do not believe that this must be so. Because readers discern the author's intention through the text itself, they don't need to know the name of the (final) author or the time of the book's final composition. They also don't need to be able to trace the specific history of the book's composition. Later I invoke the concept of the "implied author" to describe this final author/editor.[4]

There is an additional complication when speaking of the author of a biblical book. This complication arises only for those who, like myself, believe that the Bible is the Word of God. So far we have been talking about only the human authors of the biblical books. When people say that the Bible is the Word of God, they assert that God is its ultimate author. This observation raises the question of the relationship between the human authors and the divine author.[5]

Some scholars who believe that the Bible is the Word of God assert that there is no distance between the human author's conscious understanding of the meaning of his words and the divine author's intention. Others believe that the divine author's meaning might be deeper (*sensus plenior*) than what the human authors could have known.

The latter view is supported by various considerations, beginning with the NT use of OT passages. The following two examples show that the NT authors applied some OT texts in ways the OT authors could never have anticipated. By doing so, the NT authors highlight a sense of the text that is "deeper" than the conscious awareness of the OT authors.

One of the best-known NT examples of the appropriation of an OT passage concerns the use of Isa. 7:14 in Matt. 1:23. The OT passage reads as follows: "Therefore the Lord himself will give you a sign. Look, the young woman is with child and shall bear a son and shall name him Immanuel" (NRSVue). I cite the NRSVue here, rather than the NIV, because it is clear within the context that the relevant Hebrew word, *'almah*, should be translated "young woman." The NIV (and other evangelical translations) renders the word "virgin," even though this is not the primary meaning of the word *'almah*. If virgin were meant, there is a perfectly good Hebrew word that Isaiah could have used (i.e., *betulah*), and the OT context calls for the translation "young woman." The context points to an event not in the far distant future (i.e., the birth of Jesus) but in the next few years of Isaiah's life. Isaiah's statement about this birth arises in response to King Ahab's fear that the king of Syria, Rezin, and the king of Israel, Pekah, will attack him because of his refusal to support them against the threat of Assyria under Tiglath-pileser III.

---

4. See chap. 4 under "From Author to Reader."
5. See chap. 2 under "Author-Centered Literary Approaches."

The prophet urges the Judean king not to form foreign alliances but to depend on God. Isaiah is angry that Ahab does not want a prophetic sign to confirm the reliability of this message and gives one to him anyway in the form of a child born to a "young woman." That this birth will be in the next few years is made obvious by Isaiah's explanation, which immediately follows the announcement: "He [the child born to the young woman] will be eating curds and honey when he knows enough to reject the wrong and choose the right, for before the boy knows enough to reject the wrong and choose the right, the land of the two kings you dread will be laid waste" (7:15–16). In other words, the existential threat from Rezin and Pekah that Ahab fears will come to an end by the time the child reaches the age of ethical maturity.

A second example is Matthew's use of Hosea 11:1. In Hosea 11, the prophet reports God as saying, "When Israel was a child, I loved him, and out of Egypt I called my son." This statement clearly looks back to the historical exodus, because Hosea next describes how Israel responded by worshiping other gods and bringing God's judgment on themselves, though God was unwilling to destroy them completely.

Matthew applies Hosea 11:1 to Jesus's "Egyptian sojourn." Warned by an angel about Herod's decree to kill all the baby boys in the vicinity of Bethlehem, Joseph and Mary seek refuge in Egypt until God assures them that they are safe. They return only after Herod dies. After narrating this episode, Matthew concludes "So was fulfilled what the Lord had said through the prophet" and then cites "Out of Egypt I called my son" (Matt. 2:15).

My point here is not that Matthew has misappropriated these OT passages but only that their use cannot be accounted for by appealing to the conscious intention of these OT prophets. The prophets spoke better than they knew. After all, God is the ultimate author of Scripture, as Paul points out to Timothy in an oft-cited passage: "All Scripture is God-breathed and is useful for teaching, rebuking, correcting and training in righteousness, so that the servant of God may be thoroughly equipped for every good work" (2 Tim. 3:16–17). Peter also speaks to this point, saying, "Above all, you must understand that no prophecy of Scripture came about by the prophet's own interpretation of things. For prophecy never had its origin in the human will, but prophets, though human, spoke from God as they were carried along by the Holy Spirit" (2 Pet. 1:20–21). If prophecy has its origin in God, the ultimate goal in reading Scripture is to hear the voice of God.

That does not mean that the NT use of the OT is arbitrary. Isaiah might have been (at least initially) surprised to see Matthew use Isa. 7:14 to refer to Mary's pregnancy: "All this took place to fulfill what the Lord had said through the prophet: 'The virgin will conceive and give birth to a son, and they will call him Immanuel' (which means 'God with us')" (Matt. 1:22–23). But even though the future birth of Jesus to Mary, his virgin mother, was not in Isaiah's conscious intention, there are indications even in the context of Isaiah that, like all prophecy, the future expectation of a child would be multiply fulfilled and that the fulfillment would expand and intensify.[6]

The original interaction between Isaiah and Ahaz took place around 735 BC. The child, who may have been a son of Isaiah or of Ahaz (Hezekiah), would have been around twelve when the Assyrians defeated Pekah and Rezin and laid waste to their lands (Isa. 7:16), thus providing the initial fulfillment of the prophecy. However, that Isaiah anticipates future fulfillments beyond this historical moment may be seen when Immanuel is mentioned again in the next chapter (Isa. 8:6–8):

> Because this people has rejected
> > the gently flowing waters of Shiloah
> and rejoices over Rezin
> > and the son of Remaliah,
> Therefore the Lord is about to bring against them
> > the mighty floodwaters of the Euphrates—
> > the king of Assyria with all his pomp.
> It will overflow all its channels,
> > run over all its banks
> and sweep on into Judah, swirling over it,
> > passing through it and reaching up to the neck.
> Its outspread wings will cover the breadth of your land, Immanuel!

Notice that the land of Judah is now called Immanuel's land, perhaps moving the name in a royal, even messianic direction. The threat from Assyria here was realized in 701 BC, when the Assyrian king Sennacherib invaded Judah, taking many towns and threatening Jerusalem, though God kept Jerusalem from falling during the reign of Hezekiah. That the Assyrians would ultimately fail is the subject of the following lines:

> Raise the war cry, you nations, and be shattered!
> > Listen, all you distant lands.
> Prepare for battle, and be shattered!
> > Prepare for battle, and be shattered!

6. The following comments on Isa. 7 are informed by interpretive insights from Stephen Cook of Virginia Theological Seminary, in Alexandria, conveyed in print (see Cook, Strong, and Tuell, *Prophets*, 93–95) and through personal communication.

> Devise your strategy, but it will be thwarted,
> propose your plan, but it will not stand,
> for God is with us. (Isa. 8:9–10)

As Cook points out, "God is with us" in the final line in Hebrew is "*'Immanu 'el*."

Thus within Isaiah itself, readers can see an expansion of the prophecy from the child named Immanuel, born to a young woman, to a messianic/royal figure. Readers who detect the messianic expansion of Immanuel *within* Isaiah would not be totally surprised to see Matthew cite Isa. 7:14 in reference to Jesus's birth (see also Luke 1:26–38). However, readers (and Isaiah, too, if he read Matthew's use of the prophecy) might be initially surprised by the change from the Hebrew *'almah* ("young woman") to the Greek *parthenos* ("virgin"), but on reflection this expansion—or perhaps better, intensification—is a way of highlighting the special nature of this messiah in comparison to, say, King Hezekiah. But note that the Gospel writers are not the innovators here. The Septuagint translates Isa. 7:14 using the Greek word for virgin (*parthenos*); the translators "may have been influenced in their choice of the term by a perception that Immanuel was no ordinary child (see Isa. 8:10)."[7]

Hosea provides another passage in which a NT writer sees an expanded meaning. When Hosea refers back to the historical exodus, he is not thinking of his words as a prophecy as such, but the exodus story does provide a background to Jesus's life and work. The NT authors understand Jesus as the fulfillment of the entire exodus story and particularly of the prophetic anticipation of a second exodus (see Isa. 40:3–5; Hosea 2:14–15).

Further support for the idea that human-mediated revelation may have a divine intention beyond what the human author was aware of may be found in the Gospel's presentation of John the Baptist. John the Baptist was not a "writing prophet," but he was the recipient of divine revelation. Although the account of his life is in the NT rather than the OT, John precedes the time of Jesus's crucifixion and resurrection and is in the tradition of an OT prophet.

As the precursor to the coming Messiah, John is the voice in the wilderness (Isa. 40:3, quoted in Matt. 3:3) preparing for his arrival. Many people come to hear him preach, but when he sees some religious leaders, he warns them to repent in order to avoid God's coming wrath. If they don't repent, he tells them, "The ax is already at the root of the trees, and every tree that does not produce good fruit will be cut down and thrown into the fire" (Matt. 3:10). John later issues a threat concerning the one who is coming after him, saying, "He will baptize you with the Holy Spirit and fire. His winnowing fork is in

---

7. Cook, Strong, and Tuell, *Prophets*, 99.

his hand, and he will clear his threshing floor, gathering his wheat into the barn and burning up the chaff with unquenchable fire" (Matt. 3:11–12). In other words, John repeats the message that has echoed down from the exilic and postexilic prophets: God will bring violent judgment on his people's oppressors (e.g., see Dan. 7 and Zech. 14).

When Jesus comes, John recognizes him as the promised one. After he baptizes Jesus, John the Baptist is thrown in jail, where he hears reports about Jesus's ministry. Yet what he hears disturbs him because Jesus doesn't seem to be executing the judgment John predicted. Jesus is healing the sick, giving sight to the blind, raising the dead, and preaching the good news. When John hears this, he thinks, "I may have baptized the wrong person!" This is why he sends two of his disciples to Jesus to ask, "Are you the one who is to come, or should we expect someone else?" (Matt. 11:3). In response, Jesus does more of what he's been doing and instructs John's disciples to go back and tell John what they have seen.

What message is Jesus sending John? First, he affirms that he (Jesus) is indeed the right one. But he is also saying that at the present time, his mission is not to bring violent judgment on sinners but rather to heal and to preach. Looking at subsequent events in Jesus's life, readers should also realize that Jesus has heightened and intensified the warfare against evil, making the spiritual powers and authorities the object of his actions (Col. 2:13–15). This battle takes him to the cross because the powers and authorities are defeated not by killing but by dying.

Clearly, John has not understood his own words given to him by God, but he is not mistaken in his predictions. He does not realize that Jesus comes not just once but twice. And as Jesus himself describes (Matt. 24) and as Revelation announces, Jesus will come a second time to bring final judgment against human and spiritual enemies.

The NT use of the OT as well as the example of John the Baptist convinces me that the human authors of Scripture did not know the full intention of their words and likely would often have been surprised by their ultimate meaning and use. Scripture can indeed have a deeper meaning (*sensus plenior*).

Some scholarly readers of Scripture worry that this view might be used to justify imposing all kinds of foreign meanings onto a text, claiming that these "deeper" meanings are divinely intended.[8] This danger is real, which is why readers today, who are not like the NT authors and not the recipients of direct divine revelation, must justify their interpretations by ordinary means and methods, seeking to discover the human intention behind the text.

---

8. A worry expressed by Kaiser, *Toward an Exegetical Theology*, 108–14.

Reader

The act of literary communication involves an author writing a text to communicate a message to readers. I have reflected on some of the complexities involving the text and the author; I now turn to the topic of readers.

My first observation is crucial for proper interpretation. The intended readers of the various biblical books are the author's contemporaries. No biblical book was written "for the ages," but instead sought to address readers alive at the time. Since I have already complicated the notion of the author by envisioning various editions of many if not most biblical books, we must also envision multiple intended audiences for the various recensions of a biblical book. However, precise identification of the various editions of a book is a difficult and speculative process. Generally, the claim that the biblical books were not written to readers today leads simply to the important observation that the OT books in the form we have them were addressed to an ancient Israelite audience.

The fact that the OT books were written in ancient Hebrew (and a little Aramaic) should further confirm that we are not the original intended audience. However, with so many excellent translations available today, those who aren't reading the Bible in the original languages may be tempted to forget the obvious historical distance. Besides writing in an ancient language, the biblical authors used genres, literary conventions, and figurative language that were immediately familiar to their original audience but are likely unfamiliar to modern readers. Likewise, these authors refer to ancient institutions and customs that may be unknown to a modern audience or misunderstood by those who are outside the original historical context.

In sum, each biblical book was written not to modern readers but to an ancient audience contemporary with the author. The obvious implication is that readers today must look "over the shoulders" of the original audience. To put it another way, we must try our best to place ourselves in the mindset of the original audience. Of course, this way of reading requires effort to acquire the necessary knowledge. For instance, the present book seeks to explain ancient genres, literary conventions, metaphors, institutions, and customs that are unfamiliar to modern readers. Ancient Hebrew poets and storytellers communicated using conventions that were familiar to them and their original audience but are no longer used in modern writing, and bridging this historical distance is a major thrust of the present book (see esp. chaps. 4 and 5).

Once we recognize that the biblical books were not written *to* us and we try to place ourselves in the sandals of the original ancient audience, we can acknowledge that the OT books were at least written *for* us. That is, the OT remains relevant for us today. This is what we mean when we say that the books of the Bible are canonical. They are the standard of faith and practice for the church. The practical implication of this observation is that modern interpreters must read the biblical books a second time from the vantage point of twenty-first-century Christians.

A second important fact for modern readers to keep in mind is that we read the Bible from a limited perspective. As finite creatures, we have a perspective shaped by our age, gender, economic status, ethnicity, life experiences, and other factors, which influence which aspects of the text we pay special attention to and which we overlook. We naturally come to the text with questions that are unique to who we are. This observation must be qualified by two important points.

First, the human finitude that limits our perspective need not prevent us from achieving an adequate understanding of the text, for the meaning of a text is found in the author's intention as expressed in the text.

Second, our specific and limited perspective on the text brings with it strengths and weaknesses. Let me provide an illustration from my own life. A part of who I am today as an interpreter of the Bible is shaped by having a PhD in ancient Near Eastern Studies. My training enables me to approach the text with a knowledge of its ancient Near Eastern background and relevant ancient languages, including Hebrew, which gives me an interpretive advantage that most people don't have. However, I have often been in Bible studies with people who do not have a specialized knowledge of the OT's ancient Near Eastern background and yet who notice aspects of the text that I completely overlooked. In this way, I benefit from their insight while also being able to inform them about the background of a text in a way that helps them understand it better.

Let me share another example. I recently published a commentary on the NT book of Revelation.[9] Whenever I would mention that I was writing on this biblical book, those who were not trained biblical scholars typically responded by saying that the book is strange and virtually impossible to understand. To illustrate their point, they might reference Rev. 13, with its description of a seven-headed beast. However, my training enabled me to explain that the idea of a seven-headed beast representing the forces of chaos and evil was quite common in the world of Revelation and earlier. Indeed, the idea of this beast goes back to Canaanite mythology, which predates the Bible and speaks of the god Baal defeating a seven-headed monster named Lothan (biblical Leviathan; cf. Ps. 74:14; Isa. 27:1).

---

9. Longman, *Revelation through Old Testament Eyes*.

It can be unsettling to consider that our reading of the biblical text is constrained by our status, previous experience, and level of education. But the obvious solution to this problem is to recognize that interpreters need to read *in community*. We understand the biblical text better when we listen to diverse voices. If I, as a financially secure white male with an OT PhD read and listen only to others whose background is similar to mine, I may misunderstand the text or at least not understand it as fully as I could if I were exposed to other perspectives, including those of women, people of color, and those who are poorer or richer than I am or have a different or less-formal education. Their observations may not always be right, nor mine always wrong, but considering other interpretations, even those I ultimately reject as incorrect, forces me to think through my own views and makes me more aware of my own biases.

Another argument for reading in community is that biblical texts have been read and interpreted this way for centuries. Indeed, indications of biblical interpretation can be found even within the Bible itself. In a later chapter, I engage the phenomenon of intertextual connections between biblical texts, but for now I will preview an example that will be developed further later (see chap. 6, "Intertextuality"). In Dan. 9 we find Daniel reading the book of Jeremiah: "I, Daniel, understood from the Scriptures, according to the word of the LORD given to Jeremiah the prophet, that the desolation would last seventy years" (9:2). He understands Jeremiah to mean that the Babylonian exile will soon come to an end (Jer. 25:11–12; 29:10), so he turns to God in prayer, asking him to forgive the sins of the community that led to their being sent into exile. As it turns out, though, his belief that the exile would soon come to an end, at least in a definitive sense, was premature. Gabriel, the interpreting angel, transforms the seventy years of Jeremiah into "seventy 'sevens'" (9:24), extending the length of the exile far into the future.

Interpretation starts the moment the biblical text is written, though most interpretation is not written down, and even most of what is written down is lost. But in addition to OT texts interpreted by NT writers, we have examples of OT interpretation that actually precede the NT era (e.g., the Dead Sea Scrolls and other Second Temple literature). Jewish and Christian interpretation of the OT spans the centuries from the apostolic period through the Middle Ages to the Reformation and into the modern period. The history of interpretation provides a different type of community with whom modern interpreters must read the biblical text, allowing them to move outside the particularities of their cultural moment. This approach of course brings benefits and liabilities analogous to one's own individual lens of reading.

The Goal of Interpretation

What then is the goal of interpretation? I have presented the process of literary communication as an author writing a text to communicate a message to an audience. I have also shown that all three parts of this dynamic are more complex than they at first appear, and though this applies to all literature, it is especially true of biblical texts.

An OT book is rarely, if ever, the result of a single human author writing at a specific point in time. Furthermore, the author is often anonymous, and even when authors are known, they are long dead. Though we might wish to interview an author to gain a sense of the meaning of their text, they are unavailable.[10] The church's affirmation of the ultimate divine origin of the books within the canon as the Word of God raises the further question of the relationship between the divine and human intention (*sensus plenior*).

The fact that OT books have an extended history of composition also complicates the notion of the text. However, while acknowledging the composite nature of a biblical book, readers can decide to focus on its final form.

Finally, twenty-first-century readers must recognize that they are not the intended audience of the biblical books. These texts were addressed to the writers' contemporaries and require us to read them in their original context. Those who affirm the canonical status of these writings also believe that their messages are ultimately directed to us as well. But only after reading these texts while imagining ourselves as part of the original audience can we perform a second reading that asks how these texts speak to us in our present situation. And since readers are finite creatures with perspectives that are limited by their backgrounds and identities, we must also learn to read in a diverse community that includes a variety of interpreters past and present.

Ultimately, the goal of interpretation is to hear the voice of the author, first the human author and then the divine one. Having no independent access to the author, modern interpreters must perform a close reading of the text as it has come down to us. In order to read the text closely, we must consider the literary conventions of Hebrew prose and poetry. Genre plays a major role in interpretive work, which in turn leads to the question of how ancient Hebrews told their stories and wrote their poems. To better prepare us to examine these topics, however, we should briefly survey the history of the literary study of the HB.

---

10. Even if the original authors were available, one could not be sure of the accuracy of their memories or that they were conscious of all the potential meanings of their texts.

TWO

History of the Study of the Old Testament as Literature

In chapter 1 we explored the locus of meaning in a text. This focus on the text leads naturally to a survey of the history of the literary study of the Bible, which will help us situate ourselves within the context of this larger discussion. As a method, the literary study of the Bible extends back to the early church, though sadly theologians have lost sight of its importance at various times, including modern times, replacing it with a focus on the historical dimension of the text. I begin this survey with a personal story of an event that occurred around 1980; from there we will take a backward look over the field before finally looking forward to the present day.

My own involvement in literary study of the OT began at a time when the field itself was making a literary turn after over a century and a half of neglect. My doctoral adviser at Yale, W. W. Hallo, suggested that I translate and study a group of texts that he suspected formed a genre, which I eventually called fictional Akkadian autobiography.[1] At an early point in my research, I told Professor Hallo that I felt I needed to understand genre better. He wisely sent me to his friend and colleague Geoffrey Hartman (1929–2016) in the comparative literature department, who kindly discussed the issue with me, not giving me a pat description but encouraging me to begin studying genre theory from a literary perspective.[2]

---

1. Longman, *Fictional Akkadian Autobiography*.
2. Only later did I learn that Dr. Hartman is credited with alerting the American scholarly community to the work of Jacques Derrida (1930–2004). For Hartman's importance in this regard and his place among the Yale Deconstructionists (Harold Bloom, Paul de Man, and J. Hillis Miller), see Leitch, *Deconstructive Criticism*.

It did not take me long to notice the significant disconnect between contemporary literary studies and biblical scholarship on the nature of genre. In chapter 3 I expand on this observation, contrasting the prescriptive, diachronic, taxonomic, and rather rigid view of Gunkel dominant in biblical studies at the time with a descriptive, synchronic view that recognizes that texts participate in more than one genre and have fuzzy boundaries between genres. I was not the only biblical scholar to recognize the problems with the Gunkel approach to genre.[3] Over time the guild has become increasingly sophisticated in its approach to genre,[4] but even then I saw forces at work that would lead to a significant shift of focus in biblical studies, a move from analyzing the historical dimensions of a biblical text to exploring the text's literary features. Perhaps the single most influential event responsible for this reorientation was the publication of Robert Alter's *The Art of Biblical Narrative* in 1981, but there were important precursors in the preceding decade. After describing the dominant historical focus of biblical studies prior to Alter, I will discuss literary analysis.

The Historical-Critical Method

To understand the significance of the literary turn that started around 1969 and took off in earnest in the 1980s, it is helpful to remember that through the nineteenth century and most of the twentieth, biblical scholars focused on history, with biblical scholarship being something of a monolith in its historical approach during this period. Today biblical studies reflects many different perspectives and methodological approaches, as illustrated by the diversity of membership and participation in the Society of Biblical Literature. But even as recently as the 1960s and 1970s, historical criticism was the predominant acceptable approach to the text, and those who operated outside this mainstream methodology were effectively marginalized.[5]

But what is historical criticism? What are its goals, and what are its main methods and presuppositions? Historical critics study a biblical text to understand its meaning in its original context. The approach arose from a modernist, or Enlightenment, idea that one can adopt a neutral, scientific approach to the Bible. It differs from a traditional, premodern approach, which simply hands down interpretations without giving reasons and establishes mean-

---

3. See chap. 3.
4. Some recent examples include Dell, "Deciding the Boundaries of 'Wisdom,'" and Kynes, *Obituary for "Wisdom Literature."*
5. Elliott et al., *Misusing Scripture*, is a recent attempt to assert that the historical-critical method is the only legitimate way to study the Bible in scholarship.

ing on the authority of previous interpretation. To achieve a neutral stance toward interpretation, historical critics adopt what has often been identified as Troeltschian presuppositions.[6] These include (1) the principle of autonomy: critics must take a stance of suspicion toward historical sources; (2) the principle of criticism: scholars must always be open to revision of interpretive/historical conclusions; and (3) the principle of analogy: the historian must not accept as true anything that does not conform with present experience. The latter was understood in a way that cast doubt on biblical references to supernatural occurrences such as the sea crossing in the exodus tradition. J. J. Collins defends this approach as providing a common basis for both religious and nonreligious scholars to operate.[7]

The historical-critical approach to the OT was the dominant and virtually exclusive scholarly method for the century and a half prior to the rise of the literary approach, with various related methods being developed to further the project. In the nineteenth century, source criticism endeavored to identify historical sources that lay behind the final form of the text. One can see the historical impulse at work here. Starting with the biblical text, scholars worked backward to discover its previously existing, earlier forms. Although source criticism was applied to many biblical books, it was the application of this method to the study of the Pentateuch and its sources that led to the best-known and most widely accepted theory called the Documentary Hypothesis (DH), which was popularized by Julius Wellhausen (1844–1918) in the 1880s.[8] Rather than studying only the final form of the text, Wellhausen and his followers were interested in recreating the earlier literary sources of the text.

A few decades later, Hermann Gunkel used the genre theory of his day to create a diachronic form of analysis called form criticism. Again starting with the biblical text in its final form, he tried to recreate its original, oral form, which he believed had evolved and changed over time. According to Gunkel, these earlier forms could be discerned by identifying literary patterns connected to an original setting in life.

These original forms were then collected by later editors, who used them to express their own theological perspective (or *Tendenz*). The study of how the original forms were shaped and edited became known as redaction criticism (*Redaktor* is German for "editor"). While source, form, and redaction

6. Troeltsch, "Über historische und somatische Methode in der Theologie"; in English, consult Troeltsch, "Historiography." See my extensive critique in Longman, "History and Old Testament Interpretation."

7. Collins, *The Bible after Babel*. See the critiques by Levenson, *The Hebrew Bible*; and by Plantinga, *Warranted Christian Belief*.

8. Wellhausen, *Prolegomena to the History of Israel*.

criticism do not exhaust the methodological tools used in historical-critical study, they illustrate its predominantly historical, diachronic concerns.

Up until around 1980, historical criticism was the only thing that counted as true scholarship in biblical studies. After all, it was reasoned, such a neutral, scientific approach allowed everyone to discuss the biblical text on a common platform. It was acceptable for a scholar to be religious as long as the scholar bracketed out any religious beliefs when conducting academic research. Religious scholars weren't the only ones marginalized by this approach; other types of ideological interpreters, including feminist scholars (see below), were left to operate outside the mainstream.

However, the historical-critical approach was blind to its own presuppositions and lacked the neutrality it claimed to possess. The rise of postmodernism threw modernist projects into question by insisting that no neutral starting point exists. The last few decades of the twentieth century saw the emergence of alternative methods for studying the Bible, including various approaches that can be called literary. To this topic we now turn.

The Literary Turn in Biblical Studies

The late 1960s saw a decided turn from a nearly exclusive focus on the historical method to a dominant focus on literary approaches to the text that bracketed out historical interests, at least temporarily. Two scholars were especially influential in this shift toward literary interpretation; one produced a seminal article, and the other a seminal book.

The seminal article was James Muilenburg's "Form Criticism and Beyond," which was based on his 1968 presidential address to the Society of Biblical Literature. Like most later literary scholars of the Bible, Muilenburg did not disown historical approaches to the biblical text. He acknowledged that the final form of a biblical book was a composite text resulting from a long period of production. However, he felt that scholarship needed to move beyond methods like form criticism, which tried to identify earlier forms of the biblical text, and instead appreciate the texts' final form. His recognition of the high literary quality of biblical prose and poetry and his encouragement toward studying the literary style of the Bible's stories and poems influenced the next generation of biblical scholars.

The seminal book was Robert Alter's pioneering *Art of Biblical Narrative* mentioned above. Like Muilenburg, Alter did not deny that the books of the HB have a history of composition, but he also felt that the literary quality of biblical prose was worthy of recognition. His work on the conventions of

Hebrew prose, and later of Hebrew poetry, influenced and still influences the field's approach to the literary analysis of biblical texts.

These types of studies injected excitement into the field, particularly among younger scholars at the time. The focus on the historical dimension of the biblical books' composition had been so exclusive and long standing that diminishing returns came from continuing such studies. It is only a slight exaggeration to say that for the next fifteen to twenty years, precious few articles, monographs, or doctoral dissertations in biblical studies failed to include the word "literary." People were speaking in terms of a paradigm shift in the study of the biblical text. While this claim may have been overblown, the ramifications of the turn to the literary dimension were substantial and continue to be. Indeed, one of my first books, *Literary Approaches to Biblical Interpretation*, was deeply influenced by scholars such as Alter, and the present work is as well.

In the next few years, however, divisions began to appear among biblical scholars over what constituted a literary approach to biblical interpretation. Not surprisingly, biblical scholars turned to colleagues in literature departments; appropriated concepts, methods, and approaches from the study of other literary traditions; and applied them to the study of the Bible. Scholars in these departments differed among themselves and were developing new ideas during the last two decades of the twentieth century.

The various literary approaches can be divided into different schools of thought based on where their proponents believe meaning resides in the reading process. Some adopt an *author-centered* approach, others a *text-centered* approach, and still others a *reader-centered* approach to the interpretation of the biblical text. One school of thought denies that there is any determinate meaning to the biblical text. After surveying these interpretive schools, I situate my own position along this spectrum of approaches. But before we begin our survey of literary approaches and how they have influenced and continue to influence the study of the Bible, we need to understand the historical roots of literary interpretation of the Bible.

Precursors to a Literary Approach to Bible Interpretation

For those active in the guild of biblical studies in 1980, when I was just getting started, the work of Alter and others seemed new and exciting, and it was. But many who, like me, lacked historical perspective did not realize that what they were seeing and participating in was really a recovery of a fundamental unity between the study of literature and the Bible.

According to Stephen Prickett,[9] the pagan Greek literary critic Cassius Longinus (3rd cent. AD) regarded Genesis as sublime literature, though Jerome and Augustine (both ca. AD 400) struggled with the rough character of biblical narrative when judged by the standards of Latin literature. Although they applied foreign categories and literary canons to the biblical text, their comments on the text at least show that they were thinking in literary and aesthetic terms as they read the Bible. Stephen Weitzman notes that it was Matthew Arnold (1822–88) in the nineteenth century who introduced the phrase "the Bible as literature."[10]

Both the person and work of Robert Lowth (1710–87) well illustrate the intimate connection between literary and biblical studies that lasted until the beginning of the nineteenth century. Before becoming bishop of Oxford and then of London, Lowth was professor of poetry at Oxford. Like his work on the book of Isaiah, his *Lectures on the Sacred Poetry of the Hebrews* combines his skill as a literary critic and as a biblical scholar.

These examples do not provide a full account of the intimate relationship between literary study and biblical interpretation, but they do illustrate the ancient and early modern contribution of interpreters who used literary insights in their study of the OT and demonstrated an appreciation for the aesthetic nature of Scripture. They also make clear that what happened in the 1980s was not something new but was rather the recovery of a literary appreciation largely lost during the preceding century and a half.

According to Prickett, the founding of the University of Berlin in 1809 was a symbolic moment for the rift between studying the Bible as literature and theology and studying it as history,. The architect of this new university was Baron Wilhelm von Humboldt, and one of its "basic principles was to separate theology from the study of the humanities, and to place the latter firmly with the faculty of Arts (*Philosophische Fakultät*)."[11] Citing Hermann Usener, Prickett points out that this curricular change resulted in a "glacial-moraine . . . between biblical studies and the study of other literatures, both classical and modern."[12] By the end of the nineteenth century, British universities had adopted the German model.

The nineteenth century also saw the focus of biblical studies shift in a decidedly historical direction, particularly toward source criticism of the Pentateuch. What went by the name "literary criticism" was not an analysis of the text in its present final form but rather a type of textual archaeology,

9. Prickett, *Words and "The Word,"* 38–41.
10. Weitzman, "Before and after *The Art of Biblical Narrative*," 191–92.
11. Prickett, *Words and "The Word,"* 1.
12. Prickett, *Words and "The Word,"* 1.

an attempt to look behind the text to find its putative sources, often with the idea that these earlier sources were somehow more authentic or important than the final form. In the early twentieth century, interpreters can still see this historical orientation under a supposedly literary guise in the development of form criticism, which is based on a genre theory derived from folklore rather than from literary studies (for more, see the next chapter on genre). This brought the oft-quoted biting criticism of C. S. Lewis, the notable Oxford literary scholar in the mid-twentieth century: "Whatever these men may be as Biblical critics, I distrust them as critics. They seem to me to lack literary judgment, to be imperceptive about the very quality of the texts they are reading. . . . If [a critic] tells me that something in a Gospel is legend or romance, I want to know how many legends and romances he had read, how well his palate is trained in detecting them by the flavour."[13] Prickett reinforces the point: "To discuss biblical hermeneutics in the light of poetic theory is not to apply an alien concept, but to restore a wholeness of approach that has been disastrously fragmented over the past one hundred and fifty years."[14]

Author-Centered Literary Approaches

In the late nineteenth century, it was normal for literature to be analyzed according to the "genesis of the art-work in terms of 'influences' and 'sources'; to search for similar or analogous motifs or themes in earlier literature; to probe the origins of the political, cultural and social background of the period or the biographical background of the author—all in order to give a causal explanation to how the work came into being."[15]

On the surface, it seems logical to think that the meaning of a text is the result of an author's intention in writing it. Authors write texts to communicate with readers. Why else would someone write? Granted, those who write journals or diaries are writing to and for themselves, but the fact that the same person is both the author and the primary, if not the sole, reader does not disprove the assertion that authors write to communicate a message to readers.

This leads to the corresponding conclusion that readers read texts to discover the message of the author. Accordingly, one might think that the best type of interpretive strategy is to look for the intention of the author and to identify the meaning of the text with that intention. Indeed, author-centered interpretation was often associated with what might be called biographical

13. Lewis, *Fern-Seed and Elephants*, 106–7.
14. Prickett, *Words and "The Word,"* 197.
15. Bartholomew, *Old Testament and God*, 89, quoting Weiss, *The Bible from Within*, 2.

criticism. The more one can learn about the biography, social context, and psychology of an author, the better prepared one is to interpret the text that the author has produced. This approach to discovering the meaning of literary texts was the rule until the mid-twentieth century, when a more text-oriented approach to hermeneutics developed (see the next section).

During the 1960s and 1970s, E. D. Hirsch was the most ardent advocate for author-centered interpretation.[16] Hirsch believed that one needed to anchor textual meaning in the intention of the author in order to come to any determinate or established meaning of the text. Even so, he seemed to understand that readers typically have no direct access to the author in order to ask the author questions about their meaning. They must infer the author's intention from the text itself, which is why Hirsch puts a premium on genre (see below in chap. 3). Genres signal authorial intention and indicate how readers should understand the written words of the author.

Another literary scholar who maintained the importance of authorial intention during this time was Geoffrey Strickland. He too eschewed biographical criticism and focused his attention on the text, but he felt that an interpretation was merely a hypothesis about the author's intention in writing the text.[17] Hirsch, however, distinguished between the *meaning* of a text and its *significance*, believing that only the meaning of the text resides in the intention of the author, not its significance. The meaning of the text is in the mind of the author, but the significance of a literary work refers to the application that readers draw from the text based on their own background and interests.

I too identify a literary text's locus of meaning in the intention of the author,[18] but I am also aware of problems with this idea. For example, authors may fail to communicate their conscious intentions in their writing. They may write in a way that prevents even competent readers from recognizing what is in the author's mind. Authors may also not be completely aware of the signals they are sending to the reader. For example, an author may write something that unwittingly triggers associations to other texts known by the reader but unknown (at least on a conscious level) to the author.[19]

The idea that the text's meaning is connected to the author's intention brings additional complications. The first issue, identified above, is that for those like myself who affirm the Bible as the Word of God, the text has two

16. Hirsch, *Validity in Interpretation*.
17. Strickland, *Structuralism or Criticism?*, 28.
18. Postclassical narratologists have come back to an affirmation of the importance of authorial intention. See the section on "Poststructuralist Approaches" below and chap. 1 above under "Author."
19. See chap. 6 on intertextuality.

authors, human and divine. (We are bracketing out for the moment the reality of multiple human authors contributing to a biblical book over time.) Second, readers have no independent access to either the human author (who is dead) or the divine author. Although religious interpreters may believe that they are in a personal relationship with the living God through prayer and the indwelling of the Spirit, this does not give them direct access to the meaning of the biblical text apart from the usual methods of interpretation.

These complications have led many literary critics, including biblical scholars, to move away from author-centered theories of literary meaning toward text-centered approaches. To these we now turn.

Text-Centered Literary Approaches

Alter's approach to the literary study of the HB is rooted in a close reading of the text. He does not reject the idea that biblical texts, as known today, emerged from a history of composition, but he focuses his interpretation on the text before him. In this, Alter reflects the turn from an author-centered biographical approach to a text-centered interpretive approach, showing the influence of Russian Formalism and New Criticism, a predominantly English and American school of thought from earlier in the twentieth century (see more below). These interpretive schools of thought focus exclusively on the text rather than on the author or the reader.[20]

The impetus for this shift in focus is what has been called the "intentional fallacy," a term associated with Wimsatt and Beardsley.[21] Previous literary scholarship studied a text informed by an author's biography and at least implied that it was possible to get inside the author's mind. Wimsatt and Beardsley claim that such a procedure and such a goal are unachievable and that the interpreter's focus must be only on the text. They also warn of the danger of an "affective fallacy," which confuses the meaning of the text with the reader's emotional response to it.[22] They seek to develop an objective way of reading the text, a possibility that later reader-response theories rejected.

Meir Sternberg, among others, points out that people have exaggerated the danger of the intentional fallacy by suggesting that the author has nothing to do with the meaning of the text and that interpreters should not concern

---

20. The Israeli literary scholar Benjamin Harshav (*Explorations in Poetics*, 80) agrees: "Meanings are conveyed through language in texts." Harshav believes that the language's meaning must be understood in its "frame of reference" (genre).
21. Wimsatt and Beardsley, "Intentional Fallacy."
22. Wimsatt and Beardsley, "The Affective Fallacy."

themselves at all with authorial meaning. Wimsatt and Beardsley wanted to avoid the notion that an interpreter can read the mind of an author, but they do not discourage readers from trying to understand the message the author is sending to the reader, which is done by evaluating the text that the writer has produced. According to Sternberg, "As interpreters of the Bible, our only concern is with 'embodied' or 'objectified' intention."[23]

This embodied or objectified intention is ascertained through the text itself. Thus, the study of the conventions of narrative and poetry is key to interpretation. As Alter puts it, "Every culture, even every era in a particular culture, develops distinctive and sometimes intricate codes for telling its stories."[24] The key to proper interpretation then is to read the text closely while being competent in the conventions of Hebrew storytelling and poetry composition. These will be the topics of chapters 4 and 5 and illustrated in parts 2 and 3 below.

Although Alter does not engage with theory in his literary interpretations, his practice appears rooted in the type of text-oriented interpretation practiced by the Russian Formalists and the New Critics of earlier generations. The same may be said of several HB scholars active in the 1980s and 1990s, such as Fokkelmann, Berlin, and Bar-Efrat.[25]

In terms of literary theory, the most influential text-oriented scholars were associated with French structuralism. The name derives from the foundational conviction that "universal principles structure human communication."[26] These theorists, who were also practitioners, participated in what has been called "the linguistic turn" in literary study. Their work was rooted in the fundamental insights of Ferdinand de Saussure, a linguist who lectured in the first third of the twentieth century.[27] Saussure distinguishes between two levels of language, assigning them the French words *langue* and *parole*. *Langue* refers to the conventions of language, while *parole* refers to actual spoken language. In terms of linguistics, *langue* is captured by paradigms and syntactical rules as well as a lexicon; *parole* refers to actual texts or oral speech. One becomes competent in a language by learning the grammar (*langue*), which allows for comprehension and the ability to speak or write in that language (*parole*).

---

23. Sternberg, *Poetics of Biblical Narrative*, 9.
24. Alter, "How Convention Helps Us Read," 115.
25. Fokkelmann, *Narrative Art in Genesis*; Berlin, *Poetics and Interpretation*; Bar-Efrat, *Narrative Art in the Bible*. An even earlier, oft-cited precursor is Auerbach, *Mimesis*, esp. 3–23, his chapter "Odysseus' Scar."
26. Dinkler, *Literary Theory*, 71.
27. Saussure's classic work, *Course in General Linguistics*, was published after his death from class notes obtained by two of his students.

Analogously, one becomes competent in literature not by possessing an exhaustive knowledge of literature but by knowing how literature works in terms of genres and their accompanying narrative and poetic conventions. Knowledge of such genre conventions enables readers to pick up a text they have not seen before and interpret it competently.

Structuralist narratologists like Gérald Genette have investigated the *langue* of literary texts, the grammar characteristic of the novel.[28] Genette writes about the different ways in which novels present events, manipulate points of view (which he calls focalization), manage space and time, and so on. In later chapters, I draw on the insights of the French structuralist school and those influenced by them.

Before moving on, I should mention that not all structuralist thought leads to the illumination of a literary text. While the research of narratologists like Genette, the early Roland Barthes,[29] and Tzvetan Todorov[30] provides a framework for talking about literary conventions that illuminate interpretation and furnish terminology to talk about literary texts, there is also a quasi-scientific impulse that, when applied to biblical texts, leads to an esoteric and obscure analysis of the text. R. C. Culley summarizes this tendency by saying that structuralists "are seeking a method which is scientific in the sense that they are striving for a rigorous statement and an exacting analytical model."[31] In some biblical structuralist analysis, the conclusions are presented as a mathematical formula.[32] These kinds of studies are rare to nonexistent in OT scholarship today.

Poststructuralist Approaches: Deconstruction

Saussure made another distinction in literary theory that ultimately proved influential for biblical interpretation. Attempting to explain how communication occurs, he asks, How can someone say something and have another person understand that thing? He answers this question by analyzing a sign as a linguistic concept. Saussure describes a sign as composed of two parts, the signifier and what is signified. The signifier is the word, and the signified is the concept of the thing itself (the referent). On a linguistic level, "goat" is a signifier, and what it signifies is a type of ruminant mammal with cloven feet and horns curving backward. Saussure rightly highlights the arbitrary

---

28. For instance, in Genette, *Narrative Discourse.*
29. Barthes, "Structuralist Analysis of Narrative."
30. Todorov, *The Fantastic.*
31. Culley, "Exploring New Directions," 174.
32. See, e.g., Polzin's study on the book of Job, *Biblical Structuralism,* 75.

nature of the relationship between a signifier and the signified, which is easily illustrated by the fact that each language has a different signifier for the same signified item. For instance, Biblical Hebrew has several words for goat, including *saʿir* and *ʿez*. For Saussure, the system of signs is made up of differences. "In the language itself there are only differences. Even more important than that is the fact that, although in general a difference holds, in a language there are only differences, and no positive terms."[33] Though arbitrary, the sign communicates because those who share a language agree on the term for a goat.

Jacques Derrida, who exerted a wide cultural influence through the 1970s and into the 1990s, extended this analysis. One of his key points was the slippage between a sign and what it signifies, which throws into question the possibility of interpretation. Derrida was not so much engaging in interpretation as showing its limits and testing the possibility of literary communication. He asserts that there is nothing outside the system of signs, such as a transcendental or absolute signifier (e.g., author, speaker, or God himself), who can ensure the success of interpretation. One can see how turning from authorial intention (the death of the author) because of a (mis?)understanding of the intentional fallacy (see above) could lead to a focus on the text itself understood as a signifier. If the connection between the signifier and the signified is arbitrary and there is slippage between them, then reading will always face the possibility that this slippage will subvert determinate meaning. Derrida used the term *aporia* ("undecidable") to refer to this slippage, a kind of literary black hole.

Saussure believed that the relationship between a sign and its referent, or the signifier and what is signified, is arbitrary and composed of differences. Derrida's view heightens the difference between sign and referent and throws into question the possibility of literary communication. Meaning therefore is not a function of presence but of absence. Derrida uses the term *différance* to label what he means here; the word is a combination of two French words for "to differ" and "to defer." The meaning of a linguistic or literary sign is based on its difference from other signs; thus the meaning is always deferred, or delayed. With deconstruction, one enters the "endless labyrinth,"[34] and meaning is never established.

For the deconstructionist, asserting a determinate meaning in the text constitutes a will to power rather than an exposition. Such a stance is a type of logocentrism, a belief that a meaning exists somewhere out there to be discovered. According to the deconstructionist, the task of interpretation is to reveal the aporia and show the failure of interpretation.

33. Saussure, *Course in General Linguistics*, 118.
34. Lentricchia, *After the New Criticism*, 166.

Deconstruction was all the rage during the 1980s and up to the end of the twentieth century in biblical studies. David J. A. Clines is perhaps the most well-known advocate of this interpretive approach, though rather than showing that the slippage between sign and referent dismantles interpretation, he instead suggests that a text has the potential for many different interpretations. Even so, his view is anchored in the Derridean belief that a literary text has no determinate meaning.

In a 1993 study of Ps. 24, Clines compares his approach as a professional interpreter to the work of a "bespoke tailor," who cuts the cloth to make clothing according to the specifications of a paying customer.[35] Because the meaning of a text is not determined by anything like what the author intended (since that intention is inaccessible to later readers), the professional interpreter (e.g., biblical scholar, preacher) can interpret the text according to the expectations of those who have hired the interpreter. Potentially, the teacher or preacher could present the same text in different ways to different audiences.

Clines's distinguished and massive Job commentary in the Word Biblical Commentary series provides an interesting case in point. In this commentary, he acts as though there is a meaning in the text that can be reached through historical-critical or historical-grammatical interpretation. He hardly seems like someone trying to find the aporia in the book of Job. But, interestingly, he tells his readers why, and his reason fits perfectly with his idea of bespoke criticism. After all, he is being paid to produce a traditional type of commentary that conforms to what is expected for the series. He briefly explains that he could have cut the cloth differently, and he offers brief summaries of what a feminist, Marxist, and even vegetarian interpretation would look like.[36]

Paradoxically, Clines can also interpret "against the grain," by which he means presenting interpretations that arise from a hermeneutic of suspicion. In this approach, the interpreter suspects that the text is espousing a particular ideology and attempts to expose and resist the ideology presented by the narrator, who represents the author. Cheryl Exum's interpretation of Judg. 19, the story of the rape and dismemberment of the Levite's wife, is a good example of this approach as she argues against the narrator's perceived misogyny.[37] The wife (or concubine) is subjected to unbearable suffering, but Exum believes that the discourse ignores this suffering and objectifies the anonymous victim. Later I question whether she has rightly read the narrative in coming to this conclusion, but regardless, Exum's essay is a good example of interpreting "against the grain."

35. Clines, "World Established on Water (Psalm 24)."
36. Clines, *Job 1–20*, xlvii–lvi.
37. Exum, *Fragmented Women*, 176–77, in a chapter titled "Raped by the Pen."

However, there seems to be a glaring inconsistency in an approach that interprets "against the grain." If the text itself has no determinate meaning, how can one claim that the text espouses an ideology that must be opposed by interpreting "against the grain"? In the absence of an authoritative or intended meaning, there is no grain to read against.

Also problematic is the claim that since texts have no determinate meaning, readers can interpret them according to personal preference or taste or to meet the demands of a paying audience. What prevents a person from interpreting a text to produce what many, including Derrida and Clines, would consider a dangerous conclusion? Deconstructive hermeneutics tends to produce readings that comport with liberal or even progressive values. Clines, for example, offers a Marxist interpretation of Job. But why not a fascist interpretation?

Even during the heyday of Derrida and deconstruction, this worry was expressed by some Marxist critics. Indeed, a scandal rocked the intellectual world when it was discovered that Paul de Man, a member of the Yale school of deconstruction, had as a young man in Belgium been a fascist journalist during World War II. Whether this is a fair criticism of de Man as a person and mature scholar is debatable, but one wonders whether this episode contributed to declining interest in deconstruction. The terrorist attacks on the World Trade Center in New York City on September 11, 2001 (often referred to as 9/11), may also have dealt a blow to the popularity of deconstruction. Perhaps the possibility that this approach could potentially be used to put forth dangerous or destructive viewpoints also led to the abandonment of deconstruction in literary and philosophical circles.

Even before that event, I had an opportunity to ask the distinguished American philosopher Alvin Plantinga whether he or any of his Christian philosopher colleagues had interacted with Derrida's thought. He bluntly answered no and explained that they thought he was joking and not contributing to resolving the questions that philosophers were seriously trying to engage. At the time, I thought that this answer was too flippant given the influence deconstruction was having on hermeneutics, but in retrospect, perhaps he was right. In biblical studies, the kind of playful essays that had as their purpose uncovering the aporia of a biblical text were starting to disappear from the scene. They had become rather formulaic, looking for tensions to exploit in the text and then arguing that one could not decide between competing interpretations. Interestingly, the term "deconstruction" rarely appears in serious biblical scholarship anymore.[38]

---

38. Since the discipline of biblical studies lags behind literary theory, studies influenced by deconstruction continued into the first decade of the twenty-first century; see, e.g., Koosed, (Per)mutations of Qohelet.

Reader-Response and Ideological Interpretative Approaches

Reader-Response Interpretation

Depending on the advocate, what goes under the rubric of reader-response interpretation bears similarity to both the text-oriented interpretation discussed above and the belief in the indeterminacy of the text that is at the heart of deconstruction. The views of Wolfgang Iser (1926–2007) are similar to the text-oriented interpretation because he believes that the text itself constrains readers' interpretation.[39] The work of fellow-German Hans-Robert Jauss (1921–97) is similar, but he grounds his interpretation in literary or reception theory. Still, he believes that the background, interests, concerns, and questions that readers bring to a text contribute to its interpretation.[40] My own view, as expressed in chapter 1, is similar to Iser's point of view and necessitates reading in community.

Stanley Fish (b. 1938), on the other hand, illustrates the second type of reader-response theory. Because he believes that the text has no determinate meaning, he advances the idea that communities construct meaning from a text.[41] As Kevin Vanhoozer puts it, for Fish "there is no such thing as a meaning 'in' the text 'outside' the reader."[42] In his later work, Fish does acknowledge that readers' response is shaped by their participation in an interpretive community.

The work of these and other reader-response theorists has influenced OT scholarship, particularly in the area of what is called the history of interpretation. With its goal of recovering the original meaning of a text, historical-critical scholarship tends to downplay or ignore how the text has been interpreted through the ages. However, as reader-response theory implies, the original readers found meaning in a text for their own time, and subsequent readers appropriate and understand the text in a way that leads to constructive meaning relevant to their own age. Reception history examines the way biblical texts have been engaged, interpreted, and appropriated through time. Brendan Breed argues in favor of a reception-historical approach over against historical-critical/grammatical approaches because "as an open-ended process, a biblical text has no moment of purity, origin, finality, or true meaning that could constitute a necessary, universally valid boundary between the text and its later receptions."[43] Reception history,

---

39. Iser, *The Act of Reading.*
40. Jauss, *Toward an Aesthetic of Reception.*
41. Fish, *Is There a Text in This Class?*
42. Vanhoozer, *Is There a Meaning in This Text?*, 24.
43. Breed, *Nomadic Text*, 119.

according to Breed, asks not "What does this text mean?" but rather "How does this text function?"[44] At least three major publishing projects are underway in biblical studies that support the reception-history function: the Blackwell Bible Commentaries series, the *Encyclopedia of the Bible and Its Reception*, and the Illuminations Commentary Series.[45]

Ideological Interpretation

Ideological interpretation describes the practice of readers who adopt a specific perspective as they engage the text and take a type of reader-response approach derived from either Iser or Fish's starting point concerning the meaning of the text. Theoretically, there are as many different ideological readings as there are ideologies (remember Clines's vegetarian reading of Job mentioned above). In biblical studies, though, the four most common types of ideology are feminist, Marxist, queer, and postcolonial. An interpreter may approach the text from more than one of these perspectives, but below I give brief descriptions of each separately.

Feminist Interpretation

Feminist interpreters highlight issues of gender as they read the text. According to feminist literary critic Robin Warhol, "Depending on the approach, the feminist narratologist may focus on the gender of the authors, authorial (intended) audiences, actual readers, characters, narrators, and/or narratees. Feminist narratology comprises theory and practice, intervening in gender-neutral models of narrative, as well as producing gender-conscious readings of individual narrative texts."[46] Regarding the aspirations of feminist literary criticism, Warhol offers another concise statement: "A feminist narrative critic will implicitly or explicitly evaluate a text according to its relation to patriarchy: the important question about a text's value is whether on the whole it operates to support patriarchal social and cultural arrangements or subverts them."[47]

The supposition of feminist criticism is that authors and critics of literature are almost exclusively male, at least in the West. Rather than believing that the author or critic's gender is irrelevant, it is important for feminist scholarship to call out male privilege and create room for women's voices.

---

44. Breed, *Nomadic Text*, 142.
45. For the latter, see the lengthy treatment of the reception history of the book of Job in the series' premier volume, Seow, *Job 1–21*.
46. Warhol, "Feminist Narratology," 161.
47. Warhol, "Narrative Values, Aesthetic Values," 165.

Some feminist interpreters highlight passages and themes from the Bible that feature women in some way and try to address others that seem to challenge an egalitarian appropriation of the Bible's message. Still others critique the patriarchy of the text or use the text in a manner that is hard to justify solely by an appeal to the text. The book of Proverbs, for example, provokes different types of feminist approaches and attracts both praise and critique from feminist scholars. On one hand, the book is very male-centric in being couched largely as the instruction of a father to a son, but on the other hand, it also presents the figure of Woman Wisdom, who instructs all the men. Feminist readings are conflicted over the poem about the virtuous or noble woman (Prov. 31:10–31). Despite the numerous burdensome tasks the woman must perform both inside and outside the household, she is presented as a human reflex of Woman Wisdom herself.

Timothy K. Beal offers a feminist reading of the book of Esther that focuses on the instability of both gender and ethnic identity as he explores the development of characters within the book.[48] The theory of Luce Irigaray and Emmanuel Levinas provides the interpretive lens through which he reads Esther. Many readers see Esther as the mirror image of Vashti and, depending on their own theological/political viewpoint, prefer one or the other. For many, Vashti is the hero because she has the courage to resist Xerxes's command to come to his banquet so the male guests can take pleasure in her beauty, an act that leads to her erasure from her position and the story. Esther is her replacement and, according to some readings, the model of submission to men, first to Mordecai and then to Xerxes.

Beal rightly complicates this picture and sees a moment of transition in Esther's interaction with Mordecai in Esther 4. Mordecai has learned of Haman's plot to destroy the Jewish people and approaches Esther to recruit her help because of her position of influence in the Persian court. Beal notes that when Esther finally agrees to risk her life by approaching the king unannounced, she is no longer being strictly deferential and in fact devises her own strategy to defeat Haman. As Beal explains, "It becomes clear that Esther, a woman whom we begin to imagine imagining, is no longer so securely fixed as man's benchmark, no longer denied subjectivity."[49]

Another text that has attracted significant feminist attention is Judg. 19, the story of the rape of a Levite's wife. Feminist interpretation has focused attention on this text because it narrates a horrific act of sexual violence. Several feminist scholars, including Cheryl Exum (mentioned above) and

48. Beal, *Book of Hiding.*
49. Beal, *Book of Hiding,* 69, citing Irigaray, *Speculum of the Other Woman,* 133.

Mieke Bal,[50] believe that the narrative is complicit in the denigration of the woman since, they argue, she is anonymous and objectified in the story. They apply a hermeneutic of suspicion and read "against the grain" to expose the ideology of the narrator.[51] However, other feminist readers, notably Helen Paytner,[52] argue that the narrator is not complicit in presenting the woman anonymously and does so not to marginalize her but to suggest that her fate could be the fate of any woman during the period of Judges, a time of moral depravity, spiritual confusion, and political fragmentation. Paytner rightly suggests that scholars like Exum and Bal confuse the ideology of the male characters of the story with that of the narrator.

Marxist Interpretation

Marxist interpreters seek to identify class struggle in the text and apply it to issues today. Two examples of Marxist interpretation are Norman Gottwald's approach to the question of Israel's settlement in the land and the movement known as liberation theology. We will examine Gottwald first.

Gottwald represents one of the earliest attempts to apply Marxist interpretation to the biblical text to explain the emergence of Israel in the early Iron Age.[53] He seeks to understand the biblical account in its broader ancient Near Eastern context and uses many Near Eastern sources such as the el-Amarna tablets, but he makes no secret that he is reading these texts through the prism of a Marxist sociology. Indeed, his own appreciation of Marxist thought on a political level comes in his dedication to the people of Israel, whom he implicitly compares to the people of Vietnam. He later explained: "The bulk of *The Tribes of Yahweh* was written during the trauma of the war in Vietnam, and its dedicatory page contains an unabashed tribute to 'the first Israelites' who are analogized to the people of Vietnam in the common resistance to imperialist domination."[54]

More broadly, his method might be called cultural-material, but he specifically reads the biblical text through the prism of Marx. He believes that Israel's distinctive religion, Yahwism, arose from Israelite social relationships rather than vice versa. In contrast to its neighbors, Israel was an egalitarian society. Everyone was equal, at least until the idea was perverted (in his view) by the rise of the monarchy. Such an egalitarian society gave rise to

50. Exum, *Fragmented Women*; Bal, *Death and Dissymmetry*.
51. For the hermeneutic of suspicion and reading "against the grain," see the preceding sections.
52. Paytner, *Telling Terror in Judges 19*.
53. Gottwald, *The Tribes of Yahweh* (1979).
54. Gottwald, *The Tribes of Yahweh*, xlvii, "Preface to the Reprint" (1997).

monotheism and was opposed to the hierarchical society of its neighbors, which was polytheistic. If everyone has the same God, then everyone is equal; in a polytheistic system, the power hierarchy among the gods is also reflected in society.

According to Gottwald, Israel originated in a revolt of the underclasses of Canaanite feudal society. Evidence for this revolt and the emergence of Israel is seen archaeologically in the dissolution of Canaanite coastal cities in the thirteenth to the eleventh centuries BC and the appearance of small towns in the highlands to the east. Thus, Israel finds its origin in what looks like a revolt of the Canaanite proletariat class against their Canaanite oppressors. From this an egalitarian society developed, expressed religiously in the worship of a single God.[55]

Perhaps the most influential type of Marxist reading goes under the label of liberation theology, which reads the Bible as showing God's preferential treatment for the poor and oppressed. G. V. Pixley and C. Boff write that "Yahweh, the God of the Bible, is characterized by his preferential option for the oppressed."[56] As a story of liberation from Egyptian bondage, the exodus story is a favorite with liberation theologians. For C. A. Kirk-Duggan, the exodus must be read as "unfolding a divine preference for the persecuted, the disempowered, as a mode to expose, dialogue about, and eliminate classism, sexism, racism, anti-Semitism, homophobia and other experiences of oppression."[57]

Queer Interpretation

Most practitioners of queer interpretation are part of the LGBTQ+ community and seek to promote gay-friendly interpretations of biblical texts by grappling with and sometimes subverting passages that seem to censure same-sex behavior. In literary circles, queer theory developed out of gay and lesbian studies in the 1990s, particularly the work of Teresa de Lauretis.[58] *The Queer Bible Commentary*, a one-volume study Bible, focuses on issues of gender and sexuality, highlighting texts thought to be conducive to nonheteronormativity

---

55. In the preface to the reprint twenty years after the original publication of *The Tribes of Yahweh*, Gottwald engages scholarship that questioned whether monotheism developed before the postexilic period. He argues that there were actually competing religious cults among the early Israelite groups, but the increasing attraction to the worship of Yahweh was because "it offered a paradigm for networks of cooperation among groups of people who could not adequately prosper and defend themselves solely on the basis of isolated local initiatives." Gottwald, *The Tribes of Yahweh*, xliv–xlv (1997).

56. Pixley and Boff, "A Latin American Perspective," 209.

57. Kirk-Duggan, "Let My People Go!," 259.

58. De Lauretis, "Queer Theory."

and critiquing and reimagining texts thought to be problematic to the queer life.[59]

In a recent survey of the state of queer interpretation, David Stewart summarizes what he sees as seven impulses of queer interpretation. It "(1) collects interpretations and questions rather than reducing interpretations to a singular 'correct' answer—it interrogates; (2) looks for the nonheteronormative and the gender fluid; (3) resists (hetero)normativity and questions boundaries and categories—it is 'norm-critical'; (4) strains toward privileging uniqueness—it is 'anti-essentialist'; (5) resists academic norms by making room for playfulness and humor, both 'camp' and 'drag,' and eschews a single definition of 'queer,' and so (6) is a collection of 'family resemblances,' (7) saving spaces for the queer-not-yet-thought-of and the queer-to-come."[60]

Postcolonial Interpretation

Postcolonial interpretation in biblical studies emerges from the type of literary analysis practiced by theorists such as Edward Said. In his seminal book *Orientalism*, he critiques the way Western literature stereotypes Eastern cultures as "backward, uncivilized, chaotic—in terms of their legitimation of colonial control and economic exploitation."[61] In biblical studies, one needs to differentiate this type of reading from interpretations that are contextual for a majority-world perspective.[62]

Postcolonial interpretation pushes back against readings of the Bible that led to the marginalization and oppression of peoples and countries controlled by colonial powers. Impressive examples of postcolonial theory are found in *Postcolonial Perspectives in African Biblical Interpretations*.[63] One example is Robert Wafawanaka's study of how the land and conquest themes of the OT were used to justify the European takeover of African land.[64] His essay focuses on how the colonial powers appropriated the story of the conquest in the book of Joshua to provide theological justification for taking the land from indigenous peoples. Wafawanaka provides evidence that colonizers often identified themselves as Israelites and the native peoples as Canaanites and purported to be interested in introducing Christianity while really promoting imperial interests.

59. Guest et al., *Queer Bible Commentary*.
60. Stewart, "LGBT/Queer Hermeneutics," 296.
61. P. Williams, "Post-Colonialism and Narrative," 452; Said, *Orientalism*.
62. Two excellent examples are Havea and Lau, *Reading Ecclesiastes from Asia and Pasifika*; and Hwang, *Contextualization and the Old Testament*.
63. Dube, Mbuvi, and Mbuwayesango, *Postcolonial Perspectives*.
64. Wafawanaka, "'The Land Is Mine!'"

Conclusion to Ideological Interpretation

It is not my purpose in this section to offer an exhaustive description or critique of those who approach the text from an ideological perspective. I have simply offered samples of some of the most active, well-known, and interesting ideological approaches.

Labeling these as ideological readings seems to imply that all other interpretations are nonideological and neutral. The truth is that all interpreters have an ideological lens through which they read the Bible. The question is how these lenses are formed and whether the text can challenge the ideology. Most, if not all, expressions of feminist, Marxist, queer, and postcolonial readings start with an ideological approach formed outside the text and then applied to the OT as a framework for interpretation. At its most helpful, such an approach highlights themes that contribute positively to a given ideology and challenges wrong-minded interpretations that distort the text. I think here of feminist and text-oriented challenges to readings of Gen. 2 that impose a hierarchal view of gender. I find such ideological readings unhelpful, however, when they choose to read a text "against the grain" to make their point or to challenge the text itself. For instance, some queer interpreters approach the texts that prohibit same-sex unions as "clobber texts" and seek to dismiss them rather than see these texts as part of a coherent biblical theology of sexuality. One can also question Kirk-Duggan's use of the biblical exodus theme to support her conclusion that it shows divine preference for the persecuted. While God's care for the persecuted can be seen throughout Scripture, the exodus story does not really support its application to all the categories she lists. Nor does it account for the fact that it is a story about God's special people, who are not "freed" in the modern sense. Rather, the Israelites are released from bondage to Pharaoh in order to become God's servants.

New Historicism

Before leaving this survey of the intersection of literary theory and practice, I should briefly mention New Historicism, whose emergence is associated with Stephen Greenblatt (b. 1943).[65] Most often presented as a perspective rather than a method or a theory, the central premise is that literature has a historical context, and history is a literary construction. In this it is reacting against formalism and New Criticism, which seek to study the text without

---

65. The term "New Historicism" was first used in this sense in Greenblatt, *Renaissance of Self-Fashioning*.

context, and historicism, which aspires to a recovery of historical facts by a neutral interpreter. Here the lines between a literary (fictional) text and a historical text are blurred.

New Historicism is poststructural, denying that a stable coherent historical narrative can be achieved. Instead, history is regarded as unstable and best treated in small chunks or anecdotes. With these anecdotes writers try to capture lived experience, not like a short story of a king's actions, but something more eccentric that seeks to destabilize a common understanding of history. An anecdote arises from the close study of a literary fragment, which reveals something about the culture in which it is embedded. Greenblatt attempts to "speak to the dead" in the close reading of historical anecdotes. Another feature contrasting New Historicism with the old is its emphasis on the subjective nature of knowledge of the past and rejection of the Enlightenment belief that objective knowledge of the past is attainable.[66]

An example of a New Historicist approach to a biblical text is Harold Washington's fascinating study of the recent history of interpreting warfare texts and their relationship to gender in the OT.[67] Using the New Historicist insight that "text and culture are understood to be in a mutually productive relationship with one another,"[68] Washington shows how in the OT, violence expresses itself as masculinity, especially as males dominating women. He highlights how interpretations of these texts are not neutral but are affected by their "cultural and political location."[69] Describing the interpretation of texts of violence from the nineteenth century until after World War II, Washington shows how German historicism in the Rankean tradition (after Leopold von Ranke, 1795–1886), along with Prussian militarism, led scholars like Julius Wellhausen (1844–1918), Friedrich Schwally (1863–1919), and especially Hermann Gunkel (1862–1932) to extol OT militarism and hold it up as a model of masculinity. After World War II, Gerhard von Rad (1901–71) resisted Nazi attacks on the OT and reduced the strongly militaristic approach of his German scholarly predecessors.

In her New Historicist study of the book of Jonah, Yvonne Sherwood shows how professional readers of the book were influenced by their cultural, social, and political locations. Choosing three points in time, she concludes, "To the 1550s Jonah becomes a picture of dissident forces being pitched overboard and turbulent social storms calmed; to the 1780s it speaks in the sweet tone

66. Moore, "History after Theory?"
67. Washington, "Violence and the Construction of Gender."
68. Washington, "Violence and the Construction of Gender," 327.
69. Washington, "Violence and Construction of Gender," 341.

of reason, offering a biblicized transformation of *die Judenfrage*; to the 1860s it speaks in the zoological idiom of the *Origin of Species*."[70]

With this description and examples, relationships among the various literary theories discussed above become apparent. For instance, New Historicism shares some of the same concerns as reader-response approaches associated with *Rezeptionsgeschichte*, which studies how a text has been received and understood by interpretive communities at various points in history.

The Landscape Today

I started this survey of the interaction between literary theory and practice and OT/HB studies in 1980, citing the work of Robert Alter as a stimulus to literary investigation of the biblical text. Rather than being a completely new approach, Alter's work restored a Bible study method going back to early church theologians such as Jerome and Augustine, in Christian circles, and to Philo and Josephus, in Jewish circles. The study of the Bible as literature was interrupted by a historical turn that Prickett associates with the emergence of the modern university in Europe, which treated the Bible as a historical record to be analyzed historically but not from a literary or theological perspective. A review of the main themes of biblical research from 1800 to 1980 demonstrates this obsession with historical issues. Scholarly study of the Bible meant taking a document like the Torah and excavating it to discover earlier sources that were later combined into the finished literary product. Besides the history of composition, the field was also dominated by questions related to historical referentiality, weighing the evidence to determine, for example, whether the patriarchs actually existed or the exodus really occurred.

While not denying the historical dimension, Alter was interested in a different set of questions and sought to identify the literary conventions displayed in the text's final form. This shift coincided with the emergence of another focus of OT scholarship, canonical interpretation. Brevard Childs, one of the architects of this approach, denied any connection between his approach and Alter's, but it is hard to ignore that, while not denying the composite nature of the biblical text, both Childs and Alter insisted on interpreting the text's final form. Alter did this for literary reasons, Childs for theological reasons.[71]

70. Sherwood, "Rocking the Boat."
71. According to Childs, the Scripture of the church is the final form of the text, not some earlier form. See his *Introduction to the Old Testament as Scripture*, 27–83, esp. 80–83, and his *Biblical Theology of the Old and New Testaments*.

As is typical in biblical scholarship, the shift from a historical to a literary interest in the text was rather dramatic, so much so that people talked about a paradigm shift. Those of us who lived through the 1980s and into the 1990s can attest that most of the biblical studies books published at the time had "literary" somewhere in the title. Although scholars did not deny the historical dimension of the texts, they spoke of bracketing out such concerns, probably in reaction to the previous generations' obsession with history.

Alter and those who followed him were more interested in literary analysis than in theory,[72] but some biblical scholars started delving into literary theory, which led them to structuralist, deconstructive, reader-response, and ideological approaches. Theory is important, but sometimes theory can distract from or hinder interpretation.

So where is the field now? Unfortunately, there is not a simple, clear answer to this question. If there was ever a point in an earlier period when one could portray academic biblical studies as monolithic, this is certainly no longer the case. The biblical studies guild is quite fragmented and fractious throughout the world. Before the postmodern era (say before 1980), one could maintain the fiction that biblical scholars can approach their subject from a neutral, objective standpoint and marginalize those coming to the text with a stated viewpoint (e.g., evangelicals, feminists, queer interpreters, et al.). Today, most no longer hold such illusions. It is now clear that historical criticism, a supposedly neutral approach inherited from the Enlightenment, reflects an ideological viewpoint just as any other interpretive approach. The question should be not whether a biblical scholar is ideologically motivated but whether that ideology provides a more elegant interpretation than others.

The field of biblical studies is certainly not in the same place it was in the 1980s or 1990s. Generally speaking, in terms of literary approaches to biblical studies, the 1980s were dominated by Alter-type literary studies. Historical issues were bracketed out, and a text-oriented close reading of the biblical text flourished. Some early critics, such as James Kugel, a brilliant scholar in his own right, believed that Alter's approach wrongly imposed modern literary concepts on biblical literature.[73] However, Robert Kawashima, one of Alter's students, rightly points out that Alter's approach is actually deductive, discovering and then explicating OT literature from the perspective of Hebrew narrative and poetic conventions.[74] The 1990s, however, saw what I would call the hijacking of insightful exploration of Hebrew literary con-

---

72. An observation made by Bodner, *Artistic Dimension*, 3.
73. Kugel, "On the Bible and Literary Criticism."
74. Kawashima, "Comparative Literature and Biblical Studies," 326.

ventions in the interest of theory, especially the type of theory inspired by Jacques Derrida.

In 2007, a little more than a quarter century after *The Art of Biblical Narrative* appeared, the journal *Prooftexts* sponsored a retrospective on Alter's work. The issue discussed the status of literary approaches at that time. I believe that the field had not developed much in that twenty-five year interval, though since 2007 the field has shown some progress.

Already in 2007 deconstruction was seriously on the wane. Alter's biting comment is truer in 2023 than it was when he first delivered it: "Who reads Paul de Man today? Derrida is on his way to becoming a dinosaur, and even Roland Barthes, once the *dernier cri* [latest fashion] of literature studies, is looking increasingly dated."[75] Of course, Alter was talking about secular literary theory; scholarly trends take longer to die out in biblical studies, not to mention theology.

By contrast, Alter's close-reading approach, while not at the center of scholarly attention, was still influential. In his 2007 article, Alter himself cited two of his former students[76] as well as the continuing robust sales of his own earlier work. More recent evidence of continued interest in Alter's work is the excitement and ready reception shown his translation of the HB, which includes notes directing readers' attention to the literary conventions of the text.[77]

The 1990s also saw a resurgence of interest in historical questions, both in the history of composition and in issues of historical referentiality. For instance, after about a decade or more of inattention, scholars began to return to the question of pentateuchal sources,[78] but this return now included a sensitivity to literary questions. For example, in his *Reading the Fractures of Genesis*, David Carr does not automatically assume that "gaps" or "tensions" in the text are a result of different sources being brought together but allows for the possibility that they reflect narrative gapping or literary aporia.[79] Even the Documentary Hypothesis (DH), which has received revived interest and support, might in one sense be considered a literary approach. Joel Baden, for one, offers a very intelligent presentation and defense of a particular form of this theory. Over against traditional approaches going back to Wellhausen, he argues that the separation of the Pentateuch into four sources and the discernment of the compiler is a literary endeavor. He argues that the DH is "a literary solution to a literary problem." After all, "it begins with the

75. Alter, "Response," 368.
76. Partes, *Biography of Ancient Israel*; Kawashima, *Biblical Narrative*.
77. Alter, *Hebrew Bible*, initially appearing in fascicles over recent decades.
78. Emerton, "Unity of the Flood Narrative, Part II."
79. Carr, *Reading the Fractures of Genesis*.

canonical text and the literary problems that require explanation."[80] Baden is correct that the DH is primarily a literary theory, but it is also a diachronic historical approach to a literary issue.

I do not take the absence of the term "literary" in the titles of recent books and articles in the field of biblical studies as a sign that Alter-like literary approaches are dead. In my own work over the past four decades, I have incorporated this approach to the text as a matter of course. In other words, in my writing and that of many others, the literary approach is not a distinct perspective but has been folded into a larger interpretive strategy.

While avoiding the excesses of earlier decades, it may be time to reexamine the literary approach, particularly to look at literary study more broadly to see what literary critics today are saying about narrative and poetry. This may help our attempts to recover the ancient conventions that Hebrew storytellers and poets used to communicate to their ancient audiences and ultimately to us today. This is what I hope to accomplish in the present volume.

Moving On

In a 1997 review of the relationship between New Historicism and biblical studies, Stephen D. Moore observed that as a general principle, by the time biblical scholars become excited about a new literary approach and start using it, it is already becoming passé in the literature departments from which it emerged. His concrete example is New Historicism, which caught the interest of biblical scholars in the late 1990s, when literary scholars were already talking about the demise of New Historicism.[81]

Of course, there are good reasons for the time lag. After all, it is hard enough for biblical scholars to stay current in their own specialties, much less to attain and maintain expertise in another field. Furthermore, biblical studies is inherently a multidisciplinary field of study; virtually all the humanities—including linguistics, literary studies, anthropology/sociology, history, and philosophy—are relevant for the study of the Bible. When biblical scholars do engage with literary theory and practice, it is usually through reading monographs summarizing current trends in the field, supplemented by occasional articles. Biblical scholars do not typically attend literary conferences and rarely dialogue with practitioners in the field. In addition, the field of literary studies is not monolithic and can be contentious as close readers; structuralists; poststructuralists; cognitive theories; advocates of feminist,

---

80. Baden, *Composition of the Pentateuch*, 249.
81. Moore, "History after Theory?"

queer, postcolonial, and rhetorical approaches; and recently anti-mimetic theory vie for attention.

Still, we can identify positive contributions from all these different theories and some common themes. Bible interpreters can learn from many literary theories without jumping fully onto any particular theoretical bandwagon. As we do so, we must remember that virtually all these literary theories and their accompanying practices were formed in relationship to the modern novel (and more recently the postmodern novel) rather than for the study of ancient literature. For example, Genette's taxonomy of different narrator strategies is interesting (though steeped in jargon), but only two of these strategies are actually useful for the study of the HB (see chap. 4).

This variety has led me to be eclectic in how I learn from literary studies, choosing ideas and methods that help me better understand the biblical text. Since I am convinced that the goal of interpretation is to discover the author's intended message, I can learn from literary scholars who defend the idea of authorial intention, not by using authors' biographies to get into their brains but by analyzing their writerly performances. Such a view is supported by leading narratologists today.

Even though I defend the author's intention as the goal of interpretation, I fully recognize that readers have access to the author's message only through the text. I therefore also learn from literary theories that devise strategies for analyzing a text. New Criticism drives interpreters to read a text closely. Structuralism, both in its classical and postclassical forms, gives readers categories and terminology to discern and describe the literary conventions that generate meaning in a text. New Historicism reminds us, over against certain purist textual approaches, that the historical and cultural contexts of a text matter. Ideological approaches help us get out of our own ideological bubbles and consider texts from other perspectives and with different questions in mind. Even deconstruction serves a productive purpose by injecting a sense of humility into the modernist project.

In chapter 3, I begin the transition from theory to practice. I draw on insights from the field of literary studies that I find helpful in the study of OT texts. I begin by describing genre, a fundamental key to interpretation. As we shall see, genre triggers reading strategy.

THREE

GENRE TRIGGERS READING STRATEGY

A genre of literature is a group of texts that share common features. These features might be formal, linguistic, thematic, content-related, or a variety of other similarities. Assigning a genre label to a particular text requires the interpreter to demonstrate relevant similarities within a group of associated texts. "Genre" derives from a French word that also gives us the English word "generalization." Though it is a dubious practice to explain the meaning of a word based on its derivation (i.e., its etymology), the connection between the words "genre" and "generalization" helpfully reminds us that when interpreters talk about the genre of a specific text, they are *generalizing* from an individual text to a class of texts.

Authors never create entirely new types of literature; instead, they write in generic traditions that send signals to their readers about how to interpret their words. Correct interpretation (defined as reading the text as the author intended)[1] depends on identifying the genre of a particular text. In this chapter, I present a theory of genre that recognizes when a specific text is like other texts but avoids a rigid understanding of literary categories. Using structuralist terms, genre is the *langue* (conventions) of a literary culture, on analogy with the grammar of a language; the texts that participate in that genre are the *parole*, equivalent to the actual sentences of a language. To be a competent reader, one must recognize genres and how they work.

Ancient Israel and the broader ancient Near East had no explicit concept of genre, which raises the question whether we are anachronistically imposing

1. See chap. 1 for a description and defense of the author's intention as the goal of interpretation.

this concept onto ancient literature. As far as is presently known, reflection on genre, what we might call genre theory, begins with the Greeks and specifically with the philosophers Plato (ca. 428–347 BC) and Aristotle (384–322 BC).[2] The lack of evidence for genre discussions prior to this time leads some to doubt whether the ancient Near East had a concept of genre.[3] However, an author or a reader need not be conscious of the concept of genre for it to be relevant as a descriptive tool. Authors must write in specific, one might say generic, traditions for their words to make sense to readers. In addition, looking at just the HB, we encounter words that can only be understood as genre descriptions, such as "proverb," "annal/chronicle," "account" (*toledot*, Gen. 2:4 and ten other occurrences in Genesis), and a number of words in the titles of psalms, including "psalm" (*mizmor*) and "song" (*shir*).[4]

The presence of native genre designations raises the question of the appropriateness of the nonnative genre categories used in biblical scholarship. However, linguists have long understood that both native (emic) and nonnative (etic) designations have their utility, and both types of genre labels can be useful in the study of literature as long as each label clearly delineates texts that are actually similar in some way.[5]

Hermann Gunkel and the Origins of Genre Study in Modern Biblical Studies

German Old Testament scholar Hermann Gunkel (1862–1932) did not invent the concept of genre as a theoretical construct. As mentioned above, literary theorists have talked about genre from at least the time of Plato and Aristotle. But as the father of Old Testament form criticism, Gunkel initiated a line of inquiry into the biblical text that continues to the present day. The most common German term for what English-speaking scholars call "form criticism" is *Gattungsgeschichte*, roughly translated as "genre history." Form criticism seeks to identify the genre of a biblical text in order to analyze its meaning and its place within ancient Israelite society and religion (see below on *Sitz im Leben*).[6]

Gunkel took an interdisciplinary approach to the study of genre in biblical studies. In particular, the famous Grimm brothers, Jacob (1785–1863)

2. Plato in his *Republic* and Aristotle in his *Poetics*; see Orsini, "Genres."
3. Grayson, *Babylonian Historical-Literary Texts*, 5.
4. Longman, "Israelite Genres."
5. For the emic/etic distinction, see Pike, *Language in Relationship*; and Poythress, "Analysing a Biblical Text."
6. For a good example of his work, see Gunkel, *The Psalms*.

and Wilhelm (1786–1859), had an important influence on his understanding of genre. The Grimms' study of folklore and their methodology influenced Gunkel a generation later.[7] Thus, when Gunkel developed his approach to form criticism, he was using a genre theory that was already at least a generation old.

Gunkel believed that genres were pure, having an ideal form recognizable by similarities in content, theme, and structure and that each genre had one and only one setting in the life of the community (*Sitz im Leben*). He also had a diachronic understanding of genre, believing that he could analyze a passage and determine its original form, going all the way back to a prewritten oral text. In his method, genre became a tool for historical analysis, allowing him to get back to the original form of the text and its historical situation. Gunkel's understanding of the relationship between biblical genre and its setting in the social life of Israel is central to his project.

Gunkel's insistence that each genre had one and only one place or function in society influenced many other scholars but also generated lively debate. This is especially evident in research on the psalms. One of his prize students, Sigmund Mowinckel, famously argued that the book of Psalms was a libretto of sorts for a New Year festival.[8] Later, Arthur Weiser argued instead that the book was part of an annual festival reaffirming the covenant,[9] and H.-J. Kraus posited a festival that celebrated the choice of Zion as the place where God made his presence known.[10]

The desire to retrieve a supposed original form of the text and connect it to a hypothesized social setting shows the influence of Romanticism on Gunkel and this entire line of research. This influence is not without its problems. First, one may question his assumption that the original form is somehow better or more authentic than a later form of a text that has taken on accretions that render it a hybrid (*Mischwesen*). This Romantic impulse and the idealizing of a simpler original led him to believe that the most ancient expression of a text was very short and that a longer text was evidence of later accretions, which form-critical analysis could delineate.

Second, Gunkel essentially adopted a neoclassical genre theory, which G. N. G. Orsini describes as "a nineteenth-century phenomenon that held a rigid view of genres as pure and hierarchical."[11] His approach to genre can be

---

7. For Gunkel's use of the theory developed by the Grimm brothers and other nineteenth-century folklorists like P. Wendland and E. Norden, see Tucker, *Form Criticism of the Old Testament*, 4–5; and Buss, "The Study of Forms," 50.

8. Mowinckel, *Psalms in Israel's Worship*.

9. Weiser, *Psalms*.

10. Kraus, *Theology of the Psalms*.

11. Orsini, "Genres," 104.

described as taxonomic: each text is assigned to a specific genre and associated with a particular social location. Such an approach to genre can easily become prescriptive rather than descriptive. That is, instead of simply observing similarities between texts of different types (content, themes, structure, vocabulary, etc.), one invokes a list of essential characteristics that a text must display in order to qualify as a member of a genre. Gunkel's approach to genre can be criticized for being overly prescriptive and too rigid because it asserts that there is only one right genre for each text and that each genre has one and only one original setting in life.

Recent Developments in Genre Theory

While some scholars continued to operate by the standards set by Gunkel, new insights began to come into the field in the 1970s. Indeed, these new insights were part of the literary turn of that time period (see chap. 2). James Muilenburg was one of the first to suggest a shift from a diachronic, rigid understanding of genre toward a more descriptive, synchronic approach.[12] Rolf Knierem was another scholar who early on questioned what had become a widely accepted approach to the question of genre in biblical studies.[13] Over the next several decades, many biblical scholars began to work with an understanding of genre that was different from Gunkel's. With this transition, biblical scholarship moved closer to and learned from their colleagues in literary study, who already for decades had been working with a more sophisticated understanding of genre.

In contrast to previous thought, genres are not hard-and-fast categories of literature to which authors must conform when they are writing; instead, they are the result of authors consciously or unconsciously writing in the tradition of others before them in ways that their culture has come to understand as typical of certain types of communication. Authors provide signals to their audience regarding how their words should be taken and thus hopefully communicate their message successfully to their audience.[14] An obvious example of such a signal is found at the beginning of the book of Jude, which starts

12. Muilenburg, "Form Criticism and Beyond."

13. Knierim, "Old Testament Form Criticism." Other scholars who contributed to the shift from a diachronic to a synchronic understanding of genre include Doty, "Concept of Genre"; Doty, "Fundamental Questions"; Hanson, "Response to J. J. Collins' Methodological Issues"; Letzen-Dies, "Methodologische Überlegungen."

14. This view is not a return to a traditional author-centered theory of literary meaning, which purports to somehow get into the author's mind. Instead, it is a text-based approach, which analyses the author's act of writing in order to make a hypothesis about a text's meaning. See Strickland, *Structuralism or Criticism?*; and esp. Vanhoozer, *Is There a Meaning in This Text?*

by introducing the writer and the audience and includes a blessing (vv. 1–2) typical of a Greco-Roman letter.

In recent decades, genre has been described with various metaphors. René Wellek and Austin Warren liken genre to an institution (like a church or a school), which one joins and then follows the rules of the institution.[15] Todorov thinks of genres as codes that send out signals to be deciphered.[16] R. D. Abrams speaks of the communicative function of genres as "patterns of expression": authors conform to them, and readers expect them.[17]

Another helpful analogy for understanding genre is the family. No one in an extended family looks and acts exactly like anyone else in their family, but a family resemblance is often apparent. In terms of literary genres, this family resemblance may relate to content, form, or mood, though one might detect a family resemblance based on any type of similarity between two or more texts. Both Mark Sneed and Katharine Dell apply a family-resemblance approach to genre in their studies of wisdom in the OT.[18]

Will Kynes provides an especially provocative and useful analogy to explain the concept of genre. A genre is like a constellation of stars. Since antiquity, humans have looked to the skies and seen patterns among the stars. Today even many children can recognize Ursa Major (Great Bear), Orion, Canis Major (Great Dog), and more. The Big Dipper is not technically a constellation, but a pattern within the constellation Ursa Major. Similarly, literary texts, like stars, can participate in more than one genre, contra the principle of traditional form criticism that a literary text exists in one and only one genre. Kynes also points out that stars, like genres, can be grouped with different stars based on different criteria, such as size or brightness. Texts cannot be understood in strict isolation but need to be read in relationship to each other. Kynes sees genre as an "intertextual shorthand" that highlights certain significant similarities between texts and can lead to a richer reading of the text, as long as genres, which he calls "irrigation ditches,"[19] don't become dams by restricting texts to only one genre.[20]

15. Wellek and Warren, *Theory of Literature*, 226.
16. Todorov, *The Fantastic*, 11–12, 37.
17. R. Abrams, "Complex Relations of Simple Forms."
18. Sneed, "'Grasping after the Wind,'" 59, citing A. Fowler, *Kinds of Literature*; Dell, "Deciding the Boundaries of 'Wisdom,'" 155–56.
19. Kynes, *Obituary for "Wisdom Literature,"* 110.
20. Kynes, *Obituary for "Wisdom Literature,"* 140: "Rejecting the notion of a single correct genre for texts—a single pattern in which they should be read that has emerged from a solitary vantage point—and instead embracing the multidimensional subjectivity of interpretation might actually enable interpreters to produce a more objective interpretation by triangulating the text's meaning among a broader array of subjective vantage points."

Kynes also points out that genres, like constellations, have a historical dimension. Due to a difference in location and time and because stars migrate over time, the Babylonians saw patterns in the sky that are different from those that moderns see today. Likewise, modern interpreters of ancient literary texts need not restrict generic groupings to only those recognized by ancient readers. In the Bible, interpreters only occasionally get glimpses of genre categories, such as in the titles of some psalms (e.g., *miktam*, Ps. 16; etc.), but they recognize different groupings based on similarities in tone, content, and form (e.g., hymns, laments, thanksgiving psalms, etc.).[21]

Kenneth Pike uses terms derived from linguistics to refer to different sounds that would not be considered meaningful to a native speaker ("etic," from phonetic; e.g., different pronunciations of the letter *p*) and those that would be meaningful ("emic," from phonemic; e.g., the difference between *p* and *b*). Applying this terminology to genre, *miktam* is an emic category, and *kinah* (lament) is an etic one.

At first glance, Kynes's view that literary texts can participate in more than one genre and that genre categories can change over time might strike one as relativistic, but Kynes is quick to point out that this view of genre does not lead to relativism. He rightly points out that the text itself puts constraints on one's understanding of its genre. After all, he says, "Any genre grouping is constrained by the actual features of the text." In other words, it would be wrong to suggest that a text participates in a genre with other texts with which it shares no features. Assigning a text to a particular genre requires that the interpreter be able to point to actual similarities between the texts. But according to Kynes and others like him, it is also a mistake to suggest that a text can belong to only one genre, and this can also lead to a distorted understanding of a text. As he succinctly puts it, "Arguing that *Pilgrim's Progress* is not an allegory is a misinterpretation, but so is arguing that an allegory is all that it is."[22]

A More Flexible View of Genre

Genre categories, therefore, are not rigid, watertight compartments. Rather, they are classifications with fuzzy edges or boundaries.[23] And if genres are not rigid categories, then they aren't strictly taxonomic and cer-

21. I do not believe that Kynes would agree with me on this particular point since he argues that the category "Wisdom literature" is not helpful because it is a recent invention (Kynes, *Obituary for "Wisdom Literature"*). See my critique in the essay titled "Scope of Wisdom Literature."
22. Kynes, *Obituary for "Wisdom Literature,"* 140.
23. Longman, "Israelite Genres," 183.

tainly not hierarchical. Assigning a text to a genre simply draws attention to a perceived relationship between texts that may improve our understanding of them.

There are additional implications of this view of genre: (1) genre analysis should concern itself with the final form of the text and not be used to speculate about a supposed earlier "pure" form; (2) genres do not have only one *Sitz im Leben*; and (3) texts can participate in more than one genre on both a vertical and a horizontal level. Each of these points merits further consideration, in particular the third, which is especially germane to the present project.

First, traditional form criticism operated with a rigid understanding of genre and sought to find an ideal pure form. If a text exhibits features considered foreign to its supposed genre, they were assumed to be accretions to a purer, more original expression of the genre, and the task of the interpreter was to recover that original form. In contrast to this view, contemporary genre theory emphasizes a flexible understanding of genre that recognizes that genres have fuzzy edges. This perspective leads to a synchronic rather than a diachronic view of genre.

Second, Gunkel's insistence that each genre has only one social location (*Sitz im Leben*) is widely recognized as too restrictive. Indeed, there may be other *Sitze* that are more relevant to a genre, such as a literary location (*Sitz in der Literatur*).

Finally, interpreters should realize that a text may participate in more than one genre, both vertically and horizontally. Vertically, a text can be associated with a variety of genres depending on whether the text shares many or just a few features with groups of other texts. Todorov says it is possible to speak of genres on a scale that ranges from one text ("jedes Werk stilt eine eigene 'Gattung' dar") to the maximum ("alle Texte gehören zu einer 'Gattung'").[24] Taking Ps. 98 as an example, we can attempt a selective naming of the vertical genres that this text participates in, moving from a broad genre classification (many texts sharing a few common traits) to a narrow one (a small cluster of texts sharing many common traits).

A Genre Analysis of Psalm 98

Psalm 98 Is a Poem

A fuller discussion of poetry appears in chapter 5, but for now we can say that Ps. 98 clearly displays features that distinguish it from prose. Instead of

24. Cited by Hempfer, *Gattungstheorie*, 137.

sentences and paragraphs, the psalm breaks into cola (units), each consisting of two to four Hebrew words that display some form of parallelism (an echoing effect within a poetic line) within each two-cola line (see "Parallelism" in chap. 5).

> Make a joyful noise to the LORD, all the earth;
> > break forth into joyous song and sing praises.
> Sing praises to the LORD with the lyre,
> > with the lyre and the sound of melody.
> With trumpets and the sound of the horn
> > make a joyful noise before the King, the LORD. (98:4–6 NRSVue)

In the third stanza, the poet employs personification as the inanimate creation joins in the celebration of God:

> Let the floods clap their hands,
> > let the hills sing together for joy. (98:8 NRSVue)

Psalm 98 Is Lyric Poetry

Beyond a few shared stylistic features, not all poetry is alike. The term "lyric poetry" refers to poems in which poets express their inner thoughts and feelings. Psalm 98 is such a poem, as opposed to an epic poem (e.g., Exod. 15; Judg. 5) or a dramatic or didactic poem (e.g., Job 3–37).

Psalm 98 Is a Hymn

The book of Psalms contains various types of lyric poems, though some might prefer to see them as different genres rather than as types of lyric poems. Most agree, however, that there are at least four types of psalms, which are defined by their mood and orientation toward life. Walter Brueggemann famously describes the first three types as follows: *hymns* are psalms of orientation, sung when everything is going well; *laments* are psalms of disorientation, sung when life is falling apart; and *thanksgiving* psalms are psalms of reorientation, sung when God answers the lament and reorients the worshiper to life.[25] To this list, Pemberton adds psalms of *confidence*, psalms sung when God does not answer laments. In these situations, he does not want his people to lament indefinitely; rather, he wants them to come to trust him amid and despite their suffering and problems.[26]

---

25. Brueggemann, *Message of the Psalms*, 25–167.
26. Pemberton, *After Lament*.

Psalm 98 clearly reflects the first of these four types of psalms, the hymn. The first stanza calls on Israel to praise the Lord, who has won a victory on their behalf in the *past* (vv. 1–3). The second stanza calls on all inhabitants of the earth to praise God, who is their king in the *present* (vv. 4–6). The final stanza calls on the whole creation, animate and inanimate, to praise God, who is coming to judge in the *future* (vv. 7–9).

Psalm 98 Is a Hymn Celebrating the Divine Warrior

Various types of hymns appear in the psalms. Psalm 29 worships God as the one behind the power of the storm; Ps. 47, as king enthroned and reigning over the nations; Ps. 46, as the one who dwells on Zion. Psalm 98's presentation of God as victor, king, and judge relates to God as warrior. It is therefore accurate to call Ps. 98 a divine-warrior victory song.

Psalm 98 and Psalm 96

Reading Ps. 98 alongside Ps. 96 we see many similarities of mood and content that justify regarding these two as a genre in their own right. Both Pss. 96 and 98 begin with the composer urging worshipers to sing "a new song" to the Lord because he has saved them (96:1–3; 98:1–3). Both psalms acknowledge God's kingship (96:10; 98:4–6) and proclaim that God will judge the world in righteousness (96:13; 98:9).

Psalm 98 as a Unique Poem

Though similarities are apparent between Ps. 98 and other psalms, in the final analysis Ps. 98 is its own uniquely powerful psalm, not exactly like any other. Indeed, studying the psalm alongside other similar ones highlights the uniqueness of Ps. 98, which includes the crisp three-part stanza structure of three verses each that parallel each other in a way that can be summarized as follows:

> O Israel, praise God, who is your Victor in the past. (vv. 1–3)
> O inhabitants of the earth, praise God, who is your King in the
> present. (vv. 4–6)
> O all of creation, praise God, who is your Judge in the future. (vv. 7–9)

Thus Ps. 98 illustrates how a single literary text can participate in more than one genre, moving from broad genres with a few shared features (e.g., poem, lyric poetry) to a narrow genre with many features in common (e.g., divine-warrior hymn).

Psalm 98 as a Kingship Psalm

Thus far I have explored how Ps. 98 participates in multiple genres in a vertical fashion, from broad to narrow, but texts can also participate in multiple genres in a horizontal fashion, in which a specific trait is traced across many texts that share it. Psalm 98 is a divine-warrior hymn, to be sure, but it can also be grouped and studied with other psalms that speak of God's kingship. Gunkel noted a genre of royal psalms, but he treated them as distinct from other psalm types. However, Ps. 98 can be treated as a hymn, specifically a divine-warrior victory song, as well as a psalm extolling God as king. In this way, Ps. 98 participates in a genre alongside texts such as Pss. 2, 47, 93, 95, 96, and 97.

Psalm 2's Multiple Genre Participation

Kynes's constellation analogy suggests that a text might participate in differing genres over time. Having identified Ps. 98 as both a hymn and a kingship psalm, I can further illustrate this with respect to Ps. 2. This psalm was originally composed and read as a hymn of kingship, likely sung at the inauguration of the Davidic king, but after the demise of kingship at the beginning of the exile, Ps. 2 began to be read as an eschatological messianic text.

Psalm 2 has four stanzas of three verses each, and each stanza has a chiastic structure, meaning that the units form a crossing pattern (in this case *abb'a'*).[27] The first stanza (vv. 1–3) focuses on earthly kings. The composer asks why these kings vainly try to resist the Lord and his anointed king. The second stanza (vv. 4–6) changes focus to God in heaven, who ridicules them and proclaims that he has "installed my king on Zion, my holy mountain." In the third stanza (vv. 7–9) the composer keeps a heavenly focus and proclaims "the LORD's decree" (v. 7), which is addressed to him: "He said to me." This decree begins with a declaration based on the so-called Davidic covenant: "You are my son; today I have become your father" (cf. 2 Sam. 7:14). Psalm 2 has no title naming a writer, but since David was the one who received this decree, he has traditionally been regarded as the composer (Acts 4:25). The fourth and final stanza (Ps. 2:10–12) reverts to earth, where the speaker chastises the rebellious kings and urges them to submit to God and his royal son.

Regardless of whether Ps. 2 was actually composed at the time of David, the citation of the decree from 2 Samuel makes it extremely likely that it was written and originally used during the monarchy period. Most scholars think it was a song sung during the inauguration of a new king, a descendant

---

27. See "Chiasm" under "Secondary Poetic Conventions" in chap. 5 below.

of David, though it may also have been used in the context of threats from foreign powers.

However, this is not how the NT authors and Christian readers today interpret this psalm. They see the reference to God's "anointed" (messiah) as pointing to Christ (Mark 1:1 and parallels; Acts 13:33; Heb. 1:5; 5:5; Rev. 12:5; 19:15). According to the view presented in 1 and 2 Kings, the Davidic dynasty rarely lived up to the expectation of a godly king expressed in Deut. 17:14–20. Eventually, God brought an end to the dynasty, using the Babylonians to remove Zedekiah from the throne and absorb Judah into its vast empire (586 BC). The end of the monarchy surely brought a theological crisis for those who remembered the divine promise to David: "Your house and your kingdom will endure forever before me; your throne will be established forever" (2 Sam. 7:16). At this point, the faithful began to read Ps. 2 as having an eschatological significance: the "anointed one" (messiah) would come in the future, a son of David who would once again rule on the throne.

It was likely that the final form and order of the book of Psalms was established after the end of the monarchy. While I remain unconvinced of the merits of the relatively recent elaborate narrative readings of the book of Psalms as a whole (see chap. 6), the intentional placement of Pss. 1 and 2 as introductory poems to the book has been recognized since the early church.[28] In sum, as time passed after the end of the monarchy, Ps. 2 shifted from being understood and used as an inauguration psalm to being read with an eschatological sense, a future orientation that found its fulfillment in Christ.

How Genre Shapes Reading Strategy

Literary genres are modes of classification to identify types of literature that share common traits. Authors write texts and send signals to their readers regarding how to take their words. Individual texts participate in one or more genres, since authors never create texts that have no relationship with previous writings.[29] A completely unique text, if such a thing could exist, would not be understandable. How we read a text is informed by prior experiences of reading similar texts or by learning from others how certain types of texts are to be read.

A classic and obvious example of a genre signal sent from author to reader is the opening phrase "once upon a time," which communicates to readers that the text is a fairy tale, an imaginative short story with characters such as

28. So Jerome (ca. AD 400); see Janowski, *Arguing with God*, 348.
29. I discuss the relationship between genre and intertextuality in chap. 6.

witches, elves, fairies, and other fantasy creatures and often featuring magic of some sort. Among other signals, the label "fairy tale" warns readers that they are entering an imaginary space.

The same can be said of any work of fiction, including the novel. When readers recognize that they are reading a novel—perhaps informed by the cover or title page, which in modern publications often has the obvious paratextual signal "A Novel"—they are alerted to "suspend disbelief" if they are competent readers. As Umberto Eco states, "The basic rule in dealing with a work of fiction is that the reader must tacitly accept a fictional agreement, which Coleridge called 'the suspension of disbelief.' The reader has to know that what is being narrated is an imaginary story, but he must not therefore believe that the writer is telling lies."[30]

Heather Dubrow helpfully illustrates how genre identification shapes reading.[31] She creates a text and presents it as the first paragraph of a story that she titles "Murder at Marplethorpe": "The clock on the mantelpiece said ten thirty, but someone had suggested recently that the clock was wrong. As the figure of the dead woman lay on the bed in the front room, a no less silent figure glided rapidly from the house. The only sounds to be heard were the ticking of that clock and the loud wailing of the infant."

The title of this text signals to readers that the work is a murder mystery or perhaps a detective novel. With this understanding, they imagine that the woman is dead because she has been murdered. The mention of the time might later be a clue as to when the murder took place. Readers may suspect that the silent person quietly leaving the house is the killer and that the infant is wailing as a result of the violence against the woman, whom they suspect is the child's mother. As they read on, some of their initial conclusions may turn out to be wrong, but recognizing the paragraph as the opening of a mystery novel at least points readers in the right direction.

Dubrow then asks her readers to interpret the same paragraph again, but this time under a different title: "The Biography of David Marplethorpe." Now, rather than assuming there was a murder, readers may conclude that the woman died in childbirth. The silent figure might be the midwife. Determining the accuracy of the clock is relevant for establishing the time of the birth, and since this is the biography of David Marplethrope, readers assume that he is the baby and is crying because that is what babies do when they are born.

As Dubrow illustrates, whether consciously or unconsciously, we interpret according to what we believe the genre of the text we are reading is. We may

30. Eco, *Six Walks in the Fictional Woods*, 75.
31. Dubrow, *Genre*, 1–3.

be wrong, and this misidentification will distort our understanding of the text. Of course, the identification of a text's genre is often a matter of debate and is determined by how well we can discern and interpret the genre signals.

One such debate involves determining the genre of Gen. 1–3, which is often identified as either straightforward history or myth, but I believe it should instead be considered a figurative depiction of history.[32] Thus, when one reads of the creation of the woman from the man's side or rib (Gen. 2:21–23), one should not expect that males have one less rib than females or that this is how God actually made the first female, but neither should this description be understood to make no historical claim. The historical claim is that God made humanity. In this case the focus is on women, and the figurative depiction is intended to teach about the mutual and equal relationship between men and women as God created them (from the *side*, not from the head or the feet).

Even if most interpreters agree on a text's genre, there can be disagreement about how that genre functions in its ancient context. Daniel 7–12 contains four apocalyptic visions filled with imagery depicting the present condition of God's people and God's future rescue. But how should we understand the imagery, including the references to time (e.g., "time, times and half a time," Dan. 7:25; 12:7)? Do these verses point to some future three-and-a-half-year period, or are they rather a figurative way of talking about how evil grabs hold, gains traction, and then slows down and finally goes away?[33] If one believes, as I do, that numbers function in a figurative manner in apocalyptic texts, then one will adopt the second reading. In other words, knowing that a text is apocalyptic should trigger the expectation that numbers should not be taken at face value but rather understood to point to some other type of truth.

In parts 2 and 3 of this book, I present more extensive discussions of particular biblical texts and devote considerable attention to the question of genre in order to illustrate the central importance of genre to interpretation.

32. See under "Literary Reading" in chap. 7, below.
33. See Longman, *Daniel*, 190–91.

FOUR

Narrative Prose as Genre

Much of the HB is written in prose. One could call prose a "mode" of writing to distinguish it from another mode, poetry. However, one could also consider these as two different genres, with each having many subgenres. Whatever nomenclature is used, the predominant literary mode found in the HB is prose, although there is also a considerable amount of poetry. Indeed, whole books are written in poetic form (e.g., Isaiah, Song of Songs), but poetry can be found in books that are predominantly prose (e.g., Gen. 49; Exod. 15; Judg. 5), and prose appears in books that are predominantly poetry (e.g., Job; Jeremiah).

Hebrew poetry is composed of terse cola forming parallel lines, which in turn form stanzas. By contrast, Hebrew prose translates into English as sentences that form paragraphs and together create longer discourses. English translations generally reflect the difference in genre by how the text is formatted. For poetry, the cola are set on separate lines, with the second (and occasionally third or more) parallel cola slightly indented below the first line. Just a glance at the printed page of a modern English translation reveals whether a text is poetry or prose, since poetry's shorter lines leave lots of white space.

Although the border between poetry and prose is sometimes fuzzy, prose writing is generally closer to ordinary language, the way people normally talk, while poetry displays more literary artifice. This difference is one of degree, however, since even the prose of the Bible displays some amount of artifice. A literary study of the Bible's prose highlights how a story is told and what Hebrew storytelling conventions are used.

In the HB, prose serves the interest of narrative storytelling. H. Porter Abbott defines narrative as "the representation of an event or a series of events."[1] David Herman calls narrative "a strategy for creating mental representations of the world."[2] Narratologists debate whether the representation of explicit causation is a requirement of narrative. Some scholars, such as E. M. Forster, believe that for prose to be narrative, there must be explicit causation between events. For him, "The king died, and the queen died" is not narrative, but "The king died, and the queen died of grief" is.[3] Others, such as Seymour Chatman, question the necessity of explicit causation. Chatman argues that readers implicitly supply causation even when it is not explicitly stated.[4]

Prose and narrative are not synonymous terms, which is why I use the expression "narrative prose." Nonnarrative prose appears, for example, in some scientific reports, and although much of the poetry in the Bible is lyric poetry, we also see examples of narrative poetry, where poetry tells a story (see, e.g., Song 5:2–6:3). A descriptive essay is nonnarrative since it does not tell a story but merely describes what a place looks like or how a person looks, thinks, or acts. The Bible does have examples of such description, but they are rare and embedded within a larger narrative. So even though nonnarrative prose is possible, it is generally rare and largely absent from the Bible.

The fact that narrative is a representation of an event or events leads to a fundamental distinction in narratology between the events themselves (whether fictional or real) and the representation of those events. Scholars use different terms to express this distinction. For the events themselves, Russian Formalists (among the first to note the distinction) use *fabula*, but most English-speaking scholars use "story." The Formalists call the representation of the *fabula*/story the *sjuzet*, which others refer to as "discourse." The *sjuzet*/ discourse selects, orders, and comments on the *fabula*/story. To avoid unnecessary jargon, I will use the terms "story" and "discourse" to distinguish between the events and the representation of those events.

The narratives in the Bible are representations of events and therefore discourse. That they are representations of events does not mean they have no connection to actual space-time events, but it does mean that the events are presented selectively and in a way that may differ from the actual sequence of events. Written history is not a work of fiction, but it does reflect the writer's own perspective on the events being recounted. Since our focus is on the literary nature of biblical literature, the distinction between a narrative's story and its discourse involves a recognition that the discourse manipulates the

---

1. Abbott, *Cambridge Introduction to Narrative*, 13.
2. D. Herman, *Story Logic*, 5.
3. As told by Abbott, *Cambridge Introduction to Narrative*, 42.
4. Chatman, *Story and Discourse*, 45–46.

events of a story to tell it in a way that captures the imagination and shapes the reader's understanding of the significance of the events. As Kent Puckett says, "The ordering of events is . . . one way in which representation confers significance on life, one way in which discourse not only represents events but also gives value to the events it represents."[5] In countering the idea that narrative thinking (what David Herman calls "story logic") is for simple people who need help understanding complex ideas, Herman asserts, "Narrative is not a cognitive crutch for those who cannot manage to think in more rigorous ways, but rather a basic and general strategy for making sense of experience."[6]

To explore how a narrator manipulates the events of the story, I will use categories such as narrative time, characterization, focalization (point of view), setting (story world), and interpretation (ideology/theology). Using narrative time as a quick example, often the storyteller does not start at the beginning and proceed through the events in chronological order. Some narratives start in the middle (*in media res*), and others start at the end and work backward to tell the story. As I will show, most biblical stories start at the beginning and proceed to the end, but sometimes we encounter what biblical scholars call dischronologized narrative (see below on Gen. 10–11) in which a later event is mentioned before an earlier one.

The classical term for representation is "mimesis," which comes from Plato and Aristotle, but it is also sometimes referred to as "verisimilitude." Plato is critical of mimetic practices because he believes them to be a form of deceit. He understands "mimesis" as imitation, as when authors speak in the voice of another (a character or narrator) rather than speaking in their own name, something Plato felt was dangerous to society. Aristotle defines mimesis more broadly so that even authors speaking in their own name are engaged in representation. He also states that history does not have exclusive claim to truth; indeed, "mimetic representation is even considered by Aristotle superior to history, because poetry expresses the general (that which could be), while history only expresses the particular (that which has been)."[7]

The stories of the HB are deceptively familiar for three reasons. First, even in this day of increasing biblical illiteracy, some Bible stories are still well known to many people, at least in broad terms if not in detail. Many in the West have at least a vague idea of the stories of the flood, the exodus, David and Goliath, and more. Second, more English translations of the Bible are available today than ever before, including the NIV and NLT (two of

5. Puckett, *Narrative Theory*, 30.
6. D. Herman, *Story Logic*, 24.
7. Newman, "Mimesis," 309.

the bestselling English translations), which render the original in smooth and accessible English. Third, there are similarities between ancient Hebrew stories and modern stories. Like modern stories, Bible stories have plots and characters, narrators present the action from a specific point of view and organize the dialogue, and the action takes place in specific settings.

Yet in spite of these general similarities, interpreters should listen to the reminder of Robert Alter, the premier literary analyst of the Bible in my generation: "Every culture, even every era in a particular culture, develops distinctive and sometimes intricate codes for telling its stories, involving everything from narrative point of view, procedures of description and characterization, the management of dialogue, to the ordering of time and the organization of plot."[8] We will not be competent to interpret OT narrative well unless we understand its conventions and recognize some of its often-subtle differences from Western, particularly English, narratives. In the discussion that follows, I draw examples from a variety of OT stories but especially from the book of Esther.

Let us begin by exploring the role of the narrator and the narrative point of view. We will then ask whether a story's setting contributes meaning to the narrative. After that, we will talk about characters and other issues of style.

✦ EXCURSUS: NARRATOLOGY (THE STUDY OF NARRATIVE) ✦

The leading premise of this book is that the Bible in its final form has an aesthetic quality, which interpreters must take into account. I do not deny that this aesthetic quality is bound up with its grounding in history and its theological teaching, but in this book I focus on the OT's *literary* shape and make only occasional connections to questions of history and theology.

Another important premise of this book is that biblical scholars can learn from their colleagues in literary disciplines and that they will benefit if they make themselves aware of developments in the study of narrative and poetry. For this reason, I will take a moment to describe the present state of narratology.

I am not an expert in this field, but no biblical scholar is, since it is hard enough to stay on the cutting edge of specialties within one's own field. Yet I have tried to become familiar with the lay of the land through interaction with colleagues in literary disciplines and reading as widely as I can.

Narratologists today typically trace their roots to the work of structuralists from the previous generation such as the early Barthes, Todorov, and especially Genette, who

8. Alter, "How Convention Helps Us Read," 115.

attempted to construct a grammar of literature.[9] Although these scholars helped de-velop categories and terms to discuss the various features of narratives, they have been criticized by their successors for their "scientificity, anthropomorphism, disregard for context, and gender-blindness."[10] This later generation of theorists consider themselves postclassical structuralists, acknowledging their debt to the earlier generation but trying to address their perceived shortcomings.

James Phelan and Peter J. Rabinowitz, representing a rhetorical approach, define nar-rative as "somebody telling somebody else, on some occasion, and for some purposes, that something happened to someone or something."[11] Thus, they interpret the text as an act of communication rather than simply treating the text as an object, a criticism that might be leveled at scholars such as Alter influenced by New Critics. That they see the act of communication in a literary text as an interaction between author, text, and reader is clear from this statement: "Our approach assumes that texts are designed by authors (consciously or not) to affect readers in particular ways; that those authorial designs are conveyed through the occasions, words, techniques, structures, forms, and dialogic relations of texts as well as the genres and conventions readers use to under-stand them; and that since reader responses are ideally a consequence of those designs, they can also serve as an initial guide to (although misreadings are possible, not as a guarantee of) the workings of the text."[12]

This approach takes the author's intention (design) seriously. Authors write in a way to send signals to readers regarding how to take their words, but readers must be competent to understand those signals in the proper way. That there is what one might call a determinate meaning is the consequence of understanding that there can be incor-rect readings or interpretations of texts. Phelan and Rabinowitz rightly say that it is the responsibility of the actual readers to imagine themselves as the original readers if they are to arrive at a correct reading.[13]

Phelan and Rabinowitz represent their rhetorical approach admirably as inductive rather than deductive: they develop their theory from their reading of stories rather than imposing a theory on them. They are not "relativists" and do not regard all interpretations as equally valid. Yet they are self-admitted pluralists, able to learn from approaches other than their own. Indeed, Phelan and Rabinowitz are particularly attuned to the work of their colleague David Herman, who approaches narrative in the light of a theory of mind informed by cognitive linguistics, cognitive psychology, and philosophy.

Herman self-consciously builds on and moves beyond the work of classical narra-tologists like Todorov and Genette. He notes the weakness in the work of the previous

---

9. See "Text-Centered Literary Approaches" in chap. 2 and its accompanying notes.
10. L. Herman and Vervaeck, "Postclassical Narratology," 450.
11. D. Herman et al., *Narrative Theory*, 3.
12. D. Herman et al., *Narrative Theory*, 5.
13. D. Herman et al., *Narrative Theory*, 6.

generation because it was grounded in Saussurean semiotic theory, which speaks only of the sign and its signifier. Herman believes that this lacks an appreciation of how the sign points to a reference outside itself.

Herman centers his approach on the concept of "worldmaking."[14] Authors of stories create worlds in which readers take up "imaginative residence."[15] Herman focuses on fiction, but he would agree that such an understanding is still relevant for narratives that refer to real space-time events. After all, as I will explore in this volume and in the next of the series, the historical narratives of the OT are not the events themselves but representations of those events. Those representations follow the same dynamic as prose fiction, so that the author uses a narrator to select and to focalize the presentation. The author (or if one prefers, the implied author; see below) uses the narrator to present the characters' action and speech in a particular setting and so forth.

I will talk more about this later; the point here is that even though narratologists like Herman focus on fictional stories, their insights are helpful for the study of what one might consider to be historical narrative. After all, what the OT gives readers are story-like histories. Herman's understanding of narrative as "accounts of what happened to particular people and of what it was like for them to experience what happened"[16] is appropriate whether the narrative is fictional or nonfictional.

Herman is especially hard on anti-intentionalist approaches to the study of narrative.[17] He believes that the previous generation's dismissal of the author's intention is wrong minded. As I have also argued, although readers cannot get into the author's mind, they can evaluate and interpret the author's literary performance as a product of that mind. One of the biggest differences Herman has with the rhetorical approach of Phelan and Rabinowitz is his rejection of the concept of the implied author, which he believes was created to work around the idea that readers can't get into the author's mind. In this respect I agree with Phelan and Rabinowitz that, despite this criticism, the concept of the implied author is still helpful. Indeed, due to the composite nature of most biblical narrative, I argue that the implied author is an especially helpful concept.

I mention the work of Phelan and Rabinowitz, representing a rhetorical approach to narrative, and of Herman, who approaches narrative in the light of a theory of the mind, because I have found these approaches among the most helpful. In later parts of our study of narrative, I will draw on their work when discussing matters such as character, setting, focalization, and more. I will be rather eclectic myself. It's also important to be mindful that these narrative approaches are developed with a particular focus on the modern novel. Many of the terms and categories they develop are relevant to the diversity of stories in the modern period. Thus I am not only eclectic in my use of contemporary

14. D. Herman et al., *Narrative Theory*, 14.
15. D. Herman et al., *Narrative Theory*, 14.
16. D. Herman, *Basic Elements of Narrative*, 2.
17. D. Herman et al., *Narrative Theory*, 44.

narratology but also extremely selective. Indeed, regarding the terminology of narrative categories, the structuralist tradition can be criticized as excessive. As Genette himself admits, "In an area we regularly grant to induction and empiricism, the proliferation of concepts and terms will doubtless have annoyed more than one reader, and I do not expect 'posterity' to retain too large a part of these propositions."[18]

•••

From Author to Reader

Author–Implied Author–Narrator

In chapter 1, I discussed the issue of the author's role in producing meaning in a literary text. There I argued for locating the meaning of the text in the author's intention, pushing back against the anti-intentionalist arguments that started with the New Critics in the mid-twentieth century and following the lead of important twenty-first-century narratologists like David Herman. However, I also acknowledged that we cannot get into the head of an author, especially deceased authors about whom we have little or no information apart from what they have written. Nonetheless, interpreters can read what authors have written and form a hypothesis with greater or lesser probability about what they meant based on what they have written. How convincing our interpretation is depends on our ability to justify it from the text itself.

In this section, I examine how the author tells the story through a narrator. Narrators are a literary device by which an author controls the (re)presentations of events. Whether the narrator is a character in the story or outside the story, it is the literary construct that authors create to present the story. The narrator chooses how to tell the story, but since it is constructed by the author and operates at the whim of the author, the narrator gives readers a window into the author's (or the implied author's) purpose in telling the story.

The "implied author" is a concept that some theorists, beginning with Wayne C. Booth, invoke as a kind of mediating figure between the author and the narrator.[19] If one can't speak of an author's intended meaning, perhaps it is appropriate to speak of the author who is implied by the text.[20] Herman insists, however, that there is no need to think of an implied author and that it was created as a kind of "work-around" to counter anti-intentionalist

18. Genette, *Narrative Discourse*, 263.
19. Booth, *Rhetoric of Fiction*, 70–75.
20. D. Herman et al., *Narrative Theory*, 47.

arguments. I agree with Herman that once one drops the idea that it is impossible to speak of an author's intended meaning, then the idea of an implied author becomes unnecessary in most instances.

However, biblical narrative is where the concept of an implied author proves helpful. Most, if not all, narrative books of the OT are the product of more than a single flesh-and-blood author. They are a result of a history of composition and the product of more than one hand. Biblical scholarship has long recognized that the final form of the books we know today was written or redacted over a period of time. Reconstructing the history of a book's composition is often a matter of debate and some speculation, but only the most doctrinaire would defend the idea that narrative books of the OT were written by a single author. Rather, many real authors have worked on a particular book, with their work building on each other until the book reaches the form it has in the Christian canon. In one sense, the final redactor (editor) is the author since the meaning structure of the book results from the final additions, omissions, and rearrangements the final redactor has made, but interpreters can equally invoke the concept of the implied author.

For expediency, in this book I will use the word "author" to refer to the implied author, since the goal is not to get into the mind of the author[21] but to evaluate the author's written performance.[22] Accordingly, I will move on to the issue of the relationship between the author and the narrator of a literary discourse.

In terms of general narrative theory, we must recognize that the narrator may not be channeling the author's meaning and that there are different types of narrators in modern and postmodern novels. In some novels, characters serve as narrators (e.g., Laurence Sterne's *The Life and Opinions of Tristam Shandy*), while in others, the story is told by a nameless narrator who stands outside the story. Some narrators, especially if they are characters within the story, may be unreliable (e.g., Graham Greene's *The End of the Affair*). Their knowledge may be limited or simply confused. These variations in narrative strategy are important to explore when studying the wide array of literature through the ages up to the present day.

However, with one notable exception, OT narrative adopts a consistent strategy regarding the narrator. A third-person, unnamed, omniscient, and omnipresent narrator—what Genette calls zero focalization—tells the stories of the OT (focalization is discussed below). The narrator is not identified as

---

21. Scripture recognizes the impossibility of getting into the mind of another person: "For who knows a person's thoughts except their own spirit within them?" (1 Cor. 2:11).

22. For a helpful use of the concept of the implied author along these lines, see Boda, "Authors and Readers."

a character in the story but presents the action and the dialogue of the story. The biblical narrator is rightly described as omniscient because he[23] speaks of things that no human character could possibly know. For instance, he knows what people are thinking and what they are doing when no one else is around. The narrator can even inform the reader about events happening at multiple sites simultaneously. The opening chapter of the book of Esther provides an example of this: the narrator tells the reader what takes place at two banquets thrown by the Persian king while mentioning a third given by his queen of the time. Of course, no human being has such omniscience, which is why Sternberg suggests that in a sacred book such as the Bible, which includes the book of Esther, the reader doesn't ask questions about the human source of the information.[24] Of course, this leads to the conclusion either that the book is ultimately divine in origin or that, at least to some degree, it is a literary fabrication.

In some cases, the narrator is not explicitly omniscient but is omnipresent. In other words, the narrator describes what is going on in multiple locations or in places that no human observer could access. In these cases, I still consider the narrator omniscient but simply withholding information from the audience.

I believe that this narrative strategy is adopted to imply to the reader the text's divine origin. While it might not be right to say that the narrator is God, who is often also a major character in the stories of the OT, it seems obvious that readers are receiving a divine perspective as the narrator chooses what to tell and how to tell it. When the narrator evaluates (usually in a subtle way; see below) what is done or said, readers are ultimately getting a divine assessment of these words or actions.

The use of third-person omniscient narration also precludes the idea that the biblical narrator is unreliable. It assures us that there is no space between the author's perspective and the narrator's. Sternberg perceptively asserts that "omniscience in modern narrative attends and signals fictionality, while in ancient tradition it not only accommodates but also guarantees authenticity."[25]

The exception to third-person omniscient narration, alluded to above, is found in Ezra-Nehemiah in the form of an Ezra Memoir (Ezra 7–10; Neh.

23. I believe it is appropriate to refer to the OT narrator with masculine pronouns for two reasons. First, the patriarchal nature of Hebrew culture makes it unlikely that the narrator would be thought to be female. Second, for reasons explained below and attributed to Alter, a third-person omniscient narrator in literature that came to be perceived as sacred would be associated with God.

24. Sternberg, *Poetics of Biblical Narrative*, 89.

25. Sternberg, *Poetics of Biblical Narrative*, 34.

8–10)[26] and a Nehemiah Memoir (Neh. 1–7; 11–13). In this postexilic book, each of the two main characters tells his story in the first person. Not surprisingly, the question whether the historical Ezra and Nehemiah are the ones telling the story is contested in scholarship.[27] In this volume, however, I am interested in the literary effect of first-person narration.

These memoirs appear in a book that includes third-person omniscient narration. Scholars can ask the source-critical question about whether preexisting memoirs have been incorporated into a third-person text, but the more interesting question concerns the literary effect of combining these two different perspectives. The first-person speech gives a personal or subjective viewpoint; the omniscient third-person narration is objective and authoritative.[28] This insight permits comparison between the two viewpoints. Does the objective narrator affirm the perspective of the first-person speakers?

This leads to the second literary subtlety, the contrasting characterizations of Ezra and Nehemiah. The omniscient narrator consistently affirms the viewpoint of Ezra while slightly distancing himself from Nehemiah. It is not that Nehemiah is disowned by the narrator, but Nehemiah's bold, self-promoting statements are often subdued by the narrator's assessment, which may have the purpose of downplaying the importance of individual leaders in the interest of the entire community.

Since these memoirs stand in relationship to and in the context of third-person omniscient narration, we should examine the narrator's strategy. How does the narrator choose to present the story? In this way, we are also answering the question of how the *author* presents the story, because the narrator is the author's tool for communicating his message. Perhaps another way to put this is to ask about the conventions of Hebrew storytelling, since the text provides a window on such conventions. By introducing a discussion of the narrator, I have broached the question of perspective or point of view, a topic I address later in this chapter.

Narratee–Implied Reader–Actual Reader

Having considered the dynamics of the delivery of the message by the author, implied author, and narrator, I turn now to their counterparts on the reception side of the communication: the narratee, the implied reader, and the actual reader.[29]

26. Yoo, *Ezra and the Second Wilderness*.
27. This question will be addressed in the second book of my planned trilogy, which will explore matters of historical referentiality.
28. Eshkenazi, *In an Age of Prose*, 129–30.
29. According to Puckett (*Narrative Theory*, 131), Wayne Booth was the first to delineate the "classic communication model" in his *Rhetoric of Fiction*.

The narratee operates on the level of the narrator and may be thought of as the recipient of the narrator's account within the narrative. Just as the implied author is the author as understood from the text itself,[30] so the implied reader is the ideal reader that the author has in mind while writing. For OT texts, the implied reader is a person who reads Hebrew and is conversant in the genres and other conventions of Hebrew prose as well as the historical and cultural context at the time the book was written. The implied reader is more than simply a person who was part of the original target audience but one with all the competencies assumed by the text. That is what I mean when I say that the implied reader may also be considered the ideal reader.

The actual reader, on the other hand, is anyone who reads the text, which may include those without the competencies of the ideal reader. The narratee and the implied reader are constructs, whereas the actual readers are flesh-and-blood people. Phelan and Rabinowitz tell us that the best reading takes place when actual readers do their best to acquire the competencies of the implied reader: "Readers typically join (or try to join) the authorial audience, the hypothetical group for whom the author writes—the group that shares the knowledge, values, prejudices, fears and experiences that the author expected in his or her readers and that ground his or her rhetorical choices."[31]

Several biblical texts illustrate the interaction between narratee, implied reader, and actual reader. These examples indicate that there is not always a difference between the narratee and the implied reader, though on occasion that distinction becomes important. This may be seen in the book of Proverbs, where the narratee is the son of the father who does the teaching. However, the prologue of the book widens the audience so that the implied readers are not only young men but also the more mature (Prov. 1:5).

In some cases, for the first audiences of biblical texts, there was no significant difference between the narratees, the implied readers, and the actual readers, but after the time of the first audience, the actual readers are no longer the narratees or implied readers. Though he does not have these literary categories in mind, John Walton captures this point when he tells us always to remember that the books of the Bible were not written to *us* (today's actual readers).[32] The implication is that biblical authors wrote with the book's first recipients in mind.

30. I find this category helpful when considering the majority of OT narrative texts, which are the result of a history of composition or redaction.
31. Phelan and Rabinowitz, "Narrative as Rhetoric," 6.
32. Based on his affirmation that the books of the OT are canonical, Walton (*Lost World of Genesis One*, 7) goes on to say that even though these books were not written "to us," they were written "for us."

The distinction between narratee and implied reader is useful for contemporary novels. For example, in J. D. Salinger's classic novel *The Catcher in the Rye*, the narrator (Holden Caulfield) tells his story to a narratee, whom he addresses in the second person. Speaking of Maurice, an elevator operator at the hotel where he was staying and who fleeced him when he procured a prostitute for Caulfield, he says, "If you think I was dying to see him again, you're crazy."[33] Whoever "you" refers to is the narratee. The implied (ideal) reader, though, is someone who reads English and knows the idioms and references as well as the culture and politics of New York and America in the mid-1940s (without needing to look them up on Google).[34]

For the vast majority of OT prose narrative, the distinction between the narratee and the implied reader is not helpful. In the books traditionally thought to present history in some form (Genesis through Esther), the biblical narrator tells the story without specifying a narratee; thus the implied reader is the narratee. The implied (ideal) reader is the audience that is contemporary with the implied author, and readers should remember that I associate the implied author with the final author or redactor who has put the text in its final form.

This dynamic, in which the narratee and the implied reader are one and the same, is also found in other prose-narrative books. Although the book of Job is mostly poetic, the poems are speech embedded in a prose-narrative frame. The narrator introduces the characters and Job's suffering, which becomes the topic of conversation in the first two chapters. The conclusion of the book, which speaks of Job's restoration, is also narrated in prose (42:7–17). But further, the narrator also introduces and presents the poetic speeches of the characters, as in these examples:

> After this Job opened his mouth and cursed the day of his birth. Job said: (3:1–2 NRSVue)

> Then Eliphaz the Temanite answered: (4:1 NRSVue)

When Elihu makes his appearance, the narrator provides a lengthy introduction for this new character to prepare for his poetic speech (32:1–6a). So in terms of literary presentation, Job is similar to Genesis through Esther.

Daniel and Jonah too share this mix of styles. The first six chapters of Daniel are accounts of Daniel in a foreign court, while the final six chapters present four apocalyptic visions, which Daniel describes in the first person,

---

33. Salinger, *Catcher in the Rye*, 137.
34. Though, admittedly, Google can help make someone an ideal reader.

though they are introduced by a third-person narrator (e.g., "In the first year of King Belshazzar of Babylon, Daniel had a dream," 7:1 NRSVue). The book of Jonah is not so much a prophetic book as a story about a prophet and operates similarly to the prose narratives that I have described thus far.

Ecclesiastes is an exception to the pattern we have seen up to this point, however. From a literary perspective, Ecclesiastes is complex and subtle. The book is a combination of prose and poetry, and the prose is often more a description of Qohelet's thoughts than it is narrative in the sense of telling a story, as Qohelet, the main speaker and the Hebrew name for a congregational leader, reflects on the meaning of life. Still, the book, at least Qohelet's lengthy speech (1:12–12:7), has a narrative quality to it as he reflects on his search for meaning (e.g., 2:4–9).

A broad look at the book offers an interesting perspective on the dynamic of communication. The key to interpreting the book is first to recognize that it is a framed autobiography. Qohelet speaks in the first person ("I, Qohelet") from 1:12–12:7, but his autobiographical speech is framed by the words of a second voice, who speaks *about* "Qohelet" (1:2) in the prologue (1:1–11) and most notably in the epilogue (12:8–14). For good reasons, this second voice has been called the "frame narrator."[35] Tellingly, the presence of the narrator emerges briefly in the middle of Qohelet's speech: "'Look,' *says the Teacher*, 'this is what I have discovered'" (7:27 NRSVue, emphasis added).

In essence, Qohelet's first-person speech is a lengthy quote. The (frame) narrator cites the speech, which then becomes the subject of his evaluation as he speaks to his son (see 12:12). Thus the narratee is the son (see comments on Proverbs in the next chapter), but the book was not written for only the frame narrator's son. Indeed, Qohelet, the frame narrator, and his son are most likely literary constructs. The implied reader (the ideal reader of the original audience) as well as all actual readers should identify with the son in order to understand the message of the book.

As we try to identify the original audience, we must acknowledge that the attempt to date the final form of any biblical book and its hypothetical sources is usually a matter of conjecture. At this point my inquiry into the implied reader begins to intersect with historical questions that I address more fully in the second volume of this trilogy. For my present purposes, it is sufficient to remind today's actual readers that the OT books came to their final form during the OT time period. Awareness of this fact prevents us from reading meanings into the text that were not accessible to an ancient audience and

---

35. I believe the label was first used by Fox, "Frame Narrative and Composition."

allows us to appreciate the "discrete message" of the OT text. (This is a way of saying that the implied reader can't be chronologically pinpointed.)

Some readers may object and point out that Deuteronomy has a different dynamic, since the book records Moses's final sermon to the generation of Israelites who were about to enter the land. One might simply think that Moses is the narrator and his Israelite audience the narratee, but this is not the case. The sermon is actually reported by a third-person narrator, who is not participating in the narrative, which makes this text similar to all the other OT prose narratives. The book opens with "These are the words Moses spoke to all Israel beyond the Jordan—in the wilderness" (1:1 NRSVue) and concludes with a third-person account of Moses's death. Throughout the book, the narrator makes his presence known by introducing Moses as the speaker (e.g., 27:1, 9, 11; 29:1–2; 31:7, 9–10, 30; 33:1).

Others may wonder about books such as the memoirs of Ezra and Nehemiah that provide an exception to typical narration. Ezra 1–6 gives an account of the period between the Cyrus decree to release the exiles and the rebuilding of the temple and is told in typical narrative fashion. In Ezra 7, the narrator fast-forwards a few decades and introduces Ezra and his mission (7:1–10). Next, the narrator introduces (7:11) the letter that the Persian king Artaxerxes addressed to Ezra, who is commissioned to return to Jerusalem and reestablish the law (7:12–26). After this letter, however, Ezra starts speaking in the first person and continues the story of his work through chapter 9, at which point the narrator resumes his third-person account of Ezra and his activity (Ezra 10). The narrator then introduces Nehemiah briefly ("the words of Nehemiah son of Hakaliah," Neh. 1:1a), which serves as an introduction to Nehemiah's memoir, in which he tells his story in first-person narration through 7:73a.[36] At the end of Nehemiah's memoir, the narrator returns to describe a great covenant-renewal ceremony led by both Ezra and Nehemiah (7:73b–12:26). Starting at 12:27, the book ends with Nehemiah once again speaking in the first person. First, he recounts the dedication of the temple (12:27–47) and then transitions to a diatribe about atrocities committed while he was back in Persia. Upon his return, he expresses his frustration and anger at the actions required to set things right. In this chapter, the narratee seems to be God, whom Nehemiah as first-person narrator addresses: "Remember me for this, my God, and do not blot out what I have so faithfully done for the house of my God and its services" (13:14; see also 22b, 29). This prayer is reinforced in the book's final words: "Remember me with favor, my God" (13:31b).

---

36. Ezra-Nehemiah remained a single book until the Middle Ages.

The interplay between third-person narration and first-person narration in Ezra-Nehemiah is interesting, and the first-person narration certainly brings vividness to the story, but with the exception of the final chapter, the narratee/implied reader remains the same across the third-person and first-person narrations.

Focalization

Focalization is roughly equivalent to what used to be called "point of view" but is considered to be a refinement of the concept. The term was introduced into narrative theory by the pivotal structuralist scholar Gérald Genette.[37] Quoting Genette, Kent Puckett describes focalization as "'the regulation of narrative information,' which usually amounts to the ways in which information is selected and presented in relation to an explicitly or implicitly named perspective, one that may or may not be associated with a narrator."[38] The advance on the typical understanding of point of view comes with the insight that the one who speaks is not always the one who perceives; in other words, the focalizer might be someone other than the narrator.[39]

In my opinion, interpreters do not need to concern themselves with the highly developed typology of Genette and his successors for different kinds of focalization.[40] While important for analyzing modern novels, his highly technical categorization of different options for narrative focalization is relevant only as a matter of contrast. However, his basic threefold distinctions are useful: internal, external, and zero (or non)focalization. "Internal focalization" describes a story told from the perspective of a character or more than one character. "External focalization" refers to narratives where the perspective is independent of characters, and the narrator can only observe external behavior and not access the thoughts and unexpressed feelings of the characters. "Zero focalization" indicates a narrator who is not a character and whose perspective is essentially unrestricted. He speaks of "classical narrative" that "sometimes places its 'focus' at a point so indefinite, or so remote, with

37. Genette introduced the term and concept of focalization in the French (1972) edition of the book translated into English as *Narrative Discourse*, 189–94.
38. Puckett, *Narrative Theory*, 129, quoting Genette, *Narrative Discourse*, 162.
39. Puckett, *Narrative Theory*, 130.
40. Nazarov's *Focalization in the Old Testament* is perhaps the fullest use of the theory of focalization in biblical studies. He looks at focalization on three levels: selection, lineation, and presentation (verbalization). Although immensely helpful, Nazarov's application to the book of Ruth becomes overly complex by combining it with certain narratological theories. In my opinion, focalization is illuminating simply when used as a tool to delineate the final form of the narrative.

so panoramic a field (the well-known 'viewpoint of God,' or of Sirius [the brightest star] about which people periodically wonder whether it is indeed a point of view) that it cannot coincide with any character and that the term nonfocalizaton, or zero focalization, is rather more appropriate for it."[41]

Another way to think of these three different types of focalization is to consider the relationship between the knowledge possessed by the narrator and that possessed by the characters of the story. If the narrator knows *more* than the characters, then the narrative is zero focalized. If the narrator knows *less* than the characters, then it is internally focalized; and if the narrator knows *as much as* the characters, then the narrative is externally focalized.[42] External focalization reports actions and speech that would be captured by a camera if the text were a film.[43] Internal focalization reveals thoughts and feelings only if the narrating character reveals them. Zero-focalized texts allow the omniscient narrator to see into the mind of the characters.

Mieke Bal famously challenged Genette's categories of focalization, but only one of her concerns, in my opinion, is relevant for the study of the OT.[44] She proposes that so-called non- or zero focalization is really a matter of external focalization. Bal does not deny that some narratives, including the Bible, have narrators who are not characters in the story, who are omniscient in perspective, but she treats them simply as a variety of external focalization.

I agree that, when applied to the Bible, the distinction between zero focalization and external focalization is not very helpful. As far as I am aware, David Firth is the only biblical scholar (apart from Firth's student Nazarov) who uses the terminology of focalization. In his excellent commentary on Joshua, he argues that the book of Joshua demonstrates both external and zero focalization. In the first five chapters, he believes that the narrator is simply narrating the speech and external behavior of the characters. What is missing is any indication of their thinking and motivations or any evaluation of what they are doing and saying. Thus, using Genette's categories, Firth suggests that the first five chapters of Joshua are a rare use of external focalization and that only at chapter 6 does the narrator's strategy turn to zero focalization.

This is an insightful reading. Firth notes that the narrator withholds a deeper insight into the action and dialogue both by withholding knowledge

---

41. Genette, *Narrative Discourse Revisited*, 73; cited in Puckett, *Narrative Theory*, 130.

42. Nazarov, *Focalization in the Old Testament*, argues that the calculation should be between the characters and the reader, but since the reader knows only as much as the narrator and the characters reveal, I am not sure how that changes matters.

43. Jahn, "Focalization," 173.

44. Bal, *Narratology*, 132–48.

about the characters' thinking and motivation and by not providing evaluation. Yet while Firth's use of Genette's categories doesn't strike me as wrong, it does seem unnecessary and perhaps a little misleading in so far as it suggests a conscious change in narrative strategy after chap. 5. For me the omnipresence of the narrator in Josh. 1–5 implies omniscience, which then surfaces more clearly in Josh. 6. Thus it may be better to categorize it as zero focalization throughout.

As in most OT narratives, the narrator of a book like Joshua is a third-person omniscient narrator who always tells the truth but not *all* the truth. In the words of Sternberg, "The Bible always tells the truth in that its narrator is absolutely and straightforwardly reliable," but "on the other hand, the narrator does not tell the whole truth either."[45] There may be reasons why an omniscient narrator (zero focalization) is reticent to share complete knowledge. For example, he may choose to withhold information in order to create a sense of narrative suspense, to draw the reader in. But even when a narrator guards his omniscience, he remains omnipresent. In this, both zero focalization and external focalization differ from internal focalization. Even if in external narration the narrator withholds his omniscience in the interest of suspense, for example, the narrator is still observant of happenings and speech, even when characters are alone, as in Josh. 1–5.[46]

Though pre-Genette, Boris Uspensky's different "planes" are helpful for understanding for point of view. These planes are spatial, temporal, psychological, and ideological.[47] Typically in biblical narrative, the narrator is omnipresent and not restricted to a specific location as the characters in the story are. A stark example is when the character is alone, as Hagar is in the wilderness, sobbing at a distance from the young Ishmael (Gen. 21:16). A more extended instance of the omnipresent narrator occurs in the story of the rise of the first king, Saul. The narrator reports the interaction between Samuel and the elders who come to his hometown city of Ramah and request a king (1 Sam. 8:4–5). Samuel prays to God, who ultimately tells him, "Give

45. Sternberg, *Poetics of Biblical Narrative*, 51.
46. I find Firth's study "When Samuel Met Esther" to be just as insightful as his study of Josh. 1–5, but I am not convinced that the best way to speak about the narration of Esther is through the idea of shifting focalization. He is right to point out that the omniscience of the narrator is revealed only in 6:6 ("Now Haman thought to himself") and maybe in 1:11, where the narrator reveals Xerxes's motive for commanding Vashti to come to his banquet ("to display her beauty to the people and nobles"). But I think this simply confirms the narrator's omniscience, which he selectively chooses to exercise and reveal (the narrator's omnipresence is obvious throughout).
47. Uspensky, *A Poetics of Composition*. Adele Berlin uses Uspensky's work on point of view in her *Poetics and Interpretation*, 55–56. Uspensky has a fifth plane, the phraseological, that I have not found as useful.

them a king" (8:22). Immediately the narrator shifts to the location of Saul and his servant, who are looking for a lost donkey. The narrator then follows Saul and his servant as they decide to go to Ramah to consult the "man of God," Samuel, who lives there (9:6–10). In Ramah, Samuel anoints Saul and gives him a series of instructions, which Saul does not follow exactly, including going to meet Samuel at Gilgal (10:8). The narrator follows Saul home, where he withholds from his uncle that Samuel has anointed him king (10:16). The narrator again shifts his spatial focus from Saul's hometown to Mizpah (10:17), where Samuel uses the casting of lots to publicly reveal the reluctant Saul as the next king.

Uspensky's temporal plane refers to the time limitation or lack thereof imposed on the narrator. Does the narrator tell the story as it unfolds, or does he tell the story from a later period of time and reveal information about the conclusion of a chain of events? Most of the time the biblical narrator follows the development of the story as it unfolds. In this way, the story maintains suspense by keeping the reader in the dark about the outcome. In some narratives, the future is anticipated through a prophet, but the narrator still follows the temporal unfolding of the story and simply reports what the prophet says about the future. An example of this is found in 1 Kings 13:1–3, where an unnamed man of God speaks about the future destruction of Jeroboam's altar, something that happens centuries later (see 2 Kings 23:15–18). Sometimes, though, the narrator purposefully blunts the suspense by alerting the reader to something that the characters find out only later in the story. Famously, the story of the binding of Isaac begins by stating, "Some time later God tested Abraham" (Gen. 22:1). Thus the narrator tells the reader something that Abraham will not realize until he goes to Moriah, binds Isaac, and seeks to obey God's command to sacrifice Isaac as a burnt offering (22:2).

For the psychological plane, Uspensky asks whether the narrator is able to get inside the heads of the characters and report what they are thinking, even when they do not express their thoughts aloud. The narrator's ability to know the thoughts of characters displays his omniscience. Returning to Hagar alone in the wilderness, the narrator knows what she is thinking and why she puts distance between her and Ishmael: she cannot bear to watch her son die (Gen. 21:16). The verb for speaking (*'amar*) is used here, but since no one is present, the NIV rightly translates the verb as "she thought" rather than "she said." In Gen. 38, a verb more closely connected to thought is used (*chashav*): the narrator tells the reader that when Judah saw the veiled Tamar, "he thought she was a prostitute" (38:15).

Although the Hebrew narrator sometimes explicitly reports the thought of a character, on other occasions the narrator chooses not to, even when readers might expect to hear them. These are the times when interpreters read a story and find themselves asking, "Why did he or she do that?" Modern readers are often baffled about the meaning of an event or action when the narrator does not make a character's motivations explicit.

One such case occurs in 1 Kings 13, where God commissions an unnamed prophet to travel north from Judah to Bethel, a city in the Northern Kingdom of Israel, where Jeroboam, the first northern king, has just built a shrine to a calf idol (1 Kings 12:25–33). Jeroboam built the shrine out of fear that his subjects would travel to the Southern Kingdom to worship at the temple in Jerusalem and possibly shift their allegiance to the Judean king (12:26–27).

The prophet delivers a judgment oracle against the altar (13:2–3), which is accompanied by signs confirming his divine commission, including the altar splitting apart and the temporary paralysis of Jeroboam's arm. The king asks the prophet to intercede with God to heal his arm, and in return for doing this, the prophet is offered a meal and a gift from the king. The prophet refuses the king's invitation, saying, "If you give me half your kingdom, I will not go in with you, nor will I eat food or drink water in this place. For thus I was commanded by the word of the LORD: 'You shall not eat food, or drink water, or return by the way you came'" (13:8–9 NRSVue).

We are not told *why* God placed this demand on the prophet, but motivations become even more opaque as we read on. The scene shifts to the home of "an old prophet" living in Bethel who hears about the man of God (13:11). He tells his sons to saddle his donkey so that he can intercept the prophet on the road and invite him to a meal at his house. Predictably, the prophet from Judah repeats the instructions he has received from God, but then the prophet from Bethel tells him: "I also am a prophet as you are, and an angel spoke to me by the word of the LORD: 'Bring him back with you into your house so that he may eat food and drink water'" (13:18 NRSVue). The narrator immediately informs the reader, "But he was deceiving him" (13:18 NRSVue). But why? Why does the prophet from Bethel lie to the prophet from Judah?

While the prophet from Judah is sharing a meal at the house of the Bethel prophet, the latter suddenly announces: "Thus says the LORD: Because you have disobeyed the word of the LORD and have not kept the commandment that the LORD your God commanded you but have come back and have eaten food and drunk water in the place where he said to you, 'Eat no food, and drink no water,' your body shall not come to your ancestral tomb" (13:21–22 NRSVue). As the prophet from Judah is returning home, he is attacked by a lion and killed.

Again, the question arises: Why does the prophet from Bethel engage in what appears to be a form of entrapment? At such points, it is good to remember that Hebrew narrative is not always interested in providing an answer. If after looking for subtle clues in the text that may provide an answer, readers still cannot discern a motivation, they should move on and not allow themselves to be distracted from the message that the story intends to communicate. In this case, they learn that not only are people like Jeroboam listening to false prophets rather than to the voice of God, but even God's own prophets may be tempted to listen to the comforting words of a false prophet. By having the prophet from Judah repeat the divine instructions not to eat in the Northern Kingdom, the narrator emphasizes that the prophet knows what God wants him to do, but perhaps because he is hungry and thirsty, he quickly accepts the false words of the Bethel prophet.

In the book of Esther we see additional examples of the narrator's reticence to provide explicit motivations for characters' actions. In some cases, the motivations were likely obvious to the original audience without needing to be stated but are not always obvious to modern readers. In other cases, the motives were probably as obscure to the ancient audience as they are to the modern.

An example of the first type of reticence occurs when Mordecai first encounters Haman. Why does Mordecai "not bow down or do obeisance" to Haman (Esther 3:2b NRSVue)? Some modern readers may conclude that Mordecai refuses to bow because no human being deserves the type of worship that should be directed toward God alone, but bowing to a political superior was not the same as worship. Jews were not forbidden from showing respect and subordination to someone like Haman, so something else must be going on.

Then readers are left to explain the intense animosity that Haman feels not only toward Mordecai but toward all the Jewish people. "Having been told who Mordecai's people were, Haman plotted to destroy all the Jews" (3:6 NRSVue). What explains this intense hatred between the two men?

The answer comes when we realize who these men are and whom they represent. The narrator gives the clue when he first introduces them. Mordecai is introduced as "a Jew . . . whose name was Mordecai son of Jair son of Shimei son of Kish, a Benjaminite" (i.e., of the tribe of Benjamin; 2:5 NRSVue). The original audience would have detected a connection to King Saul, also a Benjaminite and a son of Kish (1 Sam. 9:1–2; cf. 2 Sam. 16:5). By introducing Haman as "the Agagite," the narrator connects Haman to Agag, the Amalekite king (Esther 3:1; cf. 1 Sam. 15). The ancient hostility between the Israelites and the Amalekites (see Exod. 17:8–16) would have been known to the first readers of the book of Esther, and in the distant past Saul had the chance to settle the score with the Amalekites and failed to do so.

Other actions in the Esther story would probably have been just as obscure to ancient readers as to modern ones. One example occurs in the aftermath of Esther's request to give a private banquet for the king and Haman. Mordecai convinced Esther to approach the king and implore him to stop Haman's plan to exterminate the Jews, although she had "not been called to come in to the king for thirty days" (4:11 NRSVue). Seeing Esther approach, the king receives her and asks, "What is it, Queen Esther? What is your request? Even to half of my kingdom, it shall be given you" (5:3 NRSVue). She asks that he and Haman join her for a banquet that very day, and he agrees.

While they are eating, the king again asks, "What is your petition? It shall be granted you. And what is your request? Even to half of my kingdom, it shall be fulfilled" (5:6 NRSVue). At this point the reader expects Esther to reveal the wicked plot of Haman and beg the king to thwart it, but instead Esther asks that the king and Haman join her for *another* banquet on the following day. At this second banquet, Esther does reveal Haman's evil plan, which leads to his destruction and the ultimate undermining of his plot to annihilate the Jewish people (7:1–10; cf. chaps. 8–10).

Why does Esther delay, waiting until the second banquet to make her request? We can speculate, but apparently the narrator does not think it important to tell us why she hesitates at the first banquet and waits for the second. But even without knowing Esther's thinking or emotions, readers can recognize a narrative explanation for the delay. Between the first and second banquets, the king finally remembers Mordecai's earlier thwarting of the assassination attempt on the king's life and exalts Mordecai (2:19–23; 6:1–11). As Haman leaves the first banquet, he is bursting with pride and looks forward to the second banquet (5:9–13). Anticipating his ultimate triumph over Mordecai, Haman arrogantly authorizes the building of a fifty-cubit-high pole on which to impale his enemy (5:14). But in the brief time between the first and second banquets, Ahasuerus honors Mordecai and even compels Haman to participate in the exaltation (6:6–11).

Seeing this turn of events, even Haman's wife, Zeresh, anticipates Haman's downfall. As he is leaving for the second banquet, she says, "If Mordecai, before whom your downfall has begun, is of the Jewish people, you will not prevail against him but will surely fall before him" (6:13 NRSVue), and indeed he does (chap. 7). Thus the time period between the two banquets, which is created by Esther delaying her request, narratively allows for Mordecai's exaltation and Haman's anticipated downfall.

Sometimes interpreters cannot be certain whether the original audience would have known a character's unexpressed motivation. The opening chapter of Esther presents an example of this in describing three opulent banquets given by the Persian court. The first banquet involves "the army of Persia and Media, the nobles, and the governors of the provinces" and lasts 180 days (1:3–4 NRSVue). This is followed by a second banquet lasting seven days for "all the people present in the citadel of Susa, both great and small" (1:5 NRSVue). While this second banquet is taking place, Queen Vashti is giving a banquet "for the women in the palace of King Ahasuerus" (1:9 NRSVue).

Why so many banquets? What reason does the royal court have for throwing such opulent parties? It is doubtful that such celebrations were constant in Persia. The first one in particular involved the gathering of leaders from all over the vast Persian Empire for six months, which would have been impractical to do often.

A modern audience cannot discern a purpose for these banquets, but perhaps the ancient audience could have. It just so happens that Herodotus (ca. 484–ca. 425 BC), a nearly contemporary Greek historian, mentions a banquet that Xerxes I gives ahead of a military campaign directed at Greece (Xerxes is the Persian emperor most likely intended by the character of Ahasuerus). Some commentators have speculated that the 180-day banquet is the same as the one mentioned in Herodotus. If so, the motivation for the feast was likely to garner support and raise confidence in the wealth and power of the Persian Empire before a dangerous military campaign.[48]

Perhaps the original readers knew of this connection, but perhaps not, since we do not know exactly when the book was written. Much of the debate about the dating of the book involves questions about its historical reliability. While the author seems to know Persian culture in general, the reliability of specific historical details is questionable. For example, the book mentions 127 provinces (1:1), but Persian sources and others speak of only 20 provinces. Another example that strikes at the heart of the book's narrative concerns the roles of Queen Vashti and Esther in the story, because historical sources name Amestris as Xerxes's wife and queen. I mention these historical issues here only to show that the lack of agreement regarding the date of composition makes it difficult to know whether the original audience would have understood the purpose of the opening banquet.

Fortunately, little is lost by not knowing why Xerxes held these banquets. In the story itself, they show that Xerxes is intent on demonstrating his wealth, authority, and generosity. So when Vashti refuses his command to show herself at the second banquet, it creates a crisis, for it undermines his demonstration of authority and power. If this banquet was a precursor to war, then the threat to the king's authority would have special urgency, but even apart from this

---

48. So Jobes, *Esther*, 60.

possibility, the insult to the king and its repercussions had to be addressed, as his advisers point out (Esther 1:13–22). In terms of the story's plot, it explains the sudden opening for the position of queen in the empire and opens the door for Esther's arrival.

Recognizing that the narrator in a Hebrew story is sometimes reticent to explain a character's motivations should make us cautious about attributing motivations to characters that are not expressed in the text either explicitly or subtly. If after close study a motive cannot be determined, it is better to move on in the plot rather than propose a motivation not apparent in the text.

Uspensky's fourth "plane" of point of view is "ideological." Here the narrator not only reports speech and action and even thought but also evaluates what he is reporting. In other words, he guides how the reader responds to the action and speech of the characters. Ideology is a system of ideas, ideals, or beliefs, which the narrator conveys in how he presents the story. When it comes to the Bible, the specific system of ideas, ideals, and beliefs of the biblical narrator encourages me to substitute the word "theological" for "ideological" as a more specific description. As Sternberg states, "The very choice to devise an omniscient narrator serves the purpose of staging and glorifying an omniscient God."[49]

The Hebrew narrator is often reticent to provide a moral evaluation of a character's actions in the story. Rarely do narrators give explicit pronouncements that a character is doing the right thing or the wrong thing. This does not mean that the narrator does not subtly lead readers toward such moral evaluations, but readers must look hard for the clues.

One example comes from Gen. 34, the rape of Dinah. Her father Jacob, after returning from his sojourn in Paddan Aram, settles his family around the Canaanite town of Shechem. When Dinah goes into town to visit some women there, the prince of the city, also named Shechem, seizes her and forces himself upon her (34:2). However, Shechem loves Dinah and wants to marry her, so he and his father initiate marriage negotiations with Jacob and Dinah's two full brothers, Levi and Simeon.

Hamor, Shechem's father, makes the following offer: "The heart of my son Shechem longs for your daughter; please give her to him in marriage. Make marriages with us; give your daughters to us, and take our daughters for yourselves. You shall live with us, and the land shall be open to you; live and trade in it and get property in it" (34:8–10 NRSVue).

According to the narrative, Jacob does not speak, but the two brothers appear to agree to the terms but add a condition. They will allow the marriage

49. Sternberg, *Poetics of Biblical Narrative*, 89.

to go forward only if the men of the city undergo the ritual of circumcision. Before the brothers announce their decision and propose this condition to Hamor and Shechem, the narrator informs us that the brothers are speaking "deceitfully because he had defiled their sister Dinah" (34:13 NRSVue). We should not necessarily see this as a negative moral evaluation, however. Elsewhere in Genesis and Exodus, the narrator approves of deceit if it leads to the survival of God's people as a separate people.[50]

The Shechemites agree to the brothers' condition, thinking that it will not only result in the marriage of Shechem and Dinah but offer additional benefits: "Let us take their daughters in marriage, and let us give them our daughters" (34:21 NRSVue). Also, Shechem and his father rhetorically ask the male population of the town, "Will not their livestock, their property, and all their animals be ours?" (34:23 NRSVue). In other words, they will completely assimilate the people and property of Jacob's family.

The men of the town agree and undergo circumcision. While they were weakened by the procedure, Simeon and Levi "took their swords and came against the city unawares and killed all the males. They killed Hamor and his son Shechem with the sword and took Dinah out of Shechem's house and went away" (34:25–26 NRSVue).

Jacob is beside himself with anger when he hears of their actions, and he confronts them: "You have brought trouble on me by making me odious to the inhabitants of the land, the Canaanites and the Perizzites; my numbers are few, and if they gather themselves against me and attack me, I shall be destroyed, both I and my household" (34:30 NRSVue).

But where do the sympathies of the narrator lie? He does not explicitly weigh in with a moral evaluation at the end of this episode, but by not letting Jacob have the last word, he appears to side with the two avenging brothers. He allows their reply to be the final statement on the matter: "Should our sister be treated like a prostitute?" (34:31 NRSVue).

While perhaps not giving full approval to the brothers, the narrator seems to side with them over Jacob. After all, as readers think about the broader implications of this story, we realize that Jacob's acquiescing to the marriage would have led to the disappearance of the chosen family, who carried the hope of a blessing to the world since the call of Abraham (Gen. 12:1–3). In addition, Jacob was not supposed to be in Shechem at this time. Before leaving for Paddan Aram, Jacob had a vision of God in a city that he named Bethel, after which he took the following vow: "If God will be with me and will watch over me on this journey I am taking and will give me food to eat

50. M. Williams, *Deception in Genesis*.

and clothes to wear so that I return safely to my father's household, then the LORD will be my God and this stone that I have set up as a pillar will be God's house, and of all that you give me I will give you a tenth" (28:20–22). By being forced to leave Shechem, Jacob finally takes his family to Bethel, where he fulfills his vow (35:1–15).

A second example in which the narrator subtly leads readers toward a moral evaluation of a character's actions comes from the opening of the exodus story. Pharaoh responds to what he sees as a threat posed by the growing Israelite population. He issues a decree to the midwives who are helping the Hebrew women give birth, ordering that all baby boys born to Israelite women must be killed (Exod. 1:15–16). After a while, Pharaoh learns that the baby boys are not being killed as he commanded, so he confronts the midwives, "Why have you done this? Why have you let the boys live?" (1:18). They respond, "Hebrew women are not like Egyptian women; they are vigorous and give birth before the midwives arrive" (1:19). In short, they lie to Pharaoh; we know this because the narrator has already informed us that the midwives "did not do what the king of Egypt had told them to do; they let the boys live" (1:17).

That they lied has led some interpreters to conclude that they sinned. After all, as the Ten Commandments later state: "You shall not give false testimony against your neighbor" (Exod. 20:16). This negative evaluation, however, does not stand up against a close reading of the episode. Even though the narrator does not explicitly give approval to their lie, he does so implicitly by stating the motivation for their actions: they "feared God" (1:17). And if that is not persuasive enough, the narrator also tells us that "because the midwives feared God, he gave them families of their own" (1:21). It would be wrong to evaluate the actions of the midwives simply through the prism of the ninth commandment. Instead, this story helps us see a possible exception to the ninth commandment: it is permissible, indeed required, that one lie to others when it is clear that the truth will lead to the harm of others, especially the people of God.

Turning to the book of Esther, readers must realize that some of the contemporary conundrums in the interpretation of this book arise because we lack awareness of narrative reticence. Many read the book looking for a hero among the characters: Is it Mordecai? Is it Esther?

Of course, it is perfectly obvious who the enemy is. Haman hates Mordecai and his people and seeks to destroy them. Readers don't need pronouncements from the narrator to know that Haman is thoroughly evil. However, the evaluation of Ahasuerus is a bit more complicated. He is no paragon of right action, to be sure. He is often drunk and easily manipulated, first by Haman and then by Esther and Mordecai. He sells out the Jews to Haman, though at that point it is not clear that he knows who the people are whom he is allowing Haman to annihilate. Then he reverses course when he realizes that Esther herself is a Jew, and he takes Haman's pogrom as an affront to his own honor.

But what about Mordecai and Esther? The picture here is also complicated, at least until the end when they both step up in the face of the threat to the Jews and manipulate Ahasuerus into allowing the Jews to defend themselves against their enemies. The complication arises because of the way the story is told. It is hard to gauge the narrator's attitude toward the thinking and behavior of Mordecai and Esther. His apparently neutral stance has led to differing assessments over the years.

Both Mordecai and Esther are introduced in Esther 2. Their names are significant for their characterization. "Mordecai" means "man of Marduk," the chief god of Babylon, and "Esther" is a form of Ishtar, the Babylonian goddess of love. These are their Persian names, though in the case of Esther we learn that her Hebrew name is "Hadassah" (2:7), which means "myrtle." Although readers certainly are not to think of them as worshipers of false gods, their Persian names show just how assimilated they are into Persian culture. Indeed, Mordecai seems to have access to high court officials such as Haman, which likely indicates that he is part of the Persian bureaucracy. His uncovering an assassination plot against the king may indicate that he is something equivalent to the secret service. That Esther was known well enough to be included in the contest to become queen also indicates that she and Mordecai were well situated in Persian society.

Now consider the contest itself. The king needs a new queen, and his advisers tell him to invite beautiful young virgins to be prepared to meet him, so that "the young woman who pleases the king [will] be queen instead of Vashti" (2:4 NRSVue). Like all the young women, Esther underwent a year of beauty preparation before going to see King Ahasuerus (2:12 NRSVue): "In the evening she went in; then in the morning she came back to the second harem in custody of Shaashgaz" (2:14 NRSVue). Without going into detail, the narrator informs the reader that the contest is not, strictly speaking, a "beauty contest," but more a sexual one, which Esther not only participates in but wins.

What does the narrator think about Esther's involvement? While readers should certainly sense no censure, no explicit approval is expressed either. Of course, her victory puts her in a position to rescue the Jews from a horrible end, just as Joseph ends up in a position to save the family of God as a result of his brothers' selling him into slavery. Is this another example of "You meant it for evil, but God meant it for good"? (Gen. 50:20, my trans.).

Because this situation bothered rabbinic interpreters, they suggested that Esther won the contest, not because she was the best in bed, but because she spent the evening reading the Torah to the king instead of sleeping with him, and the king was so impressed with her wisdom that he married her. Based on how the character of Ahasuerus is presented in the book, such an interpretation, while perhaps well intended, is very doubtful.

I would say that the reticence of the narrator indicates that, at least at the beginning of the story, the narrator is not interested in presenting Esther in either a positive or negative light. The same applies to Mordecai, her guardian, who must have allowed this to happen. But what about in chapter 4, which many see as the climactic moment in the plot, when Mordecai urges Esther to intercede with the king on behalf of the Jews? Readers have given varying moral evaluations to the roles of Mordecai and Esther. Is there a hero here? Some say Mordecai is the hero of the story, while others claim Esther. As we focus on Esther 4, we should remember that the narrator has introduced these two characters earlier, and readers should bring this previous information to bear in understanding their actions at this pivotal moment.

Haman has convinced Ahasuerus to annihilate the Jews at a date about a year in the future. The decree is proclaimed throughout the Persian Empire. When he hears the horrible news, Mordecai, the relative who has raised Esther since the loss of her parents, goes to the city gate in mourning garb to get Esther's attention. Although the whole empire knows about the plot, and the Jews are in "great mourning" (4:3 NRSVue), Esther seems oblivious. Living in the palace has apparently shielded her from outside news.

The news that Mordecai is at the city gates in mourning clothes deeply disturbs Esther, so she sends "Hathak," her attendant, to give him another set of clothes and to ask him what is wrong. Again, Esther apparently does not have the freedom to leave the palace precincts.

He tells Hathak to inform Esther of Haman's evil plan and to ask her to intercede with the king. Readers must remember that up to this point Esther, following Mordecai's instructions, has not told the king that she is Jewish (2:10, 20), which may lead us to surmise that she does not yet feel personally threatened. Whatever the reason, she hesitates to follow through on Mordecai's instructions, telling him that it is risky to approach the king without being invited, and she has not been summoned for the past thirty days. If she approaches the king uninvited and he does not extend his gold scepter toward her, she will be put to death. At this point, she does not seem prepared to put her life on the line for her people.

When Mordecai receives this message, presumably from Hathak, he then tells her "Do not think that in the king's palace you will escape any more than all the other Jews. For if you keep silent at this time, relief and deliverance will rise for the Jews from another place, but you and your father's family will perish. Who knows? Perhaps you have come to royal dignity for just such a time as this" (4:13–14 NRSVue). Upon hearing this, she tells Mordecai that she will indeed approach the king at great personal risk.

Why the change of mind? What in Mordecai's final message to Esther leads to her decision to approach the king? Are his words a personal warning to Esther or a veiled threat to reveal her connections to the Jewish people? How are readers to understand Esther's decision to risk approaching the king? Is it an act of other-serving courage or the reluctant decision of a person who knows that their life is in danger either way?

My point here is that the narrator does not seem all that interested in helping his readers make the moral evaluations needed to definitively answer these questions. Is Mordecai the hero, is Esther, or are they both heroes? The reticent narrator is not much help here and does not intend to be, because there is another hero in the book, the one who actually saves the Jews. It is neither Esther nor Mordecai, though he uses both of them. Rather, it is a character who is never named in the book. That unnamed character is none other than God himself, who makes his saving presence known through all the unexpected ironic reversals in the book, including Haman being executed on the impaling pole that he had erected for Mordecai (5:14; 7:9–10) and the destruction of the Jews' enemies on the date originally chosen for the destruction of the Jews.

Plot

Plot refers to the incidents of a story and how they are arranged. Plot is another name for what I earlier called discourse (*sjuzet*). It is constructed by the author and implemented in the text by the narrator. A plot is not a simple chronological or exhaustive accounting of an event, fictional or not. Since Aristotle, plot has been described as having a beginning, middle, and end, but this structure does not necessarily require a strict chronological telling of the story (the events themselves). Nevertheless, most biblical plots are told in chronological order. Even so, plots are highly selective in what details they include. Selectivity leads to gapping and repetition, which have literary significance (see below). Bar-Efrat well expresses the importance of plot: "If the characters are the soul of the narrative, the plot is the body. It consists of an organized and orderly system of events, arranged in temporal sequence. In contrast to life—where we are invariably confronted by an endless stream of incidents occurring haphazardly and disparately—the plot of a narrative is constructed as a meaningful chain of interconnected events. This is achieved by careful selection, entailing the omission of any incident which does not fit in logically with the planned development of the plot."[51]

Literary scholars have sometimes debated whether character or plot is the most important component of a narrative. On the surface, this discussion seems frivolous since it is hard to imagine a narrative that does not have both plot and characters. Certainly the narratives of the Bible have plots and characters. Henry James makes this point in his oft-quoted statement: "What is character but the determination of incident? What is incident but the illustration of character?"[52] It would be as impossible to summarize a plot without describing the character's actions, feelings, and speech as it would be to describe a character without engaging the plot.

The plot of a narrative is propelled by some type of conflict. Sometimes the conflict emerges at the beginning of a narrative, as when Gen. 22 begins with "Some time later God tested Abraham" (22:1). At other times, the plot conflict comes after the narrator presents preliminary information, introducing characters and situations. Indeed, readers might think of Gen. 22 as an incident within the longer Abraham narrative and see the preceding chapters as providing background and preliminary information that leads to Abraham's testing (though many of these earlier episodes also have their own plot conflict). Similarly, the Joseph narrative begins with a description of Joseph's family and specifically Jacob's special love for Joseph (37:1–3) before introducing the conflict created by the brothers' hatred for Joseph, which leads to their selling him into slavery and generates additional conflict.

The end of the plot typically involves some type of resolution. In Gen. 22 Abraham passes the test that God subjects him to and is thus blessed by God. In the Joseph narrative, the resolution culminates in Joseph's revealing his identity and saying to his brothers, "You intended to harm me, but God intended it for good to accomplish what is now being done, the saving of many lives" (50:20). After this, the action comes to an end with the report of Joseph's death, though the brothers' promise that Joseph's embalmed body will be taken back to the promised land (50:24–25) gives us the sense that the plot will continue to move forward.

In the Bible, readers can see plot functioning on more than one level. My example from Gen. 22 is an episode that functions within the broader narrative of the Abraham story (11:27–25:11), and the Abraham story is part of

51. Bar-Efrat, *Narrative Art in the Bible*, 93.
52. H. James, "Art of Fiction"; quoted in Chatman, *Story and Discourse*, 112–13.

the larger patriarchal/matriarchal narrative (11:27–37:1). My example from the Joseph narrative is on the same level as the patriarchal narrative, having a plot composed of several episodes that have their own subplots. Indeed, the historical books of the OT (Genesis through Esther) have a plot with ups and downs as the different scenes move from creation through the postexilic period. Christian readers see a continuation of that plot into the NT. Indeed, it is common to speak of the biblical text as providing a four-part drama:

Creation	Fall (the Conflict)	Redemption	Consummation
Gen. 1–2	Gen. 3	Gen. 4–Rev. 20	Rev. 21–22

Characterization

Just a selection of the characters that readers encounter in OT narratives includes Adam, Noah, Abraham, Jacob, Joseph, Moses, Aaron, Joshua, Samson, Samuel, Saul, David, Solomon, Nebuchadnezzar, Ezra, Nehemiah, Esther, and even God himself. Characters fuel the plot through their speech and actions. They make decisions that change the trajectory of the story. Some characters stay the same, but others undergo dramatic transformations. We are drawn into the account of the characters and either identify with them or contrast ourselves with them in ways that illuminate our own lives.

Characters are literary constructs. As John Frow puts it, a character in a text, including the biblical text, is "a string of words" and "a collection of dialogue."[53] This statement has nothing to do with whether the character is an actual person or whether the description reliably represents that person. To put it bluntly, the textual presentation of a biblical character is not the actual person; both fictional and nonfictional characters are *literary constructions*.

Upon reflection, the point that characters in texts are constructed figures and not actual people becomes obvious. Through the narrator, the author presents a highly selective portrait of a person, representing only the words and actions of the character that are relevant to the story. Readers know only what the narrator chooses to tell them either through narrative comment or, more often, through speech from and about that character.

Even though selectively presented, readers get to know these characters, at least the ones that play a large role in the narrative. They seem like real people; some analysts call this the mimetic function of character.[54] Since

---

53. Frow, "Character," 109.
54. See, for instance, D. Herman, *Story Logic*, 121.

E. M. Forester, such characters have been called "round" in contrast to "flat" characters.[55] Round characters undergo change as the story progresses. As an example, consider Judah in the Joseph narrative. At the beginning of the story, Judah plays a negative role. He suggests selling Joseph to the Ishmaelites (Gen. 37:27), marries a Canaanite, and after his wife's death unwittingly has sex with his daughter-in-law, who turns out to be "more righteous than" he (38:26). Later, however, he pleads in an impassioned speech to be held captive instead of his younger brother Benjamin so that his father won't die of grief at the loss (44:30–32). The narrator seems uninterested in what factors—experiential, psychological, or otherwise—led to Judah's transformation, and he offers the reader no details.

The reason for Esther's transformation is also unexplained. As Timothy K. Beal points out, at the beginning of the story, Esther is the model of submission, shown first to Mordecai and then to Ahasuerus. But at the moment of crisis, she begins to exert her own agency to rescue her people from Haman's evil plot.[56] The narrator does not tell readers why she changes, so we are left to speculate.

Access to characters is controlled within the biblical text by the narrator, who selects the information he provides. The narrator is omniscient and omnipresent (except in rare instances) but chooses when to reveal things to the narratee and thus to the implied and actual readers. The narrator often chooses not to take readers into the minds and motivations of the characters, but through a presentation of the actions and speech of characters, the narrator may on occasion *imply* motivations. Indeed, it is precisely through the representation of action and speech that the narrator shapes readers' understanding of characters. Direct physical description of characters is rare, and when it occurs, the description is in some way pivotal to the story.

Before giving biblical examples where physical description of a character is provided, I offer this contrasting example from Charles Dickens's *A Tale of Two Cities*, where the author describes a messenger on horseback: "He had eyes that assorted very well with that decoration, being of a surface black, with no depth of colour or form, and much too near together—as if they were afraid of being found out in something, singly, if they kept too far apart. They had a sinister expression, under an old cocked-hat like a three-cornered spittoon, and over a great muffler for the chin and throat, which descended nearly to the wearer's knees."[57]

---

55. Flat characters have a single trait and no development in the narrative. Those who simply move the plot along are called "agents." See Berlin, *Poetics and Interpretation*, 22–33.

56. Beal, *Book of Hiding*, 97.

57. From book 1, "Recalled to Life," chap. 3, "The Night Shadows."

Turning to the HB, readers will not find any description so extensive or so gratuitous to the plot. Perhaps "gratuitous" is too strong a word because what a person looks like and wears may contribute to the overall depiction of the character, but the HB accomplishes that much more simply, often with just one or a few words. By analogy, Hebrew narrative operates closer to the principle of "Chekhov's gun," about which the Russian playwright states, "Remove everything that has no relevance to the story. If you say in the first chapter that there is a rifle hanging on the wall, in the second or third chapter it absolutely must go off. If it's not going to be fired, it shouldn't be hanging there."[58] The narrator's reticence to give physical description of characters is extended to a similar reticence in the description of setting.

In other words, there are no free motifs in biblical narrative; when a description does appear, it is very important to the story. Saul is "handsome" and "a head taller than anyone else" (1 Sam. 9:2). Bathsheba is "very beautiful" (2 Sam. 11:2). Absalom is also "handsome" and has full and long hair (2 Sam. 14:25–26). The narrator does not seem interested in helping the reader gain a specific mental image of a character; physical characteristics are mentioned only when they play a role in the plot. Knowing Saul's height explains why the people think he will be a commanding king (only to be disappointed). Bathsheba's beauty explains David's strong attraction to her. Absalom's long hair indicates his vitality but also plays a role at the end of his story when it gets caught in a tree, leaving him vulnerable to Joab's attack (2 Sam. 18:10, 14).

One of the longest biblical descriptions of which I am aware is that of Goliath, the monstrous soldier who fights David in single combat: His "height was four cubits and a span. He had a helmet of bronze on his head, and he was armed with a coat of mail; the weight of the coat was five thousand shekels of bronze. He had greaves of bronze on his legs and a javelin of bronze slung between his shoulders. The shaft of his spear was like a weaver's beam, and his spear's head weighed six hundred shekels of iron, and his shield-bearer went before him" (1 Sam. 17:4b–7 NRSVue). This extensive description establishes a contrast with David, his opponent, who is not large enough to wear armor and approaches to fight him with a simple slingshot.

The book of Esther is also notably spare in physical descriptions of characters and settings, with one interesting exception. We are given a fairly extensive description of the seven-day banquet that followed the 180-day one. This seven-day banquet, to which Xerxes summoned Vashti, was held in "the enclosed garden of the king's palace" (1:5). "The garden had hangings of white and blue linen, fastened with cords of white linen and purple material

58. Quoted in Puckett, *Narrative Theory*, 77.

to silver rings on marble pillars. There were couches of gold and silver on a mosaic pavement of porphyry, marble, mother-of-pearl and other costly stones" (1:6). The wine was served in "goblets of gold, each one different from the other" (1:7). This description, extensive for Hebrew narrative, accentuates the wealth and power of King Xerxes as he entertains the people "from the least to the greatest who were in the citadel of Susa" (1:5). In the immediate context, this opulent setting for the banquet highlights Xerxes's assertion of wealth and power, which is undermined when Vashti refuses his summons to appear, throwing the court into a crisis that leads eventually to the choice of Esther as the new queen.

More speculatively, readers might also see a contrast with the simpler festival of Purim established at the end of the book (9:24, 26). Although several other banquets appear in the book (see the discussion of banquets under "Focalization," above), the banquets in the first and last chapters may be intended to stand in a special contrasting relationship to each other: the luxurious setting of Xerxes's banquet, which accentuates his wealth and power, contrasts with Purim, a celebration of "feasting and joy and giving presents of food to one another and gifts to the poor" (9:22).

When it comes to physical descriptions of characters, the narrator of Esther is indeed reticent, giving us only general descriptions of what people look like. Though rare, these brief descriptions are central to the plot. Indeed, the only physical description in the book is of the first and second queens. Vashti "was lovely to look at" (1:11), and Esther "had a lovely figure and was beautiful" (2:7). Readers do not learn details such as the color of their eyes or hair, the shape of their nose, the delicateness of their necks—that is, the type of description readers might find in narratives from other cultures and time periods.

Nonetheless, the mention of their beauty, though general, serves the needs of the story. The beauty of the women explains Xerxes's interest in both of them. He wants to display Vashti's beauty to his banquet guests, and Esther's beauty explains why she is included in the contest that ultimately leads to her becoming queen. So through the narrator's description of the queens' beauty, readers learn that Xerxes's interest in women is only "skin deep." Both women show themselves to be much deeper than he is: Vashti by refusing his summons, and Esther by manipulating him to thwart the genocide of her people.

Hebrew narrative shapes the reader's understanding of a character in the way the narrator and other characters refer to that person as well as how the character refers to him- or herself. In 1 Sam. 25, for instance, David encounters Nabal and Abigail. They each respond quite differently to David, and in how they are described and named, the narrator shapes their differing portraits.

The narrator introduces Nabal first as a wealthy landowner who lives in Maon, near Carmel (25:2).[59] He is named Nabal, which probably means something like "noble" (HALOT, *nabal* II) but also sounds like another Hebrew word (*nabal* I), which means "fool,"[60] a verbal connection that plays a pivotal role later in the story. He is also described as "surly and mean" (25:3), and his actions illustrate this characterization. Finally, he is introduced as a Calebite and thus associated with the noble Caleb, who along with Joshua was allowed to enter the land. V. Phillips Long wonders, though, whether it is the association with the Hebrew word *keleb* ("dog") that is more germane to the narrator's intent here.[61] In these opening verses, readers are also introduced to Abigail, Nabal's wife, who is not "surly and mean" but "intelligent and beautiful" (25:3).

David sends his men to ask for provisions, hoping that Nabal will be generous during a time of festive celebration, but in keeping with his reputation as surly and mean, he insults David's men and belittles David. When David hears of this, he intends to respond violently, but, fortunately, the "intelligent and beautiful" Abigail intercedes with David before he can act. She rushes provisions to David without her husband's knowledge. Just before Abigail arrives, the narrator reports David telling his men how "useless" it has been "watching over this fellow's property" (25:21). In the Hebrew, "this fellow" is simply the demonstrative pronoun *zeh*, which in this context is a dismissive expression of contempt.

When Abigail meets David, she acts intelligently and repeatedly refers to herself as David's "servant" (*'amah*; 25:24, 25, 28, 31, 41) and addresses David as "my lord" (*'adoni*; 25:24, 25, 26, 27, 29, 30, 31, 41), thus showing her humility as well as her understanding of the situation. In her intercessory speech, she characterizes her husband as "wicked" and says he is "like his name," suggesting the first meaning of *nabal* (fool) rather than the second (25:25). David responds by praising her "good judgment" (25:33).

Afterward, Abigail goes home and finds her husband "very drunk" (25:36), which furthers his characterization as a fool. Only when he sobers up does she tell him what has happened, at which point "his heart failed him and he became like a stone" (25:37), dying ten days later. Recognizing Abigail's intelligence and beauty, David proposes marriage.

This story illustrates how the biblical narrator shapes the reader's understanding of characters in the following ways:

59. Not the more well known Carmel, where Elijah opposed the prophets of Baal (1 Kings 18), but a town in the south near Hebron (1 Sam. 15:12). See "Setting" below.
60. See Long, *1 and 2 Samuel*, 234.
61. Long, *1 and 2 Samuel*, 234.

1. How the narrator refers to a character, how other characters in the story refer to the character, and how the character refers to him- or herself shapes readers' perception of the character.
2. The narrator may provide a brief description (i.e., "surly and mean," "intelligent and beautiful") that shapes readers' perception of the character.
3. How the narrator depicts the character's actions shapes readers' perception of the character.

Setting (Space)

Besides events (plot) and characters, biblical stories have settings. Characters act in space and in time (the topic of the next section). Through their narrators, authors create representations not only of people but also of places, and Frow's words about character apply also to setting: setting is just "a string of words."[62] Even if the setting is a real place, settings in stories are literary representations, and the narrator controls exactly how the reader imagines the place in which the characters act.

Here interpreters should see a difference between the narratee/implied reader and actual readers today, or really any reader at a historical or geographical distance from the place where the story takes place. The original readers would likely know a lot more about the setting of a biblical story than readers today, particularly readers who have never visited the land of Israel and seen the variety of environments it offers. To take one example, a resident of Jerusalem during the time of the OT would have a mental image of the city for a story that takes place in Jerusalem, a memory not available to later, more distant readers. Even later inhabitants of Jerusalem reading about an earlier time in the city's history would at least have a sense of the topography around the city. This explains why those who (like me) even today visit locations where biblical stories took place find themselves able to visualize the action with more confidence. Still, as was true of the physical description of characters, the Bible's description of setting is often sparse.

Returning to the story of David, Nabal, and Abigail, we learn that the action takes place at Carmel in Maon, where Nabal has property. Since Nabal is a descendant of Caleb, *this* Carmel must be south of Jerusalem in the vicinity of Hebron and not the mountain known by the same name, where Elijah confronted the prophets of Baal (1 Kings 18). The Hebrew word for this area is *midbar* (cf. 1 Sam. 25:1–2, 4, 14, 21), which most translations render

62. Frow, "Character," 109.

"wilderness" (NLT, ESV) or "desert" (NCV, NIV). The term "desert," however, can be misleading and may evoke the idea of a barren, sandy expanse, whereas Nabal is able to raise sheep in this area.

Also living in the wilderness, David sends ten men to Nabal to request provisions in return for the protection they provided his flocks. We are not told where they met with Nabal or the exact location of David's wilderness camp, but when Abigail intercepts David, he is in a "mountain ravine" (25:20).

After her successful intervention, Abigail returns to Nabal, who was "holding a banquet like that of a king" (25:36). After being told of his close call, Nabal dies of shock, and when David sends emissaries to ask Abigail to marry him, she returns to David's camp.

In sum, biblical stories locate the action in space. Often the location is briefly sketched and rarely with much detail: "The specification of external circumstances, setting, and gesture is held to a bare minimum"[63] (see the comments on Esther 1, above). The readers must do their best to visualize the spatial setting of the action. Readers today have limited knowledge of the locations of most biblical stories, but archaeology, historical geography, and actual visits to the lands of the Bible can enhance one's ability to visualize the settings.

Time

Abbott states that a narrative is not only a representation of events in space but also a "representation of events in time,"[64] though narratives shape or manipulate the presentation of time. We noted earlier the basic distinction between *story*, the events behind the narrative, whether fictional or not, and *discourse*, the narrative presentation of the story. For instance, narratives can engage in flashbacks or anticipations of events. A novel might start in the middle of events (*in media res*), cover a single day's activities in fifty pages, or allude to a hundred years in one sentence. Genette introduces the terms "order," "durations," and "frequency" to describe how a narrative shapes the presentation of time. *Order* refers to the presentation of the sequence, how the discourse relates to the story. *Duration* refers to the relationship between the story time and the discourse time. *Frequency* indicates that narratives may present a single event multiple times or a repeated event a single time.[65]

In OT narratives, the presentation of time is fairly straightforward: the sequence of the discourse follows the order of the story. This is true not only

---

63. Alter, *Art of Biblical Narrative*, 37.
64. Abbott, *Cambridge Introduction to Narrative*, 160.
65. Genette, *Narrative Discourse*, 33–160.

for individual episodes in a narrative but also for the overall narrative. This observation generally applies even though many OT narratives lack explicit chronological indicators of how much time passes between one action and another.

I can illustrate my point by returning to the story of David, Abigail, and Nabal. The opening verse of 1 Sam. 25 provides a transition from the previous episode, where David spares Saul's life. David swears an oath to preserve Saul's family when he becomes king and returns to his stronghold while Saul goes home (24:20–22).

First Samuel 25 begins by noting Samuel's death and his burial as well as David's moving to the Wilderness of Paran. The Hebrew of verse 1 links a series of events (Samuel's death, Israel's assembling, the burial, and David's move) with the simple copula *waw* ("and"), but the NIV rightly translates the first *waw* as "now" and the last as "then," since it is most logical that David moved to the "Desert [Wilderness] of Paran" *after* the funeral.

At this point, narrative attention turns to Nabal without any indication of how much time has passed since Samuel's burial and David's move to the region. The next thing readers know, David, through his men, asks Nabal for provisions in return for having protected his flocks. Readers are told that it is sheep-shearing time but not how long David and his men have been in the area before this time.

After David's young men ask Nabal for provisions, the narrator tells us that they were kept waiting, although we aren't told for how long (25:9). Making them wait is likely a negative reflection on Nabal, who should have been quickly forthcoming and eager to show his gratitude. When the answer comes, it is rude and demeaning toward David. When Nabal's response is conveyed to David, he tells his men to get ready to fight. The impression from the narrative is that David's response is decisive and immediate, indicating his determination.

At this point, the narrator shifts the setting from David to Abigail. One of Abigail's servants tells her what has happened. It could be that David gets his men's report at the same time that Abigail gets her servant's report. She too, we are told, "acted quickly" (25:18).

Abigail intercepts David in a mountain ravine. There is a slight flashback to a statement David made earlier expressing his determination to exact revenge against Nabal, which heightens the suspense. By her submission and the provisions she brings, Abigail successfully mollifies David and returns home to the drunken Nabal, whose heart fails him when he hears the news the next morning. At this point, readers get a specific temporal indicator: Nabal dies "about ten days later" (25:38), suggesting a prolonged period of suffering at the end. After an unspecified period of time, but probably not too long, David asks Abigail to marry him, and she agrees.

Other narratives provide time markers that are more explicit than those in 1 Sam. 25. Ezra 1–6 is a narrative account of the return from Babylonian exile through to the rebuilding of the temple. The narrative begins "in the first year of Cyrus king of Persia" (1:1) and then presents the king's decree allowing Jewish exiles to return to Jerusalem and rebuild the temple. The text seems to assume that the narratee knows the background to the decree—that is, that the Jews had been in exile in Babylon and that Persia had defeated Babylon. The narrator follows the decree (1:2–4) with an account of preparations for the return (1:5–11) as well as a list of those who make the trip back (2:1–67). We are not told precisely when the exiles departed from Babylon or when exactly they arrived in Jerusalem, but the text does say that "when they arrived at the house of the LORD in Jerusalem" (2:68), the returnees made donations for the rebuilding of the temple.

The next episode involves the rebuilding of the altar at the temple. The time indicator of "the seventh month" (3:1; Tishri [September-October]) is significant as the month when three important ceremonies occur: the Festival of Trumpets (on the first day; Lev. 23:24), the Day of Atonement (on the tenth day; Lev. 16:29; 23:26–32), and the Festival of Booths (beginning on the fifteenth day; Lev. 23:33–43). Of the three, only the Festival of Booths is mentioned in this context (Ezra 3:4), perhaps implying that the altar was not finished in time to observe the earlier festivals. Although the seventh month is mentioned, the year is not, but it is probably safe to assume that it is the seventh month in the first year after their return.

This assumption seems confirmed by the mention in the next episode that the Jewish returnees began the work of rebuilding the temple "in the second month of the second year after their arrival at the house of God in Jerusalem" (3:8). At some unspecified time after work began, they held a celebration when the foundation of the new temple was laid, though the joy of the celebration was tempered by the weeping of the older generation who still remembered Solomon's larger and more magnificent temple (3:10–13; cf. 1 Kings 6–8).

Thus far, the narrative has moved linearly from one event to the next, but Ezra 4 presents an interesting deviation. The opening of the chapter turns attention to the "enemies of Judah and Benjamin" (4:1) who, while the building is going on, seek first to help, but when rebuffed, seek to undermine the effort. According to the narrator, these attempts to undermine span "the entire reign of Cyrus king of Persia and down to the reign of Darius king of Persia" (4:5), a single verse spanning decades, and with the mention of Darius, the narrative has moved beyond the time when the temple was still being rebuilt.

Yet what is remarkable and an occasion for scholarly discussion is that the account springs even further forward to mention opposition to the Jews during the reigns of Xerxes (4:6) and Artaxerxes (4:7–23). But then the narrator returns to the time of the rebuilding of the temple with the reminder that the work on the temple was halted "until the second year of the reign of Darius king of Persia" (4:24).

Ezra 4:6–23 therefore seems to be an intrusion into the narrative flow between Ezra 4:1–5 and verse 24, where the story of the rebuilding of the temple resumes. However, this digression is ultimately both reasonable and explainable: while on the theme of opposition to the Jews, the narrator chooses to include later attempts to thwart the rebuilding of the *city* before returning to the time of the *temple* rebuilding.

Ezra 4 ends (v. 24) with the statement that the effort to rebuild the temple stalled until the second year of the reign of Darius. Ezra 5 then starts with the successful call of the prophets Haggai and Zechariah to restart the project (5:1–2). No explicit time indicator is given in the book of Ezra for the onset of the prophetic work of Haggai and Zechariah, but by saying that work on the temple ceased until the second year of Darius, the text implies that their prophetic call came in that year. This inference is confirmed by turning to the books of Haggai and Zechariah, both of whom date the beginning of their prophetic work to the second year of Darius's reign (Hag. 1:1, 15; 2:10; Zech. 1:1, 7). When the work resumes, nearby officials challenge the renewed efforts by sending a letter to Darius, who confirms that Cyrus did indeed authorize the Jews to return and rebuild their temple.

This part of the book of Ezra closes with the completion of the temple "on the third day of the month Adar, in the sixth year of the reign of King Darius" (6:15) and with the celebration of the Passover "on the fourteenth day of the first month" (6:19; Exod. 12:6, 18; Lev. 23:5).

Thus, Ezra 1–6 covers the time from the first year of Cyrus to the sixth year of Darius, from the first returnees from Babylon commissioned to rebuild the temple to the completion of the task, a period of approximately twenty-five years. The focus is on the restoration of the place of worship, moving from altar to foundation to the completed temple, and the restart of sacrificial ritual. Not surprisingly, the time indicators are closely aligned with that work.

Dialogue Management

According to David Herman, "Another relatively local principle for story world design involves the creation of mental models for speech acts performed by participants."[66] Since each narrative tradition uses dialogue in its own way, it is important to ask how Hebrew narrators present dialogue.

1. *Dialogue as shaped.* The dialogues appearing in OT narrative are not transcripts of actual speech, even if actual speech lies behind them (a question I am leaving open in this volume). Just as the presentation of action is shaped by the narrator to achieve a certain effect and to deliver a message, so too is dialogue.

2. *Dialogue as favored.* Speech plays a major role in Hebrew narrative. The narrator tends to use dialogue more than narration or description to develop character and to present the action of the story, which will become clear in the examples below and in the second half of the book. Alter puts it this way: "The biblical writers, in other words, are often less concerned with actions in themselves than with how individual character responds to actions or produces them; and direct speech is made the chief instrument for revealing the varied and at times nuanced relations of the personages to the actions in which they are implicated."[67]

The examples below also illustrate the principle that biblical dialogue is between only two characters. More than two people may be present, but even in such cases, either a single spokesperson speaks for the group or the group is portrayed as speaking collectively. The interchange between Abraham and the three visitors as well as the role Sarah plays in the story illustrates this principle. The narrator first introduces the scene that takes place near "the great trees of Mamre" (Gen. 18:1): Abraham looks up, sees three men, and rushes to them (18:1–2). He greets them and offers them hospitality (18:3–5), with the length of this speech highlighting the lavishness of the hospitality.

As a group, they respond briefly in the affirmative: "Very well . . . do as you say" (v. 5d). Abraham then goes to Sarah and gives her instructions: "Quick, . . . get three seahs of the finest flour and knead it and bake some bread" (v. 6). Abraham's words, his hurrying to the tent to give Sarah instructions, and his running to the herd to select "a choice, tender calf" show Abraham's eagerness to serve and satisfy his guests.[68]

The group then asks Abraham about Sarah: "Where is your wife Sarah?" He responds, "There in the tent" (v. 9). At this point one of the three (likely the one later identified as "the LORD," v. 13) makes a pronouncement: "I will surely return to you about this time next year, and Sarah your wife will have a son" (v. 10).

---

66. D. Herman, *Story Logic*, 171.

67. Alter, *Art of Biblical Narrative*, 6.

68. Abraham's eagerness contrasts with Lot's less enthusiastic attitude toward these heavenly visitors (Longman, *Genesis*, 237–38).

The focus then shifts to Sarah, who is in the tent and "laughed to herself as she thought, 'After I am worn out and my lord is old, will I now have this pleasure?'" (v. 12). Although the narrator makes clear that Sarah is only thinking this, speaking "internally" (*beqirbah*) and not aloud (v. 12), both the omniscient narrator and the omniscient Lord know what she is thinking. "The LORD" gives a relatively lengthy reply, challenging her doubt and reasserting the promise of a child (vv. 13–14). This is followed by Sarah's denial and the Lord's exposure of the lie (v. 15).

3. *Dialogue as managed.* Literary scholars have identified several types of dialogue management used across various narrative traditions. Using Plato's categories of diegesis (indirect presentation of speech) and mimesis (imitation of actual speech), David Herman offers this categorization: "At the diegetic end of the scale are modes such as diegetic summary ('Joe was unhappy') and indirect discourse ('Joe said he was unhappy'); at the mimetic end are modes such as direct discourse ('Joe said, "I am unhappy"') and free direct discourse ('I am unhappy,' reported as part of an interior monologue by Joe)."[69] On the same page, Herman also discusses free indirect discourse, which occurs when the character's perspective bleeds into the narrator's. This strategy is found in more-recent novels but not in the Bible.

As we consider how Hebrew narrative presents dialogue, it soon becomes obvious that the narrator uses the mimetic strategy of direct discourse a significant majority of the time. Even thought is rendered as direct discourse in the majority of cases, as Sarah's internal dialogue in Gen. 18:12 illustrates. Though rare in Scripture, speech or thought is sometimes presented as indirect discourse. One instance is seen in Gen. 38:15, which says "When Judah saw her, he thought she was a prostitute" rather than the more typical "When Judah saw her, he thought, 'She is a prostitute.'" The preference for direct discourse likely arises from the desire to render the scene more lifelike and give the impression of verbatim speech.

4. *Dialogue as brief.* As these biblical examples illustrate, dialogue interchanges are typically composed of brief speeches, often just one or two sentences. Departures from this pattern in the form of longer speeches naturally stand out and are usually pivotal to the narrative.

In the Joseph narrative (Gen. 37–50), for instance, most of the dialogue is typically conveyed through brief exchanges, but the longer speeches come at significant turning points in the plot. One of these is Joseph's interpretation of Pharaoh's dreams (41:25–36), which wins him freedom and promotion to a status that allows him to provide food for his family as well as to

69. D. Herman, *Story Logic*, 172.

test whether his brothers have changed since they sold him into slavery. A second example is Judah's speech in 44:18–34, in which he offers himself in place of his brother Benjamin, who is accused of stealing Joseph's divination cup.

The significance of this speech is related to the role that Judah plays in the Joseph narrative as a whole. Indeed, he is second only to Joseph as a major character in the story. His actions at the beginning of the story portray him as a bad person: he leads the brothers in selling Joseph to the Ishmaelites (37:26–27), he marries a Canaanite woman, and he treats his daughter-in-law, Tamar, unjustly (Gen. 38).[70]

Through Benjamin's arrest, Joseph has set up a situation in which the brothers must decide whether to repeat the evil they perpetrated against Joseph. In his lengthy speech, Judah offers himself in Benjamin's stead in order to save his father additional grief. With this speech, Judah becomes the leader of the brothers, although he is only fourth in birth order. The firstborn, Reuben, disqualified himself by sleeping with one of his father's concubines, and Levi and Simeon, born second and third, lost standing for cruelly massacring the Shechemites (Gen. 34). This narrative helps explain why the tribe of Judah—rather than that of Reuben, Levi, or Simeon—becomes the dominant tribe in later Israelite history.

5. *Dialogue as characterizing.* In some narrative traditions, an author uses style to differentiate or distinguish characters or simply to help develop the reader's understanding of the character. For instance, in *The Catcher in the Rye*, Holden Caulfield, the novel's main protagonist, sounds like a high school teenager living in New York City in the 1940s: "Her mother and father were divorced. Her mother was married again to some booze hound. . . . Skinny guy with hairy legs. I remember him. He wore shorts all the time. Jane said he was supposed to be a playwright or some goddam thing, but all I ever saw him do was booze all the time and listen to every single goddam mystery program on the radio. And run around the goddam house, naked. With Jane around, and all."[71]

Modern readers face limitations in grasping the subtleties of Hebrew and may not notice distinctive dialectical language traits. A dialectical difference factors prominently in Judg. 12:4–6, where Jephthah outs the Ephraimites by requiring them to say "Shibboleth," which they pronounce "Sibboleth." So

---

70. An earlier generation of scholars thought that Gen. 38 was misplaced in the Joseph narrative because Joseph himself plays no role in the story, which focuses solely on Judah. But Gen. 37–50 is about more than just Joseph; it is also interested in characterizing the other brothers, especially Judah.

71. Salinger, *Catcher in the Rye*, 42.

modern readers may be missing some subtle dialogue clues that the original, native speakers of Hebrew would have recognized.

But differences in dialogue style can occasionally be detected in English translation to inform us about the characters in a biblical story.[72] Samson's conversation with his father and mother in Judg. 14 reveals him as demanding and even disrespectful toward his parents. He tells them, "I have seen a woman in Timnah; now get her for me as my wife" (14:2). They respond to him, questioning his choice: "Isn't there an acceptable woman among your relatives or among our people? Must you go to the uncircumcised Philistines to get a wife?" (14:3a). His response is brusque and again demanding: "Get her for me. She's the right one for me" (14:3b).

Having given an overview of how speech is managed in the HB, I will illustrate how dialogue typically works in Hebrew narrative by looking at 1 Sam. 23:1–6, the short episode of David's defeat of the Philistines at a Judean town called Keilah. Before this episode, readers learn that David has traveled to the forest of Hereth in Judah (1 Sam. 22:5). The episode I have in mind reads as follows:

Now they told David, "*The Philistines are fighting against Keilah and are robbing the threshing floors.*" David inquired of the Lord, "*Shall I go and attack these Philistines?*" The Lord said to David, "*Go and attack the Philistines and save Keilah.*" But David's men said to him, "*Look, we are afraid here in Judah; how much more then if we go to Keilah against the armies of the Philistines?*" Then David inquired of the Lord again. The Lord answered him, "*Yes, go down to Keilah, for I will give the Philistines into your hand.*" So David and his men went to Keilah, fought with the Philistines, brought away their livestock, and dealt them a heavy defeat. Thus David rescued the inhabitants of Keilah. When Abiathar son of Ahimelech fled to David at Keilah, he came down with an ephod in his hand. (23:1–6 NRSVue, italics added)

I have put the direct discourse in italics to highlight how pervasive dialogue is in relation to the narration of action, particularly in the first part. The narrator's role in the first part of the episode is simply to serve up the dialogue. David receives a report that the Philistines are harassing the city of Keilah. Even though the narrator does not tell us who gave David this report, it is presented as direct speech. Theoretically, it could have been presented as a

---

72. Bar-Efrat, *Narrative Art in the Bible*, 64.

diegetic summary ("David heard that that the Philistines were in Keilah") or as indirect discourse ("A messenger told David that the Philistines were in Keilah"). The use of direct discourse gives the reader a sense of immediacy. It is showing rather than telling, or perhaps better, telling through showing. We feel as though we are there overhearing the conversation rather than the narrator mediating the story to us. The narrator's role, at least in these first few verses, is simply to tell us who is speaking.

After receiving this news, David then inquires of the Lord and poses a question to him in straightforward terms, "Shall I go and attack these Philistines?" The narrator then reports God's response as just as clear and straightforward, "Go and attack the Philistines and save Keilah" (more on God's speech below). The narrative implies that this inquiry and response was reported to David's men rather than their being present at the time David made the inquiry, since they question the answer. In so doing they also reveal their own fear at their present precarious position. Thus their thinking is revealed by their speech rather than expressed directly by the narrator.

David then inquires of God a second time; since readers have already heard his specific request, it is not repeated here. God's response is again presented as direct speech, "Yes, go down to Keilah, for I will give the Philistines into your hand." In this second response, God is more explicit about the outcome as well as his own involvement.

At this point, the narrator stops simply reporting speech and briefly narrates the action in a single verse. In response to the divine commission, David and his men go to Keilah, fight the Philistines, and defeat them, saving the people of Keilah and taking possession of the Philistines' livestock.

Interestingly, the episode ends not with the report of the victory but with a flashback, which modern translations often present as a parenthetical expression (see 23:6 NIV), though the NRSVue does not. Earlier we learned that Abiathar had escaped the murder of the priests at Nob and joined David (1 Sam. 22:20–23). Here we're told for the first time that Abiathar brought the ephod with him when he fled.

Though there are some questions about how the ephod is connected to divine inquiry, in this context the narrator is informing us how David inquired of the Lord. Either the ephod contained the Urim and Thummim, or it was itself a divinatory object. Regardless, we learn that the ephod is how God spoke to David. Even though God's response is reported in direct discourse, this is likely a verbal representation of what God communicated nonverbally through the ephod. David posed the question, and the answer came back twice in the affirmative: "Shall I go and attack these Philistines?" The oracular device says "Yes."

Conclusion

Narrative prose is the dominant mode (or genre) of writing in the OT. A knowledge of how Hebrew authors present their stories is key to proper interpretation, and this chapter has provided an overview of the conventions they used to construct their stories. Some of these conventions are familiar to readers of modern literature, but some are not. In our study, we availed ourselves of categories, concepts, and terms from recent narratology, recognizing that many of these scholarly tools, while helpful for the study of modern literature, are not relevant for the study of biblical literature.

We started by looking at how (implied) authors present their stories through a narrator to a narratee/implied reader and eventually to actual readers, including those of us who read the text today. Study of the narrator led us to a consideration of focalization, the management of point of view. Our attention then turned to plot and character, setting, time, and dialogue management.

Knowing how narratives work in the HB increases our sensitivity to the shape of the story and can deeply enhance our appreciation and understanding of its meaning. With that same goal in mind, we now turn to consider poetry, the other primary mode of writing (or genre) in the HB.

FIVE

Poetry as Genre

To truly understand the psalms and other poems in the OT, interpreters must understand poetry, and Hebrew poetry in particular. I could easily adapt Robert Alter's insight into story and apply it to poetry: "Every era in a particular culture . . . develops distinctive and sometimes intricate codes for telling its [poems]."[1] It is important for us to pause and consider how the psalmists wrote and understood their own poetry. Knowing how Hebrew poetry works will help us read the psalms more intelligently and enrich our understanding of the poem's message.

As we explore poetry in the OT, it will become apparent that the poetic conventions of ancient Israel often functioned on the semantic level, the level of meaning. In this chapter, therefore, I place emphasis on the semantic level of the poetry, but I will also briefly examine how poetry works on the syntactical (grammatical) and phonological (sound) levels as well.

I begin with a consideration of the three most pervasive and important poetic conventions of ancient Hebrew poetry: terseness, parallelism, and figurative language, particularly metaphor. After this, I proceed to secondary poetic devices, which are not as pervasive in the poetry but include sound plays, wordplays, and an interesting structuring device known as acrostic. Last, I discuss the absence of meter from the poetic repertoire of the Hebrew poet.

Pervasive Poetic Conventions: Terseness, Parallelism, Imagery

Terseness

Readers do not need to know Hebrew to see in an English translation that Hebrew poetry is terse when compared with narrative prose. Indeed, one need

1. Alter, "How Convention Helps Us Read," 115.

only look at a printed page of the book of Psalms and compare it with a narrative text such as Samuel, for example, to see that the psalms are laid out in poetic stanzas while Samuel has full lines of text. Readers can see the difference because of all the white space on the printed pages of Psalms. Psalms and other poetic parts of the Bible look almost as if the words have been compressed on the page, and that is actually a good way of thinking about it. Poetry is *compressed language*. A poem says a lot in few words.

Those reading Hebrew poetry in English translation may not realize that the Hebrew original typically uses fewer words than the English and so is even more terse than the translation indicates. A prose text also typically requires more English words to translate the Hebrew original, but this difference is much more pronounced in poetry. For example, the NIV translates the first poetic line of the Song of Songs as follows (1:2a):

> Let him kiss me with the kisses of his mouth— (10 words)
> for your love is more delightful than wine. (8 words)

A transliteration of the actual Hebrew words represents a fraction of the number of English words:

> *yishaqeni minneshiqot pihu* (3 words)
> *ki-tovim dodeka miyayin* (4 words)

A typical verse of Hebrew poetry in the psalms has three or four words in the first half (or colon) and three or even two in the second. The second line is almost always the same length or shorter (see below on ellipsis).

I have called the compressed nature of the Hebrew poetry "terseness," which is just another word for brevity or concision. The fact that the poet uses a few words to say a lot sends an important message to those who read and interpret it: we should slow down and carefully reflect on the words the poet uses. The poet's economy of expression means that the words are chosen carefully and intentionally.

A consequence of terseness is heightened ambiguity. After all, brevity is achieved by suppressing the use of certain parts of speech that clarify the relationships between the words. Perhaps the most obvious example is the spare use of conjunctions. In both English and Hebrew, conjunctions (e.g., "but," "and," "therefore," "however") are usually short words, but they indicate how phrases and sentences relate to one another. The relative absence of these conjunctions (compared to prose) makes clause relationships less certain. Psalm 23 opens with two cola of two words each:

"The LORD" (*yhwh*) is "my shepherd" (*ro'i*);
"nothing" (*lo'*) "will I lack" (*'echsar*). (my trans.)

The lack of conjunctions requires readers to think about the relationship between the lines. If conjunctions were used, it would likely read "Because the LORD is my shepherd, I will lack nothing" or "The LORD is my shepherd; therefore I will lack nothing." In this case, the relationship is not obscure, only vague, and requires the reader to reflect on the meaning of the poem.

Proverbs 26:7 provides a second interesting example:

> The legs of a lame person dangle,
>   and a proverb in the mouth of a fool. (my trans.)

Again, the reader must think of the relationship between the two. A simple Hebrew conjunction (*waw*, "and") stands between the two cola here, but how are they related? After some thought, it is clear that an analogy is being drawn between a lame person's legs and a proverb spoken by a fool. Both are ineffective.

Terseness is also achieved by the infrequent use of the so-called prose particle *'et*. Although this particle is not translated, it marks the direct object in a sentence and differentiates it from the subject. The absence of the prose particle in poetry heightens ambiguity by making it more difficult to determine whether a noun is the subject or the object. This difficulty is intensified because poetry does not follow the same syntactical rules that prose does. In a prose sentence, the typical word order is subject → verb → direct object, but these rules do not apply to poetry. The interpreter of poetry can usually determine the correct syntactical relationships, but it requires more effort than in prose.

Ellipsis is yet another convention that leads to brevity and potential ambiguity. In this case, an element in the first colon is omitted from the second, with the understanding that the omitted part is implied and to be read with the second colon. The verb is the part of speech most often omitted but implied, as the following example shows:

> You have put me in the depths of the Pit,
>   in the regions dark and deep. (Ps. 88:6 NRSVue)

The Hebrew verb translated "you have put me" is implicit in the line "in the regions dark and deep."

In Ps. 1:1 the opening phrase "Happy are those who" is elided (omitted) from the second and third cola:

> Happy are those who do not follow the advice of the wicked
>   or take the path that sinners tread
>   or sit in the seat of scoffers. (NRSVue)

Achieved by these and other means, terseness leads to compressed meaning. Ambiguity is not a weakness of communication but a feature that drives the reader to enter into the poem and reflect on its message, as the poet, and ultimately God, speaks to the reader through these words.

Parallelism

Semantic Parallelism

Scholars use various terms to refer to the parts of a poetic line. The line is the most basic complete unit of poetry. In most cases, a biblical verse is equivalent to a poetic line. Verse numbers were added long after the poems were composed, and those who divided each poem into verses tended to assign a verse number to each poetic line.

Psalm 125:4 follows the pattern of the most basic type of poetic line in the Psalms and the other poetic portions of the OT. English translations commonly format this verse into two parts and slightly indent the second part:

> Do good, O LORD, to those who are good,
>   and to those who are upright in heart. (NRSVue)

The two parts display a parallel structure (called "parallelism"). The second part echoes the thought of the first part and assumes the ellipsis of the opening portion "Do good, O LORD" (see the previous section). "To those who are good" parallels "to those who are upright in heart."

I call the two parts of the poetic line *cola* (sg. *colon*); since there are two cola in this verse, Ps. 125:4 is an example of a bicolon. There are also tricola in the HB such as Ps. 1:1 discussed in the previous section. On rare occasions we find examples of poetic lines with more than three cola. To facilitate discussion, I label the first colon of a bicolon the *A* colon and the second the *B* colon.

How does the *A* colon relate to the *B* colon? Theoretically, there are three possibilities, and these were first explored by the eighteenth-century British cleric and scholar Robert Lowth, who was the first to apply the term "parallelism" (a label derived from geometry) to this kind of construction. He defined the parallel line as "a certain conformation of the sentences," in which "equals refer to equals, and opposites to opposites," thus the emphasis on similarity between the cola.[2] "The correspondence of one verse, or line, with another, I call parallelism. When a proposition is delivered, and a second subjoined to it, or drawn under it, equivalent, or contrasted with it in sense; or similar to it in the form of grammatical construction, these I call parallel lines; and the words or phrases, answering one to another in the corresponding lines, parallel terms."[3]

Lowth wrote against the opposite tendency, which understood the cola as saying two different things (A does not equal B). While on the surface this view does not seem likely (look again at the examples given above), it does have some long-standing adherents. Some ancient rabbis concluded that A was not equal to B because God would not waste words repeating himself. As James Kugel explains, "This reading is laterally connected to the rabbinic conception of the Bible's sanctity, and most notably to the principle of biblical 'omnisignificance.'"[4]

Lowth's views shaped the theoretical and practical understanding of parallelism for some two centuries, though there were developments in understanding the relationship between the cola of parallel lines as evidenced by the proliferation of formal categories of parallelism. Lowth himself thought in terms of three categories: synonymous, antithetical, and synthetic parallelism.

Synonymous parallelism is the most common type, and this relation between cola seems to be what Lowth has in mind when he says "equals refers to equals." Psalm 2:1 well illustrates the formula "A equals B":

> Why do the nations conspire
> and peoples plot in vain? (NRSVue)

"Nations" is synonymous with "peoples," and the verb "conspire" corresponds to "plot." We will later revisit this verse to ask whether these two cola are truly equal, but Lowth would lead us to believe that here the poet is saying the same thing twice.

Antithetical parallelism is much rarer, apart from the book of Proverbs, presenting antonyms rather than synonyms—in Lowth's terms, "opposites [referring] to opposites."

2. Lowth, *Lectures on the Sacred Poetry*.
3. Lowth, *Lectures on the Sacred Poetry*, 1:336.
4. Kugel, *Idea of Biblical Poetry*, 104.

> The wise woman builds her house,
> but the foolish tears it down with her own hands. (Prov. 14:1 NRSVue)

In the first colon the wise woman builds her house, while in the second the foolish one tears her house down. As Kugel points out, the most common misunderstanding about antithetic parallelism is thinking that the two cola are saying opposite things. In reality, they are making the same point from two opposite perspectives.[5]

Synthetic parallelism is the label for any parallelism that is neither synonymous nor antithetic, but Lowth's third category is somewhat problematic. Kugel calls it "garbage-can parallelism" because of the many types of parallelism it includes.[6] The second stanza of Ps. 2 begins with two parallel lines that Lowth would call synonymous:

> The One enthroned in heaven laughs;
> the Lord scoffs at them.
> He rebukes them in his anger
> and terrifies them in his wrath, saying . . . (Ps. 2:4–5)

But then the third line is not obviously synonymous, though the NIV divides it into two parts as do most English translations:

> "I have installed my king
> on Zion, my holy mountain." (Ps. 2:6)

Partly because of dissatisfaction with the category of synthetic parallelism and partly in order to refine the other two types of parallelism, particularly synonymous, scholars in the twentieth century began to speak of more than the three Lowthian categories of parallelism. The secondary literature soon became peppered with labels such as staircase parallelism, metaphoric parallelism, chiastic parallelism, Janus parallelism, and more. The apex of these categorization attempts was Steven Geller's work, in which he names and illustrates numerous types of parallelism.[7]

The multiplication of categories led James Kugel to declare that there is either an infinite number of categories or only one comprehensive one such as "A, what's more, B." Kugel, and Alter after him, recognized that the poet is not wasting words by saying the same thing twice. Rather, the second colon

---

5. Kugel, *Idea of Biblical Poetry*, 13.
6. Kugel used this label in a class at Yale University in 1978, but I don't think it appears in any of his written works. He calls it a "catch-all" in *Idea of Biblical Poetry*, 12.
7. Geller, *Parallelism in Early Biblical Poetry*.

furthers, sharpens, and intensifies the thought of the first colon.[8] Continuing the mathematical analogy, the relationship between the two cola can be described as "A, what's more, B" (A < B).[9] Kugel points out how what follows the first colon always carries forward the thought of the first by sharpening, intensifying, or illustrating it. The examples below show this in more detail.

Exodus 15:2-3

Here's a portion from the Song of the Sea:

A The LORD is my strength and my might,
B   and he has become my salvation;
C this is my God, and I will praise him,
D   my father's God, and I will exalt him.
E The LORD is a warrior;
F   the LORD is his name. (15:2–3 NRSVue)

These three poetic bicola (AB, CD, EF) begin the Song of the Sea, sung after God rescued Israel from Egypt by parting the sea. None of the second cola (B, D, F) merely repeat the thought of the preceding colon, but neither are they unrelated. Rather, the second colon in each pair progresses the thought of the preceding colon in some way.

In colon A, the composer declares that the Lord gives him strength and defends him; in B he proclaims that God has used his strength to actually "save" him. In this context, modern and especially Christian readers must be careful not to spiritualize the nature of this salvation; God becomes Israel's salvation by rescuing them in a military context. A better translation of the B line might be "He has won a victory for me."

In the C colon the composer expresses his intention to praise the Lord and claims him as his God. In the second (D) line he affirms that his God is also his "father's God," and he uses a verb that might be construed as implying even more fervent worship.

In the third bicolon, the poet asserts that the LORD (Yahweh) is a warrior (E). After all, he has just fought for him at the sea. In the following colon he emphasizes that the name of his warrior God is indeed Yahweh, the name revealed to Moses, the lead singer of the poem, at the burning bush (Exod. 3).

8. Since the second colon intensifies or sharpens the thought of the first, it is often the case that the second colon presents words that occur less frequently in Hebrew and have a narrower semantic range.

9. This formulation and the thought behind it are persuasively argued by Kugel (*Idea of Biblical Poetry*) and by Alter (*Art of Biblical Poetry*).

Job 38:4–7

Near the end of the book of Job, after Job has questioned God's justice while disputing with three friends, God finally puts Job in his place. Speaking out of a storm, God challenges Job for obscuring God's plans and speaking "words without knowledge" (38:2). Then God announces that he will put Job's knowledge to the test with a series of questions that demand answers. God's first questions come in 38:4–7, questions Job cannot possibly answer because he was not present when God created the world:

A Where were you when I laid the foundation of the earth?
B   Tell me, if you have understanding.
C Who determined its measurements—surely you know!
D   Or who stretched the line upon it?
E On what were its bases sunk,
F   or who laid its cornerstone
G when the morning stars sang together
H   and all the heavenly beings shouted for joy? (38:4–7 NRSVue)

God first asks where Job was when he began the work of creation (A). Using the analogy of constructing a house, God describes the creation of the cosmos, beginning with the foundation. He follows this up with a taunting demand for Job to explain the steps of construction, which he knows Job cannot do (B).

The unanswerable questions continue, asking who marked out the dimensions of the earth (C). The analogy with building a house leads to the question in the second line, asking who stretched the measuring line to lay out the earth (D). The third poetic bicolon continues the architectural analogy, asking where the footings of the house were set and following this with a "who" question, this time asking about the laying of the cornerstone.

Lines A through F build on each other, evoking the building of the house by naming its various parts. The fourth and final bicolon describes the celebration of celestial beings. Here we see a sharpening of the poetic line in the change of verb as it moves from singing to shouting for joy. Perhaps most intriguing is the sharpening that occurs in the parallel between the "morning stars" and the "angels," associating angels with those bright celestial bodies. The creation account itself demythologizes the sun, moon, and stars (Gen. 1:14–19), which are treated as deities in the Babylonian creation account Enuma Elish. In it, the god Marduk places other gods in the skies as stars: "He made the positions for the great gods, He established [in] the constellations the stars, their likenesses."[10] But Yahweh invites us to picture the stars as angels celebrating the construction of the cosmos-house.

Psalm 2:1–3

In the earlier chapter on genre, we saw how Ps. 2 and its four stanzas of three verses each participate in the genre of a royal hymn that celebrates the inauguration of a Davidic king during the monarchical period but takes on eschatological significance after the exile. Here we will examine the relationship among the four parallel lines that constitute the first stanza.

A Why do the nations conspire
B   and the peoples plot in vain?
C The kings of the earth set themselves,
D   and the rulers take counsel together
E against the LORD
F   and his anointed, saying,
G "Let us burst their bonds apart
H   and cast their cords from us." (2:1–3 NRSVue)

The parallelism in these lines is even closer than in the previous examples and comes almost to what we might consider truly synonymous parallelism. However, a closer reading reveals a clear progression between the first and second cola of all four bicola.

The poet asks a question in the first line. Here "nations" parallels "peoples" and "conspire" parallels "plot." Some type of sharpening is likely going on even here, but we also must recognize that our understanding of the nuances of Hebrew words is sometimes vague or lacking. In such cases, interpreters should be careful not to read differences into paired cola. What is an obvious progression in B, though, is the addition of "in vain," which tells readers that the nations may conspire and plot all they wish, but in the end it will be a fruitless endeavor. The addition of "in vain" in the second colon also illustrates what some have called "compensation" or a "ballast variant."[11] The second colon elides the interrogative "why" but compensates for this shortening by adding "in vain."

In the second line, "kings" and "rulers" are parallel and provide another example showing no clear semantic progression. The obvious progression appears instead in the verbs. The kings rising up in rebellion is one thing (C),

10. Foster, "Epic of Creation," 399 (tablet 5, lines 1–2).
11. LeMon and Strawn, "Parallelism," 511.

but forming an alliance goes a step further (D). I am taking the object of the king's rebellion (E and F) as separate lines because of the parallelism between them, though they are prepositional phrases. There is clearly addition between the two cola since it names the two objects of rebellion, the first being Yahweh and the second his "anointed one," a clear reference to the Davidic king anointed at the beginning of his reign. By putting them together in this way, the poet shows a close connection between the two: a rebellion against the LORD is a rebellion against his anointed king, and vice versa.

The final parallel line in the stanza quotes the rebel kings as they proclaim their attempt at independence. They liken their subservience to the LORD and his anointed one as being in "chains." First, they assert their intention to break those chains (G), but then they intensify the thought, saying that they will cast away those broken chains (H).

Proverbs 10:1–4

Proverbs is well-known for its use of antonyms rather than near synonyms to construct parallel lines, which has been called "antithetical parallelism." But as Kugel points out, "antithetical" does not mean that these lines are saying two different things.[12] Rather, antithetical poetic lines are better thought of as saying similar things from different and sometimes opposite perspectives. Let us see how this plays out in Prov. 10:

A A wise child makes a glad father,
B   but a foolish child is a mother's grief.
C Treasures gained by wickedness do not profit,
D   but righteousness delivers from death.
E The LORD does not let the righteous go hungry,
F   but he thwarts the craving of the wicked.
G A slack hand causes poverty,
H   but the hand of the diligent makes rich. (10:1–4 NRSVue)

In the first bicolon (v. 1), the sage uses "wise" in the first colon and "foolish" in the second, and the verb "brings joy" in the first contrasted with "brings grief" in the second. The one who feels the joy of the wise son is the "father" in the first colon, and the one who experiences the grief of the foolish child is the "mother" in the second. The proverb clearly encourages the son to be wise and to avoid bringing his parents grief through foolish behavior. It would be a mistake to think, as some have done, that the first

12. Kugel, *Idea of Biblical Poetry*, 13.

colon does not also apply to the mother and that the second colon does not apply equally to the father.

The second bicolon (v. 2) is a bit more subtle than the first, though there is clearly an antithetical relationship between C and D. The first colon speaks of "treasures gained by wickedness," which in the context of Proverbs is the consequence of foolish actions. The second colon (D) speaks of righteousness, the ethical component of wisdom, having the positive outcome of delivering from death.

Although the truth claim of the third bicolon (v. 3) needs discussion,[13] the parallels between the two cola again illustrate the use of antonyms in a poetic line, with "wicked" paralleling "righteous" and unmet cravings juxtaposed with God's faithful provision for the righteous.

The final proverb (G–H) is one of many examples in Proverbs that teaches the virtue of hard work and warns against the vice of sloth. By setting laziness and diligence in parallel, the contrasting outcomes of poverty and prosperity are also set side by side.

Song of Songs 8:5b–6

Song of Songs is an anthology of love poems, most of which celebrate physical intimacy between a man and a woman,[14] and Song 8:5b–6 is a snippet of perhaps the most well-known song in the book. The woman claims to have aroused the man and then to mark the man as owned by her.

A   Under the apple tree I roused you;
B   there your mother conceived you,
C   there she who was in labor gave you birth.
D   Place me like a seal over your heart,
E   like a seal on your arm;
F   for love is as strong as death,
G   its jealousy unyielding as the grave.
H   It burns like blazing fire,
I   like a mighty flame. (8:5b–6)

The first poetic line is a tricolon (A–B–C). In the first colon, the woman reminds the man that she aroused him under the apple tree. The apple tree evokes a place that provides cover, implies a sweet smell, and even hints at fertility. The parallelism proper occurs between the second and third cola (B–C). The NIV rendering obscures the fact that the same verb (*chabal*) occurs in

---

13. For which, see Longman, *Proverbs*, 231.
14. See Longman, *Song of Songs*.

both. In the Piel this verb can mean either "to conceive" or "to be in labor"; it is questionable, though not impossible, that the first meaning is implied in the B colon while the latter is the sense in the C colon, as the NIV translates. If so, there is a clear progression from B to C. However, an argument can also be made that, in this context where sexual intimacy is at issue and the apple tree is the setting, *chabal* should be translated as "conceive" in both cola, though the progression would then be a much more subtle one of emphasis.

Next she instructs her lover to "seal" himself with her (D–E). In Israel at the time, a "seal" was typically a stamp seal that made an impression on soft clay and was used to mark one's ownership of a possession. The "A, what's more, B" meaning may be seen in her request to first place her like a seal "over your heart" (D) and then "on your arm" (E). The significance here is that she desires him both inside and outside.[15]

In the following motivation clause, the woman parallels "love" in F with the emotionally more intense "jealousy" in G. This love is strong (F), so strong that it does not yield (G). Indeed, love is as strong as death, and its jealousy is as unyielding as the grave. Such love is hot like a "blazing fire" (H), indeed a "mighty flame" (I). The latter may be an even more significant intensification if translated as "flame of Yah," as the NIV footnote and some commentators suggest.

Isaiah 1:5–6

In his opening judgment speech, the prophet Isaiah calls on the heavens and earth to hear God's judgment against his ignorant people (1:2–3), which is followed by pronouncing a "woe" over them because of their sin and corruption caused by their abandonment of Yahweh (1:4). Let us do a closer analysis of the parallelism in 1:5–6:

A Why should you be beaten anymore?
B   Why do you persist in rebellion?
C Your whole head is injured,
D   your whole heart afflicted.
E From the sole of your foot to the top of your head
F   there is no soundness—
G only wounds and welts
H   and open sores,
I not cleansed or bandaged
J   or soothed with olive oil. (1:5–6)

---

15. Hallo ("'As a Seal upon Thy Heart,'" 22) mentions the Mesopotamian practice of placing a seal on a corpse's chest and arm at burial.

This passage begins with a why question expressed as a two-part parallelism. The "why," though appearing at the beginning of both A and B in English translations, is the first word of A in Hebrew but is implied by ellipsis in B. The first colon asks sinful Israel why they continue to allow themselves to be beaten, and the second colon asks why they persist in rebellion against God. The parallelism suggests that their being beaten is a result of their rebellion, so the idea is that they should stop rebelling so that they stop suffering.

Indeed, their beating is so severe that the "whole head" is injured (C) and the "whole heart" is afflicted (D). Physically and emotionally, outside and inside, they are beaten up. It is not just their head that suffers injury, however; for from head to toe (E) there is no soundness, no health (F). Their body is covered with "wounds and welts" (G) and, worse, "open sores" (H), which have received no treatment. They have not been cleansed or bandaged as wounds should be (I), nor have they been "soothed with olive oil" (J). The whole passage graphically describes the sorry state of Israel, though they have brought this injury on themselves through their recalcitrant rebellion.

These examples illustrate that parallelism permeates Hebrew poetry and is one of its distinctive features. An interpreter must first identify the poetic lines and then observe the relationships between the cola. English translations typically mark the parallelism clearly by indenting the second colon, and I have followed the NIV formatting here. Hebrew poetry's compressed forms of expression generally trigger a response in readers by forcing them to slow down and reflect, including carefully thinking about the nature of the relationship between poetic lines. How does B further the thought of A? The variety of potential meanings cannot be reduced to simple categories, though at least some of the categories retain their usefulness.

The interpreter should approach all parallel lines with the idea that the cola have an "A, what's more, B" relationship. The parallelism may be constructed from antonyms and can therefore be described as "antithetical parallelism," or the relationship between the cola may be more complex.

One of the more complex forms of parallelism is called "Janus-faced" parallelism, after the Roman god Janus, whose two faces looked forward and backward. This construction has a middle colon with a word or phrase that has two meanings, one sense pertaining to the preceding colon and one pertaining to the subsequent colon. Scott Noegel provides an example from Job 7:6–7 of this form of parallelism:[16]

---

16. Noegel, *Janus Parallelism*, 50, cited in D. Garrett, *Job*. The translation is Noegel's.

A My days are more trifling than a weaver's shuttle.
B   They go without a *tiqwah*.
C Remember, my life is but a wind, my eyes see no more good.

Noegel points out that *tiqwah* can mean either "thread" or "hope," and he suggests that the "thread" meaning corresponds to colon A and "hope" to colon C. Duane Garrett summarizes Noegel's interpretation as follows: "In verse 6, following the metaphor of the shuttle, Job asserts the 'thread' of his life has run out. But in the next verse he says he will no longer see any good, implying he has no 'hope.'"[17]

Of the many labels used to describe the various types of parallelism, the only categories that seem completely useless are "synthetic" and "synonymous parallelism." "Synthetic" seems to refer to any type of parallel relationship that is not synonymous or antithetic. And although the term "synonymous parallelism" rightly indicates that the parallelism is built on near synonyms, it also suggests the inaccurate idea that the second colon is merely restating the first using different words. Instead, in nearly every case, something new is added by the second colon.

Grammatical Parallelism

Parallelism functions not only on a semantic level, the level of meaning, but also on a grammatical level and, at least occasionally, on a phonological level. Geller cites the Russian Formalist Roman Jakobson to this effect. Jakobson believes that parallelism, especially grammatical and phonological, is a function of all poetry, not just biblical poetry:

> Pervasive parallelism inevitably activates all the levels of language—the distinctive features, inherent and prosodic, the morphological and syntactical categories and forms, the lexical units and their semantic classes in both their convergences and divergences acquire an autonomous poetic value. This focus upon phonological, grammatical, and semantic structures in their multiform interplay does not remain confined to the limits of parallel lines but expands throughout their distribution within the entire context; therefore the grammar of parallelistic pieces becomes particularly significant.[18]

We will examine the syntactical and morphological relationships between the cola in an attempt to identify grammatical parallelism, but to make the

17. D. Garrett, *Job*.
18. Jakobson, "Grammatical Parallelism," 423; cited in Geller, *Parallelism in Early Biblical Poetry*, 1.

underlying Hebrew syntax clearer to English readers, I have rendered the Hebrew more literally, which may sound awkward compared to the smoother renderings of published translations. For example, the NIV translates Ps. 3:4 as follows:

A I call out to the Lord,
B   and he answers me from his holy mountain.

Following the Hebrew syntax more closely, we get the following:

A My voice to the Lord I call out,
B   and he answers me from his holy mountain.

In the Hebrew we see a grammatical connection between colon A and B through the verb that ends A and the verb that begins B. There is a morphological variation in that the verb in A is an imperfect, while the verb in B is a *waw*-consecutive (see the excursus on verbs in poetry, below).

In the NIV, Ps. 1:1 reads:

Blessed is the one
    who does not walk in step with the wicked
or stand in the way that sinners take
    or sit in the company of mockers.

A more literal rendering of the Hebrew syntax reads as follows:

A Blessed is the one who does not walk in step with the wicked,
B   and in the way of sinners does not stand
C   or in the seat of mockers sit.

Notice how the B and C cola reverse the syntactical pattern established in colon A. After the opening "blessed is the one," the prepositional phrase follows the verb in colon A, but in B and C the prepositional phrase precedes the verb.

In Song 1:2–3 there is an interesting grammatical linking between the second colon of one line and the first colon of the next:

A Let him kiss me with the kisses of his mouth!
B   For your love is better than wine.
C Your anointing oils are fragrant;
D   your name is perfume poured out. (NRSVue)

The Hebrew syntax of B and C can be represented as follows:

> Pleasing [*tovim*] is your love more than wine;
> the fragrance of your perfumes is pleasing [*tovim*].

By placing "pleasing" (*tovim*) at the beginning of one colon and at the end of the next, the psalmist provides a sense of closure.

English translations such as the NIV, ESV, NLT, and NRSVue, which are intended for general reading, do not seek to mirror the Hebrew syntax and morphology because doing so would create unnecessarily difficult renditions. Highlighting grammatical parallelism through more literal translation of the Hebrew original makes the poetic structure and the connections between lines clearer but rarely, if ever, adds to the reader's overall understanding of the poem.

Before leaving the topic of grammatical parallelism, I should mention a recent attempt to ground the definition of Hebrew poetry in the syntax of the poetic line. Building on Michael O'Connor's complex and thorough study of the syntactical constraints of the poetic line,[19] Robert Holmstedt moves the discussion to the relationship within a poetic line. He identifies "syntax as the generating mechanism of line relations,"[20] using the categories of apposition and nonapposition to analyze the relationship between lines. He suggests that this insight renders the concept of parallelism problematic and obsolete. I agree with him if he is arguing against parallelism as described by Lowth and the "A equals B" approach, but otherwise he seems to be only reinforcing on the semantic and syntactical level the approach put forward by Alter and Kugel, which I am following here.

Imagery

Imagery is figurative language, and though it is not restricted to poetry, it appears only sparingly in prose. The story of Samson includes figurative language, employing analogies to express Samson's great strength. When Samson kills a lion, we are told that "he tore the lion apart with his bare hands as he might have torn a young goat" (Judg. 14:6), as if tearing apart a young goat is an easy task! When Delilah ties up Samson with seven fresh bowstrings (thus breaking his Nazirite vow not to touch dead matter) and the Philistines attack, he snaps his restraints "as easily as a piece of string snaps when it comes close to a flame" (16:9). And finally, when Samson is tied with new ropes, he snaps "the ropes off as if they were threads" (16:12).

19. O'Connor, *Hebrew Verse Structure*.
20. Holmstedt, "Hebrew Poetry," 632.

Figurative language is also used in Gen. 1–11 to speak of the deep or primeval past. As I will argue in chapter 7, these chapters are a figurative depiction of historical events. For example, the creation "days" of Gen. 1 must be figurative, since there was no sun, moon, or stars, which are necessary for a literal twenty-four-hour day, an insight recognized by some since the early church. Augustine, for instance, writing around AD 400, stated that the days of creation were not actual "solar days."[21] As Origen (ca. AD 185–253) put it, "To what person of intelligence, I ask, will the account seem consistent that says there was a 'first day' and a 'second day' and a 'third day,' in which also 'evening' and 'morning' are named, without a sun, without a moon, and without stars, and even in the case of the first day without a heaven?"[22]

The picture of God, a spiritual being, blowing on dust as if he had lungs to create the first human is also obviously figurative (Gen. 2:7). The flood story is likewise filled with hyperbole in terms of the extent of the sin, the scope of the flood, the size of the ark, and more.[23] The density of figurative language in Genesis lessens once the narrative introduces Abraham (with the *toledot* of Terah, 11:27) as narrative time slows drastically and narrative space narrows from the whole world to one man.

So although imagery is not unique to poetry, it is definitely more pervasive in poetic texts. As Brent Strawn puts it, "Poetry traffics in imagery."[24] Along with terseness, parallelism, and secondary poetic devices (see below), imagery helps readers recognize Hebrew poetry. M. H. Abrams calls imagery an "ambiguous" term and quotes C. Day Lewis, who speaks of imagery as "a picture made out of words."[25] This picture can be painted in various ways, but one of the most common ways is through comparison using either simile or metaphor. The difference between these two is that simile expresses the comparison using "like" or "as" while metaphor does not. Instead, metaphor expresses the comparison by saying that one thing is another (e.g., "He is a wizard at chess" rather than "He is like a wizard at chess").

Another term sometimes used to speak of imagery is "trope." A trope uses words or phrases in a way that differs from their ordinary meaning. We may recognize a trope when we can't make sense of an expression if taken in its ordinary, literal sense. An initial reading may even lead us to conclude that the statement is false. For example, the famous opening line of Ps. 23 ("The LORD is my shepherd") is false unless we realize that the psalmist is

---

21. Augustine, *Literal Interpretation of Genesis* 5.5.12.
22. Origen, *First Principles* 4.3.1; quoted in Cunningham, *Darwin's Pious Idea*, 381.
23. Longman and Walton, *Lost World of the Flood*.
24. Strawn, "Imagery," 306.
25. M. Abrams, *Glossary of Literary Terms*, 78.

not saying God tends a certain type of four-legged ruminant mammal (more on this verse below).

The classical theory of tropes can be traced back to at least Aristotle and finds a more fulsome expression in the work of Quintilian, but discussion of the nature and affect of tropes has continued through the centuries to the present day. As W. Martin points out, "What Quintilian said of tropes remains true today: 'This is a subject which has given rise to interminable disputes among the teachers of literature, who have quarreled no less violently with the philosophers than among themselves over the problem of the genera and species into which tropes may be divided, their number and their correct classification.'"[26]

While my discussion occasionally dips into this debate over different perspectives on imagery, I focus mostly on issues helpful for interpreting and understanding biblical texts and especially on the types of tropes found most commonly in the OT. At the end of the nineteenth century, W. W. Bullinger famously cataloged over two hundred different types of tropes, or figures of speech,[27] but we will focus on seven: metaphor, simile, metonymy, synecdoche, anthropomorphism, personification, and hyperbole.

Metaphor

Metaphor is certainly the most discussed form of imagery in poetry, both in general and in Scripture. Metaphors create a comparison between two things that are alike in some way but different in others. Metaphors are similar to similes (see below) but do not make the comparison explicit by using "like" or "as" as similes do. Since classical times (Aristotle, Quintilian), metaphor has been understood as a "condensed simile."[28]

In classical theory, metaphor was mostly thought of as a linguistic decoration, nothing more. It was believed that a metaphor could be replaced with a nonfigurative statement that exhaustively and exactly expressed the same semantic content. But a metaphorical expression *cannot* be replaced by a paraphrase, nor can interpreters be certain whether they have read too much or too little into a metaphor. Even if readers could replace a metaphor on a semantic level, metaphors communicate more than just ideas. Like imagery in general, metaphors also arouse emotions and stimulate imagination. They appeal to readers' whole selves, not just to their brains. Metaphors also catch readers' attention and have the capacity to shock them by comparing two

26. Martin, "Metaphor," 863.
27. Bullinger, *Figures of Speech.*
28. M. Abrams, *Glossary of Literary Terms*, 192.

things that initially seem very different from each other. In fact, metaphors are recognizable because of this shock value. Readers trying to interpret a metaphor using the ordinary sense of words discover an obvious disjunction between the literal meaning of the statement and the writer's intended meaning.

I. A. Richards offers some helpful terminology for analyzing metaphors. He describes metaphors as having a vehicle and a tenor.[29] The *vehicle* is the part of the comparison not used in its ordinary sense, and the *tenor* is the part of the comparison that the vehicle helps the reader understand better by unpacking the relationship between the two. In Ps. 23:1 ("The LORD is my shepherd"), "shepherd" is the vehicle and "the LORD" is the tenor.

This particular metaphor, "The LORD is my shepherd," illustrates several points I have made so far about metaphor. First, the comparison should shock the reader, though this too-familiar biblical passage may have lost the shock value it once had. When we try to think about it anew, we realize that this metaphor compares things that are fundamentally different. The LORD is the creator of everything, a spiritual being of unlimited power and knowledge, whereas shepherds, especially in ancient Israel, were not considered inherently noble or to have great physical or mental abilities, and because they were outside with their flocks for long periods of time, they also washed infrequently.

However, as the psalmist expounds on the metaphor throughout the rest of the psalm, a clear similarity emerges between the relationship of the Lord to his people and the shepherd to his sheep. But even with the help of the remainder of the psalm, interpreters cannot exhaustively and exactly paraphrase the metaphor, though they can make a beginning.

Like a shepherd, the Lord guides his people, and as a shepherd leads his sheep to water and rest, so the Lord provides for his people. A shepherd protects his sheep from predators, and the Lord protects his people from dangers, represented in the language of the psalm as "the darkest valley" (23:4), also itself a metaphor.

The metaphor stimulates the reader's imagination by evoking mental images of sheep lying down in green pastures, walking by quiet waters, and being guided through dark valleys. But along with stimulating readers' imaginations, the metaphor also arouses emotions in a way that a prose paraphrase cannot. If nothing else, the metaphor evokes a feeling of comfort and confidence amid a turbulent life.

---

29. Richards, *Philosophy of Rhetoric*. Lest this language be understood to suggest a one-way road from vehicle to tenor, see Harshav, *Explorations in Poetics*, 44.

To this point, I have treated Ps. 23 only as a pastoral poem. This approach is not necessarily misleading, but there is an important point that twenty-first-century readers should remember if they want to see the depth of the metaphor in its original setting. Max Black points out that a metaphor evokes a "system of associated commonplaces" between the focus (his term for "vehicle") and the frame (his term for "tenor"). In other words, the interpreter brings together everything that he or she knows about the focus and the frame,[30] what John Frow and others call "encyclopedic knowledge."[31] This leads to an important interpretive principle to bear in mind when reading OT metaphors: we must ask, What encyclopedic knowledge would the original readers have been able to bring to bear on the metaphor? Or, to apply this question to the present example, What was thought and known about shepherds at the time the psalm was written?

Of course, at this historical distance, what we know about shepherds in ancient Israel and the broader Near East is limited to what we read in texts from the OT time period. I remember, while a seminary student, being taken out to the Judean wilderness to meet a Bedouin shepherd on the premise that our group would be seeing an authentic example of the type of shepherd evoked by Ps. 23. I am sure that it was more authentic than a visit to a shepherd in, say, Wisconsin would have been, but my expectations still crumbled when I approached the shepherd's tent and saw a television antenna sticking out and the shepherd wearing a Washington Redskins (now Commanders) T-shirt.

However, modern readers who do study ancient texts to enhance their "encyclopedic knowledge" of the shepherd metaphor in Ps. 23 will also encounter the use of this metaphor elsewhere in the Bible (e.g., Pss. 77:20; 78:70–72; Ezek. 34) and in the broader Near East to refer to a king or other leader of people. From this we can appropriately conclude that Ps. 23 is not a simple pastoral poem but a royal psalm. The Lord is the shepherd of his people like a king is the shepherd of his people. With this background into the nature of metaphor, let us now look at some further examples.

Psalm 22

Psalm 22 is the lament of a person who feels abandoned by God and under attack by his enemies. Here I focus on the metaphors used to characterize those who are attacking the psalmist. They are bulls, lions, and dogs. These are the *vehicle*, and the context, particularly verses 6–8, supplies the *tenor*, the enemies whom the composer likens to wild and dangerous beasts.

30. Black, *Models and Metaphors*, 28.
31. Frow, *Genre*, 107.

A Many bulls surround me;
B   strong bulls of Bashan encircle me.
C Roaring lions that tear their prey
D   open their mouths wide against me.

E Dogs surround me,
F   a pack of villains encircles me;
G   they pierce my hands and my feet. (22:12–13, 16)

Metaphor works powerfully with parallelism here. In A, the enemy is likened to many bulls; in B, they are not just any bulls but the notoriously strong ones from the region of Bashan, in the Upper Transjordan (now Golan Heights; Deut. 32:14; Ezek. 39:18; Amos 4:1). In C, the psalmist compares the enemy to lions that roar and tear their prey; in D, these lions are attacking the psalmist himself. In E, the enemy is compared to yet another predator, a pack of dogs ready to attack. Even in today's culture, where we are more likely to think of dogs as cute household pets, we can still understand the danger presented by a pack of wild dogs (cf. 1 Kings 14:11; 16:4; 21:23–24; 2 Kings 9:10, 36). The F colon explicitly identifies the dogs as villains, human enemies who not only threaten but actually harm the psalmist (G).

The poet draws on the concept that enemies are dangerous animals, which allows him to describe them as bulls, lions, and dogs who threaten him. He appeals to God with these images that show threat and evoke fear in order to implore God to save him. In his plea for help, the psalmist once again returns to the image of the enemy as dangerous beasts.

> But you, LORD, do not be far from me.
> You are my strength; come quickly to help me.
> Deliver me from the sword,
> my precious life from the power of the dogs.
> Rescue me from the mouth of the lions;
> save me from the horns of the wild oxen. (22:19–21)

Song of Songs 4:1–5:1

Song of Songs 4:1–5:1 is one of the longer poems in this anthology of love poetry.[32] Scholars have identified it as a *wasf* (or *watsf*), a descriptive poem based on similarities with nineteenth-century Arabic love poetry. In this *wasf*, a man describes the physical beauty of the woman, starting with her head and working down her body. I focus here on the high point of this

---

32. Longman, *Song of Songs*, 48–49.

description, which speaks of her garden and, more specifically, the spring or fountain in the garden.

A You are a garden locked up, my sister, my bride;
B　 You are a spring enclosed, a sealed fountain.
C Your plants are an orchard of pomegranates
D　 with choice fruits,
E　 with henna and nard,
F　 nard and saffron,
G　 calamus and cinnamon,
H　 with every kind of incense tree,
I　 with myrrh and aloes
J　 and all the finest spices.
K You are a garden fountain,
L　 a well of flowing water
M　 streaming down from Lebanon. (4:12–15)

The vehicle in A is an exotic garden, which contains an abundance of fruits, spices, and aromatic shrubs and trees. In the B colon, the focus sharpens to a spring in the garden itself. Both have not been entered: the garden is locked and the fountain sealed. The tenor is not explicit in the passage, but the interpreter who pays attention to context and knows of the use of garden imagery in the ancient Near East will understand that the garden and its fountain tactfully allude to the woman's vagina.

In terms of literary context, the *wasf* starts with the woman's head (hair, teeth, lips, temples) and moves down her body to her neck and breasts before coming to her garden. The best understanding of the *wasf* genre is that the poem is a prelude to lovemaking, so a reference to the woman's most private bodily space makes sense. Elsewhere in the Bible (e.g., Prov. 5:15–20) and in the literature of the ancient Near East,[33] both a garden and a fountain can serve as a metaphor for a woman's vagina. That the garden is locked and the fountain sealed means that she has not yet been entered, has not had sexual relations.

This metaphoric description of the woman's body cannot be paraphrased, and my description of the image is neither exhaustive nor able to capture the feeling that the metaphor intends to evoke. We can at least say that the man's speech expresses his desire for intimacy and perhaps intends for the reader to find similar words to express his desire for intimacy with his beloved. As the

33. Paul, "A Lover's Garden of Verse"; Fox, *Song of Songs*, 283–87.

poem continues, the woman responds to the man's implicit desire to enter her garden with a poetic "Yes!" (Song 4:16) followed by the man's celebration (5:1).

Ecclesiastes 12

The last chapter of Ecclesiastes also contains powerful metaphorical language:

A Remember your Creator
B   in the days of your youth,
C before the days of trouble come
D   and the years approach when you will say,
E   "I find no pleasure in them"—
F before the sun and the light
G   and the moon and the stars grow dark,
H   and the clouds return after the rain;
I when the keepers of the house tremble,
J   and the strong men stoop,
K when the grinders cease because they are few,
L   and those looking through the windows grow dim;
M when the doors to the street are closed
N   and the sound of grinding fades;
O when people rise up at the sound of birds,
P   but all their songs grow faint;
Q when people are afraid of heights
R   and dangers in the streets;
S when the almond tree blossoms,
T   and the grasshopper drags itself along
U   and desire no longer is stirred.
V Then people go to their eternal home
W   and mourners go about the streets. (12:1–5)

This complex metaphor only implies its tenor in A–E, but the contrast between the "days of your youth" and the "days of trouble" clearly refers to the aging process. The following verses liken growing old and approaching death to a house with four groups that live in the house (the vehicle of the metaphor). I unpack this metaphor in the paragraphs that follow.

First, the poet pictures a nice sunny day that turns stormy (F–H). This description evokes a melancholic reaction. Qohelet, the speaker, intends to communicate that aging is not a happy prospect. Recent research also suggests that the imagery is provided by eschatological literature that pictures the end of time as storm and darkness (Isa. 13:10; Amos 5:8; 8:9).[34]

In the next section (I–L) readers hear about the inhabitants of a house, which are divided into four groups, two male and two female. One male group and one female group are servants, and one male group and one female group are owners. The NIV translation masks the gender, but the Hebrew makes clear that "the keepers of the house" and "the strong men" are male, and "the grinders" and "those looking through the window" are female. All four groups languish, just as bodies weaken with age.

These four groups may also point to specific aspects of aging. The most obvious are the grinders and those looking through the window, both female. Those who grind grain are servants, and those who have time to look through the windows are women of leisure, probably the owners. In terms of the body, "grinders" suggests teeth; particularly in an ancient culture with poor dental care and coarse grains, people often lost teeth as they aged. Looking through a window implies sight and represents a person's vision worsening with age. The male servants are the keepers of the house, and their owner counterparts are the strong men. The strong men stoop, perhaps suggesting one's posture bending forward with age. The servants tremble, as the hands of older people often do.

The next few verses take the reader outside the house, beginning with the doors, which on analogy may refer to bodily orifices that shut up as one gets older (constipation?). At this point, readers are still in the metaphorical realm outside the house, but the description of weakening abilities is more direct. Lines N–P refer to hearing. One's hearing often gets worse with age, and sudden noises can startle. As one grows old, fears increase, whether of heights or public threats. The next section (S–U) returns to a more figurative description. The almond tree with its white blossoms surely suggests the graying or whitening of one's hair, and the reference to desire no longer stirring reminds one of diminishing sexual interest. The middle colon—the grasshopper dragging itself along—remains opaque to me, though the idea of a grasshopper that was energetic in its prime but now drags itself along surely gestures toward the slowing of one's movements in old age.

The final line, speaking of one's "eternal home" (the grave) and "mourners," reminds the reader that the text is speaking of the aging process and approaching death. At the end of his speech, Qohelet puts a cap on what he has been saying throughout his speech (1:12–12:7): Life is hard, and then you die. End of story.

---

34. Sherwood, "'Not with a Bang but a Whimper.'"

Nahum 3:4–7

The book of Nahum is an oracle against a foreign nation, in this case Assyria. Assyria's capital city, Nineveh, serves as a synecdoche, a part for the whole (see below).[35] The verses preceding this excerpt are a "woe oracle" based on a funeral dirge pronouncing the demise of the city (v. 1). This segues into an "event-vision" that prophetically pictures the future fall of the city to an invading army (vv. 2–3). This event-vision culminates with a motivation for the judgment described metaphorically as the sin of a prostitute. The prophet then envisions the fight for the city and the mounting pile of corpses (v. 4). The city falls

A all because of the wanton lust of a prostitute,
B   alluring, the mistress of sorceries,
C who enslaved nations by her prostitution
D   and peoples by her witchcraft.

E "I am against you," declares the LORD Almighty.
F "I will lift your skirts over your face.
G I will show the nations your nakedness
H   and the kingdoms your shame.
I I will pelt you with filth,
J   I will treat you with contempt
K   and make you a spectacle.
L All who see you will flee from you and say,
M 'Nineveh is in ruins—who will mourn for her?'
N   Where can I find anyone to comfort you?" (3:4–7)

In the OT, cities are often likened to women, both positively and, as here, negatively. Nineveh is a prostitute, showing prodigious lust by trying to dominate others and profit from them. She uses not only her natural charms but also the love charms of a witch.

Since Nineveh is a prostitute, she deserves the punishment that prostitutes received in that culture, including public shaming. At this point, the interpreter benefits from the "encyclopedic knowledge" I referred to above, in this case the knowledge of how prostitutes were dealt with. The judgment oracle, beginning with the divine statement "I am against you" (v. 5), then goes on to describe how prostitute-Nineveh will be exposed and made vulnerable to others. The city will also be pelted with filth (i.e., feces) and abandoned.

35. See detailed analysis of this passage in Longman, "Nahum," 814–17.

Simile

A simile creates an analogy by using a comparative term such as "like" or "as" or a verb such as "liken" or "resemble." My examples from the Samson story presented above are similes. Although similes may be found in many prose passages, the examples presented below come from poetic literature. After discussing these examples, I will offer some summarizing comments.

Job 3:16

> Or why was I not hidden away in the ground like a stillborn child,
>   like an infant who never saw the light of day?

Being subjected to great physical and emotional suffering, Job breaks his silence after his three friends come and sit with him for seven days. Whether as a lament or a complaint, Job expresses his anguish by wishing he had never been born: "May the day of my birth perish, and the night that said, 'A boy is conceived!'" (3:3). But short of that, he wishes that he had died at birth: "Why did I not perish at birth, and die as I came from the womb?" (3:11). Job goes one step further and wishes that he had been "hidden away . . . like a stillborn child" (3:16). The reason for this wish is made explicit in the second colon (A, what's more, B): a stillborn has an advantage over a child who dies shortly after birth in never having seen the light of day (see also Eccles. 6:3).

Psalm 1:3-4

> They are like trees
>   planted by streams of water,
> which yield their fruit in its season,
>   and their leaves do not wither.
> In all that they do, they prosper.

> The wicked are not so
>   but are like chaff that the wind drives away. (NRSVue)

Psalm 1 opens with a blessing on those who do not associate with the wicked and find pleasure in meditating on the law of the Lord (1:2). Such persons are like trees—not just any trees, but trees planted by streams of water. This continuous supply of water invites readers to picture fertile trees; the B and C lines further inform us that these trees produce fruit, suggestive of a productive life. Indeed, these trees never lose their leaves.

The poet then begins to contrast the opening image with that of wicked persons. While the righteous are like well-watered, productive trees, the wicked are like chaff, the dry and inedible husk of a grain seed, such as wheat. While

the trees are firmly planted, the chaff is blown around by the wind, suggesting rootlessness.

Psalm 78:65

Then the Lord awoke as from sleep,
  as a warrior wakes from the stupor of wine.

As discussed above, metaphor typically is a more shocking or attention-
grabbing expression than simile. Because of the presence of "like" or "as," a
simile is not technically a trope since interpreters can understand all the words
according to their ordinary sense. However, there is surprise value in the simile
here, which is striking because the analogy seems to border on the irreverent.

Psalm 78 is a poem of remembrance, which looks back on the history of
God's people so that the next generation "would not forget his deeds but
would keep his commands. They would not be like their ancestors—a stub-
born and rebellious generation, whose hearts were not loyal to God, whose
spirits were not faithful to him" (78:7–8). The psalm's conclusion indicates
that it celebrates the choice of David as king and of Zion as the place where
God makes his presence known (78:65–72).

The striking simile that begins this final section follows a stanza recounting how the generations before the monarchy tested God and caused him
to respond in anger by giving "his people over to the sword" (78:62). After
a period of absence, God again made known his presence to his people.
God's appearing is first described as someone awaking from sleep. This image
catches readers' attention because they know that God does not sleep, but his
absence made it seem as though he were asleep and needed to be awakened
to action. In good "A, what's more, B" fashion, the second colon takes this
thought further. The Lord is identified specifically as a warrior, and his sleep
is likened to the stupor of a drunk.

This simile calls on the interpreter to reflect, first, on what a soldier is like
when roused from a drunken stupor. I think it is fair to say that such a person
could be dangerous and violent. Thus the poet wants readers to think about
God in this context. God had been absent, but the time has come for him to
make his presence known, specifically as a warrior: "He beat back his enemies;
he put them to everlasting shame" (78:66).

Song of Songs 4:4

Your neck is like the tower of David,
  built with courses of stone;
on it hang a thousand shields,
  all of them shields of warriors.

This interesting simile is an earlier part of the *wasf* that was discussed above in reference to the metaphor of the garden and the garden fountain. The early part of the *wasf* is a series of similes, but the focus of my discussion here is the woman's neck. The man compares her neck to the tower of David and then describes that tower as constructed from courses of stone and adorned by a thousand warrior shields.

This comparison reminds readers of the importance of the "encyclopedic knowledge" that is assumed by the poet but sometimes eludes modern readers, though we can make some guesses in order to interpret it. We can visualize a tower constructed of stone, but this simile refers to a specific tower associated with David. We cannot be sure whether such a tower actually existed or is merely a product of the poet's imagination; David's name implies a kind of dignity and importance in and of itself. Hanging shields are mentioned, a practice for which there is no evidence, but the image may be intended merely to make readers imagine shields hung ornamentally on the outside of the tower. But what is the man trying to say about the woman's neck by conjuring this image in the reader's mind?

To answer this question, I first want to point out how the New Living Translation (NLT) renders this verse. I was the translator in charge of the Psalms and Wisdom literature and am mentioning our discussion of this verse because it reflects the process all interpreters must go through in coming to an understanding of a metaphor or simile.

> Your neck is as beautiful as the tower of David,
> jeweled with the shields of a thousand heroes. (Song 4:4 NLT)

I am not going to defend or criticize this rendering. Though I was in charge, I did not make the final decision but was part of a small group of scholars and stylists who also had a voice. Regarding the parallelism, observe how the four poetic lines (see the NIV translation above) have been collapsed into two, thus leaving out the "courses of stone" and combining "a thousand shields" and "shields of warriors" into "shields of a thousand heroes."

The NLT unpacks the simile for the reader. The translators decided that the simile concerns the beauty of the woman's neck and that the shields allude to jewels, perhaps a necklace, enhancing the beauty of her neck. As one who was part of the discussion, I can attest that this approach was intentional and was applied in several places in the NLT translation. Though not without some internal controversy, we decided that if the "everyday reader," with no understanding of the historical setting and without immediate access to a commentary, would have no inkling as to the meaning of a metaphor or simile,

the translation would provide some help. I believe that this decision is justifiable for the type of translation the NLT intends to be (functional equivalent)
and on the principle that all translations are interpretations.

But as with all translations, there is a cost and potential liability with this
strategy. For one thing, it stifles readers' own thought process by preventing
them from working through the comparison on their own. Perhaps even more
important, it gives the impression that a comparison like this is reducible to
a single word, which may not even be the best word, since in my own view
the comparison is also designed to communicate the dignity of her neck and
perhaps even her confident posture. However, I do think that the translation
is correct in its understanding that the shields on the tower are intended to
evoke the image of a necklace around her neck.

Lamentations 1:1

> How deserted lies the city,
>   once so full of people!
> How like a widow is she,
>   who once was great among the nations!
> She who was a queen among the provinces
>   has now become a slave.

The book of Lamentations is composed of five poems, each a separate
chapter in modern translations. The first four are acrostics, and the fifth is
acrostic-like (see "Acrostics" below under "Secondary Poetic Conventions").
The first verse begins with the first letter of the Hebrew alphabet (*aleph*),
setting the tone for the first poem and indeed the whole collection. The poet
mourns the sad state of Jerusalem, which once bustled with people but after
the destruction of 586 BC is now virtually empty.

The second parallel line echoes the first, creating a comparison by means
of a simile between the city and a woman, specifically a widow. A widow, of
course, is a woman who was married but is now alone after the death of her
husband. The city is like a widow, bereft, lonely, and sad. This simile creates
personification by representing the city as a person (see "Personification" later
in this section). The second colon, though, reverts to the city, with "who once
was great among the nations!" echoing the previous "once so full of people!"

By picturing the city like a widow, the poet seeks to evoke pity in the reader.
Readers feel sorry for women who have lost their husbands, particularly since
widows were especially vulnerable in ancient culture. Interestingly, the implied
reader (addressee) of the poems of Lamentations, including the first poem, is
God himself ("See, LORD, how distressed I am!" 1:20). The poet knows that

the people's present plight is the result of God's judgment against them (1:8; et al.); he also believes that the only way out is for God to take pity on them and restore them (5:19–22).

Proverbs 26:8, 11, 18–19

Like tying a stone in a sling
    is the giving of honor to a fool.

As a dog returns to its vomit,
    so fools repeat their folly.

Like a maniac shooting
    flaming arrows of death
is one who deceives their neighbor
    and says, "I was only joking!"

Proverbs often use similes to communicate important observations, instructions, admonitions, and prohibitions. These three excerpts from Prov. 26 call on the interpreter to ask how X is like Y. My first example is particularly difficult because the translation of the Hebrew is uncertain.[36] If we suppose that the NIV got it right, the comparison seems to be about stupidity. It is stupid and futile to tie a stone into a sling so that one can't actually throw it, and the same is true about giving honor to a fool. It's just the wrong thing to do as well as not being fitting.

The next proverb alludes to dogs' strange and disgusting habit of returning to their vomit and eating it. Just as dogs will eat what they have just thrown up, so fools will repeat their mistakes instead of learning from them (a major teaching in Proverbs; e.g., 10:17; 12:1).

The third proverb, formatted in the NIV as four cola,[37] compares someone who deceives their neighbor and tries to cover it up by claiming that it was a joke to a mentally unstable person who shoots deadly flaming arrows. It's unclear whether the cover-up comes before or after the deception is discovered, but either way, the proverb warns that doing so will cause a lot of damage and almost certainly end the relationship.

Nahum 2:4

The chariots storm through the streets,
    rushing back and forth through the squares.
They look like flaming torches;
    they dart about like lightning.

---

36. Longman, *Proverbs*, 465–66.
37. One could argue that the line is really composed of two relatively lengthy cola.

Nahum prophesies the downfall of Nineveh, the Assyrian capital city, which takes place in 612 BC but is foretold by Nahum years or even decades earlier. Nahum 2:4 occurs in the middle of what has been called an "event-vision" or a "dramatic word-vision," where the prophet describes the future defeat of the city as if it were happening before his very eyes.

The attacking army's chariots are described here as they rush through the streets and city squares. Though the attackers are not mentioned by name, this anticipates the fall of the city to the combined forces of the Babylonians and Medes. The poet-prophet describes the appearance of the chariots as like "flaming torches" and "lightning." These similes vividly emphasize both the speed of the chariots and their destructive power. The implied addressees are the inhabitants of Nineveh (e.g., Nah. 2:1, "An attacker advances against you, Nineveh"), who should be frightened by this eventuality, though the real readers were likely Judeans, who would rejoice at the fall of the city that was the center of Assyrian domination.

Metonymy and Synecdoche

While metaphor is a trope that trades on comparison, metonymy and synecdoche are tropes generated by association or contiguity. Rather than comparing two things, metonymy and synecdoche refer to a thing by means of something else with which it is associated. W. Martin describes metonymy (I suggest that it also describes synecdoche) as "a trope in which one expression is substituted for another on the basis of some material, causal, or conceptual relation."[38] These tropes occur in everyday speech when we use "the White House" to refer to the president of the United States or do a "head count" to determine the number of people. Metonymy and synecdoche are more difficult to understand than metaphor and simile, but the examples below will clarify the concepts.

Theorists differ on two points regarding these tropes.[39] First, they debate the relationship between metonymy and synecdoche. Is synecdoche a type of metonymy, or is it a separate category? Although treatments of metonymy and synecdoche differ, the question is ultimately unimportant for our purposes. The name one puts on a certain biblical expression is not as important as identifying and properly interpreting the trope. Acknowledging the rather fuzzy use of these terms in the general literature, I will treat metonymy and synecdoche together in this section but will apply the synecdoche label to a particular type of relationship of association or contiguity, that of a part for

38. Martin, "Metonymy," 876.
39. See Martin ("Metonymy," 876–78) for the details of these theoretical disagreements.

the whole (see below for examples). To simplify our discussion, I will use the term "metonymy" to refer to both metonymy and synecdoche unless I am speaking specifically about, or giving examples of, a part for the whole.

A second controversy concerns whether metonymy is even a trope or figurative language at all. Although I think it is such, deciding the issue is not important for my analysis. Earlier we observed that similes too can be treated as nonfigurative, though the close relationship between simile and metaphor led me to treat them as related concepts.

Many different types of associative or contiguous relationships fall into the category of metonymy. Along with the basic idea of a part for the whole, there is a container for what it contains, a producer for the product, a place for something that happened there, a building for an institution, a person for that person's descendants, a cause for an effect, and an effect for a cause. In all these types, metonymy is achieved by ellipsis or deletion and thus avoids unnecessary words, a feature of poetic language in general. To use a nonbiblical example, instead of saying "I am reading a novel by Sterne," one could say "I am reading Sterne at the moment," the name of the author standing for his literary work.

Besides making language more concise, metonymy can contribute to vividness and a sense of precision or particularity. Metonymies can also slow down reading, causing the interpreter to reflect on their meaning. Figurative language can become frozen and conventional through repeated use to the point that we may not be aware that we are speaking figuratively. "The leg of a table" illustrates this in the case of metaphor, and "the crown" is a conventional metonym.

I will now provide some examples of various types of metonymy, without attempting to be exhaustive, for many different forms of association or continuity can create a metonymy.[40]

The following passages use a person to designate a people or a place:

> Oh, that salvation for Israel would come out of Zion!
> When the LORD restores his people,
> let Jacob rejoice and Israel be glad! (Ps. 14:7)

> The high places of Isaac will be destroyed
> and the sanctuaries of Israel will be ruined;
> with my sword I will rise against the house of Jeroboam. (Amos 7:9)

> Do not prophesy against Israel,
> and stop preaching against the descendants of Isaac. (Amos 7:16b)

40. For a rather full taxonomy of biblical metonymy, see the classic work by Bullinger, *Figures of Speech*, 538–656.

In the psalm, "Jacob" refers to "the people of Israel" in a way that is not only concise but also evocative: these terms remind readers of the patriarchs and the promises that God gave to Abraham, which are passed down to Jacob from his father and grandfather. Jacob's new name, Israel (Gen. 32:28), could be analyzed as a metonym, but since it is the standard term for the land and the people who dwell in the land, it has become frozen and is not recognized as a trope. The use of "Jacob" to refer to the people of Israel, often in parallel with "Israel" as here, is rarer, does not reflect the name change, and is therefore recognizable as a metonym.

Even rarer, indeed unique, is Amos's use of the name "Isaac" to refer to Israel. The first of the two passages from Amos (7:9) is a divine judgment oracle against sinful Israel; the second quotes the Bethel priest Amaziah's attempt to censure Amos, who is speaking out against Israel. In these passages, "Isaac" functions as "Jacob" does in Ps. 14. One wonders why Amos would choose to use the name "Isaac" in this context. Few if any commentators remark on this question. It is not as if Isaac is associated with false places of worship in the patriarchal narratives. Perhaps it is because, in contrast with Abraham and Jacob, Isaac plays a rather insignificant role in Genesis. He is mostly a transitional figure between his father, Abraham, and his son Jacob. Especially in his dealings with Jacob, Isaac is rather clumsy and even spiritually insensitive. This may stand behind Amos's unusual metonymy here.

Zion is a metonym of another sort in Ps. 14. Here a place stands for the building located on it, since Zion is the mountain on which the temple stands. When Zion is mentioned, one thinks of the temple, the place where God made his presence known from the time it was built around the tenth century BC.

In the third colon of Amos 7:9, "my sword" is a metonym for war. As an instrument of war, it here stands for war itself. Of course, since it is God who speaks about taking up the sword, this metonym is clearly used in a figurative way. What God is saying is that he will bring conflict and battle to the dynastic house of Jeroboam, the first ruler of the Northern Kingdom. Jeremiah also uses "sword" as a metonym for war, often in conjunction with famine and plague, as in Jer. 14:12: "Although they fast, I will not listen to their cry; though they offer burnt offerings and grain offerings, I will not accept them. Instead, I will destroy them with the sword, famine, and plague."

Another type of metonym speaks of an effect by citing the means or instrument by which the effect is achieved. Readers can see this in how body parts associated with speech are used to refer to speech:

> The tongue of the righteous is choice silver,
>   but the heart of the wicked is of little value. (Prov. 10:20)

Here "tongue" refers to one's words, and "heart" refers to one's inner self, with perhaps an emphasis on cognition. Tongue, lips, and speech are often paired with heart in Proverbs (16:23; 26:23, 24–26) since typically one's speech reveals a person's inner character.

> Truthful lips endure forever,
>> but a lying tongue lasts only a moment. (12:19)

In this antithetical parallelism, both lips and tongue stand for speech.

Psalm 23:4 presents another kind of metonym: objects associated with the task of shepherding stand for the Shepherd, God himself:

> I will fear no evil,
>> for you are with me;
> your rod and your staff,
>> they comfort me.

Of course, a shepherd's rod and staff don't comfort anyone, but the shepherd who wields them can bring comfort.

A slightly different kind of metonym emerges when a cause stands for an effect. Notice, for instance, how wrath stands in the place of judgment. God's wrath leads to judgment, so the word "wrath" can stand for judgment, as in the first parallel line in Mic. 7:9:

> Because I have sinned against him,
> I will bear the LORD's wrath.

Yet another example of a cause (alcoholic drink) standing for an effect (actions associated with drunkenness) comes from Prov. 20:1:

> Wine is a mocker and beer a brawler;
> whoever is led astray by them is not wise.

Anthropomorphism

Some metaphors and metonyms create anthropomorphisms, another form of figurative language. Anthropomorphisms describe God in human terms, and numerous examples can be found in OT narrative texts as well as poetry. The depiction of God in Gen. 3 is a prime example. In this story of the first human rebellion against God, the narrator depicts God as "walking in the garden in the cool of the day" (v. 8) and seemingly unaware of Adam's location: "The LORD God called to the man, 'Where are you?'" (v. 9).

The opening verse of Ps. 98 provides an example of anthropomorphism in poetry:

> O sing to the LORD a new song,
>> for he has done marvelous things.
> His right hand and his holy arm
>> have gotten him victory. (98:1 NRSVue)

"God is spirit" (John 4:24) and has neither hands nor arms, but these idioms stand for God's power in battle. They are metonyms or, if one prefers, synecdoches (parts for the whole).

Personification

According to E. Fowler, personification is "a device that brings to life, in a human figure, something abstract, collective, inanimate, dead, nonreasoning, or epitomizing."[41] The use of personification has various purposes, but vividness is one of them. As with metaphor and simile, giving human form to something nonhuman causes readers to pay attention, read closely, and ask in what way the personification is appropriate for what is being personified.

Some of the Bible's most striking and developed personifications are of humans themselves. This form of personification treats a group as an individual. Two examples come from Lamentations, which personifies the Judeans in the aftermath of the Babylonian destruction of Jerusalem. The book opens with a dirgelike description of a weeping widow:

> How deserted lies the city,
>> once so full of people!
> How like a widow is she,
>> who once was great among the nations!
> She who was queen among the provinces
>> has now become a slave. (1:1)

Here Jerusalem is likened to a widow, but the city itself stands for the people as a whole. Jerusalem, the queen, has become a widow and a slave. The vibrant city is now deserted; the great city, now enslaved. The poet reflects on the aftermath of the destruction by Nebuchadnezzar's army and the exile of leading citizens as well as the incorporation of the nation into the Babylonian Empire.

41. E. Fowler, "Personification," 1025.

> Bitterly she weeps at night,
>   tears are on her cheeks.
> Among all her lovers
>   there is no one to comfort her.
> All her friends have betrayed her;
>   they have become her enemies. (1:2)

The widow's response is to weep in sadness. She has been betrayed by her lovers; her friends have become her enemies. Surrounding nations that might have helped her, and perhaps with whom Judah was in alliance (Egypt!), have offered no support against the Babylonians.

The following verses go in and out of the personification, sometimes speaking of the widow and sometimes speaking more literally of Judah and its inhabitants. Indeed, in Lam. 1:9c–16 (and again, vv. 18–22), the widow herself speaks and gives voice to the suffering of Jerusalem as she pleads to God for pity:

> "Look, LORD, on my affliction,
>   for the enemy has triumphed." (1:9b)

Neither the suffering widow nor the poet are under any illusions. The widow Jerusalem suffers because of her sins:

> Jerusalem has sinned greatly
>   and so has become unclean.
> All who honored her despise her,
>   for they have all seen her naked;
> She herself groans
>   and turns away. (1:8)

The widow herself acknowledges the truth of the charge:

> "The LORD is righteous,
>   yet I rebelled against his command.
> Listen, all you peoples;
>   look on my suffering.
> My young men and young women
>   have gone into exile." (1:18)

The poet's ultimate purpose is to paint Jerusalem's suffering in such moving terms that it elicits God's pity and leads him finally to relent in his judgment. The use of the personification of a widow lends vividness and pathos to the composer's intention.

Lamentations' third and lengthiest poem presents another personification of God's suffering people, "the man who has seen affliction" (3:1a). Speaking in the first person, the man of affliction describes the torment that he receives "by the rod of the LORD's wrath" (3:1b). He describes his divinely inflicted suffering in very Job-like terms:

> He has made my skin and my flesh grow old
>   and has broken my bones.
> He has besieged me and surrounded me
>   with bitterness and hardship.
> He has made me dwell in darkness
>   like those long dead. (3:4–6; see also vv. 7–18)

As with the widow, the poet's personification of the suffering people of God elicits the reader's pity as it concretizes it in the man of affliction. Unlike the widow, though, the man of affliction registers hope amid the suffering:

> Yet this I call to mind
>   and therefore have hope:
> Because of the LORD's great love we are not consumed,
>   for his compassions never fail.
> They are new every morning;
>   great is your faithfulness.
> I say to myself, "The LORD is my portion;
>   therefore I will wait for him." (3:21–24, see also vv. 25–42)

Though expressing hope, the man of affliction calls on the community to acknowledge the sin that led to their suffering and to repent. God still has not forgiven them:

> Let us examine our ways and test them,
>   and let us return to the LORD.
> Let us lift up our hears and our hands
>   to God in heaven, and say:
> "We have sinned and rebelled
>   and you have forgiven." (3:40–42)

In the remainder of this central poem (vv. 43–66), the man of affliction again appeals to God's pity due to the depth of his suffering and the taunts of his enemies. He beseeches God to restore him and to punish his enemies.

Sometimes the OT personifies God. Besides the anthropomorphism discussed in the previous section, the OT on at least one occasion describes God not simply as if he has a human body with hands, arms, eyes, and feet but as a specific character. I am thinking here of the rather striking figure of Woman Wisdom in the book of Proverbs.

This is not the place for an extensive treatment of the topic,[42] so I will focus my comments on Prov. 9. In this pivotal chapter between the book's discourses and the proverbs per se, the implied reader must make a choice with whom to dine, Woman Wisdom or (yet another personification) Woman Folly. The poet first describes Woman Wisdom before she speaks through her servants:

> Wisdom has built her house;
>   she has set up its seven pillars.
> She has prepared her meat and mixed her wine;
>   she has also set her table.
> She has sent out her servants, and she calls
>   from the highest point of the city,
>   "Let all who are simple come to my house!"
> To those who have no sense she says,
>   "Come, eat my food
>   and drink the wine I have mixed.
> Leave your simple ways and you will live;
>   walk in the way of insight." (9:1–6)

By this time, readers of the book have already been introduced to Woman Wisdom (Prov. 1:20–33; chap. 8), but even from this short section, they can observe that Woman Wisdom, at a minimum, represents God's wisdom. Yet I will go further. Based on the location of her house at the "highest point of the city,"[43] I believe that she stands for God himself (9:3).

Why personify God and his wisdom as a Woman? Answering this question will also help explain some of the poetic effects of the personification. The Hebrew word for wisdom (*chokmah*) is feminine, which may have influenced the poetic choice. Perhaps wisdom is a quality not reserved for only women but notable among women. There may also be an intentional jab at Egyptian wisdom, *ma'at*, which is represented as a goddess. But the most likely reason of all is that the implied readers of the book of Proverbs are men, for whom the idea of entering into an intimate relationship with a woman would be provocative and inviting. The composer presents a picture that encourages

---

42. See Longman, *Fear of the Lord*, 14–24.
43. In the ancient Near East, the abode of the gods is in the mountains. God instructs Israel to build the temple on Mount Zion: "Great is the Lord and greatly to be praised, in the city of our God. His holy mountain, beautiful in elevation, is the joy of all the earth, Mount Zion, in the far north, the city of the great king" (Ps. 48:1–2 NRSVue).

such an intimate relationship, while also discouraging an intimate relationship with the other woman, Folly, whose meal looks deceptively enticing.
That her house is also "on a seat at the highest point of the city" (9:14) tells
us that she too is a personification of deity, but she represents all the false
gods who try to seduce people away from the true god (for more on Prov. 9,
see chap. 10 below).

Finally, the poets of the OT personified inanimate objects. Earlier I cited
Ps. 98:7–9, where creation itself—the sea, rivers, and mountains—joins in
the praise of God (see "Psalm 98 as a Unique Poem" in chap. 3 above). Here
I cite Ps. 114:

> When Israel came out of Egypt,
>   Jacob from a people of foreign tongue,
> Judah became God's sanctuary,
>   Israel his dominion.
> The sea looked and fled,
>   the Jordan turned back;
> the mountains leaped like rams,
>   the hills like lambs.
> Why was it, sea, that you fled?
>   Why, Jordan, did you turn back?
> Why, mountains, did you leap like rams,
>   you hills, like lambs?
> Tremble, earth, at the presence of the Lord,
>   at the presence of the God of Jacob,
> who turned the rock into a pool,
>   the hard rock into springs of water.

This lively hymn celebrates the exodus and the entry into the promised land.
The sea that parted (Exod. 14) and the Jordan that dried up (Josh. 3–4) are here
personified as fearful of God and his power. They run away at the presence
of God. Reading this personification of the sea and the river in its original
context brings depth to its impact on the original audience. The surrounding
nations often associated the waters (i.e., the sea and rivers) with anti-creation
gods (Tiamat, Yam, Lothan [= Leviathan]), whereas mountains are associated
with God, and thus they celebrate God's presence.

Hyperbole

Hyperbole is a type of figurative language in which exaggeration is used
for rhetorical effect. Sometimes exaggeration can lead to deception, as when
a businessperson falsely inflates the value of his assets or income in order to

get a bank loan. Hyperbole is different because the exaggeration is intended not to deceive but to emphasize a point.

Let me illustrate using an everyday conversational example. I tend to pack heavily when my wife and I travel. When she tries to lift my suitcase and says "Your bag weighs a ton!" I know that she is not trying to deceive me into thinking that my suitcase actually weighs two thousand pounds. She is simply emphasizing that the heavy books I've packed are making my suitcase hard to carry.

Both OT poetry and narrative provide examples of hyperbole, and failing to recognize hyperbole can lead to some significant interpretive and theological errors. Consider the following examples from the book of Psalms.

A Surely I was sinful at birth,
B   sinful from the time my mother conceived me.
C Yet you desired faithfulness even in the womb;
D   you taught me wisdom in that secret place. (Ps. 51:5–6)

Psalm 51 is a powerful and well-known penitential prayer. The title sets it in the aftermath of the prophet Nathan's confronting David after his sin with Bathsheba. Yet as typical with the psalms, the prayer itself downplays its specific historical inspiration so that it may be used as a template for people who face similar, though not necessarily identical, situations.

The psalm opens with the composer's appeal for mercy in light of his sin. In verses 3–6 he acknowledges his sinfulness. In verses 5–6 he uses hyperbole to emphasize the depth and pervasiveness of this sin. In good "A, what's more, B" fashion, the hyperbole intensifies in the second line. In A he states that he has been sinful since birth, but in B he takes the origins of his sin back to the time his mother conceived him. Perhaps one might believe that the psalmist, like all people, is sinful since birth, but to take the statement that he is sinful since conception at face value stretches credulity.[44]

The hyperbole in the second set of parallel lines is too far-fetched to allow a literalistic understanding. Colon C claims that God wants the fetus to be faithful, and D says that God teaches the fetus in the womb ("that secret place"). It is hard to believe that the composer actually thinks the reader will take these statements in a nonfigurative way, as if the fetus could properly fear God before consciousness.

---

44. Some theologians might wrongly use this verse as a prooftext to support the idea that Adam's sin is imputed to a person at conception. This is not to deny that the Bible teaches what theologians call "original sin" (for which, see Longman, *Confronting Old Testament Controversies*, 66–73), but Ps. 51:5–6 is not relevant to the question.

  A For he spoke and stirred up a tempest
  B   that lifted high the waves.
  C They mounted up to the heavens and went down to the depths;
  D   in their peril their courage melted away. (107:25–26)

The opening of Ps. 107 calls on readers to thank God for rescuing them from various types of trouble and suffering. The stanza where verses 25–26 occur refers to seagoing merchants who face threats from volatile seas. The hyperbole comes in the second parallel line, which speaks of either the tempest or the waves produced by the tempest mounting "up to the heavens" and extending "down to the depths." Readers realize that the tempest or the waves did not actually extend from the heavens to the depths, but the hyperbole definitely highlights the threat posed by the storm.

Next is an instance of poetic hyperbole from the Prophets.

  A We would have healed Babylon,
  B   but she cannot be healed;
  C let us leave her and each go to our own land,
  D   for her judgment reaches to the skies,
  E   it rises as high as the heavens. (Jer. 51:9)

In this oracle against Babylon, Jeremiah speaks of the excessive punishment that will be levied against Babylon. The judgment against Babylon is so great that it is described as reaching up to the heavens.

Hyperbole is found not just in poetry but also in prose, and failure to detect its presence can lead to significant problems in interpretation or create unnecessary obstacles to understanding. Sometimes the hyperbole is local, in a verse or a phrase. An example is the quoted reason why the wilderness generation feared going into the land after the spies' report. They said that the people in the promised land "are stronger and taller than we are; the cities are large, with walls up to the sky" (Deut. 1:28). By saying that the walls rose as high as the sky (or heaven), the scouts register their belief that the walls are formidable, not that they believed the walls actually extended to heaven.

The first of two more extensive examples of hyperbole in the Bible comes from the book of Joshua. Reading the description of the conquest in the first twelve chapters of Joshua would lead one to conclude that the Israelites under Joshua conquered the entirety of the promised land.[45] The summary

---

45. For the view that Josh. 1–12 and Judg. 1 present alternative and conflicting views of the conquest, see the discussion and counterarguments of Woudstra, *Book of Joshua*, 8–13.

statements in Josh. 11–12 especially give this impression: "So Joshua took the entire land, just as the LORD had directed Moses, and he gave it as an inheritance to Israel according to their tribal divisions. Then the land had rest from war" (Josh. 11:23).

But did Joshua actually take the whole land? When we turn to Josh. 13 and subsequent chapters that narrate the distribution of the land to the various tribes, we learn that large tracks of land are still held by Canaanites (e.g., Josh. 13:1–7; 16:10), a reality that becomes especially clear in Judg. 1.

Some scholars reading in an overly literal way claim to see a contradiction between Josh. 1–12 and the second half of Joshua along with Judg. 1. But it is better to recognize the hyperbole and understand Josh. 1–12 as not simply a neutral and straightforward account of the conquest but one shaped by hyperbole to celebrate the initial fulfillment of the Abrahamic promise of land (Gen. 12:1). This view is supported by Lawson Younger's study of hyperbole as typical of ancient Near Eastern battle reports.[46]

A second example of hyperbole in narrative is found in the flood story. Of course, attributing hyperbole to Gen. 6–9 is controversial, but the language of the story itself makes such a position defensible. Despite attempts to make the flood story an account of a local or regional flood, the most natural reading indicates an immense worldwide flood of impossible proportions. The waters "rose greatly on the earth, and all the high mountains under the entire heavens were covered. The waters rose and covered the mountains to a depth of more than fifteen cubits" (7:19–20). Remembering that the ark came to rest on Mount Ararat, a mountain nearly 17,000 feet tall, the amount of water required would be impossible, but the hyperbole is not intended to be understood literally. Hyperbole pervades the flood story, including the description of the extent of sin: "The LORD saw how great the wickedness of the human race had become on the earth, and that every inclination of the thoughts of the human heart was only evil all the time" (6:5). The size of the ark that carried Noah, his family, and representatives of all the animals on earth is also hyperbolic: "The ark is to be three hundred cubits long, fifty cubits wide and thirty cubits high" (6:15).[47]

---

46. Younger, *Ancient Conquest Accounts.*
47. For a fuller treatment of hyperbole in the flood story and its theological meaning, see Longman and Walton, *Lost World of the Flood.*

✦ EXCURSUS: VERBS IN HEBREW POETRY ✦

Before we move on to discuss secondary poetic conventions, let us examine one of the challenges confronting a translator of Hebrew poetry: accurately rendering the tense of Hebrew verbs into English. The difficulty arises because Hebrew does not have tense like English verbs but instead has two aspects, typically called perfect and imperfect. Hebrew prose narrative operates by fairly clear principles. Perfect aspect is completed action, so past tense, and imperfect aspect is incomplete action, thus either present or future. The so-called *waw*-consecutive (where the imperfect verb is prefixed by the conjunction *waw*) is also past tense.

Principles that generally apply to prose texts don't seem to apply to poetic texts, which generates debate about how best to render Hebrew verbs into English. Differing conclusions in this debate result in differing English translations. Consider these varying renderings of Ps. 3:5–6 (the verbal aspect is identified in square brackets):

> I lie down [perfect] and sleep [imperfect];
>> I wake again [perfect], because the LORD sustains [imperfect] me.
> I will not fear [imperfect] though tens of thousands
>> assail [perfect] me on every side. (NIV)

Notice how the NIV translators render both perfect and imperfect verbs as present or future in English. Contrast the NIV's translation with the same passage in the ESV (or any other version):

> I lay down and slept,
>> I woke again, for the LORD sustained me.
> I will not be afraid of many thousands of people
>> who have set themselves all around me. (ESV)

Rather than translating both perfect and imperfect verbs as presents and futures, the ESV chooses to translate most of the verbs using the past tense (e.g., "slept," "woke," "sustained," "set"). However, neither translation consistently follows the principles used to render perfects and imperfects in prose texts. Applying those principles to this Psalms passage yields the following:

> I laid down and sleep;
>> I woke again, because the LORD sustains me.
> I will not fear though tens of thousands
>> assailed me.

This translation is possible but reads a bit more awkwardly than either the NIV or the ESV. What are readers to make of the use of verbal aspect in poetry? Some scholars suggest that poetry uses an archaic form of the verb. Others believe that the choice of verb is a function of parallelism, perhaps grammatical, and varies for poetic rather than semantic reasons.[48] Other scholars insist that the verbal system functions similarly to prose. Until a satisfying answer to this question is found, the best approach is simply to translate according to context or, as the NIV seems to be doing in this passage, render all verbs in the timeless present. As Tania Notarius states, "An atemporal perspective, namely, a zero temporal location or a basic ambiguity concerning the temporal location is quite typical of biblical poetic discourse."[49] Fortunately, as the sample passage above illustrates, regardless of what English tense is used in translation, there is little or no discernible difference in meaning.

◆◆◆

Secondary Poetic Conventions

Terseness, parallelism, and figurative language are the primary conventions of Hebrew poetry and are used pervasively by the poets of ancient Israel, but they are not the only literary features that signal that a composition is poetic. There are also what I call secondary poetic conventions. These appear only occasionally, ornamenting the language of the poet with various plays on the sound or meaning of words. Of the many such features, I will discuss only some of the more striking ones, including various structuring devices (refrain, *inclusio*, merism, chiasm, and acrostic) and various sound plays.[50]

Refrain

A refrain is a repeated phrase or line in a poem that serves at least one but usually two purposes. The first is emphasis. The poet emphasizes a theme or point by repeating it. In Ps. 136, the worship leader repeatedly drives home the lesson that, because of who God is and what he has done for his people, God's "love endures forever." Indeed, that phrase occurs as the second colon in each of the poem's twenty-six poetic bicola (each forming a verse). The first three bicola begin by calling on the congregation to "give thanks" to God (vv. 1–3), followed by a declaration of his works, beginning with creation (vv. 4–9), the exodus (vv. 10–15), the guidance through the wilderness and conquest (vv. 16–22), and more (vv. 23–26). The Hebrew word for "love" used here is *chesed*. Although the exact nuances of this word are debated, it is connected to the type

---

48. Buth, "Hebrew Tense-Shifting in the Psalms."
49. Notarius, "Poetic Discourse and the Problem of Verbal Tenses," 68.
50. For extensive treatment of secondary poetic devices in Hebrew, see Watson, *Classical Hebrew Poetry*.

of love and loyalty that God promises through his covenant. The common—and likely—belief among interpreters is that the first colon in each verse was spoken by the worship leader, with the congregation responding with the refrain.

Inclusio

Some refrains, while emphasizing an important theme, also provide a sense of closure to a poem or to a section of a poem. This usage may also be called an *inclusio*, or envelope structure.

Psalm 8 provides a good example of a psalm that begins and ends with the same refrain. The poem opens with "Lord, our Lord, how majestic is your name in all the earth!" (v. 1). And after recounting with wonder the glory of God's work of creation and how he has conferred dignity and purpose on humanity, the poet concludes by repeating the opening exclamation: "Lord, our Lord, how majestic is your name in all the earth!" (v. 9).

The presence of a shared refrain is what leads scholars to conclude that Pss. 42 and 43 are actually a single psalm. That refrain, appearing twice in Ps. 42 (vv. 5, 11) and again as the concluding verse of Ps. 43 (v. 5), sets the tone for the psalm and also provides closure to the three sections (42:1–5, 6–11; 43:1–5):

> Why, my soul, are you downcast?
>   Why so disturbed within me?
> Put your hope in God,
>   for I will yet praise him,
>   my Savior and my God.

Merism

Poets create merisms when they refer to the poles or extremes of a matter in order to include everything along the spectrum between the poles. Below are some examples.

> Surely the lowborn are but a breath,
>   the highborn are but a lie. (Ps. 62:9a)

The psalmist means that everyone from the highest born to the lowest born is ephemeral.

This verse speaks of Israel's enemies:

> The Lord says, "I will bring them from Bashan;
>   I will bring them from the depths of the sea." (Ps. 68:22)

From Bashan in the east and from the sea in the west and from all the areas in between, God will bring all of Israel's enemies into judgment.

> The sun will not harm you by day,
> nor the moon by night. (Ps. 121:6)

God will protect them all day and all night.

Chiasm

One of the best-known secondary poetic conventions is the word-order play known as chiasm, named after the Greek letter *chi*, which is shaped like an X. Chiasms form an *abb'a'* crossing pattern. This can happen on the verse level, as in Song 1:2b–3a, where *tovim* (good) begins and ends the couplet:

> *ki-tovim dodeka miyayin*
> *lereach shemaneka tovim*

> For good is your love more than wine;
> as for the scent, your oils are good. (my trans.)

A chiastic pattern can also be discerned in a larger portion of text. Of Ps. 2's four stanzas, for example, the first (vv. 1–2) and the last (vv. 10–12) are set on earth and the middle stanzas (vv. 4–6 and 7–9) are set in heaven. Although chiasm is an important structuring device in Hebrew, it is probably not as prevalent as some interpreters insist that it is, claiming to find it everywhere in their analysis of Hebrew poetry.

Acrostics

An acrostic is a poem in which each unit (typically a line or verse) begins with a successive letter of the Hebrew alphabet. In other ancient Near Eastern literature, the first letters of a sequence of lines may create a sentence or spell the composer's name,[51] but in Hebrew, the acrostics are only alphabetic, patterned after the order of letters in the Hebrew alphabet.[52]

---

51. The best-known Babylonian example is the Babylonian Theodicy, in which the first signs of each line form an acrostic. (Instead of spelling words with letters, Akkadian uses signs to represent syllables.) The acrostic identifies the composer, a rare thing in Akkadian literature, and also seems defensively to assert the composer's orthodoxy: "I, Saggil-kinam-ubbib, the exorcist, am a worshipper of god and king."

52. This structure is also known as an alphabet primer, or abecedary (= a-b-c-d-ary).

Nine psalms are acrostics, usually with a different letter beginning each verse, from the first letter of the Hebrew alphabet (*aleph*) to the final letter (*taw*). Since there are twenty-two letters in the Hebrew alphabet, acrostic psalms generally have twenty-two verses, but Ps. 119, the so-called Giant Psalm, has twenty-two stanzas of eight verses each, and all eight verses in each stanza begin with the same Hebrew letter. Most English translations show this by placing the Hebrew letter at the top of the stanza.

Psalms 9 and 10 together form a single acrostic, which strongly suggests that these two psalms were originally one. Psalms 111 and 112 are each complete acrostics but thematically related, Ps. 111 describing God's character, and Ps. 112 describing the blessed man, who reflects the divine characteristics described in the preceding psalm. The remaining acrostic psalms are Pss. 25, 34, 37, and 145.

There are no acrostic structures in Job, Ecclesiastes, or the Song of Songs, but the poem of the virtuous woman that ends the book of Proverbs (31:10–31) is an acrostic. Perhaps the most ambitious use of the acrostic form appears in the book of Lamentations. Each of its five chapters is a separate poem, with twenty-two verses in chapters 1, 2, 4, and 5 and sixty-six verses (3 × 22) in chapter 3. Reading in the Hebrew shows that chapters 1, 2, and 4 are relatively simple acrostics, though their lines vary in length. The poet composes a longer acrostic in chapter 3 by beginning each three-line cluster with the same Hebrew letter. Perhaps the most interesting fact is that though the concluding chapter (5) has twenty-two poetic lines, it is not an acrostic.

Besides simply observing that the OT contains acrostics, one needs to ask how they function. Lacking the Hebrew equivalent of Aristotle's *Poetics*, scholars must try to deduce an answer from the evidence. Some believe that acrostics are mnemonic devices. This may be so, but it is hard to believe that Ps. 119 was easier to memorize because it is an acrostic.

Acrostics evoke a sense of order and completion to a poem. After reading Ps. 119, interpreters end their reading with the sense they have a complete description of the psalmist's love for the law. Proverbs 31 describes the virtuous woman completely, from *A* to *Z*, so to speak. It may also be significant that almost all the poems in which an acrostic appears have a connection with the Bible's wisdom tradition.

The claim that acrostics communicate a sense of order and closure and perhaps also resolution is supported by examples of incomplete or broken acrostics. Lamentations is an interesting case in point. I noted that the first four chapters are complete acrostics, though of differing lengths, and the middle chapter (3) is three times the length of the other chapters. Its greater length may be intended to attract readers' attention and signal its importance, and in the middle of this chapter, we find a message of hope for the future (3:21–42). The fact that the final chapter is not structured as an acrostic may be intended to signal that the hoped-for resolution is still in the future. This view seems to be reinforced by how the final chapter, and thus the book, ends:

> Why do you always forget us?
> Why do you forsake us so long?
> Restore us to yourself, LORD, that we may return;
>   renew our days as of old
> unless you have utterly rejected us
> and are angry with us beyond measure. (Lam. 5:20–22)

Nahum 1:2–8 provides a different sort of broken acrostic, but it too communicates a lack of order. Nine of the first eleven letters in the Hebrew alphabet appear in their proper order in these verses, but some letters are omitted. Most of these nine letters appear at an interval of one bicolon (or half line), but two nonacrostic bicola intervene between the first letter (*aleph*) and the second letter (*bet*). After these first eleven letters, the acrostic starts to fall apart until it disappears. Some scholars think this disturbed acrostic is the result of textual corruption, and they seek to repair it through emendation.[53] Yet it is probably more likely that the poet intentionally broke the acrostic pattern so that the poem's form would support the picture of God conveyed in these verses. The poem describes the appearance of God the Warrior, in whose presence the sea dries up and the mountains quake, and by whose power apparently even acrostics break apart.[54]

Sound Plays

Many poetic traditions use rhyme to generate interest and coherence in a poem, but not so in Hebrew. The reason is simple: rhyme is much too easy to generate in a language where most feminine nouns end in -*ah* and plurals are consistently formed with an -*im* or -*ot* ending. Sound plays do occasionally occur, but it is hard to know exactly what the original audience would have heard or observed. One fairly certain example appears in Prov. 30:20:

> *ken derek 'ishah mena'aphet*
> *'akhelah umachatah phiha*
> *we'amerah lo'-pha'alti 'awen*

---

53. So Gunkel, "Nahum 1."
54. A more detailed analysis of the acrostic in Nah. 1 is presented in chap. 11, below.

This is the way of an adulterous woman:
She eats and wipes her mouth
and says, "I've done nothing wrong."

Several of the consonants in this verse can be categorized as labials—that is, consonants formed by the lips (m, p, b). It appears to be no coincidence that the content of the verse directs attention to the woman's lips. Unfortunately, such poetic devices cannot be reproduced in English translations without sounding awkward or stilted.

Voice

During our exploration of narrative (chap. 4), I identified the following communication dynamic:

Author—Implied Author—Narrator→Narratee—Implied Reader—Actual Reader

What is the communication dynamic in biblical poetry? In attempting to answer this question, I have found Elaine James's concept of "voice" a helpful starting point.[55] The following discussion is inspired by James but not necessarily a perspective James would fully endorse.

Like all literary texts, biblical poems have authors, or composers. Here I will refer to the author as the poet. As with biblical narrative, the idea of an implied author/poet is helpful because of the possibility that the poem before us is a composite. Unlike narrative, a poem has no narrator who controls the action and reports the speech of the characters. Instead, the poet is the voice of the poem, unmediated by anything like a narrator. I will use "voice" or "poetic voice" to refer to the poetic equivalent of the narrator, since the voice can, at least theoretically, be different from the author. For instance, the poet may construct a character who does not represent the poet's own perspective (e.g., the opinions of Job's three friends). The poetic voice directly addresses someone, an audience basically comparable to a narratee. James helpfully distinguishes the following audiences: the poems of the book of Psalms speak to God, those in the Song of Songs and Job speak to other characters in the book (Job to his three friends, etc.), and prophetic poetry "primarily speaks to an audience as or on behalf of God. It is God's voice."[56]

Narratee, of course, is not an appropriate label for a poetry audience, so I will instead refer to the one addressed by the poem as the addressee. This is,

55. E. James, *Invitation to Biblical Poetry*, 16–51.
56. E. James, *Invitation to Biblical Poetry*, 29.

or at least can be, different from the intended audience of the poem, which I will call the implied reader. As with narrative, the actual readers are those throughout history who read the poem, including us.

Poet—Implied Poet—Voice→Addressee—Implied Reader—Actual Reader

I will later apply this taxonomy when appropriate to specific poems in chapters 9–11.

✦ EXCURSUS: A WORD ABOUT POETIC METER ✦

Poetic traditions from many different cultures, both ancient and modern, display meter. Language is naturally rhythmic, but meter is highly regularized rhythm. Since meter characterizes many poetic traditions, biblical scholars have often assumed that the poetry of the Bible must also have meter. This belief goes back to ancient times, when Jewish scholars such as Philo and Josephus and early church fathers such as Origen, Augustine, and Jerome attempted to describe Hebrew meter using categories known from Latin poetry (e.g., iambic pentameter).[57] Kugel quotes Jerome as saying: "What is more musical than the Psalter? Which, in the manner of our Flaccus or of the Greek Pindar, now flows in iambs, now rings with Alcaics, swells to a Sapphic measure or moves along with a half-foot? What is fairer than the hymns of Deuteronomy or Isaiah? What is more solemn than Solomon, what more polished than Job? All of which books, as Josephus and Origen write, flow in the original in hexameter and pentameter verses."[58] More recently other metrical schemes have been proposed for the poetry of the Psalms and other poetic literature in the OT.[59]

Back in the 1970s and 1980s, HB scholars were on the hunt to uncover the nature of Hebrew meter. The assumption was that since most poetry has meter, or at least most poetry of which Western scholars are aware (Greek, Latin, English, etc.), then ancient biblical poetry must have meter as well.

None of the attempts to discover and describe meter in the OT has convinced a majority of scholars. At best, Hebrew biblical meter remains undiscovered, but it is more likely that Hebrew poets did not use meter in the construction of their poems.[60]

✦✦✦

57. Kugel, *Idea of Biblical Poetry*, 129, 140–41, 147.
58. "Preface to Eusebius," PL 27:36; cited in Kugel, *Idea of Biblical Poetry*, 152. Kugel explains that Jerome's citation of several different metrical forms actually betrays his "insecurity with any one meter" (153). Maybe so, but it also demonstrates his belief that if it's poetry, it must be metrical.
59. For a nice summary of quantitative, accentual, syllabic, and accentual syllabic meter, see McConnell, "Meter."
60. See Longman, "Critique of Two Metrical Systems."

SIX

Intertextuality

From the very beginning of biblical interpretation, the relationship among biblical books has received significant attention. The study of this topic takes many forms, some of which are reviewed below. In the past few decades, it has often been influenced by an insight about the nature of texts that goes by the name "intertextuality." As a literary phenomenon, it is a proper topic for our present project.

In the past two chapters, we have explored the conventions of Hebrew narrative and poetry, concentrating our focus on the analysis of individual passages. In this chapter, we will consider how scholars think about the relationships between biblical texts. We will consider not just discrete texts but also the intertextual blending/reuse of texts. This blending may be within types (narrative prose or poetry) or across types (a poetic text picking up a narrative idea). In the process, we will encounter differing ideas about how intertextuality works.

Every Text a Mosaic

In the 1960s, Julia Kristeva set the literary world abuzz by pointing out that every text is a mosaic of previous texts. As she later put it, "Any text is constructed of a mosaic of quotations; any text is the absorption and transformation of another."[1] She originally referred to this "mosaic" as intertextuality, though she later used the term "transposition" to differentiate the concept from what she called a "banal sense of the 'study of sources'"[2] (see

1. Quote from Kristeva, "Word, Dialogue, and Novel," 37.
2. Kristeva, *Revolution in Poetic Language*, 59–60.

below on the difference between synchronic and diachronic intertextuality). Kristeva certainly had her precursors, particularly Bakhtin and his concept of dialogism;[3] indeed, I suggest in what follows that the phenomenon of intertextuality provides the basis for similar forms of biblical interpretation under different names, going back to the earliest attested interpreters of the Bible. Nonetheless, her observation has attracted considerable attention in broader literary circles as well as in biblical studies. I use the term "observation" intentionally because that is what Kristeva offers. Intertextuality is not a method, though it can lead to a certain type of close reading of a text. In Kristeva's sense, it is more of an insight into the nature of texts—less of a method than a theory about how language and literature work.

Kristeva and those who follow her line of thinking believe that this insight highlights the instability of a text's meaning and undermines the idea of an author. In her view, the author of a text is not fully aware of the previous texts that his or her text has absorbed. In other words, Kristeva supports an anti-intentionalist approach to the meaning of a literary text since the author cannot grasp the referent of his or her own writing.

However, even if Kristeva is correct and a text is a pastiche or mosaic of previous texts, her conclusion does not follow. An author might unconsciously or consciously absorb previous texts in producing his or her text and yet still have an intention different from them. In other words, the intention or meaning of an earlier, absorbed text does not determine the meaning of the text into which it is absorbed. The meaning is as intended by the author of the text under study. Indeed, a later author might actually quote, allude to, or echo an earlier text in a way that clearly goes beyond the intention of the earlier author. This happens in the way the NT sometimes uses the OT (a form of intertextuality; see below). Again, the *author's intention* is the ground of meaning in the text, and later interpreters have access to that intention only by drawing inferences from the text itself.[4]

Diachronic and Synchronic Approaches

Intertextual studies today may be divided between diachronic and synchronic approaches, and often these two appear to be in conflict with each other.[5] As the names suggest, the former takes into account the relative chronology of texts in intertextual relationship. A later text either consciously or

3. Bakhtin, *Dialogic Imagination*.
4. See the earlier discussion in chap. 2 under "Author-Centered Literary Approaches."
5. See the helpful discussion in Kynes, "Intertextuality."

unconsciously absorbs a previous one. Such an approach is author-centered in that the interpreter cares about the intention of the second author's use of the earlier text. Such a diachronic approach precedes Kristeva. Those who adopt a historical-critical or historical-grammatical approach to the text are comfortable with this diachronic type of reading. Indeed, as Sweeney has pointed out, such study flows from traditional historical-critical methodologies such as redaction or tradition-criticism.[6]

But scholars more directly influenced by Kristeva disregard the second author's intention behind the reuse of a text and are not interested in chronological distinctions among texts. From her dismissive comment about "sources," quoted above, we see that Kristeva privileges a synchronic understanding of intertextuality, so determining the relative dates of texts is irrelevant. As Timothy Sandoval puts it, "Rather than focusing on quests for sources and influence, contemporary discussions of intertextuality often involve thoroughgoing claims about textuality in general and thereby shift considerably the terms of the discussion of intertextuality itself."[7] His strongest argument against diachronic analysis and in favor of a synchronic approach is that the former is a modernist approach to literature, whose time has passed. He asserts, "One cannot unring the bell of poststructuralism,"[8] by which he means that we must reject authorial intention and recognize the instability of meaning. Apparently Sandoval did not get the memo from his secular colleagues in literary theory, many of whom were rejecting this kind of anti-intentionalism at the time he was writing.[9]

Needless to say, I find this type of understanding of intertextuality unconvincing. Indeed, I would argue that a synchronic reader-oriented intertextual approach has a faulty theoretical basis that can lead to all kinds of fanciful interpretations. As intimated above, I approach intertextuality by wedding it to hypotheses about authorial intention based on textual analysis. I find diachronic approaches more illuminating, though often admittedly speculative.[10]

A diachronic approach can provide helpful controls on interpretation, but like all interpretation, it does not lead to absolutely certain conclusions. Its results range from possible to probable to nearly certain. While readers can't get

6. Sweeney, "Intertextuality in Exodus–Numbers," 43.
7. Sandoval, "Amos, Proverbs, and Intertextuality," 136–37.
8. Sandoval, "Amos, Proverbs, and Intertextuality," 138.
9. See chap. 2 under "Text-Centered Literary Approaches."
10. Some, such as Benjamin Sommers (A Prophet Reads Scripture, 6–31), suggest that this type of diachronic approach be called not "intertextual" but rather "inner-biblical" exegesis, in the spirit of Michael Fishbane's groundbreaking work Biblical Interpretation in Ancient Israel. This suggestion, however, seems merely semantic and does not account for the fact that diachronic connections are indeed intertextual.

into an author's mind, they can draw hypotheses from the writer's performance with varying degrees of certainty.[11] In a diachronic approach to intertextuality, interpreters must make a textual argument that a later text is intentionally using an earlier one in some way. Scholars differ when describing the nature of that use, and it is more an art than a science to identify it. One of the most influential figures in delineating such use is Richard Hays, who divides such textual borrowing into three categories: quotation, allusion, and echo. In his words,

> These terms are approximate markers on the spectrum of intertextual linkage, moving from the most to the least explicit forms of reference. Generally speaking, a "quotation" is introduced by a citation formula (e.g., "as it was written"), or it features the verbatim reproduction of an extended chain of words, often a sentence or more, from the source text. An "allusion" usually imbeds several words from the precursor text, or it at least in some way explicitly mentions notable characters or events that signal the reader to make the intertextual connection. It is difficult to separate the concept of allusion from notions of authorial intentionality; the meaning of a text in which an allusion occurs would be opaque or severely diminished if the reader failed to recognize the implied reference to the earlier text. "Echo" is the least distinct, and therefore always the most disputable, form of intertextual reference; it may involve the inclusion of only a word or phrase that evokes, for the alert reader, a reminiscence of an earlier text.[12]

There is nothing particularly sacrosanct about this three-part categorization,[13] and the boundaries between the categories are fuzzy, but determinations of intertextuality ultimately rest on one's ability to make a disciplined, text-oriented argument that the later text's author was mindful of the earlier text. However, this task presupposes another: establishing the relative dates of two texts. Sometimes biblical scholars can reach consensus when assigning dates to biblical texts, but often there are disagreements. If two scholars disagree over the chronological relationship between two texts, it is likely that they will also disagree over the nature of their intertextual relationship.

Daniel and Jeremiah

An example where readers can be virtually certain regarding the relative dates of two texts in intertextual relationship is the connection between Dan. 9

---

11. See the earlier discussion in this chapter and in chap. 2 under "Author-Centered Literary Approaches."

12. Hays, *Echoes of Scripture*, 10. See also Hays, *Reading Backwards*.

13. Sommers (*A Prophet Reads Scripture*, 10–18) uses four categories: allusion, influence, echo, and exegesis.

and Jer. 25 and 29. Daniel begins chapter 9 by telling readers that he "understood from the Scriptures, according to . . . Jeremiah the prophet, that the desolation of Jerusalem would last seventy years" (9:2). This causes him to pray to God for restoration, which surely means that he thinks the seventy-year period is nearing completion.

Daniel does not quote the relevant texts from Jeremiah, but he makes a clear allusion to Jer. 25:11–12, which anticipates a seventy-year Babylonian exile, and perhaps 29:11. The date of composition for the book of Daniel is vigorously debated, but it surely is later than the passages in Jeremiah. The *literary* chronology is that Daniel's realization and prayer occur in the first year after the Babylonian defeat (9:1; so 539/538 BC), while the word of the Lord to Jeremiah comes in "the fourth year of Jehoiakim son of Josiah, . . . which was the first year of Nebuchadnezzar king of Babylon" (25:1; thus 605–604 BC). The Dan. 9:2 text presents Daniel as reading Jeremiah.

The Jeremiah text takes on new meaning in the book of Daniel, or perhaps the Daniel text exposes the figurative nature of the number 70. When Gabriel comes in response to Daniel's prayer, he essentially says, "Not so fast." Gabriel interprets the seventy years of Jer. 25:11–12 as "seventy 'sevens'" (Dan. 9:24). In other words, Judah will not return to a preexile independent status in the near future.

Qohelet and Solomon

A second example of a diachronic relation where the relative dates of the texts in question are clear is the connection between the book of Ecclesiastes and the earlier historical books. In an earlier study, I explored intertextual relationship between the character named Qohelet in Ecclesiastes and the picture of Solomon in 2 Kings.[14] The date of the book of Ecclesiastes can be established with a high level of confidence to the postexilic period,[15] and the final form of the book of Kings dates to the exilic period, so the study of Ecclesiastes in the light of Kings is a diachronic intertextual study.

Solomon is not mentioned by name in Ecclesiastes, but from the beginning of the history of interpretation, scholars have noticed that the figure of Qohelet reflects characteristics comparable to that king. This has led many to conclude, wrongly I believe, that Qohelet is Solomon. What are these characteristics that Qohelet and Solomon have in common? I will name only the most salient.

I must begin by differentiating the two voices found in the book of Ecclesiastes: Qohelet's voice and that of a second unnamed wise man. Neither is

---

14. Longman, "Qohelet as Solomon."
15. Likely the late postexilic period; see Longman, "Determining the Historical Context."

given a proper name (more on "Qohelet" below), but these two characters can be differentiated by whether Qohelet is speaking in the first person ("I, Qohelet") or whether the voice is speaking about Qohelet in the third person ("he, Qohelet"). Once we have distinguished these two voices, we can observe that 1:12–12:7 presents Qohelet's first-person speech as he searches for the meaning of life and then offers advice following his failure to find it. The most obvious shift from the first-person speech of Qohelet to third-person speech about Qohelet comes in the so-called epilogue (12:8–14). There it appears that this second person is evaluating Qohelet for his own son (12:12) and then giving his son advice on how to succeed where Qohelet has failed: by fearing God, obeying his commandments, and living in light of God's future judgment (12:13–14).

Determining the voice in the opening of the book (1:1–11) is more difficult. Certainly 1:1 is an editorial superscription and 1:2 is third-person speech about Qohelet, which cites Qohelet. Ecclesiastes 1:3–11 is either Qohelet's first-person speech or a second person obviously talking about Qohelet. Because 1:12 is a typical ancient Near Eastern introduction to an autobiography, it seems most reasonable to attribute the preceding speech to the second wise man as he sets the mood for Qohelet's reflections in 1:12–12:7. Because the words of the second wise man precede and follow Qohelet's speeches, thus framing in Qohelet's words, scholars sometimes speak of this second voice as "the frame narrator." These observations suggest that the authorial voice of the book is that of the frame narrator, who is quoting the words of Qohelet so that he can evaluate his thinking for the benefit of his own son. This observation is confirmed by the one momentary appearance of the frame narrator amid Qohelet's speech ("says the Teacher," 7:27).

But what are the intertextual links between Ecclesiastes's portrait of Qohelet and Solomon in the book of Kings? For starters, the superscription identifies Qohelet as the "son of David, king in Jerusalem" (1:1). Solomon is of course David's son, but "son" can also indicate any one of David's many descendants that followed him on the throne until the demise of the dynasty in 586 BC. Jennifer Barbour suggests that Qohelet is a composite of many of David's royal descendants and not just one.[16] She is right that many of Qohelet's characteristics could apply to other Davidic descendants. Certainly other Davidic kings besides Solomon were known for their wealth, their building projects, and their pursuit of pleasure.

However, one feature of Solomon is not shared with the other Davidic kings mentioned in the book of Kings: his wisdom. In Kings, Solomon is a

16. Barbour, *Story of Israel*.

ruler given special wisdom by God and renowned for his adept use of this gift (1 Kings 3:1–28; 4:29–34; 10:1–13). Qohelet claims, "I have increased in wisdom more than anyone who has ruled over Jerusalem before me" (Eccles. 1:16). He also says, "I applied my mind to study and to explore by wisdom all that is done under the heavens" (1:13; see also 2:12–16). Solomon is also known as a producer or collector of proverbs in the book of Proverbs, and Qohelet uses proverbs in Eccles. 7 and 10. In fact, the nickname Qohelet reinforces this connection to Proverbs. The name is formed from the common Hebrew verb "to assemble" (qhl), which in its participial form can mean "assembler" and may provide a linguistic connection to Solomon in 1 Kings 8, where the same verb is used several times of Solomon's gathering/assembling the people to dedicate the newly built temple (vv. 1, 2, 14, 22, 55, 65).

Although these connections between Qohelet and Solomon have led many interpreters through the years to argue that Qohelet is the historical Solomon, there are many reasons why such a conclusion is wrong.[17] Although the figure of Qohelet is constructed to make readers think of Solomon, there are also plenty of signals discouraging them from a straightforward identification. These signals may be subtle, but they are clear.

First, we must ask why the writer does not refer to himself by the name Solomon. The choice of the name Qohelet seems intended to associate him with Solomon without identifying him as such.

Further, some passages are awkward when read in relationship to Solomon. What kind of boast is it, for instance, for Solomon to say that he is wiser than "anyone who ruled over Jerusalem before me" (1:16), when only David and some Jebusite kings preceded him? What's more, in several passages Qohelet even speaks as if he is *not* the king (4:1; 5:8–9; 10:20).

Readers should therefore not identify Qohelet as Solomon but should instead recognize that the author of the book is making an association between Qohelet and Solomon. Why does the author of the book want his readers to recall Solomon as they follow Qohelet in his search for meaning "under the sun" (Eccles. 1:3, 9, 14)? Such a strategy warns readers against thinking that they can find meaning in things such as pleasure, wisdom, work, or wealth if only they had more. Perhaps they simply don't yet have enough money to find satisfaction, but they would if they had more. However, Solomon had more money, wisdom, and pleasure than anyone else, and even he could not find meaning in those things. To use Qohelet's words, "What more can the king's successor do than what has already been done?" (2:12). Also, Solomon did not continue to fear God and obey his commandments; at the end of his

17. For those reasons, see Longman, *Ecclesiastes*, 4–9.

life, he died a broken shell, his kingdom being split into two. The intertextual connection between Qohelet and Solomon undergirds the argument that the meaning of life cannot be found in anything but God alone.

Job and Psalm 8

A third intertextual connection, one that is obvious even though the relative dates of the two texts are not certain, may be seen in the relationship between Job's speech in Job 7:17–21 and Ps. 8, particularly verse 4. To give context, I cite the entire first stanza of Ps. 8 followed by the Job passage.

> LORD, our Lord,
>   how majestic is your name in all the earth!
> You have set your glory
>   in the heavens.
> Through the praise of children and infants
>   you have established a stronghold against your enemies,
>   to silence the foe and the avenger.
> When I consider your heavens,
>   the work of your fingers,
> the moon and the stars,
>   which you have set in place,
> what is mankind that you are mindful of them,
>   human beings that you care for them? (Ps. 8:1–4)

> What is mankind that you make so much of them,
>   that you give them so much attention,
> that you examine them every morning
>   and test them every moment?
> Will you never look away from me,
>   or let me alone even for an instant?
> If I have sinned, what have I done to you,
>   you who see everything we do?
> Why have you made me your target?
>   Have I become a burden to you?
> Why do you not pardon my offenses
>   and forgive my sins?
> For I will soon lie down in the dust;
>   you will search for me, but I will be no more. (Job 7:17–21)

That there is an intertextual connection between these two passages has long been recognized and discussed, though their chronological order is uncertain. If we take the psalm title at face value, Ps. 8 is Davidic, leading us to conclude that the psalm is no earlier than the time of David, whereas the text from Job is completely undatable. The opinion that Job is an early book is based only on the early setting of the story, which really says nothing about the actual date of composition.[18] Most scholars believe (rightly in my opinion) that Ps. 8 predates the speech in Job, and Job's speech seems either to parody or "weaponize" this psalm.

Assuming our chronological conclusions are correct, Job's cry "What is mankind that you make so much of them, that you give them so much attention?" (7:17) strongly alludes to the psalmist's question "What is mankind that you are mindful of them?" (Ps. 8:4a). A verbal similarity is apparent in Hebrew: the verbs used in "human beings that you *care for* them" (Ps. 8:4b) and in "that you *examine* them every morning" (Job 7:18a) derive from the Hebrew root (*pqd*). Though the other Hebrew words used in the two passages differ, the question in both instances is the same.

Job's use, as I mentioned, comes across as a parody or, more likely, a weaponization of the psalm. The psalm expresses wonder that God has endowed humanity with glory. But Job, in the midst of his suffering, which he believes comes from the hand of God, sarcastically wonders why God in his greatness bothers to harass humanity. On the surface, this use seems to be a parody of the psalm: God's attention does not reflect the exalted status of humanity but demonstrates God's pettiness and leads to our suffering. But Will Kynes makes an excellent case that Job's statement is better seen as an attack on God.[19]

Up to this point my readings have been clearly diachronic in approach, even in the last example where I cannot be absolutely certain about the texts' relative dates. However, another way of thinking about intertextuality and authorial intention allows something more like a synchronic approach while still retaining a focus on authorial intention. I begin with a reminder of something that I mentioned in the first chapter: Scripture, by virtue of being the Word of God, is ultimately authored by God. He speaks to his people through the pages of Scripture, though he uses human authors with all their individual distinctive qualities. I believe that this affirmation reflects the self-attestation of Scripture and the historic position of the Christian church, which recognizes the canonical status of these particular writings. I also acknowledge that many do not share this fundamental belief and may not be able to follow my reasoning here, so for now I simply assert my conviction.[20]

18. See Longman, *Job*, 24–27.
19. Kynes, *"My Psalm Has Turned into Weeping,"* 63–79.
20. I justify this belief in the volume on theology and the OT.

Belief in the divine authorship of all of Scripture underwrites another type of intertextual study that is sometimes called "canonical interpretation" or "biblical theology." It involves a kind of synchronic reading that moves both forward and backward in Scripture. In such intertextual connections, a later text makes an obvious reference to an earlier one (see above on quote, allusion, and echo) and causes us to read the earlier text differently.

Revelation and Genesis 3

For a brief example, consider how the writer of Revelation understands the serpent of Gen. 3:1a, which reads, "Now the serpent was more crafty than any of the wild animals the LORD God had made." Putting ourselves in the position of the original audience, the serpent would have been understood to represent an embodiment of evil. In that time and place, walking serpents were common symbols of evil.[21] However, the original audience would not have understood the serpent to be Satan or the devil, who is never mentioned in the OT.[22]

In Revelation we read of a heavenly struggle between the angel Michael and his angelic army against the dragon, who is described in a way that alludes to Gen. 3:1: "The great dragon was hurled down—that ancient serpent called the devil, or Satan, who leads the whole world astray. He was hurled to the earth, and his angels with him" (Rev. 12:9).

Reading forward, interpreters learn that the serpent of Gen. 3, who symbolizes embodied evil, continues to challenge God, is ultimately cast down to earth, and eventually suffers God's ultimate judgment (Rev. 20:7–10). Reading backward, we learn more than was revealed to the original audience about the serpent in Gen. 3—namely, that the serpent is a symbol of not only evil in general but of Satan, the devil. For this reason, most Christians read Gen. 3 and identify the serpent as Satan. Such a move is not so much wrong as simply too quick if it leads us to assume that this identification would have come naturally to the original audience of Genesis, which is unlikely.

Colossians and Proverbs 8

A second example of synchronic intertextuality comes from Paul's Letter to the Colossians: "The Son is the image of the invisible God, the firstborn over all creation. For in him all things were created: things in heaven and on

---

21. Walton, "Genesis," 34–35.
22. Stokes, *The Satan*. On the identity of the accuser in Job, see Longman, *Job*, 82–83.

earth, visible and invisible, whether thrones or powers or rulers or authorities; all things have been created through him and for him. He is before all things, and in him all things hold together" (Col. 1:15–17). This celebration of the Son goes on, but for my purposes I will restrict the discussion to these three verses and to only one set of intertextual relations, with Prov. 8:22–31:

> The LORD brought me forth as the first of his works,
>   before his deeds of old;
> I was formed long ages ago,
>   at the very beginning, when the world came to be.
> When there were no watery depths, I was given birth,
>   when there were no springs overflowing with water;
> before the mountains were settled in place,
>   before the hills, I was given birth,
>   before he made the world or its fields
>   or any of the dust of the earth.
> I was there when he set the heavens in place,
>   when he marked out the horizon on the face of the deep,
> when he established the clouds above
>   and fixed securely the fountains of the deep,
> when he gave the sea its boundary
>   so that the waters would not overstep his command,
> and when he marked out the foundations of the earth.
>   Then I was constantly at his side.
> I was filled with delight day after day,
>   rejoicing always in his presence,
> rejoicing in his whole world
>   and delighting in mankind.

According to Paul, Jesus is the "firstborn of creation," which echoes Woman Wisdom's claim that she was given birth before anything was created: the Lord brought her "forth as the first of his works." Paul goes on to say that all things were created in, through, and for the Son. That Woman Wisdom observed God's creation is obvious from her description, but I believe it likely that Woman Wisdom also participated in the work of creation. This assertion depends on the translation of a rare Hebrew word in verse 30 (*'amon*). The NIV understands the word as an adverb ("constantly"), but more likely it means something like "craftsman" (NKJV).[23] Thus Woman Wisdom is seen as active in creation in the same way as God's preincarnate Son. Furthermore,

23. See Longman, *Proverbs*, 196.

Colossians mentions "thrones, powers, rulers, and authorities" (cf. 1:16), which arguably echoes an earlier claim by Woman Wisdom:

> By me kings reign
>   and rulers issue decrees that are just;
> By me princes govern,
>   and nobles—all who rule on earth. (Prov. 8:15–16)

Paul is making a conscious reference back to Prov. 8 for the purpose of associating Jesus with Woman Wisdom. He is not identifying Woman Wisdom with Jesus, as if Prov. 8 were some type of prophecy. But this connection does allow Paul to say elsewhere that in Jesus "are hidden all the treasures of wisdom and knowledge" (Col. 2:3). This association with Woman Wisdom highlights the relational nature of wisdom. In Prov. 9 the reader is urged to choose whether to dine (have a relationship) with Woman Wisdom or Woman Folly, which in its OT context is a choice between a relationship with Yahweh or with a false god. Due to the association between Jesus and Woman Wisdom, however, the Christian reader can view it as a choice between Jesus and anything or anyone else.[24]

The Editing of the Psalms in an Intertextual Context

I conclude this chapter with a negative example of intertextual analysis, one that misleads rather than illuminates. The example comes from recent studies of the book of Psalms. I contend that these studies are misguided on two counts, both connected to literary approaches to OT interpretation. First, they are the result of an overzealous narrative approach to the book, and second, they make a wrong-minded intertextual connection to the Davidic covenant.

I acknowledge that the book of Psalms in the masoretic tradition invites a type of intertextual reading of several psalms, particularly when a psalm includes a title referencing a character or episode from another biblical book. Although these titles were clearly added by later editors, they are nonetheless part of the current canonical Hebrew text, though English translations sometimes obscure this fact.

Not every psalm has a title, though they are so common that those without a title are sometimes called "orphan" psalms. And not every title provides the same information, the varied content including musical notations, genre indicators, liturgical directions, tunes, authorship ascriptions, and on thirteen

24. For more on this, see Longman, *Fear of the Lord*, 246–50.

occasions notes that place the psalm within a specific historical context, typi-
cally an episode from David's life. This last-described type of title gives the clearest basis for an intertextual
reading. Psalm 51 illustrates this point with its lengthy title that assigns it
a specific authorship and historical situation: "A psalm of David. When the
prophet Nathan came to him after David had committed adultery with Bathsheba" (NIV). This notice encourages us to read Ps. 51 in the light of 2 Sam.
11–12, which tells the story of David's adultery with the wife of Uriah and his
subsequent confrontation by Nathan. The contents of the psalm fit extremely
well with a Davidic response to the prophet's rebuke. It begins as follows:

> Have mercy on me, O God,
>   according to your unfailing love;
>   according to your great compassion
>   blot out my transgressions.
> Wash away all my iniquity
>   and cleanse me from my sin. (51:1–2)

Although this is the type of prayer someone in David's situation might
utter, we should notice that the language is not specific to that situation. There
is no mention, for example, of the particular nature of David's sin (i.e., adultery). It appears that David wrote this psalm in the aftermath of the prophetic
confrontation, but he composed it in a way that allows other worshipers to
use his prayer for similar, though not necessarily identical, situations.[25]

Besides the psalms with historical notices in their titles, an additional sixty-
one psalms name David as the author without specifying any historical context. Even without historical details, the connection with David encourages
an intertextual reading. For instance, Ps. 131 names David as the author and
reads as follows:

> My heart is not proud, LORD,
>   my eyes are not haughty;
> I do not concern myself with great matters
>   or things too wonderful for me.
> But I have calmed and quieted myself,
>   I am like a weaned child with its mother;
>   like a weaned child I am content.

25. Of course, the historical authenticity of the titles is debated, but the question whether the
historical David wrote the psalm is irrelevant to the literary (explicitly intertextual) connection being
drawn between the psalm and the narrative in 2 Sam. 11–12. In general, these intertextual readings
do not depend on the titles being historically reliable, but that is a topic for another occasion.

Israel, put your hope in the LORD
both now and forevermore. (131:1–2)

Reading Ps. 131 informed by details from David's life leads us to two occasions when David spares Saul's life (1 Sam. 24 and 26). Having already received the promise that he would be Israel's next king (1 Sam. 16), David had two opportunities to hurry things along, but he chooses not to bring about the fulfillment of God's promise through violence. Psalm 131 expresses the heart of a person who is content to wait on God's timing and does not try to manipulate a situation to gain an advantage.

Keeping in mind that the psalms are more than historical memoirs, I believe that reading the psalms in light of the information provided by their titles creates legitimate opportunities to pursue intertextual connections. However, I also believe that some attempts to read the book of Psalms intertextually are misguided and result in an incorrect intertextual reading driven by an overzealous narrative impulse.

In 1985 Gerald Wilson published *The Editing of the Hebrew Psalter*, which initiated a long string of investigations into whether the order of the psalms could be described as having a narrative structure or whether it was merely an anthology as had been widely held previously. It is not my purpose here to provide a detailed critique of Wilson and those following in his footsteps; instead, I wish to raise questions about this line of thinking. I will clarify the nature of this approach by describing the work of Wilson and of Peter C. W. Ho, a recent follower of Wilson's thinking.

Wilson's 1985 book was the published version of his Yale dissertation, which was supervised by Brevard Childs, who is known for a canonical approach to interpretation.[26] Childs's canonical approach advocates a form of intertextuality in which any biblical book is read in the context of the whole Bible. This canonical approach led Childs to suspect that there might be some kind of intentional order to the psalms, and as his doctoral advisor, Childs encouraged Wilson to pursue the idea.[27]

Wilson discovered that the seam psalms (psalms standing at the beginnings and ends of the Psalms' five books) are significant, at least those connected to the first three books. He was struck by how a number, but not all, of the seam psalms relate to David and in particular to the Davidic covenant (2 Sam. 7).

---

26. Wilson, *Editing of the Hebrew Psalter*.

27. In his highly regarded introductory textbook, Childs asks, "What significance can be attributed to these elements of the present form of the Psalter? In what way does the final editing of the Psalter testify as to how the collectors understood the canonical material to function for the community of faith?" (*Introduction to the Old Testament as Scripture*, 512–13).

Wilson rightly identified Ps. 1 as the introduction to the entire book of Psalms, which then made Ps. 2 the first seam psalm, a psalm that clearly relates to the Davidic covenant with its quote of 2 Sam. 7:14 (see Ps. 2:7). But here his first problem arises: most scholars regard Pss. 1 and 2 together as introductory psalms, which makes Ps. 3 the first seam psalm. As its title indicates, Ps. 3 is indeed a Davidic psalm, but it does not celebrate the initiation of the Davidic covenant as Wilson's hypothesis would require. Instead, the psalmist calls on God to deliver him from his enemies, which is Absalom and his army according to the title.

The first actual seam between two books is found at Pss. 41 and 42. Wilson believes that Ps. 41 (and not 42) is relevant to his thesis. The genre of Ps. 41 is debated, but I think it is more likely a lament than a statement of confidence in the Davidic covenant, as Wilson suggests.[28] In the seam between books 2 and 3, again only one of the two relevant seam psalms fits Wilson's schema. Psalm 72 does bear a relationship to the Davidic covenant. It is a blessing on the king, calling on God to make the king sensitive to the plight of the oppressed. However, rather than being named a psalm of David, it is called a psalm "of Solomon." One might see it as "passing the baton" from David to Solomon and then to other royal descendants.

At the seam between books 3 and 4, again only one of the two psalms is relevant. Wilson characterizes Ps. 89 as marking the demise of Davidic kingship. Indeed, it is bleak, talking in terms of God's renunciation of the covenant (v. 39) and covering the king with shame (v. 45). But again, Wilson mischaracterizes the psalm: Ps. 89 is less a statement about the ultimate failure of the covenant and more a lament calling on God to restore his favor (vv. 46–52).

The seam psalms between books 4 and 5 do not fit in Wilson's thinking. He sees here a transition from a focus on the human monarchy in the first three books to an emphasis on divine kingship in the last two. Wilson thus perceives in the book of Psalms a movement from the initiation, continuation, and failure of the Davidic kingship to its culmination in divine kingship. In this way, the book of Psalms has a trajectory toward a messianic reading.

I don't think Wilson has made his case. His use of the seam psalms is questionable, he selectively determines which psalms are important, and he often interprets them incorrectly in support of his theory. If all the seam psalms were relevant, he would have a stronger case, but they are not. Further, considering psalms outside the seam psalms works against his thesis that there is an intentional narrative movement from the initiation, continuation, and demise of the Davidic covenant to a messianic king. Psalm 132 is one example.

28. Longman, *Psalms*, 190.

According to Wilson's approach to the Psalms, Ps. 132 is after the demise of the Davidic covenant signaled by Ps. 89. But here in the section that purportedly has moved on from the Davidic king, the psalmist appeals to God that he "remember David and all his self-denial" (v. 1). The appeal that God not reject David, his "anointed one" (v. 10), presumes that the Davidic covenant has not yet been rejected. Furthermore, the psalm ends with a divine blessing on David: "I will make a horn grow for David and set up a lamp for my anointed one" (v. 17). Far from moving away from David, God still speaks of him as his "anointed."[29]

Many followed Wilson's approach in the decades after he published his arguments and sought to remedy the weaknesses in his proposal that I have mentioned. However, despite applying the same narrative/intertextual approach to the psalms, no two scholars exactly agree on the overall structure of the book of Psalms.[30] One recent attempt comes from Peter C. W. Ho, writing thirty-five years after Wilson's book.[31] He offers a very well researched, detailed, and densely written argument, but I believe that he, like Wilson, fails to make a convincing case and encourages a problematic reading of the book in the process. Below I raise some questions, especially regarding the intertextual reading that he does between the book of Psalms as a whole and David's story in Samuel-Kings.

The fact that Ho's approach is extremely complex makes it hard to do it justice in a short compass, but I believe that this is also a strike against it. The very complexity of his proposed structure suggests that readers, both ancient and modern, would not see it.

Ho sets out three research goals at the beginning.[32] First, he asks, "What are the main organizing techniques of the Psalter?" His answer to this question is quite complex and multilayered. He asserts that thirteen "Formal Techniques" bind the book together: book divisions, prologue, epilogue, symmetrical/concentric structures, five Davidic collections (3–41, 51–70 [+86], 101–103, 108–110, 138–145),[33] Elohistic/YHWH psalms, acrostics and alpha-

---

29. Before his untimely death, I asked Wilson about this. He replied that Ps. 132 is in a group (Psalms of Ascent), and the editors' hands were tied. This strikes me as too convenient an answer.

30. For some well-known examples, see Zenger, "Bei kanonischer Psalmenauslegung"; Zenger, "Das Buch der Psalmen"; Zenger, "Der Psalter als Buch"; McCann, *Introduction to the Book of Psalms*; Creach, *Yahweh as Refuge*; Mitchell, *Message of the Psalter*; deClaissé-Walford, *Reading from the Beginning*.

31. Ho, *Design of the Psalter*. A briefer and more recent description of his approach can be found in Ho, "Macrostructural Design."

32. Ho, *Design of the Psalter*, 5.

33. The designation "Davidic collections" is generally accurate, but within these five collections, Pss. 33, 66, 67, and 102 do not have a Davidic ascription, and Pss. 86, 122, 124, 131, and 133 do have a Davidic ascription but are typically not included in these collections.

betical psalms, superscriptions, historical superscriptions, postscript (72:20),[34] doxological postscripts/motifs, numerical devices, and symbolism. Ho lists nineteen "Tacit Techniques" that bind the book together: leitmotifs in the prologue, central motifs of a group, genre motifs, chain-linking concatenation, networking, distant binding, composite psalms, intertextual reading, theological developments, messianic and eschatological perspective, a shift from individual to communal psalms, an interlocking framework, Pss. 18 and 144, narrative and prophecy fulfillment, a pan-Psalter occurrence scheme, figurative/metaphorical devices, *maqqeph*, nexus word, and alternation.[35] The quantity of techniques Ho identifies to support his thesis gives him multiple tools by which to draw connections, but their number and complexity make one wonder how a reader, ancient or modern, could possibly detect all these connections unless they were writing a doctoral dissertation on it.

Ho's second programmatic question is "How is the Psalter organized macro-structurally?" He rightly believes that Pss. 1–2 provide a prologue to the book of Psalms as a whole and identifies what he considers to be three major themes (law, messiah, and Zion) that reverberate through the rest of the book. He is correct that these themes are in the prologue, but he is selecting only those he finds relevant to his point. Other themes in these two opening psalms are blessing on the righteous, judgment on the wicked, God's providential oversight, the nations' resistance, God's kingship (apart from the messiah), and probably more. Indeed, one could argue that some of these other themes are more prominent in the prologue than Zion and messiah are.

Using the Techniques listed above, Ho then claims that there are three main sections to the Psalter (books 1 [Pss. 3–41], 2–3 [42–89], 4–5 [90–150]). Each of these three sections contains four groups. The complexity increases when Ho suggests that the book of Psalms can be read concentrically, linearly, and contemporaneously and argues that the five Davidic collections mentioned above have a unifying metanarrative.

Ho's third and final research question asks, "Is there a consistent, coherent, and overarching logic to the design and arrangement of the Psalter?" His conclusion is announced at the beginning of the book: "The Psalter is an intertwining structure of at least three narratives expressed via the garbs of Hebrew poetry. The first is a larger metanarrative of God's purpose expressed through

---

34. Ho believes that the postscript signals the end of Davidic kingship, but what it actually signals is the end of the Davidic collection; the present order does not tell us that the psalms have been reordered during that time. Also, Ps. 132 is just one example showing that the Davidic kingship is not at an end after either Ps. 72 or Ps. 89.

35. For a convenient summary of these Formal and Tacit Techniques, see Ho, *Design of the Psalter*, 35–37.

the prophetic understanding and unfurling of the Davidic covenant. Within this metanarrative, two smaller narratives representing the life-journeys of the Davidic king and the *chasidim* of God to the paradisiacal garden-city of bliss."[36]

At this point, Ho's study becomes intertextual. He reads the Psalter in the light of the story of David and his covenant in Samuel and Kings. On this basis, he asserts that the book of Psalms "traces the establishment, fall, and 're-establishment' of the Davidic promises via an ideal anointed king."[37] Here Ho's thesis is similar to Wilson's and thus open to the same criticisms. For instance, it does not seem right to think of Ps. 72:20 or Ps. 89 as asserting the fall of the Davidic dynasty and giving way to an ideal Davidic king when Ps. 132 disrupts this interpretation by focusing on a present king rather than an eschatological one. Also, by the time the Psalms were finally edited in the postexilic period, after the demise of the human monarchy, kingship psalms like Ps. 2 would be read eschatologically rather than as establishing the Davidic king.

Ho's tour de force offers some interesting connections, but I remain unconvinced of the effort to read the Psalter as a continuous narrative. I agree with other recent scholars who, though a minority, insist that we continue to view the book of Psalms as an anthology.[38] It perhaps contains an identifiable prologue (Ps. 1–2) and a doxological conclusion (Pss. 146–150) and may show a general trajectory from lament to celebration,[39] but the forty-year search for a coherent structure to the whole book of Psalms has not yielded a view capable of persuading a significant number of scholars. This, in my opinion, is an argument against the validity of the effort. Attempts prior to 1985 are not completely absent but are few in number. If there were a meaningful structure, one assumes it would have been discovered by now and be widely accepted.

What motivates the pursuit of this question today? Even though Psalms scholars can't agree on a particular structure, it is likely that most think some structure does exist. In response, I suggest the following. Human beings have a narrative impulse. Give us an assortment of disparate points, and our first reaction is to try to find connections. In extreme cases, this predisposition

36. Ho, *Design of the Psalter*, 6.
37. Ho, *Design of the Psalter*, 337.
38. For instance, see the extensive treatment by Willgren, *Formation of the "Book" of Psalms*, and the interesting work of Yarchin, "Were the Psalms Collections?" Based on manuscript evidence, Yarchin wonders whether the masoretic ordering of the Psalms was settled or whether there were variants. If the latter is true, it leads one to doubt whether the masoretic arrangement of the Psalms is meaningful in the way Wilson, Ho, and others insist. David Willgren (now David Davage) has a helpful review of Ho's *Design of the Psalter*.
39. On this view, which goes back to the early church, see Longman, *Psalms*, 33–36.

becomes obsessive and is classified as a form of mental illness with the technical labels *apophenia* or *pareidolia*. This human impulse may move us to find connections among things that really are related, but at other times it drives us to try to find common elements and piece together things that don't belong together and vary too widely to be related.

PART TWO

• • •

The ANALYSIS of ILLUSTRATIVE PROSE- NARRATIVE TEXTS

Having completed our discussion of the theory of literary meaning and our exploration of genre as well as narrative and poetic conventions, we turn now to the practice of literary analysis. Although I have already given numerous textual examples to illustrate the conventions of Hebrew narrative and poetry, parts 2 and 3 provide more sustained literary readings of prose and poetic passages.

I have chosen texts from a representative variety of genres found in the OT. In chapter 7, I look at four key narrative passages from the Torah: the story of the first sin (Gen. 3), the flood story (Gen. 6–9), the binding of Isaac (Gen. 22), and the story of Egyptian bondage (Exod. 1). In chapter 8, I examine episodes from the so-called historical books, including 1 Sam. 17 and Neh. 13.

As part of a literary approach to the OT, I undertake a close reading of relevant prose texts in light of the conventions discussed in chapter 4. This literary focus requires that for now I bracket out as much as possible historical questions and theological issues that could distract us, but they are treated in my other volumes.

SEVEN

Literary Readings of Prose Narratives from the Torah

In this chapter, I explore four narrative episodes from the Torah, beginning with Gen. 3. Based on the context provided by Gen. 1 and especially Gen. 2, I conclude that the genre of Gen. 3, and indeed of Gen. 1–11, is a figurative depiction of a historical event, and I do a close reading of the story in light of this conclusion. My excursus on the genre of the flood story (Gen. 6–9) follows from my analysis of Gen. 3. I then move to the artistically powerful and disturbing story of the binding of Isaac (Gen. 22), known as the Akedah (from 'aqad, bind). After my own literary reading, I consider a recent, and I believe problematic, literary reading of the Akedah. Finally, I turn to the opening chapter of the exodus story.

Genesis 3: The First Sin

Genre

In chapter 3 I laid out my understanding of genre. Authors write in generic traditions that signal to readers how to take their words. Thus, genre triggers reading strategy. Texts participate in genres, often more than one, though some genres can be more illuminating for interpretation than others. In this chapter I argue that Gen. 3 presents a figurative depiction of a historical event. Understanding the genre of Gen. 3 is key to proper interpretation and avoids some embarrassing misinterpretations, particularly the idea that the creation account intends to inform the reader exactly how God created everything.

Recognition of the genre of a text arises through interaction with the text itself. Although texts may sometimes carry with them paratextual signals,[1] these are rare in the OT. Thus genre identification must arise from a hermeneutical spiral of repeated readings to come to a more precise understanding of the genre. Because repeated exposures help solidify our conclusions about a text's genre, I could have expressed my conclusions about the genre of Gen. 3 *after* presenting my literary exposition of the text rather than before it.

Because Gen. 3 is an episode in a longer narrative in the book of Genesis (and beyond), my discussion of its genre must include genre signals from the surrounding context, particularly the previous two chapters. I will seek to justify my conclusion that the author intends for readers to understand that historical events are being described in figurative language.

One feature characteristic of Genesis as a whole is its use of the *'elleh toledot* ("this is the account") formula throughout (Gen. 2:4; 5:1; 6:9; 10:1; 11:10, 27; 25:12, 19; 36:1, 9 [which may be part of the same section signified by 36:1]; 37:2). The full formula is "this is the account of X," where X is a person's name and the formula introduces the next section of Genesis focusing on X's offspring. The one exception to this pattern is the first occurrence of the formula (Gen. 2:4), which names "the heavens and the earth" instead of a person.

The *toledot* formula signals to readers that the book is composed of previously existing sources. In one case, the source is identified as a "written" account (5:1). The author intends readers to understand that the work is based on testimony handed down (either in written or oral form) from a previous age.[2]

The consistent use of the *toledot* formula throughout Genesis is a strong indicator that the genre is the same throughout the book. However, textual signals indicate some differences between the historical narratives of Gen. 1–11 and those of Gen. 12–50. The early part of Genesis uses figurative language more extensively than the later part does. Some representative examples from Gen. 1–2 are the nature of the days and the way the human was formed.

From at least the time of the early church, theologians have recognized the figurative nature of a creation that takes place over the course of one week. Augustine, writing around AD 400, states that the days of creation are not actual "solar days."[3] As Origen (ca. AD 185–253) puts it, "Who would be so

1. This is a term devised by Genette (*Paratexts*) to refer to additional material, outside the text itself, that may refer to matters like author or genre. The titles appended to many of the psalms are a rare example of paratextual material in the OT.
2. That the author gives the impression of speaking of historical events does not mean that he is successful. That, however, is the subject of the volume on the OT as history. Here I simply mention how the author wants us to take his writing.
3. Augustine, *Literal Interpretation of Genesis* 5.5.12.

foolish as to believe that the days of creation are literal days when there is not even sun, moon, and stars until the fourth day!"[4] Biblical literalists might protest that God could use some light source other than the celestial bodies; yet there can be no "evenings and mornings" without a sun that sets and rises. The best reading understands that the author is not interested in telling the reader the how or how long of creation but is instead using the trope of a regular work week to celebrate God's creation of everything, including human beings.

It has long been recognized that the days of the creation week have an interesting literary relationship with each other. The first three days describe the creation of realms, and the second three days provide inhabitants to fill those realms. So the sun, moon, and stars of day 4 fill the realm of the light and darkness of day 1; the birds and fish of day 5 fill the sky and sea of day 2; and the animals and humans of day 6 fill the land of day 3.

Day 1	Day 2	Day 3
light and darkness	sky and sea	land

Day 4	Day 5	Day 6
sun, moon, and stars	birds and fish	animals and humans

That this presentation of the creation is not intended to give the actual sequence of creation is confirmed by the fact that the second creation account (Gen. 2:4–25) presents a different order of creation. There God creates the first human before the emergence of vegetation and before the animals, whom God presents to the first human to name. Some modern translations (most notably the ESV) try to harmonize the sequence by using the pluperfect tense to suggest that these events happened before the creation of the first human, but the Hebrew is most naturally rendered with the simple past. Translating *'erets* as "land" rather than "earth" in Gen. 2:5 is also strategic, but these extraordinary efforts at harmonization are necessary only if we assume that the author intended to communicate the actual creation sequence instead of representing it figuratively.

A second striking example of figurative description that should be obvious to any readers, ancient or modern, is the account in Gen. 2:7 of God's creating the first human: "Then the LORD God formed a man from the dust of the ground and breathed into his nostrils the breath of life, and the man became a living being." This verse describes God as picking up some dust

4. Origen, *First Principles* 4.3.1.

and breathing on it to form the first human. That the author intends this to be taken figuratively is clear from the fact that "God is spirit" (John 4:24) and does not have lungs. Yes, God can do anything, including take on human form, but why would he do so here? The most natural reading understands that God is being described anthropomorphically, a type of figurative language, and this interpretation is confirmed by the fact that other ancient Near Eastern creation accounts also describe the forming of the first humans from a terrestrial element (clay) and a divine element, either the blood of a demon god (Enuma Elish) or the blood of a god and the spit of the divine assembly (Atrahasis). None of these creation texts is intended to tell readers how humans were actually made but instead simply claims that either God (Genesis) or Marduk (Enuma Elish/Atrahasis) brought humans into existence.

The choice of elements in the creation accounts also communicates something about humans at their emergence. The other Near Eastern accounts convey the idea that humans are evil from the start and also the object of divine contempt. By contrast, the biblical account says that humans are creatures (dust) who have a special and dignified relationship with God their Creator (via breath). But in both types of creation accounts, the events are expressed in figurative language.

Literary Reading

The preceding discussion of genre focused on Gen. 1–2, which I argue is a figurative depiction of history. This genre identification arises from interaction with the text and is based on signals the author sends to the reader. Since Gen. 3 is a continuation of the creation story begun in the previous chapters, particularly Gen. 2, I suggest that an ancient audience would have understood this story as a figurative depiction of a historical event. Origen came to the same conclusion about Gen. 3 that he did about Gen. 1: "Who is so silly as to believe that God, after the manner of a farmer, 'planted a paradise eastward in Eden,' and set in it a visible and palpable 'tree of life,' of such a sort that anyone who tasted its fruit with his bodily teeth would gain life; and again that one could partake of 'good and evil' by masticating the fruit taken from the tree of that name?"[5]

Now let's take a closer look at the story itself to see how the author communicates a message to readers in a way that recalls my discussion in part 1 of the dynamics of literary communication.

Author—Implied Author—Narrator→Narratee—Implied Reader—Actual Reader

---

5. Origen, *First Principles* 4.2.1.

Readers today are the "actual readers," who are reading the text of Gen. 3 to understand the message of the actual author. The author and modern readers stand outside the text, but the author's purpose in writing is to communicate a message to readers.

In chapter 1, I acknowledged that the concept of the author is complex. First, the book of Genesis, indeed the entire Torah, is anonymous. Later tradition associates the Torah, or more likely an earlier form of the Torah, with Moses (e.g., Josh. 1:7, 8; 2 Chron. 25:4; Ezra 6:18; Neh. 13:1), but virtually all scholars, including very conservative ones, allow for post-Mosaic editorial activity. For Genesis, the idea of an author is further complicated by evidence that the book is based on earlier oral or written sources (*toledot*), and Gen. 3 is part of the *toledot* of "the heavens and the earth" (Gen. 2:4a).

At this point, I find the concept of the implied author helpful. The final form of Gen. 3 may well be the product of a long compositional history, but as we read the text, the implied author's presence and intention can be discerned.[6] The implied author creates a narrator who describes the setting, manages the speech and actions of the characters, and arranges the temporal dimension of the narrative's events. This narrator selects what to tell the reader and shapes the story accordingly.

As is typical of Hebrew prose writers, the narrator of Gen. 3 is a third-person omniscient observer. The narrator is not a character and does not participate in the story. In its present form, Gen. 3 continues the narrative of Gen. 2.[7] The characters, the man and the woman, are the focus of interest and have already been introduced in Gen. 2. Both were created by God and enjoy an intimate relationship with each other, feeling no shame as they stand naked in one another's presence (2:25). This implies a state of innocence; they have nothing to hide from each other.

Genesis 3 introduces a new character, the serpent. His entry into the narrative is totally unanticipated, a surprise. Surprise turns to suspense as readers wonder what to make of the interaction between the serpent and the woman. As is typical of much Hebrew narrative, the story moves forward through direct speech. Because there are four main characters in the chapter (serpent, woman, man, God), there is the possibility of a three-way or even four-way conversation, but the narrator pares down the dramatic dialogue to two parties.

The narrator provides a short and salient description of the serpent before it speaks. It is "more crafty than any of the wild animals the LORD God had

---

6. I earlier spoke of God as the ultimate author of Scripture, but a fuller discussion of this dimension of the text awaits the volume on theology and the OT.

7. Genesis 3 begins with the conjunction *waw*, which in this context can be translated either "and" or "now" and suggests a connection with the preceding chapter.

made" (Gen. 3:1). The word "crafty" (*'arum*) can have a positive meaning, such as "prudent" (e.g., Prov. 1:4; 8:5, 12; 12:16, 23), but here the context requires a shadier rendering. "Crafty" or "shrewd" captures the tenor of the serpent's speech: "Did God really say, 'You must not eat from any tree in the garden'?" (Gen. 3:1). On the surface, the question is ridiculous: if the man and woman could not eat from *any* tree in the garden, they would have starved. But as the plot unfolds, this initial question becomes part of a strategy to manipulate the man and the woman to rebel against God's actual command.

The woman immediately sets the serpent straight by her response that God said they could eat the fruit from the trees in the garden (3:2; cf. 2:16–17) with one exception: the fruit of the tree "in the middle of the garden" (3:3; cf. 2:9), "the tree of the knowledge of good and evil," cannot be eaten. However, she adds to the divine proscription by claiming that God said "You must not touch it" (3:3), which God did not say. The addition to God's command (cf. 2:17) is clearly important and shows that the woman is already playing fast and loose with God's words. She seems to be "fencing in the law" by adding to it in this way.

Furthermore, readers would already be struck by the absence of the man from the scene (though we soon discover that he is not physically absent), and this is not because of some presumed patriarchy.[8] After all, it was the man who actually received God's instructions even before the woman began to exist in the narrative world of Gen. 2 (see vv. 15–17).

The serpent now openly challenges the truth of God's instructions to the man and the woman by saying, "You will not certainly die" (3:4), which is contrary to what God told the man (2:17) and what the woman clearly understood (3:3). He then implies that God has an ulterior motive for threatening the man and the woman this way: "For God knows that when you eat of it your eyes will be opened, and you will be like God, knowing good and evil" (3:5).

On the surface, the idea of knowing what is good and evil sounds positive. After all, one must know what is good and what is evil in order to be good and avoid evil. But the original readers would understand the nuance of "to know" in this context: knowledge that is not intellectual but experiential. Indeed, Adam and Eve already know intellectually that it is evil to eat that fruit, but by eating it, they exert their moral autonomy and actually participate in evil.

The next paragraph (3:6–7) shifts from direct speech to reported action. The omniscient narrator reveals to the reader the inner thinking of the woman: "The woman saw that the fruit of the tree was good for food and pleasing to

8. The emphasis in Gen. 1–2 is on the equality and mutuality between the man and the woman. See Longman, *Genesis*, 65.

the eye, and also desirable for gaining wisdom." Then the narrator tells readers the consequence of her transformed thinking: "She took some and ate it. She also gave some to her husband" (3:6). At this point, for the first time in the episode, we learn that the man is present but has apparently remained silent during this entire exchange. The narrator does not evaluate the man's silence, but because it was the man who originally received God's instruction not to eat from this tree, his utter silence throughout the scene should make readers realize that the man is as culpable as the woman. Thus readers should not be surprised to learn that the results are negative for both of them. Earlier they could stand naked before each other without shame, but now they quickly cover themselves.

After using what is handy (fig leaves) to cover themselves, Adam and Eve hear God walking in the garden. The narrator notes that it is the "cool of the day" (3:8). One gets the impression that this activity is common: the cool of the day is considered the optimum time for a stroll. The description of God's activity and speech in this chapter seem remarkably humanlike,[9] including God's apparently limited knowledge of the man's location as he calls out to him, "Where are you?" (3:9).

The man responds to God by telling him that he hid because he was naked. God further questions the man, knowing that such self-awareness can only result from a sense of shame, the consequence of eating from the prohibited tree. The man defends himself by blaming the woman, and since he further describes her as "the woman you put here with me" (3:12), he ultimately blames God. God then questions the woman: "What is this you have done?" (3:13). She too responds by shifting blame to the serpent: "The serpent deceived me, and I ate."

God does not bother interviewing the serpent but simply announces judgment on all three culprits in reverse order to their interrogation. Thus God first announces a curse on the serpent, who will now slither: "You will crawl on your belly and you will eat dust" (3:14); this implies that until this time the serpent had legs and walked. He also informs the serpent that he will put enmity between him and his offspring, on the one hand, and the woman and her offspring, on the other. Although the serpent will be able to harm the woman's offspring ("you will strike his heel"), the woman's offspring will bring an end to the serpent ("he will crush your head"; 3:15).

God then turns to the woman. The consequences imposed on her pertain to her two most intimate relationships, as a mother and a wife. Regarding children, the consequences include increased physical suffering during childbirth.

9. See chap. 5 under "Anthropomorphism."

Regarding her husband, the consequences include the emotional toll that could have physical repercussions. The key to understanding this latter punishment is determining the meaning of the Hebrew word here translated "desire" (*teshuqah*). This Hebrew word is rare, occurring in only two other places in the Bible, Gen. 4:7 and Song 7:12. In the Song of Songs passage, the desire is clearly romantic; in the Gen. 4 passage, the desire is not for intimacy but for control. This negative meaning is more appropriate to the context of Gen. 3: the woman will desire to control the man, but he will respond by forcibly controlling her.

Instead of cursing the man directly, as he did the serpent, God curses the ground so that it will adversely affect the man. Note that the punishment spoken to the man brings negative consequences for all people, just as the punishment leveled at the woman will result in emotional pain for the man as well. The curse on the ground means that the man's work will not be as easy as it was before the rebellion. Now human toil will be "painful" (3:17), arduous (3:19), and accompanied by obstacles (the ground "will produce thorns and thistles for you"; 3:18), making it difficult to cultivate and produce food crops.

The final and most devastating consequence of human disregard for God's instruction is the certainty of death. God explicitly warned of this penalty when he first spoke of the tree (2:17). Not only will people need to work the ground, but their bodies will also return to the ground. Alluding to man's creation as depicted in 2:7, God says to the man, "For dust you are and to dust you will return" (3:19).

After the announcement of these punishments, we are told that the man named his wife "Eve," with the explanation that she will be "the mother of all the living" (3:20). Up to this point, she had simply been referred to as "the woman."

There is uncertainty about when "Adam" is used formally as the man's name and when it is used generically as the Hebrew word for man, since *'adam* means "man" in the sense of human. English translations vary widely in how the word is treated. The NIV and ESV begin translating *'adam* as a personal name at 2:20, the NLT at 3:20, and the NRSVue at 4:25. The NRSVue's handling of the word has the strongest argument in its favor, since prior to 4:25 *'adam* appears with the definite article, "the man." Regardless of these variations, most important is the observation that "Adam" means humanity, though interpreters may differ as to the significance of that meaning.

In the final paragraph of the episode (3:21–24), the narrator reports the execution of the judgment: Adam and Eve are expelled from the garden of Eden. Significantly, however, before they are cast out, we are told that God made "garments of skin" for them (3:21). Claiming that this involved some kind of sacrificial atonement ritual stretches the meaning, but it is legitimate to see this act as an expression of God's grace toward his sinful human creatures. God helps them amid their newly acquired vulnerability and thus communicates that he will continue to pursue a relationship with them. The continuing narrative in subsequent chapters confirms this.

◆ EXCURSUS: THE GENRE OF THE FLOOD STORY (GEN. 6–9) ◆

The story of the flood offers another example of a historical event depicted figuratively.[10] Some try to treat the flood as a straightforward presentation of a historical event, as either a local flood or a worldwide flood. However, those holding the local view must work overtime to turn this flood whose "waters rose greatly on the earth, and all the high mountains under the entire heavens were covered" (7:19) into a regional flood. And those holding the worldwide view face not only the challenge of believability but also the absence of geological evidence for a worldwide flood. Of course, these problems lead others simply to dismiss the story as a myth or a legend.

In this excursus, I am not directly addressing the historical question of what reality, if any, stands behind the story of the flood. I am more interested in the figurative language used to tell the story. If we recognize that Gen. 1–11 as a whole is a figurative depiction of history, we are more likely to realize that the flood story is told using hyperbole.[11] A select list of hyperbolic elements in the flood story includes the following: (1) the extent of human wickedness: "every inclination of the thoughts of the human heart was only evil all the time" (Gen. 6:5); (2) the size of the ark—"three hundred cubits long [450 feet], fifty cubits wide [75 feet] and thirty cubits high [45 feet]" (6:15)—bigger than any wooden ship built even in the modern period; (3) the extent of the destruction God announces: he will "destroy all life under the heavens, every creature that has the breath of life in it. Everything on earth will perish" (6:17); (4) the amount of animals Noah must collect: he is to take "seven pairs of every kind of clean animal, a male and its mate, and one pair of every kind of unclean animal, a male and its mate, and also seven pairs of every kind of bird, male and female, to keep their various kinds alive throughout the earth" (7:2–3); (5) the sudden amount of water: "all the springs of the great deep burst forth, and the floodgates of the heavens were opened" (7:11); (6) the height of the flood waters, which covered not only all the "mountains under the entire heavens" (7:19) but also "the mountains to a depth of more than fifteen cubits [22½ feet]" (7:20).

This type of figurative depiction of a historical event is consistent with what readers see throughout Gen. 1–11, and recognizing that the author intends his audience

10. For more detail, see Longman and Walton, *Lost World of the Flood*.
11. See chap. 5 under "Hyperbole."

to understand this keeps one from rejecting the flood story out of hand or proposing sometimes tortuous readings to harmonize the text with either a local or worldwide flood interpretation.

♦♦♦

Genesis 22: The Binding of Isaac

Genesis 22 presents one of the most intriguing stories in the OT, not only for its content but also for how the story is told. Paying attention to the conventions of Hebrew storytelling illuminates its meaning and keeps us from drawing false conclusions about what we are reading. I first offer a literary commentary on the story and then address what I believe is a problematic interpretation.

Up to this point, the story of Abraham has focused on his response to the delayed fulfillment of the promise of descendants (12:1–3). In previous episodes, we have seen Abraham sometimes respond with trust and confidence (Gen. 13), but in the majority of cases, his initial reaction is fear, resulting in misguided attempts to fulfill the promise on his own.

Finally, however, the promised heir, Isaac, is born (21:1–7). Genesis 22 opens with a rather vague indicator of the passage of time: "And it came about after these things" (my translation of 22:1; cf. the NIV: "some time later"). "These things" includes the events of chapter 21: the birth of Isaac, the expulsion of Hagar and Ishmael (21:8–21), and the making of a treaty between Abraham and Abimelek at Beersheba (21:22–34). By the time Abraham forces Ishmael and his mother, Hagar, to leave, Isaac is weaned (21:8), but we are not told his exact age at that time or how much time has passed between this story and the events of Gen. 22. "A bit later" is a rough indication of how much time has passed before the present story.

Surprisingly, the omniscient third-person narrator informs readers right at the start of the story that God was testing Abraham (22:1). Why would the element of suspense be removed from the story, if not completely, then certainly to a significant extent? I can only think that it is because what God asks Abraham to do is so horrific that the narrator thinks it is too much to ask of the reader and so provides some relief. Perhaps also the narrator is simply stating the obvious since by the time the story is written, but not at the time of Abraham, it is well known that God does not ask for human sacrifice in worship (Jer. 19:5; 32:35). So readers know from the start that God is testing Abraham, but how and to what purpose?

The test begins with a brief exchange in which God gets Abraham's attention by simply stating his name: "Abraham!" The patriarch responds to this one-word exclamation with a one-word (in Hebrew) reply: "Here I am" (*hinneni*). God then presents his demand, which begins "Take your son, your only son, whom you love—Isaac." He does not simply say "Take your son, Isaac," but goes out of his way to describe him in a way that will intensify the sacrifice that God is about to ask Abraham to make. Isaac is not just any son, even though having to sacrifice any child is bad enough! No, Isaac is Abraham's *only* son, the son intended to be the heir to the covenantal promises, the son that Abraham feared would never be born and yet was born in his advanced old age. Worst of all, God mentions that Abraham loves his son, something about which Abraham needed no reminding.

This is the son God tells Abraham to sacrifice as a whole burnt offering (*'olah*). What is Abraham's immediate reaction? What must he be thinking? Does he have a sleepless night as he wrestles with this demand? We will never know because the narrator, who could have told us, withholds this information. He merely recounts Abraham's actions the next morning: he saddles his donkey, cuts wood for the sacrifice, summons two servants and Isaac, and heads off to where God told him to go for the sacrifice. By moving directly to these actions rather than giving us a window into Abraham's mind, the narrator emphasizes Abraham's complete obedience. Despite previously having shown little confidence that God would fulfill his promise of a descendant, Abraham has now come to a place where he trusts God unreservedly.

Readers are given what looks like a more specific time indicator in verse 4: Abraham sees Moriah after a three-day journey. He started from Beersheba in the southwest (21:22–23), and later tradition associates Moriah with the eventual location of the temple (2 Chron. 3:1), so some conclude that Abraham has come into the vicinity of the city later known as Jerusalem. As he draws near to his ultimate destination, Abraham gets off his donkey and addresses the two servants he has brought with him: "Stay here with the donkey while I and the boy go over there. We will worship and then we will come back to you" (Gen. 22:5). The statement "*we* will come back to you" seems to imply that Abraham has hope even at this stage that he may not have to carry out God's deadly command.

This suggestion of hope is furthered by the interchange between Abraham and Isaac (22:6–8). According to the narrator, Abraham gives the wood to Isaac to carry but carries the knife and the fire himself. How much wood would be needed for such a burnt offering is an interesting question, since it would likely take more than one person could carry, regardless of age, even if it is only the kindling. Clearly, Isaac is no longer a child; his ability to carry the wood suggests that he is probably an adolescent or young man. Jewish tradition places him at fourteen, which is too specific but nonetheless supports the general point. To get the materials up the mountain, Isaac would need to display cooperative action with a father now well over one hundred years old.

As they walk, they talk. Isaac asks the obvious question, "The fire and the wood are here, but where is the lamb for the burnt offering?" (22:7). Abraham responds, "God himself will provide the lamb for the burnt offering, my son" (22:8). The omniscient narrator chooses not to tell the reader what Abraham is thinking, but it seems unlikely that he is thinking "And it is you!" As the narrator will soon inform readers, Abraham is willing to see the sacrifice of Isaac through to its completion, so I cannot say that Abraham knows for a fact that God will provide an alternative sacrifice, but I suspect he harbors hope that God will. In Abraham's response, readers are also introduced to the important thematic word "provide" (r'h, see below).

When Abraham and Isaac reach the right spot, the narrator describes Abraham's actions in a methodical, nonemotional manner. He builds an altar, arranges the wood, and binds Isaac and places him on top of the altar. He takes a knife "to slay his son" (22:10). As with his preparations to leave Beersheba (22:3), the narration communicates Abraham's unquestioning obedience and willingness to go through with the deed even though the passage implies that he hopes for a different outcome. Perhaps his hope encourages him to follow the divine instructions. Still, at this point, he has no reason to have confidence that God will stay his hand.[12]

However, before Abraham can strike, the angel of the Lord, who turns out to be the Lord himself, intervenes by calling his name twice: "Abraham! Abraham!" And Abraham responds, "Here I am" (22:11). This sequence repeats the dialogue pattern that opened the chapter, but there God called Abraham's name only once (22:1). The twofold calling of his name here communicates urgency as Abraham was about to bring down the knife on his son.

At this point, the angel of the Lord reveals to Abraham what readers have known from the very beginning: God's instruction to sacrifice Isaac was part of a test. The narrator allows God to do the revealing: "Do not lay a hand on

12. I am aware that the author of Hebrews (11:19) states, "Abraham reasoned that God could even raise the dead," and so was willing to go through with the deed. However, in my opinion it is methodologically inappropriate to use this NT passage to interpret the OT text or to think that it gives one an actual insight into Abraham's thought process. The NT often uses the OT text in surprising ways as it reads the OT from the perspective of the NT and through the prism of first-century hermeneutical practice. See the masterful treatment of this subject by Enns, *Inspiration and Incarnation*. It would be a mistake to think that Abraham had in mind the afterlife, since the earliest text that anticipates it clearly is Dan. 12:1–3. Still, though we should be careful about claiming to read Abraham's mind here, it is possible that he was thinking that God could raise Isaac from the dead as God raised the son of the widow of Zarephath (1 Kings 17:7–24).

the boy. Do not do anything to him. Now I know that you fear God, because you have not withheld from me your son, your only son" (22:12).

The narrator next manages the action by reporting that Abraham sees a ram caught by its horns in a thicket. Abraham recognizes that this ram is the provision he had expressed hope for in his earlier conversation with Isaac (22:8), so he names the place "The LORD Will Provide" (22:14). The ram substitutes for the life of his son Isaac.

Abraham's obedience to God then prompts a second speech from the angel (22:15–18). The speech's importance for this episode is emphasized by its climactic placement at the end of the test; the speech's importance for the entire Abraham story is made clear by its length and by the fact that, although it reiterates earlier divine-promise speeches (esp. 12:1–3), it adds a significant twist.

The emphasis in this second angelic speech is on the promise of descendants, on the blessing of those descendants, and on how "through [Abraham's] offspring all nations on earth will be blessed" (22:18; see 12:3). What this story clarifies is that, while the fulfillment of the promises depends on faith (see 15:6), obedience is the essential manifestation of that belief. The angel could not be clearer: "Because you have done this, . . . I will surely bless you" (22:16–17) and "Through your offspring all nations on earth will be blessed, because you have obeyed me" (22:18). Though I am shading into theological commentary here, James's much later argument ("Faith without works is dead," James 2:26 NASB) is clearly illustrated by the Abraham story (see James 2:14–24).

The narrator then concludes the episode by telling us "Abraham returned to his servants, and they set off together for Beersheba. And Abraham stayed in Beersheba" (Gen. 22:19). Sensitivity to intentional omissions by the narrator leads to the question What about Isaac? Where did he go? Did he go with Abraham back to Beersheba? When the narrator says that Abraham went back, is he expecting us to assume that Isaac was with him? Or was Isaac so traumatized by his experience on the mountain that he did not return with Abraham?

Isaac's absence from this verse creates room for discussion and has led some to conclude that he did not return with Abraham because of his traumatic experience (see below on Middleton). However, I believe that Isaac's return with his father is implied by the text, and later events in Genesis seem to support this. Isaac appears to be living with Abraham when Abraham sends his servant to Haran to find Isaac a wife (Gen. 24), and Isaac is present with Ishmael at the burial of their father (25:9).

The bottom line is that this story focuses on Abraham throughout; it is not a story about Isaac. This does not mean that readers can't try to fill in some gaps concerning Isaac's age and therefore raise possibilities regarding his cooperation with his father, but we must be careful not to turn this into a story about Isaac. The narrator is extremely clear that Abraham's obedience is the important issue here.

◆ EXCURSUS: MIDDLETON ON GENESIS 22: ◆
AN ALTERNATIVE LITERARY READING

A close reading of a biblical text attends to gaps in the narrative that arise from the narrator's intentional reticence to divulge motivations, thoughts, emotions, and more. The third-person omniscient and omnipresent narrator can, of course, choose to enter the mind of his characters and at times certainly does so. But the narrator's ability to share the inner life of his characters means that he is intentional when he does not. Typically, such gaps entice readers to enter the story and fill them in. In such instances, the narrator prods the reader toward certain conclusions about a character's inner life.

Of course, misunderstandings can arise. Readers may fill in gaps incorrectly, or a gap may be so large that surmising a character's motivations or thoughts leads to uncontrolled speculation. The thoughts, motives, or emotions we impute to a character must be justified by an appeal to the text. In a previous chapter I discussed those who choose to read "against the grain"—that is, against the obvious perspective of the narrator and the constraints of the text.[13] But similar missteps can also be made by those trying to read *with* the grain.

I believe that respected OT scholar Richard Middleton has made some missteps in his recent book, *Abraham's Silence*, in which he offers an unprecedented interpretation of Gen. 22 that, despite his protestations to the contrary, runs against the grain of the text. Even if one denies that he is reading against the grain of the text, he is obviously reading against the grain of the long tradition of interpretation, as he himself acknowledges.[14]

Middleton claims to offer an approach consistent with the text's own native features: "I will nevertheless attempt to stay close to the text itself—that is, I am attempting not a midrashic reading (with creative filling in of the gaps) but rather a nuanced literary or rhetorical reading of textual details (closer to the Jewish notion of *peshat*)."[15] Yet although Middleton claims not to fill in the text's gaps creatively, he nevertheless reads

---

13. On this, see chap. 2 under "Poststructuralist Approaches: Deconstruction."

14. Middleton interacts in particular with the interpretations of Walter Moberly and Jon Levenson, whose readings resonate with mine. See Moberly, *Bible, Theology, and Faith*; Levenson, *Death and Resurrection of the Beloved Son.*

15. Middleton, *Abraham's Silence*, 165. Midrash and *peshat* are Jewish modes of reading that involve imaginatively filling in gaps in a text.

them with surprising results. He argues that Abraham would pass the test only if he protested God's command to sacrifice Isaac; Abraham does not protest and so does not pass the test.

What has led Middleton to question the standard interpretation of this passage? He mentions two concerns. The first is ethical. He cannot understand how the God we know from the rest of Scripture would command Abraham to sacrifice his son. Later verses make clear that God does not command human sacrifice. In fact, in Jer. 19:5, which Middleton cites, God declares that such a notion never entered his mind. But as I pointed out in my own literary analysis, we are informed from the outset that this is a *test* of Abraham, and as such, God has no intention of letting Abraham follow through with it. Is God deceiving Abraham into thinking that he is commanding the sacrifice in earnest? Well, yes, that is how such a test works. At the time of the patriarchs, though, it appears that God had not yet made clear that he is not the type of deity who requires or wants human sacrifice. Even in Middleton's interpretation, the way God commands Abraham gives the impression that God does indeed expect this sacrifice to be performed (so it *has* entered God's mind in that sense). Otherwise, why would Middleton think that Abraham can pass the test only if Abraham protests?

This brings us to the second reason leading Middleton to question the idea that Abraham passes the test only if he is willing to sacrifice Isaac. Middleton rightly points out that elsewhere in Scripture, God invites his people to protest. Readers can see this in the lament psalms and especially in Job. So Middleton asks, Where is the protest that would mean Abraham has passed the test? I will respond to this concern after reviewing and critiquing Middleton's close reading of the text.

The first textual feature to which Middleton draws attention is the way God refers to Isaac when he gives the command to sacrifice him. In particular, Middleton comments on the reference to Isaac as Abraham's "only son," the son whom he loves (Gen. 22:2). But wait a minute, Middleton exclaims, Isaac is not Abraham's only son; what about Ishmael? He is right to say that this highlights the fact that Isaac is Abraham's only "remaining son" now that Ishmael has been sent away.[16] He then suggests that "whom you love" is not asserting that Abraham loves Isaac but rather questioning "Do you really love him?" Middleton implies that the test will give the answer. "If you love your only remaining son, you will certainly protest my command to sacrifice him, but if not, you won't. Which will it be?"

But this is not the most persuasive way to understand the phrases Middleton examines. As suggested in my analysis of the text, the emphasis on "your only son" and "whom you love" highlights the enormity of the divine command. Isaac is Abraham's only son who is with him and who is the heir to the promises, the other being sent away because he is not the heir. Isaac is the one whom Abraham loves, and the test is whether that love

16. Middleton, *Abraham's Silence*, 172.

will prevent Abraham from loving and trusting God fully.[17] This is the choice Abraham is called to make.

Middleton is stunned that the narrative does not register any protest or lament on Abraham's part. Instead it moves quickly to a description of the next morning, when Abraham gets up early, loads his donkey, and calls his two servants and Isaac. Then he cuts wood and finally sets out. I interpreted Abraham's actions as expressing his utter trust in God, but Middleton sees this as the beginning of Abraham's failure: God really wants Abraham to protest rather than to obey. Yet such an interpretation clearly runs "against the grain." God gives a command, and despite the inner turmoil and anguish that this no doubt caused Abraham, he obeys it. The narrator purposefully does not let us into the mind of Abraham but focuses only on Abraham's actions to emphasize his obedience. Perhaps Abraham does lament, pray, and protest, but this is not what the narrator wants the reader to know or pay attention to.

In the description of these preparations Middleton sees a deliberate delaying tactic by Abraham: Why did he cut wood only after making all the other preparations if not to allow God time to change his mind? Middleton concludes that the lengthy three-day journey was intended to give Abraham time to come to his senses and protest or even refuse the divine command. But this seems like a rather sneaky way for God to test Abraham, who has a history of mistrusting God. It seems much more likely that God is interested in Abraham's willingness to trust him rather than resist his command. The whole Abraham story follows his journey of faith and how he responds to obstacles that threaten the fulfillment of the promises God has made to him. It is more in keeping with this trajectory to regard this episode as a test of Abraham's trust in God, which he passes by showing unreserved obedience rather than by resisting and protesting God's command.

Besides his misconstrual of the purpose of God's initial command, Middleton makes other problematic interpretive moves. Perhaps the other most significant obstacle to his attempted reinterpretation of this episode is the second angelic speech, which so clearly affirms Abraham's obedience to God's command to sacrifice Isaac. Middleton concedes the enormity of this obstacle to his interpretation when he says, "A surface reading may, indeed, suggest [the traditional understanding of Abraham's obedience]."[18] However, I would say that most times the surface reading is the correct one, especially when the text on its surface presents such a clear statement: "Because you have done this and have not withheld your son, your only son, I will surely bless you" (22:16–17). Middleton

---

17. Middleton notes that the word "love" (*'ahav*) is used in later chapters of Genesis for distorted loves of one sort or another, but this meaning should not be read back into Gen. 22. What makes those later loves problematic is the *object* of those loves (e.g., Isaac for savory food; 27:4, 9) or the *excluding nature* of those loves (e.g., Jacob loving Rachel but not Leah; Jacob loving Joseph and Benjamin but not the other sons).

18. Middleton, *Abraham's Silence*, 214.

wants to understand this as God's decision to bless Abraham *in spite of* his failure to pass the test, as God being gracious toward Abraham *in spite of* his unwillingness to protest. Middleton's reading forces the speech to mean the exact opposite of what it says.

Middleton highlights the role played by the genre of lament in the OT to support his interpretation of Gen. 22. He draws on Walter Brueggemann's insightful analysis of the three main types of psalms: hymns (orientation), laments (disorientation), and thanksgiving prayers (reorientation).[19] People sing laments when life goes wrong, and those laments are often directed toward God. Middleton also cites Job, who in his disputation with the three friends often turns to God with a lament. In both Psalms and Job, God does not criticize the lament or the one expressing it. So Abraham's failure to cry out to God in this way strikes Middleton as wrong and failing God's test.

In response, I would say that there is a weakness in Middleton's understanding of what Psalms and Job teach us about how to respond to suffering, and Middleton also fails to consider Abraham's long history of protest earlier in his life. As Glenn Pemberton points out, Brueggemann's treatment of the psalms fails to answer the question "What if God does not answer lament?"[20] What if suffering persists? In such cases, does God want those in pain to lament without ceasing?

Rather than unending lamentation, the Bible offers a better alternative. Pemberton points to a fourth type of psalm that expresses confidence. Psalms such as 23 and 131 express trust in God in the midst of suffering and in spite of circumstances. The same pattern of lamentation turning to trust occurs in Job. At the end of the book, after God confronts him, Job repents not of any supposed sin that may have led to his suffering, since there was none, but of his accusations against divine injustice (Job 40:8). At that point, Job decides to stop his laments and to suffer in silence, not knowing whether God will restore his fortunes.

To these examples I would add Lam. 3. In this lament, the man of affliction suffers greatly (3:1), but eventually it says this about his situation:

> Let him sit alone in silence,
>   for the Lord has laid it on him.
> Let him bury his face in the dust—
>   there may yet be hope.
> Let him offer his cheek to one who would strike him,
>   and let him be filled with disgrace. (3:28–30)

These biblical texts suggest that while lament and protest have a legitimate role, a proper response to suffering does not end with them. Eventually, God desires us to trust him in the midst of pain. And that is what Abraham does over the arc of his life journey.

---

19. Brueggemann, *Message of the Psalms*, 25–167.
20. Pemberton, *After Lament*.

He protests repeatedly against God's apparent failure to follow through on his promises (see esp. Gen. 15 and 17), but here in Gen. 22 he comes to trust God fully.

In conclusion, I reaffirm my admiration for Middleton as an interpreter, but I think that in this case he approaches the text, perhaps unconsciously, as a problem to be solved rather than as a text to be expounded. Despite his claim to the contrary, he solves it by reading against the grain. Since he does so in the name of a close literary reading, it demonstrates how gaps can be "filled in" in more than one way but that some ways of reading are less convincing than others. Perhaps how hard one needs to work to justify a particular reading is an indication of the weakness of one's interpretation. This is especially true when the reading goes against a long-standing interpretive tradition, which in the case of Gen. 22 goes back even to Heb. 11:17–19 and James 2:20–24.[21]

♦♦♦

Exodus 1: Bondage in Egypt

Exodus 1 begins the story of the exodus from Egypt. Closely reading this episode in light of the conventions of Hebrew narrative helps us navigate its interpretation and appreciate the power of the story.

Although the Torah is divided into five books, readers should not forget that this division results from its length; being too large to fit on only one scroll, five were needed (thus the term Pentateuch, "five scrolls"). The importance of this observation for my literary study is that the Torah should be viewed as a single literary composition.[22] Therefore, I need to start with a comment about the context of Exod. 1.

The immediately preceding episode is an account of the death of Joseph (Gen. 50:22–26). Although that death provides closure to what today is the book of Genesis, Joseph's final speech to his brothers makes clear that the story will continue: "I am about to die. But God will surely come to your aid and take you up out of this land to the land he promised on oath to Abraham, Isaac and Jacob. . . . God will surely come to your aid, and then you must carry my bones up from this place" (50:24–25).

As Exodus begins, the narrator draws an intertextual link to Gen. 46:26 to remind readers that Jacob's family had years earlier immigrated to Egypt (Exod. 1:1–5). The narrator provides only indirect hints about how much time

21. I agree with Midddleton that the NT does not always engage in what we consider a historical-grammatical interpretation, but Hebrews and James do show a reading that certainly can be defended from Gen. 22 itself.

22. I am speaking of the final form of the Torah and make no comment at this point about the history of composition of the Torah.

has passed since the death of Joseph and his brothers, but it has been long enough that "the Israelites were exceedingly fruitful, they multiplied greatly, increased in numbers and became so numerous that the land was filled with them" (1:7). Readers can only speculate about how much time has passed from the death of Joseph to the present situation, but an intertextual references to Genesis are clearly evident.

First, the wording of Exod. 1:7 reminds attentive interpreters of the language of Gen. 1:28, where the verbs "be fruitful" (*prh*), "increase in number" (*rbh*), and "fill" (*ml'*) occur. But the more relevant antecedent is found in Gen. 12:2, where God promises Abraham that he will make him into a "great nation," establishing an expectation of what is to come.

Now with this background, readers are introduced to the first speaking character, who is identified as a "new king to whom Joseph meant nothing" (Exod. 1:8), a description that anticipates trouble to come. Notice that the narrator carefully avoids actually naming this king, likely because he does not want to give any lasting memory to him as an individual or because "Pharaoh" was considered a god.[23] This unnamed king then speaks, giving voice to his anxieties about the Israelites' presence in Egypt (1:9–10). To the Israelites, particularly in light of Gen. 1 and 12, their population growth represents God's blessing and the hope for things to come, but to Pharaoh, the Israelites' increasing numbers represents a significant threat. The new king's speech marks him as nervous, fearful of a large foreign population within Egypt, and uncertain about the Egyptians' ability to defend themselves should the Israelites choose to rise against them. He therefore urges his people to "deal 'shrewdly' with them" (1:10).

The narrator then steps in to inform readers of Pharaoh's plan. The Egyptians put the Israelites to forced labor to build "store cities for Pharaoh" (1:11). But the resilient Israelites multiply even more, prompting worse treatment from the Egyptians. The narrator describes the Egyptians' treatment of the Hebrews as ruthless and harsh (1:13–14).

When Pharaoh's desire to neutralize the perceived threat posed by the Israelites is still not achieved, he takes additional, even more drastic steps. The narrator communicates this new strategy through dialogue, reporting Pharaoh's instructions to two Hebrew midwives, Shiphrah and Puah. Notice that although the narrator does not give the name of the pharaoh, readers learn the names of the midwives whose actions no doubt led to a desire to remember their names.[24]

23. Walton, Matthews, and Chavalas, *IVP Bible Background Commentary*, 74–75.
24. A well-known ambiguity is whether Shiphrah and Puah are themselves Hebrews or Egyptians serving as midwives to the Hebrews.

Pharaoh's spoken instructions are as clear as they are ruthless. When the women go to assist a Hebrew woman in childbirth, they are to kill any newborn boy. Hebrew literature does not always, or even often, report the motivation for a character's actions, but here the narrator tells readers that the midwives, at great risk to themselves, chose not to follow Pharaoh's instructions because they "feared God" (1:17). Fearing God more than they feared Pharaoh, they let the boys live.

However, their actions—or, more accurately, their inaction—cannot escape Pharaoh's notice, and he calls them in for interrogation. "Why have you done this? Why have you let the boys live?" (1:18). They may fear God more than Pharaoh, but they know better than to tell Pharaoh the truth, so they lie: "Hebrew women are not like Egyptian women; they are vigorous and give birth before the midwives arrive" (1:19).

Not only is motivation rarely reported in Hebrew narrative, but explicit evaluation by the narrator is also minimal, and this passage is a classic example. The lack of explicit commendation leads some commentators to suggest that the midwives sinned by breaking the ninth commandment, which forbids false witness. However, rather than tell, the narrator shows readers that the midwives' lie has God's approval. Because they acted out of fear of God, "he gave them families of their own," and as for the Israelites, they "increased and became even more numerous" (1:20–21).

But Pharaoh is not to be thwarted in his determination to harm the people of God. He next issues a decree that Hebrew boys be thrown into the Nile. This command sets up the next episode, which is the birth of Moses, the future deliverer of God's people, but we will end our study of Exodus at this point.

EIGHT

Literary Readings of Prose Narratives from the Historical Books

In this chapter, I offer two more close literary readings of prose narratives. The first is from the account of David's fight with Goliath. This story is told with energy and vividness. The second text is from Neh. 13, a passage that is interesting in many respects and provides a contrast of sorts with the typical mode of OT narration. Probably the biggest difference is that the account is told in the first person by Nehemiah himself.

1 Samuel 17: David and Goliath

The books of Samuel are among the most literarily sophisticated in the OT, and the story of David and Goliath is one of the most memorable in the OT. In much of the OT, the narrator advances a story largely by presenting dialogue, but here the narrator does so by presenting the action, particularly in the first part of the chapter. The narrator also departs from telling the story through dialogue by revealing Goliath's emotional reaction to David—"He despised him" (1 Sam. 17:42)—something we could also have deduced from his words to David: "Am I a dog, that you come at me with sticks?" (17:43). The story is told from a third-person omniscient point of view, though the focalization is predominantly from the Israelite perspective.

The first paragraph of the story (vv. 1–3) sets the scene of the confrontation between the Israelites and the Philistines. The Philistines are said to be encamped on one side, at a place called "Ephes Dammim, between Sokoh and Azekah." The Israelites, with their leader Saul, are encamped "in the Valley of Elah." Verse 3 further clarifies the setting of this confrontation: the armies are on opposite hills with a valley between them. Neither army has a topographical advantage. The Israelites are on the east side of the valley; the Philistines are on the west, coming from the Mediterranean coast and threatening to invade further eastward.

At this point, the first character featured in the story steps forward, Goliath. Hebrew narrative is notoriously spare in giving physical descriptions of its characters, but here the narrator devotes four lengthy verses to Goliath (vv. 4–7). He is "six cubits and a span" tall (over 9 feet), wearing a bronze helmet and a coat of armor "weighing five thousand shekels" (about 125 pounds). He has bronze greaves (shin guards). In terms of weapons, both offensive and defensive, he has a bronze javelin and a spear of large proportions with a six-hundred-shekel iron point (about 15 pounds), and his shield bearer walks ahead of him. Goliath is a huge man and heavily armored. The length of the description indicates how important it is to the story. The intent is to contrast Goliath with his opponent, David—soon to be introduced as inexperienced and unarmored—and show that the latter is clearly outmatched and outgunned.

The narrator then turns from Goliath's appearance to his speech, how he taunts the Israelite army and challenges them to send out a representative to fight him, with the victor determining which army wins. In the face of Goliath's aggressive and boastful speech, the Israelites are "dismayed and terrified" (v. 11).

The narrator next introduces David, but instead of giving a physical description as he did for Goliath, the narrator identifies David by his place in Jesse's family (vv. 12–15). Readers have already met David in the preceding chapter, both when Samuel secretly anointed him as the future king of Israel and then as a young man playing the lyre for a tormented Saul (16:18–23). David's apparent earlier introduction to Saul will raise a problem later in chapter 17. The narrator now tells readers that David is the youngest of Jesse's eight sons, three of whom are presently serving in the Israelite army. Apparently too young to join them, David instead stays behind to care for his father's flocks. However, he also acts as a messenger between Jesse and David's older brothers at the battlefront.

After mentioning that Goliath has been taunting the Israelite army for forty days (17:16), the number signifying a long time rather than precisely forty days, the narrator takes readers to Jesse's home, where the father instructs his youngest son to deliver food to his brothers and their military leader (vv.

17–19). When David arrives at the camp, he finds his brothers heading toward the front lines to face the Philistine army. At that moment, Goliath renews his challenging taunt, and the Israelites again react with fear (vv. 20–24).

The narrator then has the Israelite soldiers report that Saul has made promises to the one who kills Goliath. That person will be given wealth, the king's daughter, and tax exemptions. David does not hear this from the Israelite warriors but from "the men standing near him" (vv. 25–27).

Eliab, David's oldest brother, reacts with anger toward David, accusing him of coming to watch the battle and neglecting the sheep. He tells David, "I know how conceited you are and how wicked your heart is" (v. 28). It is difficult to know how to take Eliab's accusation. Perhaps at this point in his life, David comes across to his brother as overconfident. Or perhaps Eliab is frustrated and feels shame that he himself does not have the courage to stand up to Goliath. Whatever the motivation for the accusation, David takes exception, sounding like a typical little brother to a belittling older brother: "What have I done? . . . Can't I even speak?" (v. 29). David then continues to make inquiries.

When Saul hears about David's interest in the challenge and the reward, he sends for him. David confidently volunteers to take on the giant, but Saul reacts skeptically. David is a "young man," implying inexperience, and Goliath "has been a warrior from his youth" (v. 33). David then counters by citing instances when he protected his father's flock from a lion and a bear. He will kill Goliath to protect Israel, just as he killed these fierce predators to protect the sheep. One naturally hears in this the analogy, later made explicit, that the leader of a people is like the shepherd of a flock of sheep (2 Sam. 5:2). It is also important to note that David attributes his past and future success to the Lord, who rescued him from the attacking beasts and will aid him against Goliath, whom David disparagingly calls "this Philistine." Saul then commissions David: "Go, and the LORD be with you" (1 Sam. 17:37). As readers soon find out, the Lord will indeed be with David.

Readers should see a contrast here between David and Saul, Israel's divinely appointed king. Saul is earlier described as especially tall (1 Sam. 10:23) and therefore perhaps best positioned to physically challenge Goliath. But he has already shown himself to be less than up to the task. Initially hesitant to take on the role of king (1 Sam. 10–11), Saul forfeited the possibility of a dynastic line by showing a lack of trust in God when he refused to wait for Samuel to arrive and offer the pre-battle sacrifices (1 Sam. 13). Then he lost the kingship by not obeying God's command to do away with the Amalekites when he had the chance (1 Sam. 15; cf. Exod. 17:16; Deut. 25:17). One would have expected Saul to step up and face Goliath in the power of the Lord instead of listening to Goliath's taunts day after day until an inexperienced country boy takes up the challenge. The best Saul can do is provide David with armor and weapons, but David is so inexperienced that even these are no help. Instead, David takes his shepherd's staff, a sling, and five smooth stones—weapons he has used in his role as shepherd to protect his flock.

As Goliath approaches David, he sees nothing more than a boy "glowing with health and handsome" (17:42) and is filled with contempt for him. Regarding it as a personal insult, he asks, "Am I a dog, that you come at me with sticks?" (17:43). Goliath sees David as an unworthy opponent and expects to dispatch him easily.

David responds by letting Goliath (and readers) know that he comes against him in God's power rather than in his own strength. He does not claim the ability to defeat Goliath himself but gives God the glory and declares that his victory over Goliath will demonstrate to all "that it is not by sword or spear that the LORD saves; for the battle is the LORD's" (17:47). Slinging a stone, David hurls it at Goliath, hitting him in the forehead and causing him to collapse facedown on the ground. David then uses Goliath's own sword to cut off his head.

This scene suggests the interplay between divine sovereignty and human responsibility. David gives glory to God, but God does not win the victory apart from David's actions. Indeed, David exhibits cunning in his approach to the contest. Attacking Goliath head-on would likely have been a suicide mission. By standing at a distance and hitting him in the head with a stone, David is able to stun Goliath so that he can dispatch him with a sword. Still, David recognizes that this victory is God's as surely as if God had struck Goliath with lightning from heaven.

At this point readers may recall the agreement that if the Israelite champion defeats the Philistine champion—in this case, if David defeats Goliath—then the Philistines will become their subjects (17:9). Rather than submit to the Israelites, however, the Philistines flee the scene. The Israelites, emboldened by David's victory, pursue and slaughter the Philistines and plunder their camp (17:52–53). David keeps Goliath's sword as a trophy for himself but brings the giant's head to Jerusalem.

The account ends in an unexpected way that raises some questions. The narrative goes back to the time preceding the contest, when Saul asks Abner, his general, "Whose son is that young man?" Abner has no clue and is tasked with finding out (17:55–56). After David's victory, Abner brings David before King Saul, who asks him, "Whose son are you, young man?" David's response brings the story to a close: "I am the son of your servant Jesse of Bethlehem" (17:57–58).

At first glance, Saul's ignorance is hard to explain, since in the immediately preceding chapter David is described not as an inexperienced shepherd but as "a brave man and a warrior" (16:18), and he plays the lyre for Saul on a regular basis (16:14–23). How should we understand the relationship between these two stories? Should we consider this the clumsy result of bringing together two stories without concern for contradiction? It's hard to be dogmatic, but at least a couple of answers are possible. The first is that Saul knows full well who David is, but after David's victory Saul is trying to identify his father in order to apply the tax exemptions promised to the family of the one who defeats Goliath (17:25). However, this does not explain why David in the first story seems already to have a reputation as a warrior. Perhaps the best solution is to suggest that the narrative here is not concerned with being chronological but is arranged thematically to introduce David as the future psalmist of Israel and warrior extraordinaire.

Nehemiah 13: Nehemiah's Angry Disappointment

The last chapter of the book of Nehemiah completes the memoir of Nehemiah himself. I include an analysis of this chapter as an example of a type of narrative that is different from what is found in much of the rest of the OT. Based on the previous examples we have looked at, one can see that Hebrew narrative typically uses third-person omniscient narration. In two cases, however, biblical narrative uses first-person narration: the Ezra memoir (Ezra 7–10; Neh. 8–10) and the Nehemiah memoir (Neh. 1–7; 11–13). In chapter 13 Nehemiah describes what he thinks and does after returning from Persia for the second time, continuing the memoir of the previous chapters that culminates in a covenant renewal ceremony led by both Ezra and Nehemiah (Neh. 8–12).

Nehemiah 13 begins with a remembrance of the earlier covenant ceremony when the Torah was read. He recalls in particular the law that "no Ammonite or Moabite should ever be admitted into the assembly of God" (Neh. 13:1; Deut. 23:3). On this earlier occasion, as Nehemiah reminisces, "They excluded from Israel all who were of foreign descent" (Neh. 13:3). In other words, in the immediate aftermath of the renewal ceremony, the Israelites obeyed the Deuteronomic law. But Nehemiah goes on to describe how the priest Eliashib, who was in charge of the temple storerooms, allowed a foreign associate, Tobiah, to use a large room that was intended to store provisions for the temple ritual (13:4–5).

Nehemiah makes clear that he was not around when this happened. He says that he had returned to Persia in the thirty-second year of Artaxerxes, the king who had previously appointed Nehemiah as governor of Judah some twelve years earlier. Presumably, Nehemiah had finished his term in office and was reporting back to the king. After an unspecified amount of time in Persia ("some time later," 13:6), Artaxerxes gives Nehemiah permission to return to Jerusalem. Nehemiah gives the impression that he had left things in good order when he departed Jerusalem for Persia, but upon his return he finds that matters have fallen into disarray in his absence.

Nehemiah, characterized in previous chapters as an aggressive, take-charge leader, immediately sets about to rectify the situation. He begins by throwing Tobiah and his possessions out of the temple storeroom. Based on Nehemiah's own description, we can picture an angry Nehemiah physically throwing Tobiah out on his ear and tossing his possessions out into the street: "I was greatly displeased and threw all Tobiah's household goods out of the room" (13:8). Because a ritually unclean Gentile had occupied the room, Nehemiah then purifies it and restores it to its former use as a storeroom for temple provisions.

But Tobiah's appropriation of the temple storeroom is not the only violation that has occurred in Nehemiah's absence. Support for the Levites had ceased in his absence, and they were forced to abandon their temple duties and work in the fields to feed themselves and their families (13:10–11). He chastises the officials responsible and summons the Levites to return to temple service. Nehemiah then assigns trustworthy people—"Shelemiah the priest, Zadok the scribe, a Levite named Padaiah," and "Hanan son of Zakkur"—to be in charge of the storeroom provisions and make sure that the supplies were distributed to the Levites working at the temple (13:13).

Up to this point, Nehemiah has been recounting his actions upon his return, but in 13:14 he turns to God with the following petition: "Remember me for this, my God, and do not blot out what I have so faithfully done for the house of God and its services." Nehemiah asks both for divine recognition for his actions and that his efforts not be in vain.

At first glance, Nehemiah's appeal to God might strike readers as potentially self-serving, perhaps putting Nehemiah's character in a negative light. It certainly contrasts with Ezra's earlier penitential prayer, in which he asks God to forgive sins that he himself did not actually commit, but he nevertheless accepts the burden of guilt and chooses to identify with the sinful community (Ezra 9:6–15). Yet readers should not be quick to evaluate Nehemiah negatively here. His attitude is actually similar to that expressed in some laments in the book of Psalms, where the psalmist calls on God to judge the wicked but to count the righteous (including the psalmist) as innocent:

Vindicate me, LORD, according to my righteousness,
    according to my integrity, O Most High.
Bring to an end the violence of the wicked
    and make the righteous secure—
you, the righteous God
    who probes minds and hearts. (Ps. 7:8b–9)

O that you would kill the wicked, O God,
    and that the bloodthirsty would depart from me—
those who speak of you maliciously
    and lift themselves up against you for evil!
Do I not hate those who hate you, O LORD?
    And do I not loathe those who rise up against you?
I hate them with perfect hatred;
    I count them my enemies.
Search me, O God, and know my heart;
    test me and know my thoughts.
See if there is any wicked way in me,
    and lead me in the way everlasting. (Ps. 139:19–24 NRSVue)

Nehemiah differs from the psalmist because he has been put in a position of authority and power that allows him to execute God's judgment and
set things right, but his appeal to God to recognize his actions on God's
behalf appears to be justifiable, even though his speech might at first seem
self-serving.

Nehemiah does not stop with addressing violations by and against the
priests. He next tackles a broader problem that has developed in his absence:
transgression of the command to rest on the Sabbath. The fourth commandment not only requires God's people to observe the Sabbath (Exod. 20:8–11;
Deut. 5:12–15) but functions as a sign of the Mosaic covenant (Exod. 31:12–
18). A covenantal sign was like a brand, reminding God's people of the relationship established between them and God and fundamental to their identity.

Nehemiah's charge arises from his own observation: "In those days I saw
people in Judah treading winepresses on the Sabbath and bringing in grain
and loading it on donkeys" (Neh. 13:15). Nehemiah begins a diatribe against
the nobles of Judah, rebuking them for permitting commerce on the Sabbath:
"What is this wicked thing you are doing—desecrating the Sabbath day?
Didn't your ancestors do the same things, so that our God brought all this
calamity on us and on this city? Now you are stirring up more wrath against
Israel by desecrating the Sabbath" (13:17–18). Here Nehemiah impresses on
the Sabbath breakers the seriousness of their violation. He reminds them

of the horrific past consequences of this type of wicked behavior. After all, violating the Sabbath is what led to the exile in the first place.

Nehemiah's speech does not completely correct the problem. Sellers continue trying to bring goods into the city on the Sabbath. Even after he orders the gates of Jerusalem to be kept shut on the Sabbath, some sellers camp outside the gates, waiting for them to open. In response, Nehemiah goes out and personally threatens them: "Why do you spend the night by the wall? If you do this again, I will arrest you" (13:21). They stop, and Nehemiah commands the Levites to guard the gates. At this point, Nehemiah again stops to address God, asking him to remember him and show mercy toward him since he has been standing up for God's law against those in the community who are breaking it: "Remember me for this also, my God, and show mercy to me according to your great love" (13:22b).

But Nehemiah is still not yet done instituting reforms to correct violations that have cropped up in his absence. He observes certain "men of Judah who have married women from Ashdod, Ammon and Moab" (13:23). The children from these unions cannot even speak "the language of Judah" (13:24). Nehemiah tells us that he took drastic measures against these men, accosting them both verbally and physically. He rebukes them with a lengthy reported speech that again ties the present sin to the past sins that led to the exile in the first place:

> "You are not to give your daughters in marriage to their sons, nor are you to take their daughters in marriage for your sons or for yourselves. Was it not because of marriages like these that Solomon king of Israel sinned? Among the many nations there was no king like him. He was loved by his God, and God made him king over all Israel, but even he was led into sin by foreign women. Must we hear now that you too are doing all this terrible wickedness and are being unfaithful to your God by marrying foreign women?" (Neh. 13:25b–27)

He concludes his critical diatribe by reporting that he personally drove away one of Joiada's sons, who had married the daughter of the Gentile antagonist Sanballat the Horonite (13:28). By permitting this marriage, Joiada was allowing the priestly line to be corrupted, since a priest's wife must be from the people of Israel (Lev. 21:13–15). Nehemiah calls on God to remember this, with an implicit call to punish them. He then purifies the priests and Levites and sets them to their divinely given tasks. With this, Nehemiah closes the book, calling on God: "Remember me with favor" (13:31).

In sum, chapter 13 concludes Nehemiah's memoir and the whole of Ezra-Nehemiah on a note that promotes his godly work. The chapter furthers the characterization of Nehemiah as an energetic, task-oriented implementer of God's restoration of Jerusalem and Judah. The chapter also indicates that the covenant ceremony of Neh. 8–12, celebrating the rebuilding of the wall and the restoration of the law in the land after the exile, is not the end of the story. Disobedience rears its head again. The book of Nehemiah narrates the latest period recorded in the OT. It is telling that the writer of the book chooses to end it, not with the celebration of the covenant ceremony, but with a story of continued trouble and the people's continued unfaithfulness to God's covenant.

PART THREE

• • •

The ANALYSIS
of ILLUSTRATIVE
POETIC TEXTS

We turn now to a selection of poetic texts. In chapter 9, we will look at an assortment of psalms that exemplify lyric poetry. I have chosen texts from the four main types of psalms: a hymn (Ps. 46), a lament (Ps. 77), a thanksgiving prayer (Ps. 67), and a psalm of confidence (Ps. 23). We will consider the genre, poetics, and voice of each psalm. The poetics section examines how parallelism ("A, what's more, B"), various kinds of imagery, and secondary devices generate meaning in a poem.

Chapter 10 presents samples from the three books generally regarded as wisdom or didactic literature. For Proverbs, I analyze an extended discourse (9:1–8, 13–18) and a selection of short, pithy proverbs (14:1–7). For Ecclesiastes, I take a portion of Qohelet's reflections (9:11–12). And for Job, I look at the beginning of Yahweh's challenge to Job (38:2–7).

In chapter 11, the final chapter of part 3, I focus on prophetic and epic poetry. For the prophetic, I look at the opening of the prophet Nahum with its stirring depiction of Yahweh the warrior (1:2–6). For epic poetry, I chose a section of Deborah's song celebrating a victory over the Canaanites (Judg. 5:19–27).

NINE

Literary Readings of Poetic Texts from the Psalms

The book of Psalms is a collection of poems used in corporate worship. The final form of the book contains 150 poems. They were originally meant to be sung and performed with musical accompaniment, but they can also be read and studied as individual poems with sensitivity to the poetic conventions described in chapter 5. These poems are of different types or (sub)genres, and since texts can participate in more than one genre (see chap. 3), different interpreters and even the same interpreter may provide various names for the genres. However, there is wide agreement on the four categories of psalms: hymn, lament, thanksgiving, and psalm of confidence. We will look at an example from each of the four categories, describe the type and its relationship to the other types, and then provide a poetic analysis.

Earlier I introduced the concept of voice in poetry.[1] The following chapters look at poetry from different poetic traditions in the OT, and in the various types of poems, voice functions differently. The following study of specific psalms demonstrates that the voice of each poem, while almost certainly originating in response to a specific experience or event in the poet's life,[2] does not embed that experience or event in the content of the psalm. Rather, the psalms seem to have been written for communal use (and only secondarily for private use) to be shared by those who have had experiences that are similar but not identical to those of the composer. For instance, Ps. 3 in its

---

1. See chap. 5 under "Voice."
2. The historical titles give that impression for the handful of psalms that have them: Pss. 3, 7, 18, 34, 51, 52, 54, 56, 57, 60, 63, 142.

title names David as the author as he struggles with the betrayal by his son Absalom (2 Sam. 15–17). However, in the psalm itself David calls on God to rescue him from unnamed enemies without identifying Absalom specifically. In this way, any who feel unjustly attacked can use the psalm as a template for their own prayer. This communal aspect is illustrated in 1 Chronicles when David gives a psalm to Asaph and his associates, who oversee communal worship (16:7–37).

As I will show below, the voice of the psalms can often be clearly associated with the worship leader, who addresses either God or the congregation or alternates between both. Though many psalms fit this pattern, there are other possibilities. For instance, sometimes the psalmist seems to be speaking to himself (e.g., "Praise the LORD, my soul; all my inmost being, praise his holy name," Ps. 103:1). But even this bit of self-reflection was likely done in front of the congregation, perhaps with the hope of bringing the community along with him. Indeed, the last stanza of this psalm explicitly exhorts the angels and all God's works to praise God (103:20–22).

Psalm 82 is also an interesting case study. Most of it (vv. 2–7) is an oracle in which God exhorts the "gods" (probably a reference to angels) to get busy protecting the marginalized or risk losing their immortal status (v. 7). The oracle is framed by the poet's introduction and conclusion, and in the conclusion he calls on God to act on his threat: "Rise up, O God, judge the earth, for all the nations are your inheritance" (v. 8).

The next two chapters will include a section on context to position those poems within their respective books, but in this chapter I do not try to situate a psalm within the context of the whole book of Psalms. In chapter 6 I argued against the idea that individual psalms have a meaningful and intentional placement within the larger book, which I regard as an anthology.[3] In this respect, my work differs from scholars such as Wilson and Ho.

But now let us look at examples of the four main types of psalms by identifying their genre (hymn, lament, thanksgiving, psalm of confidence), describing their poetic shape, and analyzing the voice with which they speak.

Psalm 46: Hymn

Genre

Walter Brueggemann famously describes hymns as psalms of orientation. They are prayers sung when life is going in the right direction. These prayers

---

3. See chap. 6 under "The Editing of the Psalms in an Intertextual Context."

express joy in God, in others, and in oneself. The expression of this joyful attitude is what unites these hymns, although there are different reasons for the celebration expressed by these hymns. Psalm 46 rejoices in Zion as the place where God makes his protecting presence known to his people (for other Zion hymns see Pss. 48, 76, 84, 87, 122).

Poetics

A God is our refuge and strength,
B   an ever-present help in trouble.
C Therefore we will not fear, though the earth give way
D   and the mountains fall into the heart of the sea,
E though its waters roar and foam
F   and the mountains quake with their surging. (vv. 1–3)

The first stanza begins by giving expression to the central idea of the poem, that God is present to protect his people. It expresses this idea with poetic intensification: the A colon's affirmation of God's protection ("God is our refuge and strength") is furthered in the B colon's declaration that his protecting presence is continuous ("ever-present") at the most important time, when his people are "in trouble."

Hebrew poetry tends to employ fewer conjunctions, which raises the level of ambiguity when trying to determine the relationship between lines. However, with the conjunction 'al-ken ("therefore"), verse 2 begins with a clear indication of its relationship to what precedes.[4] Because "God is our refuge and strength, an ever-present help in trouble," the community ("we") will not fear. God will protect us.

The next two poetic lines then figuratively depict situations of utter chaos. In the second line, the first colon (C) communicates chaos as the earth gives way or "shakes" (hiphil of mwr II), likely referring to an earthquake. The second colon (D) evokes a more specific and intensified picture of geological chaos: the mountains fall into the sea. In Hebrew and also in broader ancient Near Eastern conception, mountains symbolized solidness and permanence, even the place where the gods dwell. By contrast, the sea was associated with chaos and even evil. An equivalent expression today might be something like "when all hell breaks loose." The bicolon in verse 3 develops and specifies the picture in verse 2b, describing the waters of the sea as roaring and foaming (E) and the mountains as quaking in response (F).

---

4. A similar causal relationship is communicated without the conjunction in Ps. 23:1, which is discussed below in the final section of this chapter.

G There is a river whose streams make glad the city of God,
H   the holy place where the Most High dwells.
I God is within her, she will not fall;
J   God will help her at break of day.
K Nations are in uproar, kingdoms fall;
L   he lifts his voice, the earth melts. (vv. 4–6)

In Hebrew the first colon (G) of the second stanza starts with the word "river" (*nahar*). The previous stanza spoke of the chaotic, uncontrolled, and dangerous sea, but this river, by contrast, runs between its banks in a controlled manner and brings life and sustenance. The river makes glad "the city of God," a clear reference to Jerusalem. The second colon of this line (H) sharpens the reference from "the city of God" to "the holy place where the Most High dwells," meaning that part of Jerusalem known as Zion, the location of the temple. That we are dealing with figurative language here is obvious because there has never been a literal river flowing through Jerusalem.

Readers already know that the city's security is because God is its "refuge and strength," and the second colon of verse 4 (H) mentions the holy place where God dwells. The first colon of verse 5 (I) drives home the point by saying "God is within her," which is why "she will not fall." Colon (J) presumes that the city and its inhabitants need God's help and proclaims that such help is coming soon ("at the break of day"). Verse 6 (cola K and L) speaks of the chaos of the nations. They are in an uproar, and they fall (K). In this they are like the waters that roar and foam (E, v. 3a). But in the response stated in L, God simply speaks ("lifts his voice") and the chaos ends ("the earth melts"). Here we should note that "earth" is an intensification of "kingdoms," and thus the melting of the earth is a reference to the eradication of the threatening enemies.

M The LORD Almighty is with us;
N   the God of Jacob is our fortress. (v. 7)

Cola M and N form a poetic line that brings the first half of the poem to a close. It constitutes a refrain that the last verse of the poem will repeat. Together the two cola provide a good example of "A, what's more, B" parallelism, but they also provide a restatement of the foundational idea of the psalm: God is present with his people in the city and thus will provide protection for them. The first colon (M) uses God's warrior title "LORD of hosts/armies" (translated rather insipidly by the NIV as "LORD Almighty") and says that he is with them. The following colon (N) speaks of God as the God of Jacob, meaning the God of "Israel," Jacob's divinely given name. Rather than simply saying that God is present "with us," the poet proclaims God as "our fortress." The semantic parallelism of the line is also buttressed by the syntactical parallelism. The two cola relate to each other as a kind of grammatical chiasm. Translating according to the Hebrew syntax, an *abb'a'* pattern appears:

  a The LORD of hosts
   b is with us;
   b' a fortress to us
  a' is the God of Jacob.

    o Come and see what the LORD has done,
    p   the desolations he has brought on the earth. (v. 8)

After the first occurrence of the refrain, the poet invites the audience to "Come and see what the LORD has done," telling them that they will see "the desolations he has brought on the earth." The purpose of the divinely wrought desolations is expressed in verse 9. In contrast to the stichometry of the NIV, I suggest that this verse is a tricolon rather than two bicola, so I format it as follows (using the NIV translation):

    Q He makes wars cease to the ends of the earth.
    R   He breaks the bow and shatters the spear;
    s   he burns the shields with fire. (v. 9)

Granted, this change makes the Q colon appear unusually long, but in the Hebrew it is not much longer than the R colon, which itself is not much longer than the S colon. This reflects a typical poetic pattern in which the second and subsequent cola are shorter rather than longer than the first. The Q colon states that God ends wars across the earth, and the R and S cola add that he does so with violence. Bow and spear, typical offensive weapons, and shields, defensive devices, may be metonymic for warriors or armies. God the warrior protects his people from attacking enemies by destroying them.

    T He says, "Be still, and know that I am God;

    U   I will be exalted among the nations,
    V   I will be exalted in the earth." (v. 10)

In verse 10 God speaks climactically, suddenly, and perhaps unexpectedly. The NIV's "he says" that introduces God's proclamation is not in the Hebrew, but it makes clear what is obvious, since the speaker demands that the raging nations "Be still, and know that I am God." This I consider a monocolon (T), followed by a nearly synonymous poetic bicolon (U and V). The verb "I will be exalted" ('*arum*) stands at the beginning of both cola, but the intensification takes place in the ending prepositional phrases: the "earth" (U) has an even wider scope than "the nations" (V).

The poem then ends with a reiteration of the refrain that first appeared in v. 7, reminding us of the central point of the poem:

w The LORD Almighty is with us;
x   the God of Jacob is our fortress. (v. 11)

Such reiteration creates a refrain and brings a strong sense of closure to the poem as well as providing a final and emphatic declaration of the protecting presence of God with his people.

Voice

Readers can know nothing about the specific historical situation that gave rise to the composition of this hymn. It celebrates God and does not speak of any specific threat but seeks to engender confidence in God in case any danger or crisis emerges. In other words, it speaks of a hypothetical or potentially future threat. Thus, as with psalms in general, this historically nonspecific poem has timeless relevance and significance.

The title attributes the psalm's composition to the "sons of Korah" (see also Pss. 42, 44–45, 47–49, 84–85, 87–88) but does not allow readers to pinpoint a specific historical moment for the composition of the psalm. Little is known about the sons of Korah. Korah was a descendant of Kohath, the son of Levi (Exod. 6:16, 18, 21), and thus a cousin of Aaron the high priest. In Num. 16 Korah along with some Reubenites rebelled against Moses and Aaron, the divinely appointed leaders of Israel at the time, and he was killed by divine judgment. However, Korah's descendants apparently continued to serve God, and in at least one place, they are mentioned as singers. At the time of King Jehoshaphat, "some Levites from the Kohathites and Korahites stood up and praised the LORD, the God of Israel, with a very loud voice" (2 Chron. 20:19).

Regardless of whether one of the sons of Korah is the actual or even the implied author, the composer seems to be writing this psalm for use in public worship. The worship leader speaks in the first-person plural to identify with the congregation and lead them into an affirmation of confidence. Hence he begins, "God is our refuge and strength" (v. 1). At one point he uses imperatives to appeal directly to the congregation: "Come and see what the LORD has done" (v. 8). Later he speaks on God's behalf to give the congregation a sense of confidence: "Be still, and know that I am God; I will be exalted among the nations, I will be exalted in the earth" (v. 10).

Psalm 77: Lament

Genre

According to Brueggemann's helpful schema, laments are the emotional opposite of hymns; they are poems of disorientation, sung when life is falling apart. The one who laments has issues with other people, themselves, and sometimes God. Many laments, including Ps. 77, conclude on a note of resolution, perhaps an expression of confidence or even praise, but not all do so (Ps. 88 is a well-known example). Laments often express dark thoughts and in some cases even express hatred toward those who have harmed them (e.g., Ps. 69:22–28). As with hymns, the reasons for laments can vary: an attacking army (e.g., Ps. 7), sickness (e.g., Ps. 6), or guilt (often called penitential psalms: e.g., Pss. 6, 32, 38, 51, 102, 130, 143). Psalm 77 suggests that God is the cause of the composer's unspecified distress, and with brutal honesty typical of laments, the psalmist unabashedly voices anger toward God. Even so, the psalmist does not express his anger publicly as the wilderness generation did and brought God's judgment on themselves (e.g., Num. 11:1–3). Instead, he talks to God privately. However, God remains silent in the first stanza.

Poetics

A I cried out to God for help;
B   I cried out to God to hear me. (v. 1)

The NIV's rendering is a bit interpretive, though not necessarily wrong. The following translation helps to bring out the relationship between the two cola more clearly:

> My voice to God, and I cry out;
>   my voice to God that he hears me.

Both cola begin the same way (*qoli 'el-'elohim*), but the verb "to cry" (*sa'aq*) is only in the first colon. The NIV translation does not express the sharpening of the second colon in the Hebrew but instead gives the impression that the A colon is the more specific of the two by giving the reason why the psalmist is calling—he wants God's help. In the Hebrew, colon A says that the psalmist cries out to God, and colon B says that he wants God to actually hear him. The Hebrew verb *'azan* in the hiphil has the sense not just of hearing but of acting on what is heard. Based on the context, the NIV brings out the idea that the psalmist is calling to God for help, but this is only implied in the Hebrew rather than made explicit.

There are two ways to understand the structure of verse 2, which further develops the psalmist's appeal to God. One might legitimately take it to be two bicola:

c When I was in distress,
d   I sought the Lord;
e at night I stretched out untiring hands,
f   and I would not be comforted. (v. 2)

On this understanding, the first colon of each bicolon names a time of distress (C and E), and the second colon of each bicolon describes the psalmist's action (D) or emotional state (F).

The relationship between C and E would be clearer if we translate the opening of C (*beyom*) not as a temporal indicator ("when") but as "in the day of" distress, thus paralleling "day" (C) with "night" (E) and forming a merism meaning all day and all night long. However, this understanding results in very short cola in the first bicolon (C and D, two morphemes each) in contrast to the second bicolon (E and F, five and three morphemes respectively).

A second way of arranging the lines avoids this problem. The verse may contain a tricolon, which is how the NIV takes it.

g When I was in distress, I sought the Lord;
h   at night I stretched out untiring hands,
i   and I would not be comforted.

This understanding results in cola that are better balanced in length. Again, by translating G as "In the day of distress, I sought the Lord," readers can see more clearly the sharpening in H with "night" coming after "day" (G) along with the intensification of the image of prayer from seeking in G to extending the hands untiringly in H. The idea that his hands are "untiring" as they are thrust upward into the air in prayer shows persistence, a praying without ceasing, even in the face of God's silence.

Verse 3 (J and K) continues to express the negative condition of the psalmist as he repeatedly turns to the Lord but receives no response.

J I remembered you, God, and I groaned;
K   I meditated, and my spirit grew faint. (v. 3)

Remembrance, an important theme running throughout this psalm, first appears here. But the psalmist's first remembrance of God apparently brings groaning rather than rejoicing. The second colon (K) intensifies by saying that this remembrance is not a momentary thought but a prolonged meditation and that the psalmist's persistence does not bring help but emotional weakening.

This leads to the psalmist's first open accusation against God:

L You kept my eyes from closing;
M   I was too troubled to speak. (v. 4)

The psalmist declares that God caused his sleepless nights. The Hebrew of L is vivid and graphic: "You grabbed the guards [i.e., lids] of my eyes." Deprived of rest, he finds himself speechless.

The psalmist then reveals what he was thinking:

N I thought about the former days,
O   the years of long ago;
P I remembered my songs in the night.
Q   My heart meditated and my spirit asked: (vv. 5–6)

He turned to the past: "former days," indeed, "years of long ago." What he remembered were the songs he sang in better times. The contrast with his present pain is unbearable. A similar thought is expressed in Pss. 42–43 (actually a single psalm, despite the chapter division), in which the psalmist contrasts the pain of his present with "how I used to go to the house of God under the protection of the Mighty One with shouts of joy and praise among the festive throng" (Ps. 42:4). Here the contrast leads the poet to further meditation (see also v. 3) followed by a series of accusations against the Lord:

R "Will the Lord reject forever?
S   Will he never show his favor again?
T Has his unfailing love vanished forever?
U   Has his promise failed for all time?

v Has God forgotten to be merciful?
w   Has he in anger withheld his compassion?" (vv. 7–9)

Previously the psalmist addressed God in the second person ("you"), but in this series of six acerbic questions that in essence cast doubt on God's veracity and dependability, the psalmist refers to God in the third person ("he"), perhaps because these questions are so biting. He feels rejected by God and asks whether God will reject him forever (R) and thus not show his favor again (S). In T through W, he asks whether God has abandoned his unfailing love, promise, mercy, and compassion—all qualities God commits himself to when he enters into a covenant with his people. Notice that the psalmist asks questions instead of making assertions, allowing God the opportunity to refute them.

The next stanza shows a change of attitude that is also based on remembrance, but remembrance of a different type. First, however, we must sort out the lexical conundrum presented in verse 10. English Bibles vary widely in their translation of this verse, as can be seen by comparing the NIV with the NRSVue:

x Then I thought, "To this I will appeal:
y   the years when the Most High stretched out his right hand." (v. 10
   NIV)

x And I say, "It is my grief
y   that the right hand of the Most High has changed." (v. 10 NRSVue)

Since I am giving a literary analysis rather than a full commentary, I will simply acknowledge that an argument can be made on lexical grounds for either translation. If the NIV is right, then verse 10 belongs to the stanza that follows, in which case, the "this" in X to which the psalmist appeals is specified in Y: God's salvific actions, the products of his right hand. If the NRSVue is correct, then verse 10 belongs to the preceding stanza as its concluding verse. Y then specifies what causes the psalmist's grief: God's salvific and protecting right hand has changed in how it treats the psalmist.

Although verse 10 is obscure, verses 11–12 are clear as the psalmist again remembers.

z "I will remember the deeds of the LORD;
AA   yes, I will remember your miracles of long ago.
BB I will consider all your works
CC   and meditate on all your mighty deeds." (vv. 11–12)

Z and AA repeat the verb "remember" in both cola, but the first is in the causative (hiphil) and the second in the intensive (piel). This intensification of the verb corresponds to a clear heightening of the verbal object, moving from "deeds of the LORD" to "miracles of long ago." The Hebrew word translated "your miracles" or "your wonders" (*pil'ekha*) connotes something beyond the ordinary. A similar heightening occurs between BB ("works") and CC ("mighty deeds"). (In verses 16–20 the psalmist develops at length what may be the most spectacular of God's past deeds.) In CC, the verb "meditate" (*sych*) appears for the third time, but as with the other thematic verb, "remember" (*zakar*), the psalmist moves from meditations/remembrances that brought about negative doubts about God to those leading to a positive confidence in God, which is expressed in the next stanza.

DD Your ways, God, are holy.
EE   What god is as great as our God?
FF You are the God who performs miracles;
GG   you display your power among the peoples.
HH With your mighty arm you redeemed your people,
II   the descendants of Jacob and Joseph. (vv. 13–15)

The meditation on and remembrance of God's mighty deeds leads the hitherto depressed psalmist to proclaim that God's ways are holy (DD), which in turn evokes the rhetorical question asserting God's uniqueness among the gods (EE). Again the psalmist declares that God performs miracles/wonders (FF; see v. 11b). In the second colon of this bicolon (GG), the psalmist makes clear that these acts reveal God's power not just to Israel but also to all the peoples on earth. In HH the mighty deeds are in particular acts of redemption for his people, who in II are identified as the descendants of Jacob and Joseph. This reminds readers of the role of the patriarchs and of the promises passed down from Abraham that God will bless Abraham and his descendants and through them all the peoples of the earth (Gen. 12:1–3). This stanza sets up the next, which dramatically recalls the most stirring act of divine power and redemption in the history of God's people, the crossing of the sea.

JJ The waters saw you, God,
KK   the waters saw you and writhed;
LL   the very depths were convulsed.
MM The clouds poured down water,
NN   the heavens resounded with thunder;

oo   your arrows flashed back and forth.
PP   Your thunder was heard in the whirlwind,
QQ   your lightning lit up the world;
RR   the earth trembled and quaked.
SS   Your path led through the sea,
TT   your way through the mighty waters,
UU   though your footprints were not seen.

VV   You led your people like a flock
WW   by the hand of Moses and Aaron. (vv. 16–20)

This stanza ends with a climactic bicolon after four concise tricola. The bicolon makes clear what is suggested throughout and was surely understood
by the original readers: the mighty deed described here is none other than the
crossing of the sea, the climactic moment of the exodus (Exod. 14–15) and
the salvation event par excellence of the HB.

The first tricolon personifies the waters of the sea as an opponent in conflict
with God. Upon seeing God (JJ), the waters respond by writhing (KK) and
convulsing down to their foundations (LL, "the very depths"). The poet thus
mythologizes a past event by presenting it as a battle not between God and
Egypt but between God and the sea. "Mythologizes" is the right word here
because of the well-known motif in the Mesopotamian (Marduk versus Tiamat) and Ugaritic (Baal versus Yam) cultures of the creator god fighting and
defeating the god of the sea, who represents chaos and anti-creation forces. In
this tricolon, the subject ("waters") is repeated verbatim in the first two cola
and then replaced in the third colon with a rarer word, "depths" (tehom), a
term that harks back to the creation account (Gen. 1:2).

In the next two tricola (MM–RR), the poet associates God with the power
of the storm. In the first, clouds pour down water (MM), thunder booms in the
sky (NN), and God's arrows flash (OO), certainly a reference to lightning. The
next tricolon (PP–RR) again features God's thunder (PP) and lightning (QQ),
which result in the convulsions of the earth itself.

The fourth and final tricolon turns attention to God's making a path
through the sea (SS) and a way through the mighty waters (TT). The "mighty
waters" (mayim rabbim) is itself a resonant mythological allusion to the waters of chaos (Pss. 29:3; 93:4; Isa. 17:12–13; Jer. 51:55).[5] God's path through
the waters of chaos left no observable evidence of his presence ("though your
footprints were not seen," UU).

5. Mays, "Some Cosmic Connotations."

The climactic final poetic line, a bicolon rather than a tricolon, stands in contrast to the violence of God's battle with the waters of chaos described in the preceding stanza. The image is one of tranquility as God, through the agency of Moses and Aaron, leads his people through the waters as a shepherd leads his flock.

Voice

The title of Ps. 77 names Asaph as the composer (see also Pss. 50, 73–76, 77–83), though for the purpose of literary analysis, whether he is actually the composer is not relevant. Asaph is known in the historical books as one who presented music before the Lord when the ark was brought to Jerusalem during the time of David (1 Chron. 15:16–22). David appointed him along with Heman and Ethan to be in charge of the music at the tabernacle, and they and their descendants continued in this role after Solomon built the temple (1 Chron. 6:31–47).

This psalm reflects a turbulent period in the composer's life, but it is written in a way that allows later readers to use the psalm as a template for their own prayers in similar but not necessarily identical situations. That is, by identifying with the speaker, later worshipers can use his words to articulate their own struggles and their own potential resolution.

It is striking that the psalmist alternates between speaking *of* God in the third person and speaking *to* God in the second person. In the first stanza (vv. 1–2), the composer addresses an unnamed other (the congregation?) and describes his difficult night prayers. In the second stanza (vv. 3–6), the poet addresses God directly as his first remembrance of God turns bitter: he accuses God of being the one troubling him so that he cannot sleep.

This leads the psalmist to level further cutting accusations against God in the form of rhetorical questions (vv. 7–9) posed in the third person (e.g., "Will the Lord reject forever?" v. 7). As I mentioned in my poetical analysis, these accusations boil down to a charge that God has not kept his covenant promises. Such a charge is quite bold and may explain the shift to the third person.

The next stanza (vv. 10–13) marks a transition from accusation to meditation on and remembrance of God's former deeds. The stanza starts by referring to God in the third person, "I will remember the deeds of the LORD," as if the poet is talking to himself or others. He then turns to God and again speaks to him directly: "I will remember your miracles of long ago" (v. 11).

The next two stanzas stay in the second person for the most part, though verse 13 first speaks to God, acknowledging God's holiness (v. 13a), before apparently turning to the congregation with a rhetorical question: "What god is as great as our God?" (v. 13b).[6] The psalmist continues to praise God by citing the crossing of the sea, extolling the Lord by recounting how he rescued the Israelites from the Egyptians.

Psalm 67: Thanksgiving Psalm

Genre

Thanksgiving psalms are what Brueggemann names "psalms of reorientation," sung after God answers a lament and restores order in the life of the singer. They typically respond to some specific act of deliverance or blessing. Although Ps. 67 is perhaps not the clearest representative of a thanksgiving poem (Ps. 30 provides a good example), it is appropriate to see it as participating in this subgenre, and it displays many of the important elements characteristic of this type of psalm. Although this psalm petitions God for blessing, it also acknowledges that God has done so already with the harvest (L–M) and expresses hope for future blessings as well.

Poetics

A May God be gracious to us and bless us
B   and make his face shine on us—
C so that your ways may be known on earth,
D   your salvation among all nations.

E May the peoples praise you, God;
F   may all the peoples praise you.
G May the nations be glad and sing for joy,
H   for you rule the peoples with equity
I   and guide the nations of the earth.
J May the peoples praise you, God;
K   may all the peoples praise you.

L The land yields its harvest;
M   God, our God, blesses us.
N May God bless us still,
O   so that all the ends of the earth will fear him.

6. The Hebrew has "What god is great like God"; NIV adds "our," for which a contextual argument can be made.

The poem begins with a bicolon (A–B) that recalls the blessing bestowed on the community by the high priest:

> The LORD bless you
>   and keep you;
> the LORD make his face shine on you
>   and be gracious to you;
> the LORD turn his face toward you
>   and give you peace. (Num. 6:24–26)

The psalm most likely reflects the earlier priestly blessing, though the chronology is not that important. In Numbers the priest blesses the community, but here the worship leader petitions God on behalf of the community for blessing (see below on voice), and the requests are also shorter and in a different order in the psalm. The psalmist asks God to extend grace and bless the community (A) and to be favorably present with them (B).

The second bicolon (C–D) encourages God to bless the people (A) so that God's "ways may be known on earth." Here D sharpens C by specifying the type of ways God should make known on the earth (i.e., his salvation, or in an OT context, his victory) and by narrowing "earth" to "the nations."

The second stanza opens and closes with the same refrain (E–F, J–K). The first colon of each appeals to God with the vocative. The subject "peoples" and the verb "praise" are repeated verbatim in each colon. Although these lines are highly repetitive, the second colon of each pair is made emphatic with the addition of "all." The lines between the refrains form a tricolon (G–I), the opening colon of which picks up and expands on the idea of the peoples praising God by saying that they are glad and sing for joy (G). The second and third cola give the reason for their joy and praise: God rules with equity (H) and guides them (I).

The concluding stanza (L–O) acknowledges God's blessing and asks that it continue. The concrete expression of God's blessing is the harvest, which gives God's people sustenance. Rather than the typical movement from general to specific in the second colon, the more specific reference to harvest (L) precedes the more general one about blessing (M). God can bless in many different ways, but here his blessing manifests itself in providing an abundant harvest. The poem concludes with a request for continued blessing (N), with the subsequent colon (O) providing the rationale for why God should do this: so the nations may fear God.

Although this can be categorized as a thanksgiving psalm, it has connections with wisdom as well. The focus on blessing and evoking a blessing is typical of wisdom as is the idea of the fear of God. Specifically, the hope is that people will obey God because they recognize that he is their creator.[7]

Voice

No composer is named in the title of Ps. 67, but whoever composed it did so "for the director of music." In other words, whatever the specific inspiration for the composition of the psalm, it was intended for use in the public assembly. The other parts of the title—"With stringed instruments. A psalm. A song"—also imply a public performance. Of course, this primary purpose does not preclude private use of the psalm, just as church hymns today, though primarily used in public worship, can also be sung in private worship.

Thus, the speaker of the psalm (voice) is the worship leader, who begins with a blessing that resembles the high-priestly blessing. He pronounces the blessing over the congregation with whom he identifies—"May God be gracious to *us* and bless *us*" (v. 1a)—with the hope that God will hear and respond.

In the second stanza (E–K), the poet now explicitly addresses God ("you, God"), requesting that not just the people of Israel but all nations would praise God because he rules with equity and guides the nations.

The final stanza (L–O) shifts the addressee again as the worship leader reverts to speaking to the congregation. First, he asserts that God has indeed blessed them with an abundant harvest (L–M). Then in the final cola of the poem, the leader again confers a blessing on the people, asking that God continue giving abundant harvests, which will in turn lead the other nations to fear God (N–O).

Psalm 23: Psalm of Confidence

Genre

In Walter Brueggemann's triad of psalm types—hymn (orientation), lament (disorientation), and thanksgiving (reorientation)—the latter is sung when God answers the lament and is in the process of restoring a person to their previous condition (reorientation). But what if God does not resolve the crisis that led to the lament? Should one just continue lamenting? This may be the right approach in some cases, but Psalms offers another way to respond, by moving to trust in the midst of suffering and trouble. Glenn Pemberton has identified these as psalms of confidence.[8] And there is no more powerful example of such a psalm than Ps. 23.

---

7. For the concept of the fear of God in the OT, see Longman, *Fear of the Lord*, 12–15.
8. Pemberton, *After Lament*.

Poetics

Psalm 23 is perhaps the best-known psalm of confidence, a reputation due largely to its poetic power. Its focus is on God as shepherd and his people as his sheep. Indeed, this theme is expressed in the opening verse, which could be considered a bicolon in which B expresses the consequence of A:

A The LORD is my shepherd,
B   I lack nothing.

But perhaps better is to take this opening line as a monocolon, whose premise is developed in the rest of the psalm.

The LORD is my shepherd, I lack nothing.

In either reading, the lack of a conjunction between the two parts creates some ambiguity, but the relationship is most likely cause and effect: "*Since* the LORD is my shepherd, *therefore* I lack nothing."

Verses 2 and 3 then expand the shepherd metaphor:

C He makes me lie down in green pastures,
D   he leads me beside quiet waters,
E   he refreshes my soul.
F He guides me along the right paths
G   for his name's sake.

In the Hebrew, lines C and D share a similar syntactical pattern, which binds them together. It differs from the NIV by placing the prepositional phrases before the subject and verb. An English translation mimicking the Hebrew would look something like this:

In green pastures he makes me lie down,
   beside quiet waters he leads me.

As a shepherd provides for and guides his sheep, so God provides for and guides his people. The imagery creates a picture that evokes a sense of calm trust. The third colon of this poetic line (E, "he refreshes my soul") breaks from the metaphor momentarily and speaks directly about the effect the shepherd-like God has on his follower.

The following bicolon speaks of God the Shepherd's guidance of the sheep along "right [i.e., straight] paths," which fits with a wisdom motif portraying the path of wisdom as straight (Prov. 3:6; 4:11; 11:5) and the path of folly as crooked (2:15; 10:9). The Hebrew word for "right" or "straight" is related to the Hebrew ethical term for "righteousness," so readers should likely hear a double entendre here in which physically straight paths also suggests morally righteous paths. The final colon (G) is a purpose clause explaining why God provides, guides, nourishes, and refreshes: it is for his own reputation, his own name's sake.

Verse 4 may be formatted in the following way to make the relationship between the cola clearer:

H Even though I walk through the darkest valley,
I   I will fear no evil,

J for you are with me;

K your rod and your staff,
L   they comfort me.

Between the two bicola, a single colon (J) pivots from one to the other. In the first bicolon, the first colon (H) imagines a situation of great distress. The opening of the poem describes how God the Shepherd provides for, leads, and guides his sheep, including the psalmist, who is speaking in the first person. Here the poet acknowledges that his path (a metaphor for life) can go through dangerous places. The "dark valley" metaphor does not identify a specific threat, thus allowing later readers to see their own particular life situations expressed in the poem.[9] In the second colon (I), the psalmist declares that, despite the threat, he will not fear the evil that he faces. The pivot colon proclaims why he will have no fear: "You," God, are present "with me." The shepherd does not abandon his sheep when trouble comes.

In the next bicolon, the first colon (K) communicates God's presence in a way that makes the shepherd metaphor explicit by way of synecdoche. The shepherd's tools for protecting and guiding are tokens of God's presence. With his rod and his staff, a shepherd can both gently guide the sheep and fend off predators, enabling the psalmist as God's sheep to experience comfort in the face of danger.

9. Due to the enduring influence of the KJV, some may expect to read "through the valley of the shadow of death." With rare exceptions (see the ESV), this reading is largely thought to be an error, which has been corrected by comparative philology. Of course, the threat of death is a good example of walking through one of life's dark valleys.

The final two verses shift metaphors from God as shepherd to God as host, though it is likely that the poet thinks of the shepherd as the host.

M You prepare a table before me
N   in the presence of my enemies.
O You anoint my head with oil;
P   my cup overflows.

Lines M and O address God directly in the second person.[10] God prepares a table for a meal and anoints the psalmist's head with oil for refreshment.[11] The second colon of the first bicolon (N) declares that the table is set in the presence of enemies. With this second acknowledgment of a continuing threat, the composer again signals that he is writing a psalm of confidence. In the second colon of the second bicolon (P), the psalmist uses the metaphor of the cup of salvation or blessing (Pss. 16:5; 116:13; 1 Cor. 10:16)[12] to express the happy consequences of God's hosting.

The psalm ends with a lengthy bicolon.

Q Surely your goodness and love will follow me all the days of my life,
R   and I will dwell in the house of the LORD forever [Heb.: "for length of days"].

The clearest parallel between Q and R is in the expression of time that ends each colon: "all the days of my life" (Q) parallels "for length of days" (R). The NIV and almost all other translations of R have "forever," feeling the pressure of a long-standing rendering dating back to the KJV. Such a translation makes the expression in R seem like an intensification of Q, moving from the composer's lifetime to something beyond, but the Hebrew does not support this idea. Instead, the progression is from the psalmist speaking of God's action toward him (Q) to speaking of his own response to God's action (R). In Q, he proclaims that God's goodness and love (the term *chesed* is something more like covenantal/loyal love) will follow him. These divine attributes, strikingly personified here, are a kind of metonymy for God himself. If the shepherd image is still operative, as I think it is, then perhaps they are like the sheepdogs that keep the sheep in line. In his response, the psalmist

10. The verb in M is an imperfect second-person singular verb, while the verb in O is in the perfect aspect.
11. Applied to soothe and perhaps clean the skin in the dry climate of Israel.
12. The opposite is the cup of judgment: Isa. 51:17, 22; Jer. 25:15–17; Ezek. 23:31–34; Mark 14:36; Rev. 16:19.

declares that he will dwell in God's house for his whole life (R). Since God's house, the sanctuary, did not include residences, this is a poetic way of saying that he is determined to stay in God's presence.

Although the focus of this volume is literary analysis, Ps. 23 raises an important historical consideration. Knowing the historical context helps us determine the original meaning of the shepherd metaphor. In the historical setting in which Ps. 23 was composed, that of ancient Israel, there is abundant evidence that the shepherd is a metaphor for a leader, particularly the king (cf. 2 Sam. 5:2; Ezek. 34), and this is also supported by the broader ancient Near Eastern context.[13]

Voice

The title of Ps. 23 simply states "A psalm of David," so David is at least the implied author, if not the actual author. The connection with David is of interest because David himself was a shepherd of sheep in his youth (2 Sam. 7:8) as well as a shepherd of people as king (2 Sam. 5:2). The psalm was surely written by someone intimately acquainted with shepherding. But the poems in the Psalms were not written to be personal memoirs and do not include particulars from the composers' lives so that they can be read in more than one way.

Regardless of its authorship, Ps. 23 is found in a collection of poems used in corporate worship. We might imagine a worship leader praying this psalm before a congregation and speaking on their behalf or an individual offering this as a personal prayer to God. Either way, the psalm's voice expresses confidence in God as a provider, protector, and leader.

There is an interesting shift of address between verses 3 and 4. The psalm begins by addressing the Lord in the third person: "The LORD is my shepherd. . . . He makes me lie down." This could be seen as an affirmation of confidence by the worship leader to the congregation or as a personal declaration of confidence by an individual. Verse 4 transitions to the second person as the composer addresses God: "I will fear no evil, for you are with me. . . ." Again, the voice of the psalm could be that of the worship leader speaking on behalf of the people or of an individual speaking on their own behalf. The second-person address makes the psalm seem more like a prayer. Yet the poem ends by resuming third-person address with its declaration "I will dwell in the house of the LORD for length of days" (my trans.).

---

13. Although the value of historical context may be obvious to some, not all scholars consider the historical context to be relevant, and as I have learned from personal experience, this can be the source of strong disagreement.

TEN

Literary Readings of Poetic Texts from Wisdom Literature

Having looked at selected psalms, I now turn to passages from the Wisdom literature—particularly Proverbs, Ecclesiastes, and Job—to examine them in light of the poetic conventions described in chapter 5. This is not the place to defend at length the classification of these three books as wisdom, although I address the question briefly elsewhere in the book.[1] As with my study of Psalms in the previous chapter, I will ask questions about genre, voice, and poetics, and we will see that in these books poetic voice operates differently from the Psalms. In addition, I add a section on context, which I did not have in the chapter on Psalms, because the context created by the book as a whole shapes the interpretation of individual passages in these books more than it does in the Psalms. My representative passages are Prov. 9:1–6, 13–18; 14:1–7; Eccles. 9:11–12; and Job 38:2–7.

Proverbs 9:1–6, 13–18: Woman Wisdom or Woman Folly?

Context

These two poems occur at a pivotal point in the book of Proverbs, and their significance depends in large measure on their placement in the book of Proverbs, so I have begun my analysis with a section on context. Because

---

1. See chap. 3 under "Recent Developments in Genre Theory"; see also Longman, *Fear of the Lord*, esp. 276–82.

of the importance of context in this case, these poems stand in contrast to the psalms discussed in the previous chapter, whose literary context within the larger psalter had no significance.

Proverbs 9:1–8 and 9:13–18 appear at the end of the first major part of the book and provide a crucial transition to what follows. Indeed, these two poems provide an interpretive lens through which the second half of the book should be read. Proverbs 1–9 constitutes a series of speeches. These are typically lectures given by a father to his son, but on occasion, as here, they come from a woman whose name is Wisdom, a character who personifies the very life the readers are urged to pursue. In Prov. 2:20–33 Woman Wisdom speaks directly to her male audience; in Prov. 8 her speech is introduced by the narrator (on which see below under "Voice"). After assessing the voice and poetics of these two poems, I will return in the conclusion to the significance of context and will reflect on the possible function of the passage that sits between these two poems (9:7–12).

Genre

Traditionally, at least from the mid-nineteenth century, the book of Proverbs has been classified as Wisdom literature, but recently this genre identification has been questioned, most notably by Will Kynes,[2] and I both agree and disagree with Kynes's assessment. Both of us believe that texts can participate in more than one genre, and while there are differences in Proverbs, Job, and Ecclesiastes that allows them to participate in other genres, all these books have wisdom as a central focus in one way or another. In the case of Proverbs, the preamble (1:1–7) announces that the purpose of the book is to teach wisdom, and it does so through discourses (lectures, speeches) and pithy aphorisms.

Two such discourses are Prov. 9:1–6 and 9:13–18, which form a pair. Although these discourses are lengthy compared to the succinct proverbs that follow in chapters 10–31, they are brief compared to the longer example in 2:1–22. I call them discourses, speeches, or lectures because typically they are the words of a father to his son, urging him to acquire wisdom and instructing him in right behavior. He is to stay on the path of wisdom, which leads to life, and avoid the path of folly, which leads to death.

In a few discourses, the main speaker is not the father but Woman Wisdom, and in one discourse (9:13–18), the main speaker is Woman Folly. These women address the broader public, but their poetic voice seems implicitly to

2. Kynes, *Obituary for "Wisdom Literature."*

be associated with the father, whose words provide an introduction.[3] In Prov. 1, the poetic voice introduces Woman Wisdom in verses 20–21 as speaking in the public square, and verses 22–33 turn out to be one long exhortation to enter into a relationship with her or suffer the consequences. In Prov. 8, the poetic voice again alerts us to Wisdom's speech in the public square, where paths meet at the high point of the way. Then in a lengthy speech (8:4–36), Wisdom introduces herself as the epitome of the virtues of wisdom, speaking of her involvement in the creation of the cosmos and urging her listeners to pay attention to her in order to find life.

The poetic voice also introduces the speeches of Woman Wisdom and Woman Folly that form the two poems we are analyzing. Though their speeches are short, the purpose of the poetic voice is to focus attention on their invitations, which are described below.

Voice

We do not know the identity of the actual author of these poems. Although the opening verse of the book of Proverbs mentions Solomon by name, it is clear that Solomon did not write every part of the book. Other contributors mentioned include the wise (22:17; 24:23), Agur (30:1), and Lemuel (31:1). Also mentioned are the "men of Hezekiah" (25:1), who apparently added more proverbs of Solomon hundreds of years after Solomon's death. Because 10:1 announces that the proverbs that follow are from Solomon, we can infer that the previous material, including Prov. 9, is not Solomonic. However, none of this ambiguity about authorship bears on the meaning of Prov. 9, and in the absence of a personal name, I will simply refer to the author by the title poet or sage.

The first poem begins with the poetic voice introducing Woman Wisdom and her actions. The voice is not named or identified, but since the dominant voice in the preceding discourses is the father's, perhaps we can assume that it is the father who introduces the Woman to the men who are walking along the road. He also introduces and gives a direct quotation from the Woman to the men who are walking by (see G, I–L below). Her speech is an invitation to the men to join her in a meal that she has prepared. The narrator interrupts her speech (see H) to identify her addressees as "those without sense."

The second poem (9:13–18) also begins with the poetic voice introducing a character, this time a woman named Folly. In contrast to Wisdom, who has already appeared earlier in the collection, Folly makes her first and only

---

3. This discussion of voice here anticipates the next section and shows that voice and genre are interrelated, voice helping us identify the genre(s) a text participates in.

appearance here. The poetic voice presents her in very uncomplimentary terms, introducing and quoting her invitation to presumably the same group of men, those who are immature ("simple") and lack sense. While the poetic voice does not evaluate or comment on Woman Wisdom's invitation, he issues a harsh warning to those tempted to accept Woman Folly's invitation to dine (see below).

The poetic voice and the two women speak to men who are passing by, who form the implied audience. Those who hear or read Prov. 9 are the actual audience and identify with the men who are the implied audience.

Poetics

A Wisdom has built her house;
B   she has hewn her seven pillars.
C She has slaughtered her animals; she has mixed her wine;
D   she has also set her table.
E She has sent out her female servants; she calls
F   from the highest places in the town [city, NIV]
G "You who are simple, turn in here!"
H   To those without sense she says,
I "Come, eat of my bread
J   and drink of the wine I have mixed.
K Lay aside immaturity and live,
L   and walk in the way of insight." (Prov. 9:1–6 NRSVue)

M Folly is an unruly woman;
N   she is simple and knows nothing.
O She sits at the door of her house,
P   on a seat at the highest point of the city,
Q calling out to those who pass by,
R   who go straight on their way,
S   "Let all who are simple come to my house!"
T To those who have no sense she says,
U   "Stolen water is sweet;
V   food eaten in secret is delicious!"
W But little do they know that the dead are there,
X   that her guests are in the realm of the dead. (Prov. 9:13–18)

Wisdom was personified as a woman earlier in Proverbs (1:20–33; chap. 8), so we should not be surprised to encounter her again here. As we read, we are able to be more specific about the role Wisdom plays in Proverbs and in this poem in particular. She is a builder, not a destroyer, just like a human woman who is wise (14:1). She has built her house (A), which has "seven pillars" (B), with B sharpening A. Hers is no ordinary house; it has seven (a number symbolizing totality) pillars, an architectural feature of grandeur and permanence.[4] The poetic voice thus presents her as an industrious woman of substance.

Her industriousness extends to the preparation of a sumptuous meal of meat and wine. This is a banquet beyond the ordinary. Meat was not a staple in the ancient Near East but was a delicacy enjoyed only by the wealthy or on special occasions.[5] The wine is also special, being "mixed," likely with honey or spices. She has prepared not only the meal (C) but also the table at which she will entertain her guests (D).

We next learn that Wisdom has not prepared this meal for only herself or her household: she takes on the role of hostess and invites guests to join her (E). Showing again that she is a woman of substance, she sends her servants to gather the guests. The second colon of this poetic bicolon (F) reveals that her house is in a significant location, "the highest point of the city" (NIV). The location of Woman Wisdom's home furthers our understanding of whom she represents. Only one house was permitted on the highest point of the city, and that was the temple. Therefore, Woman Wisdom stands not just for any wisdom, but for God's wisdom, and by metonymy, for God himself.

The next bicolon (G–H) fits together by the parallel between "simple" (better rendered "immature") and "those without sense." Such persons belong neither to the wise nor to the fools, but their future hangs in the balance based on their choice. Woman Wisdom wants them to join her for a meal so that they will go the right way, toward wisdom rather than folly. The underlying metaphor illustrated by the Woman is hospitality. To accept Woman Wisdom's invitation to a meal is to accept an invitation for relationship. As is true today but even more so in the ancient Near East, dining with someone deepens the relationship. Since Woman Wisdom is a personification of God's wisdom and God himself, to dine with Woman Wisdom is to enter into a relationship with Yahweh.

In her invitation, she beckons the immature to come to her house and consume the food (earlier identified as meat) and drink the mixed wine, the banquet she has prepared. Accepting this invitation will create a relationship between Woman Wisdom and the invitee, the banquet surely representing the wisdom that Yahweh offers in the guise of Woman Wisdom.

4. The suggestions of Patrick Skehan ("Seven Columns") that the seven pillars represent the seven planets known at the time, and thus the cosmos, or that they refer to seven previous hypothetical speeches strike me as overly speculative and lacking justification.

5. Whybray, *Book of Proverbs*, 144.

The final bicolon of Woman Wisdom's speech exhorts those who accept her invitation to change their life by giving up their immature ways (K) and adopting a constructive manner of living (L). The "way" is a metaphor for one's life and conduct. But there is more than one way to live: the way of folly and the way of wisdom (here called "the way of insight") are polar opposites. The simple, or immature, have not fully blossomed into either way of life, but without correction, their way will lead to folly. Woman Wisdom wants to make sure that the immature become wise rather than foolish.

After an intervening passage (vv. 7–12), which is discussed below, we are introduced to Woman Folly, a figure who stands in contrast to Woman Wisdom. This passage is her first and only appearance in the book of Proverbs. While Wisdom was first introduced as a builder, Folly is described as unruly (M)— that is, someone who is disruptive and cannot be controlled. Wisdom serves a constructive role, while Folly destroys and tears down. She does not bring order, but chaos. Not only that, but she herself is immature ("simple") and ignorant (N).

She too has a house where she sits and from which she issues an invitation to dine. Woman Wisdom's magnificent house has seven pillars, but we hear only of the door of Folly's house, in front of which she sits (O), though the second colon of this line specifies that her seat is at the "highest point of the city" (P). On the surface, this location sounds similar to that of Woman's Wisdom's house and thus suggests deity, though Folly represents the false gods that vie for the attention of God's people. However, the NIV and NRSVue obscure a difference in the Hebrew. Wisdom's location is more literally translated "the pinnacle of the heights of the city" (*'al-gappe merome qaret*, v. 3), which perhaps suggests a point higher than merely "the highest point of the city" (*merome qaret*, v. 14), the spot occupied by Folly, though both phrases still suggest divine status.

The next line (Q–R) announces Folly's invitation and names the recipients, those passing by (Q), who are going straight on their way (R). Path/way is a metaphor for the journey of life, and walking on a straight path may refer to the immature people who have not yet fully committed to wisdom but have also not yet chosen folly. Woman Folly of course wants to change this.

Folly's invitation (S) is exactly the same as Woman Wisdom's (G). In the second colon (T; cf. H) the poetic voice breaks in to identify the invitees as those who lack sense, another way to refer to the immature. That the identical invitation comes from both women highlights the competition between them. They are appealing to the same group, both the implied audience of men who are passing by and the actual audience of later readers. A decision must be made.

When Woman Folly speaks again (U–V), she tells those passing by about the food and drink she is offering. Woman Wisdom's meal of meat and mixed wine sounds luxurious and delectable, but Folly's is bland (water and food). She hopes that the guilty pleasure of consuming her meal (water that is stolen and food eaten in secret) will lure men into a relationship by appealing to their baser instincts. Likely too, this meal stands for the "knowledge" that folly will impart to them. While Wisdom's teaching is always public (8:1–3), Folly tries to hook people by suggesting that her knowledge is secret. Of course, the wary listener is already wondering whether there is any real substance to the meal she offers.

If there is any doubt about what Woman Folly is actually offering, the poetic voice steps in with the concluding line of the poem and removes all uncertainty (W–X). Those who accept her invitation and go to her house will join others who have already done so: the dead (W). This Hebrew word is not the more common word for dead but rather suggests the ancestral shades (*repha'im*). The second colon (X) makes clear that the dead referred to here are those who accepted her invitation ("her guests") and as a result are in the "realm ["depths"] of the dead [Sheol]."

Conclusion

The two poems in Prov. 9 form a contrasting pair. In the first poem, Woman Wisdom invites people to join her in a sumptuous meal at her grand house at the pinnacle of the city's highest point. In the second poem, Woman Folly invites the same group to join her in a secret meal at her home located at the highest point of the city. Those invited—the implied audience of passersby and the later actual audience who identify with the passersby—must decide between the two invitations. The poetic voice clearly urges acceptance of Wisdom's offer.

I have suggested that the location of these two women's homes connects them with the divine realm. Woman Wisdom represents Yahweh and his wisdom; Woman Folly stands for any false god (Baal, Astarte, Marduk, Ishtar) whom the Israelites might be tempted to worship in place of Yahweh. Of course, actual readers today are not tempted to worship one of these ancient Near Eastern deities, but the choice of dining with Folly can stand for putting anything or anyone in the place of God. The NT associates Woman Wisdom with Christ (John 1:1–3; Col. 1:15–20), and Christians who read Prov. 9 in light of the NT might think of dining with Woman Wisdom as equivalent to entering into an intimate relationship with Christ.[6]

6. To be developed in my volume on the OT and theology.

The obvious similarities and contrasts between Prov. 9:1–6 and 9:13–18 are clear, but it is not clear how the intervening passage, 9:7–12, relates to these two passages, and one cannot be dogmatic about any explanation that is offered. Proverbs 9:7–9 advises advice-givers to instruct the wise and avoid interacting with mockers because it is counterproductive. Then 9:10–12 echoes an earlier admonition in 1:7 regarding "the fear of the LORD" being "the beginning of wisdom" and is perhaps intended to give a sense of closure, an *inclusio* at the end of this first major part of the book of Proverbs. R. W. Byargeon notes that just as the invitations from Wisdom and Folly provide a contrast and summon us to make a choice, so this intervening section also sharply divides into two ways, the way of wisdom and the way of the fool/mocker. In his opinion, verses 1–6 and 13–18 are "illustrative," while verses 7–12 have the "indicative" contrast. In other words, "each type of individual mentioned in 9:7–12 corresponds with the two women in Proverbs 9."[7]

It is significant that these two poems appear in the final chapter of the discourse section of Proverbs, before the proverbs themselves (Prov. 10–31). The proverbs teach and encourage wise attitudes, behaviors, and speech, while warning about foolish ones. Many of the proverbs just seem like good advice, such as "Lazy hands make for poverty, but diligent hands bring wealth" (10:4). Proverbs like these lead some, including scholars, to downplay the theological meaning of the book of Proverbs, some even suggesting that the book, or at least parts of it, is secular.[8] The personification of Wisdom and Folly in Prov. 9, however, shows that wisdom and folly are theological to the core. And an interpreter who reads Prov. 10:4 in context could say that hard work is not just wise on a practical level but shows that one is acting like a proper worshiper of Yahweh. Laziness reveals the opposite, that the person not only lacks practical wisdom but is acting like one who worships false gods.

Proverbs 14:1–7: Assorted Proverbs

Context

We have already discussed the two-part structure of the book of Proverbs. and 14:1–7 occurs in the second part of the book, which is subdivided as follows:

7. Byargeon, "Structure and Significance," 373.
8. This is the view of Walter Brueggemann, which he expressed in one of his early writings; see *In Man We Trust*, 81–82.

10:1–22:16	First Solomonic Collection
22:17–24:34	Sayings of the Wise
25:1–29:27	Second Solomonic Collection (added by the men of Hezekiah)
30:1–33	Sayings of Agur
31:1–9	Sayings of Lemuel
31:10–31	Poem of the Virtuous Woman

As the preceding outline indicates, Prov. 14:1–7 is a part of the first Solomonic collection. But is there any structure within this collection that relates one proverb to another, or are they only loosely connected? The answer to this question is debated and has some influence on interpretation.

Although there are older examples,[9] efforts to find an underlying structure to the proverbs in chapters 10–31 began to proliferate around 1980 and seem to have peaked around 2000. Elsewhere I have offered a more substantial critique of these attempts;[10] here I will say only that I am not persuaded that the sage editors of the collection intended readers to recognize connections between proverbs that would affect the meaning of individual proverbs. My main objections are twofold. First, those who have argued for a deeper structure employ far too many and varied criteria to draw those connections. Knut Heim, for instance, uses phonological, semantic, syntactic, and thematic repetition in order to find coherence between units of proverbs.[11] Human beings are notorious for the ability and the inherent tendency to imagine connections between even random bits of data.[12] Imposing meaning on all the different types of repetition is particularly problematic in a book like Proverbs, which employs a limited basic vocabulary related to wisdom and folly, making repetition inevitable rather than meaningful.

My second objection stems from the first. Scholars appeal to a wide variety of criteria for grouping related proverbs into units, but they rarely agree with each other. For example, Bruce Waltke treats Prov. 14:1–7, 8–15, and 15–32 as units,[13] but Heim treats 14:5–12 as a unit, which cuts across Waltke's pattern. Waltke explains this by saying that Heim "was misled" because the union between the first two units of chapter 14 is "so skillful."[14] This suggests to

9. E.g., Boström, *Paronomasi i den äldre hebreiska maschallitteraturen.*
10. Longman, *Proverbs,* 38–40.
11. Heim, *Like Grapes of Gold.*
12. This is similar to the attempt to read the book of Psalms as a cohesive book rather than as an anthology, an approach I critique in chap. 6 under "The Editing of the Psalms."
13. Waltke, *Proverbs: Chapters 1–15,* 583. He treats 14:15 as a "Janus" verse, to be read with what precedes and what follows it.
14. Waltke, *Proverbs: Chapters 1–15,* 583.

me that the units are not as clearly delineated from each other as some would claim, and attempts to delineate such units are overly clever. Given the lack of agreement on the exact divisions of meaningful units, using a neighboring proverb to interpret another proverb will inevitably be misleading. I believe that the proverbs of chapters 10–31 are randomly organized[15] and should be interpreted individually within the context of the book as a whole. The context of chapters 10–31 is of course the long theological shadow cast on them by the discourses in chapters 1–9. So in contrast to Waltke, who treats 14:1–7 as a chiasm by (in my opinion) mislabeling the main point of the verses, I treat each proverb individually.

Genre

While discussing the genre of the two poems in Prov. 9 (see above), I addressed the question of the genre of the book of Proverbs as a whole. I also mentioned the two-part structure of the book of Proverbs, and while not every part of Prov. 10–31 is well represented by the selection from Prov. 14:1–7,[16] these verses are largely typical of the contents of that section. The proverbs in 14:1–7 are short, pithy observations, admonitions, and prohibitions intended to instruct a person in how to act, speak, and think in order to navigate life well. However, they teach more than just how to navigate life on a practical level. They also encourage ethical behavior and should be read in the context of the admonition to "fear God/the LORD" and the need to enter into a relationship with Woman Wisdom. In other words, the speech, actions, and attitudes of the wise reveal that they are in a proper relationship with God.

Different genres make different types of truth claims, and proverbs do not claim always to be true. Many proverbs are true only when applied to the right situations. This can be seen most clearly in the proverbial pair at 26:4–5, where verse 4 warns against answering a fool according to his folly and verse 5 encourages one to do so. It is not enough to know the proverbs; one must also be able to read people and situations well enough to determine which proverb applies at the moment.[17]

Not only are proverbs generally not statements of universal truth, but they also do not make promises or offer guarantees. This is simply not what

---

15. The random nature of the collection may result from what was likely a prolonged period of collection. This also explains why some proverbs appear more than once. See Snell, *Twice-Told Proverbs*.

16. The book of Proverbs contains more than just proverbs. For instance, it ends with a lengthy connected poem (31:10–31) about the "wife of noble character" (*'eshet chayil*, v. 10), or "virtuous woman" (KJV).

17. Longman, "To Answer or Not to Answer."

proverbs do. Rather, they instruct a person on the best route to a desired conclusion, all other things being equal.

Voice

Earlier I addressed the issue of actual authorship of the book of Proverbs as a complicated matter since the book was not written by one person at one time. This raises questions about the authorship of any particular part. Proverbs 10:1 provides the heading for the part of Proverbs that includes 14:1–7, and it credits Solomon. I see no reason to doubt that the historical Solomon authored and/or collected proverbs, perhaps including these. However, I also see no difficulty in believing that Proverbs is a collection accumulated over a long period of time, with some portions possibly Solomonic and others not. Authorship ultimately has no impact on the meaning of any given proverb.

The discourses of Prov. 1–9 are mainly presented as addresses of a father to his son or of Woman Wisdom to all in general, expanding the audience of the book beyond the "simple/immature" and "young" (1:4) to the "wise" and "discerning" (1:5). The proverbs in chapters 10–31 retain the sense of a father or Woman Wisdom speaking to young men, but it is probably not too much of a stretch to think that the final form of the book speaks to the entire community. Certainly the wisdom contained in the book is relevant to women as well as men, though women may need to apply Proverb's teaching *mutatis mutandis* to gain insight from the book.[18] In the final analysis, perhaps the best way to think of the communication arc in these proverbs is from the sages to the community.

Poetics

A The wise woman builds her house,
B   but with her own hands the foolish one tears hers down.
C Whoever fears the LORD walks uprightly,
D   but those who despise him are devious in their ways.
E A fool's mouth lashes out with pride,
F   but the lips of the wise protect them.
G Where there are no oxen, the manger is empty,
H   but from the strength of an ox come abundant harvests.
I An honest witness does not deceive,
J   but a false witness pours out lies.
K The mocker seeks wisdom and finds none,

---

18. Longman, *Fear of the Lord*, 208. Thanks to Amy Felt for this insight.

L   but knowledge comes easily to the discerning.
M Stay away from a fool,
N   for you will not find knowledge on their lips. (Prov. 14:1–7)

The opening poetic line (A–B) of Prov. 14 is in many ways typical of the book. It is a brief observation about the effect that a wise woman and a foolish woman have on their houses, the wise woman having a positive influence and the foolish woman a negative one. In this way the proverb pushes readers toward wisdom and away from folly. The proverb is presented in what has traditionally, and not wrongly, been called antithetical parallelism, the parallelism resulting from the pairing of antonyms rather than near synonyms. In fact, the first six of the seven verses in this passage are in antithetical parallelism. Antithetical parallelism is particularly appropriate for Proverbs, which pits wisdom, righteousness, and godliness over against folly, wickedness, and ungodliness.

Even so, as James Kugel points out, the basic principle of "A, what's more, B" still works here as well.[19] The first and second cola of an antithetical proverb are neither simply saying the same thing nor just stating opposite things. Rather, they are talking about the same truth from opposing perspectives. Here the antonyms are wise woman/foolish woman and builds up/tears down, but each woman acts on her own house. In this context, "house" means more than just the physical structure; it is not as if the wise woman actually constructs her house and the foolish woman physically tears hers down. Rather, "house" stands for "household," the functions and social relationships within the house.

In Hebrew, both cola begin with the subject (wise woman/foolish woman) but differ grammatically after this. In the first colon, the verb occurs immediately after the subject, while in the second colon, the verb occurs at the end. In the first colon, the direct object is made explicit with a noun ("her house"), while in the second colon, the house is referred to by a pronominal suffix (rendered in the NIV as "hers"). The second colon adds a prepositional phrase ("with her own hands") after the subject and before the verb to underline the self-destructive behavior of the foolish woman.

The second parallel line in this section (C–D) is also antithetical, contrasting walking uprightly with being devious in one's ways, and fearing the Lord with despising the Lord. The central metaphor of the verse is the path, an image that appears frequently in Proverbs. Those with the right attitude toward God, who fear God, walk uprightly and travel in straight life paths; those who

19. Kugel, *Idea of Biblical Poetry*, 13.

despise God are devious in their ways and walk in crooked life paths. Again, the observation leads to advice: fear the Lord and walk on straight life paths.

The third parallelism (E–F) puts a fool's mouth in antithesis to the lips of the wise. The book of Proverbs often refers to speech using the metonymy of mouth, lips, or other body parts associated with speech. The parallel between the verbs is less directly antithetical. One might have expected "lashes out with pride" to be countered by an expression referring to humble speech, but this seems to be assumed. Instead, the second colon talks about the consequences of wise speech; it protects the speaker. This of course raises the question "Protection from what?" Proverbs often speak in open-ended language that may be fulfilled in multiple ways. In this case, it suggests protection from a multitude of potential threats.

In many ways, the middle proverb of the passage (G–H) is the most interesting and enigmatic. Again, the proverb is antithetical: the first colon (G) imagines a manger devoid of food for oxen or other animals and contrasts this in the second colon with the beneficial effect of an ox on the harvest (H). The first colon seems to express a tautology. If there are no oxen, then the manger where animals feed would of course be empty. The absence of oxen implies that the manger would be well-ordered and clean due to a lack of grain. But an ox helps generate abundant harvests by pulling a plow or wagon and thus would more than repay any grain that it eats and any care or maintenance it requires. This proverb likely originated in a rural, cattle-rearing setting, but its message and application extend beyond this context.

The following line (I–J) presents an obvious statement by way of antithetical parallelism. Honest witnesses do not deceive, so if witnesses do deceive, they are by definition not honest! And of course, a false witness lies; that is the very definition of a false witness. This obvious truth is perhaps one of the most repeated themes of the book of Proverbs (6:16–19; 10:18; 12:17, 19, 22; etc.), the repetition underlining its importance. Wisdom tells the truth, particularly in legal contexts; fools lie and try to mislead others.

Out of an appropriate concern to make the English translation smooth and understandable, the NIV departs from the syntax of the original. In the Hebrew, the line begins with "honest witness" and ends with "false witness," an *abb'a'* pattern that provides a strong sense of closure:

> An honest witness does not deceive,
> > but pours out lies a false witness. (my trans.)

In the sixth poetic line, the mocker is opposed to a discerning person. These are categories related to the fool and the wise, respectively. Mockers are the worst type of fools because they scoff at the truth and those who hold it. Of course, the result is that they cannot learn from their mistakes and are unwilling to listen to instruction. No wonder they come up empty. On the other hand, discerning persons grow in knowledge, a close synonym of wisdom. Indeed, knowledge comes easily to them. This observation is intended to encourage people toward discernment and away from mockery.

The previous six parallelisms worked with antonyms. The seventh (M–N) uses neither antonyms nor synonyms. Lowth would categorize this line as an example of synthetic parallelism, which, as I mentioned elsewhere, Kugel rightly dubs "garbage-can parallelism."[20] Perhaps it is a monocolon, but it may evince the pattern "A, what's more, B," or, in this case, "M, what's more, N." M begins with the admonition to stay away from a fool, and N gives the reason or motivation for the advice: "for you will not find knowledge on their lips."[21]

Ecclesiastes 9:11–12: Time and Chance

Context

The macrostructure of Ecclesiastes is based on voice (see below). In the large central part of the book (1:12–12:7), someone named Qohelet speaks about his exploration of the meaning of life and gives advice when he fails to find it under the sun. His fundamental conclusion is that life is difficult for humans, and the end of life is death. He envisions no afterlife, and this is one of the main reasons why he feels that life is meaningless. Given the meaninglessness of life, one should grab whatever enjoyment one can find (*carpe diem*: 2:24–26; 3:12–14, 22; 5:18–20; 8:15; 9:7–10).

Qohelet's speech does not identify a specific audience; he seems to be addressing whoever will listen. The Hebrew word Qohelet means "one who gathers" or "assembles," from which come the popular translations "Preacher" (KJV + 23 versions), going back to the Greek and Latin, or "Teacher" (NIV + 18 newer versions). The first assumes a religious congregation, the latter a classroom. I believe that it is misleading to label Qohelet as either a preacher, which would be anachronistic, or a teacher. Rather, the nickname Qohelet is an attempt to associate this otherwise unidentified and likely fictional character with Solomon. Solomon was a well-known figure by the time the book of Ecclesiastes was written in the late OT time period. Qohelet tried to find

20. See chap. 5 under "Parallelism."
21. I am translating the simple *waw* conjunction as "for" based on context and with the support of most modern Bible translations.

the meaning of life in wealth, wisdom, pleasure, work, and power—all things that the historical Solomon possessed and excelled in. By the time Ecclesiastes was written, everyone knew the story of Solomon, who started well early in his reign but by the end was an apostate, and the nation of Israel divided into two kingdoms upon his death. The story of Solomon is an object lesson against those who put first anything other than God. If Solomon could not find the meaning of life in wisdom, pleasure, work, and power, then who else can? After all, "What more can the king's successor do than what has already been done?" (2:12b).[22]

But Qohelet is not the only speaker in the book, nor is his voice the closest to the (implied) author's message. A second voice can be discerned, one distinguishable from Qohelet's because Qohelet speaks in the first person ("I, Qohelet"), whereas the second voice speaks *about* Qohelet in the third person ("he, Qohelet"). This second voice is most obvious in the so-called epilogue (12:8–14), where he gives his son (mentioned in 12:12) an evaluation of Qohelet and then presents the final lesson of the book.

Qohelet starts speaking in the first person in 1:12—"I, the Teacher, was king over Israel in Jerusalem"—a typical opening line for ancient Near Eastern autobiographies.[23] While 1:12–12:7 is clearly in the voice of Qohelet, and 12:8–14 in the voice of the second wise man talking to his son, the status of 1:1–11 is debated by interpreters. Since 1:2 quotes Qohelet, I think that we should assign the entirety of 1:1–11 to the second wise man. In support of this view is the fact that 1:2 is repeated in 12:8, the first verse spoken by the second wise man in the epilogue. In other words, both prologue (1:1–11) and epilogue (12:8–14) are in the voice of the second wise man, whose words frame Qohelet's. For this reason, some commentators, myself included, refer to this second wise man as the frame narrator.[24] These observations have implications for understanding the genre of the book.

Genre

Based on the observations presented in the preceding section, I suggest the following outline of the macrostructure of Ecclesiastes:

> Frame narrator's prologue (1:1–11)
>
> Qohelet's autobiographical reflections (1:12–12:7)
>
> Frame narrator's epilogue (12:8–12)

22. See Longman, "Qohelet as Solomon."
23. This was the subject of my dissertation, published as *Fictional Akkadian Autobiography*.
24. Fox, "Frame Narrative and Composition."

Seeing this structure helps readers understand that the authorial message is not the message expressed by Qohelet but the message of the frame narrator. In essence, Qohelet's speech is a long quotation, a view confirmed by the one time the frame narrator makes his presence known within Qohelet's section: "'Look,' *says the Teacher*, 'this is what I have discovered'" (7:27, emphasis added).

I begin by recognizing Ecclesiastes as Wisdom literature. Two people present themselves as sages—Qohelet and the frame narrator—and the topic is finding the meaning of life. The book is a framed autobiographical reflection, where the second wise man is using Qohelet's reflections to teach his son a lesson about the meaning of life.[25]

The reason the frame narrator introduces his son to Qohelet's thinking is to warn him about "under the sun" thinking. After all, Qohelet has tried to find the meaning of life by observing what goes on "under the sun," but his observations have not been informed by God's revelation, and so he comes up empty. The frame narrator tells his son that Qohelet is right in concluding that it is not possible to find ultimate meaning with a strictly "under the sun" perspective. Therefore, in the last two verses of the book, the father points his son to the right path for a meaningful life: "Now all has been heard; here is the conclusion of the matter: Fear God and keep his commandments, for this is the duty of all [hu]mankind. For God will bring every deed into judgment, including every hidden thing, whether it is good or evil" (12:13–14).[26]

Voice

I have already discussed the interplay of two voices in the book of Ecclesiastes—Qohelet and a second wise man—and have assessed their impact on the interpretation of the book. The frame narrator—the second wise man—presents Qohelet's reflections to his son and evaluates them at the end. The actual readers of the book identify with the implied reader, the son, to hear the message of the frame narrator, whose viewpoint is to be associated with the (implied) author. My selected passage is in the voice of Qohelet, in which he makes two observations, each beginning with a prose statement and concluding with a poetic reflective observation.

25. As with Proverbs, the father-son dynamic is another feature suggesting that Ecclesiastes is Wisdom literature.

26. The NIV puts these verses in poetic format, but I am not convinced that they are poetry.

Poetics

I have seen something else under the sun:

A The race is not to the swift
B   or the battle to the strong,
C nor does food come to the wise
D   or wealth to the brilliant
E   or favor to the learned;
F but time and chance happen to them all.

Moreover, no one knows when their hour will come:

G As fish are caught in a cruel net,
H   or birds are taken in a snare,
I so people are trapped by evil times
J   that fall unexpectedly on them. (Eccles. 9:11–12)

The first prose statement announces an observation: "I have seen something else under the sun" (9:11). The observation is then described with a bicolon (A–B), followed by a tricolon (C–E), and concluding with a monocolon (F). There are syntactical and semantic parallels between the bicolon and the tricolon. The syntactical parallelism is seen in that all five cola have the following structure:

Negative ("not")—Prepositional Phrase ("to the X")—Subject

Each of the last three cola add the adverb *gam* ("also," "likewise"), prefixed by the conjunction *waw*. A translation more closely reflecting the Hebrew word order is as follows:

Not to the swift the race,
   Not to the strong the battle,
And likewise not to the wise food,
   And likewise not to the brilliant wealth,
   And likewise not to the learned favor. (9:11, my trans.)

Qohelet observes that people do not get what their various abilities deserve, which fits into his frequent theme that there is no justice in the world. The opening bicolon denies the guarantee of success in a race or a battle to those who have the requisite physical abilities, whether speed (A) or strength (B). The next tricolon speaks of mental abilities—wisdom (C), brilliance (D), and learning (E)—which do not ensure food, wealth, or favor to those who possess these qualities. Life is unfair and unpredictable, and Qohelet concludes in a climactic monocolon that "time and chance" ultimately prevail.

While 9:11 acknowledges that skill does not guarantee the expected reward, 9:12 asserts that life and its tragedies are random and unpredictable. Earlier, Qohelet states that God has created everything for its proper time (3:1–8), but in the same context (3:9–11), he also admits that God has not shared this knowledge with humans. Qohelet finds this predicament extremely frustrating.

Like 9:11, Eccles. 9:12 begins with a prose statement: "Moreover, no one knows when their hour will come." "Their hour" refers to the time of their death, a theme that also pervades Qohelet's thought, since in his mind, the finality of death renders all possible purpose in life impossible. Qohelet has no sense of an afterlife.

Qohelet sets up an analogy between fish and birds on one hand and human beings on the other. Fish swimming along in the water are suddenly captured by a fisherman's net (G). Birds flying high through the sky can be captured by a snare when they land (H). The net and the snare bring a sudden end to their life journeys. The NIV translation of G and H follows the syntax of the Hebrew, and readers can see the grammatical parallelism: both G and H begin with a comparative ("as"), then the subject followed by a verb (both lines have different forms of the verb *'achaz*, caught, taken), and ending with a prepositional phrase. The adjective of G ("cruel") is elided but implied in H. In other words, the snare that takes the bird is also a cruel instrument. Colon I moves from fish and birds to humans. Like these animals, they too are trapped (a different but similar verb, *yqsh*) by "evil times." The J colon continues the thought of I by making explicit that this sad end is "unexpected."

Job 38:2–7: God Challenges Job

Context and Genre

In spite of recent challenges,[27] Job is generally regarded as another major example of Wisdom literature alongside Proverbs and Ecclesiastes. I believe this traditional designation is correct since the book's major question is "Who is wise?" But Proverbs, Ecclesiastes, and Job each represent a different type of Wisdom literature. Job is a debate about wisdom in which each of the human participants (Job, the three friends, and Elihu) claims to be able to accurately

27. Dell, "Deciding the Boundaries of 'Wisdom.'"

diagnose Job's predicament and propose the best way forward. In this, they all present themselves as sages who are able to help a person avoid trouble or, in this case, resolve life's problems.

Each of Job's three friends tells him that he suffers because he has sinned and that he can end his suffering by repenting. Elihu, though he presents himself as having the answer that the three friends failed to provide, essentially argues the same point. Job himself knows they are wrong; his suffering is not due to his sin. He believes that he suffers because God is unjust, and his remedy is to confront God and lay the charge against him that God has treated Job unfairly. At first, Job does not think such a confrontation is possible or will work, but by the end of his speeches, he seems confident that he can put God in his place (31:35–37).

Job finally gets his audience with God, but in retrospect he should have been careful what he wished for. My sample passage is the beginning of Yahweh's speech to Job, where instead of Job putting God in his place, God puts Job in his place. Yahweh speaks to Job out of a whirlwind (38:1) and bombards him with a series of questions Job cannot possibly answer, thus reminding Job of who is the creator and who is the creature. Job sees that he is wrong to accuse God of injustice (40:8) or demand that God explain himself, and Job claims to have gained a more intimate knowledge of God through the experience: "My ears had heard of you but now my eyes have seen you" (42:5). After Job decides to withdraw his challenge and suffer in silence, God chooses to restore him (42:7–17).

Voice

Like the book of Ecclesiastes, Job is a multivoiced book as each character offers a different perspectives on Job's situation. Clearly, Yahweh's is the authoritative voice in the book, and the selected passage is where God's voice is first heard at the start of two weighty speeches.

Poetics

A "Who is this that obscures my plans
B   with words without knowledge?
C Brace yourself like a man;
D   I will question you,
E   and you shall answer me.

F "Where were you when I laid the earth's foundation?
G Tell me if you understand.

H Who marked off its dimensions?
I   Surely you know!
J Who stretched a measuring line across it?
K On what were its footings set,
L   or who laid its cornerstone—
M while the morning stars sang together
N   and all the angels shouted for joy?" (Job 38:2–7)

God opens with a question that asserts Job's ignorance. He rhetorically asks, "Who is this that obscures my plans?" (A), knowing full well that it is Job. The word translated "plans" (*'etsah*) in the NIV is better rendered "counsel," but the important thing to recognize is that *'etsah* is the product of wisdom. Up to this point, Job has refused to affirm that God is the one who has *'etsah*; instead Job utters "words without knowledge" (B). The "what's more" aspect provided by B fills out the means by which Job has been obscuring God's *'etsah*.

God then issues a challenge to Job, telling him, "Brace yourself like a man" (C). The Hebrew of Job 38:3 hints at a military connotation: "Gird up your loins like a warrior," an image of a warrior gathering up his robes for combat. In the second (D) and third (E) cola of this tricolon, God then tells him the form of combat: this battle will be with questions and answers instead of swords and shields.

Job 38:4–7 then presents the first series of questions, which center around God's creation. His creation of the earth is likened metaphorically to the building of a house with its foundation, dimensions, footings, and cornerstone. God asks Job whether he was present when God laid the earth's foundation (F) and then taunts him in the second colon by demanding a reply if he has understanding (G). Of course, Job does not understand and cannot possibly understand because he was not there, and that is God's point.

God persists in pressing his point in the next parallel line (H, I, and J) by asking who marked the earth's dimensions (H) by stretching out a measuring line (J). The I colon ("Surely you know!") may be read as a Janus line that connects to both H and J, again taunting Job for his lack of knowledge.

The following bicolon (K–L) continues the house metaphor, speaking of creation's footings (K) and cornerstone (L) and asking where they were set and laid respectively. Again, Job has no clue.

The final parallel line of this unit (M–N) describes God's cheerleaders during his creation. The most interesting aspect of this line is the parallel between "morning stars" and "angels." This parallel trades on the ancient Near Eastern mythical idea that the stars are really spiritual beings. In Enuma

Elish, the Babylonian creation story, Marduk places the gods and goddesses in the heavens as celestial bodies: "He made the positions for the great gods, He established (in) constellations the stars, their likenesses."[28] Here in Job, God associates his angelic servants with the stars and imagines them praising God throughout the creation process.

28. Foster, "Epic of Creation," 399 (tablet 5, lines 1–2).

ELEVEN

Literary Readings of Poetic Texts from the Prophets and Epic Poetry

I conclude my survey of selections of poetic texts by analyzing an example from the prophets and another from what I will call epic poetry. My prophetic example is the magnificent opening to the book of Nahum, which extols God as warrior (1:2–6), and my example of epic poetry comes from the Song of Deborah (Judg. 5:19–27). Readers will notice many similarities with the poetry studied in the previous two chapters, and as before, I will look at the context of these texts, their genre and voice, and their poetic conventions.

Nahum 1:2–8: The Coming of the Warrior

Context and Genre

The superscription to Nahum refers to the book as a "prophecy [*massa'*] concerning Nineveh" and "the book of the vision [*chazon*] of Nahum the El-koshite" (1:1). The word translated "prophecy" can also be rendered "oracle," an utterance or writing where God speaks through a human intermediary. In the book proper, Nahum speaks about God (as in my sample text) but also speaks in God's voice (1:12–13, 14; 2:13; 3:5–7). *Massa'* may also point to a more specific type of prophetic oracle, since it often connects to what one might call war oracles against a foreign nation. Examples occur in various prophecies (Isa. 13:1; 14:28; Zech. 9:1; etc.), including the whole book of Nahum, which inveighs against the city of Nineveh, the capital of Assyria.

Nahum is a "vision" in both the broad and narrow sense. Prophets are visionaries, seeing what God intends for the future. Nahum also has examples of what can be called "event visions," which describe actions that will take place in the future (2:3–10 [4–11 MT]; 3:2–3).

My sample text is the first unit of the book, which I identify as a hymn that extols God as a warrior. This prophetic book is a war oracle against a foreign nation, specifically Assyria, represented metonymically by its capital, Nineveh. Contrary to the translation of the NIV in colon Y, however, Nineveh is never mentioned in this opening poem (see below), though it is implied in a series of judgment oracles, taunts, and insults against this predatory nation. The hymn also predicts the future good coming for God's people, Judah (U, V, W).

Voice

Although Nahum sometimes speaks about God and sometimes for God, in this text he speaks about God, describing him as a warrior who has great strength and will defeat his enemies. In essence, the passage is a hymn that celebrates God's military power. Like the psalms, this hymn is not historically specific, offering no information we can use to fill out its original context in greater detail.

This raises questions: To whom is the prophet speaking? Who is the implied audience? This opening poem mentions no specific audience. In 1:9, the prophet does address someone or something in the second person: "What are you plotting against the LORD?" (1:9 CEB; see also vv. 11–14). Only when read in light of the larger context does an answer become clear: although Nineveh is not named in the hymn (the superscript in 1:1 is not a part of the prophecy itself), it does appear in 2:8. However, the NIV supplies the name "Nineveh" in 1:8 (Y) in place of the Hebrew phrase "those who rise against him," which, though an accurate understanding of the context, lessens the suspense intended by delaying the identification until 2:8. Only in light of this later identification does it become clear toward whom these judgment oracles are directed and who will be the recipient of God's judgment.

But it is unlikely that anyone in Nineveh ever read this prophecy. In other words, the implied audience was not the actual audience. The actual audience was the original people of God. This also explains why the enemy, Nineveh, is sometimes addressed in the third person (e.g., v. 10) and why the people of Judah are sometimes addressed in the second person (e.g., 3:15 [2:1 MT]). This interesting use of voice in the book of Nahum is a bit complicated.

However, it creates suspense and also provides comfort and assurance to the actual audience, Judah, by affirming that the nation oppressing them will soon be overthrown.

Poetics

A The Lord is a jealous and avenging God;
B   the Lord takes vengeance and is filled with wrath.
C The Lord take vengeance on his foes
D   and vents his wrath against his enemies.
E The Lord is slow to anger but great in power;
F   the Lord will not leave the guilty unpunished.
G His way is in the whirlwind and the storm,
H   and clouds are the dust of his feet.
I He rebukes the sea and dries it up;
J   he makes all the rivers run dry.
K Bashan and Carmel wither
L   and the blossoms of Lebanon fade.
M The mountains quake before him
N   and the hills melt away.
O The earth trembles at his presence,
P   the world and all who live in it.
Q Who can withstand his indignation?
R   Who can endure his fierce anger?
S His wrath is poured out like fire;
T   the rocks are shattered before him.

U The Lord is good,
V   a refuge in times of trouble.
W He cares for those who trust in him,
X   but with an overwhelming flood
Y he will make an end of Nineveh;
Z   he will pursue his foes into the realm of darkness. (Nah. 1:2–8)

The poem starts out as a standard acrostic, lines beginning with consecutive letters of the Hebrew alphabet. Thus the poem opens with *aleph* (A; 1:2a), *bet* (G; 1:3b), and *gimel* (I; 1:4a), but the fourth letter of the alphabet, *dalet*, is missing. Instead, the line begins with *aleph* (K; 1:4b). The next line resumes the acrostic with *he* (M; 1:5a) and *waw* (O; 1:5b). *Zayin* is missing (the line beginning with *lamed*), but then comes *chet* (S; 1:6b), *tet* (U; 1:7a), *yod* (W; 1:7b, ignoring the initial *waw* conjunction), and *kaph* (Y; 1:8aβ). After this, the acrostic ceases, having gone about halfway through the alphabet. Another unusual feature of this acrostic is that the opening *aleph* line is three times longer than the others, which are all bicola. After reviewing the parallelism and imagery in the poetic lines of the poem, I will comment on the significance of the broken, or incomplete, acrostic pattern.

The first two lines (A–D) are two bicola and are connected by recurring use of the verb *naqam*, which appears as a *qal* participle in the first three cola. The first occurrence in A is translated "avenging" since it is adjectival, though a more stilted rendition that preserves the Hebrew order would be "God is jealous, and avenging is Yahweh [the LORD]" in an *abb'a'* pattern. The second occurrence, which in the Hebrew begins the colon, is translated "takes vengeance" (B). The third occurrence (C) again begins the colon in the Hebrew and is translated similarly to B. The repetition of the verb *naqam* creates cohesion within the first bicolon (A–B) and between the first bicolon and the second (C–D) and places emphasis on the fact that God takes vengeance.

Colon A states that God is jealous and avenging: he is possessive of those who are his own (which turns out to be Judah, though not yet mentioned) and will avenge them when they are harmed. The second colon (B) reaffirms that God takes vengeance and adds the fact that he is filled with wrath. The next and closely related bicolon makes clear that God's vengeance and anger are directed against his foes (C–D), later specified as Assyria's capital city, Nineveh.

The third bicolon (E–F) begins with the proclamation that God is "slow to anger but great in power" (E). Considering that the first two bicola emphasize God's anger, this is an important reminder that God is not one who easily or quickly loses his temper. Variations of this expression are found elsewhere in the Bible (Exod. 34:6; Num. 14:18; Neh. 9:17; Pss. 86:15; 103:8; 145:8; Jer. 15:15; Joel 2:13); in such contexts, the emphasis is on God's love or mercy. But here the context is God's judgment, so the second colon of this line (F) tells us that, even though God is long-suffering, he will not fail to judge the guilty (cf. Exod. 34:7; Num. 14:18).

The next line (G–H) describes God in the image of an ancient Near Eastern storm god like Baal or Marduk, associating him with "the whirlwind and the storm" (G). Like Baal, he rides the clouds, surely referring to a dark storm cloud. The clouds serve as his chariot (H). A storm god like Baal fought the divinized waters in the person of Yam (both Ugaritic and Hebrew for "sea"). In the Ugaritic myth, the god Yam is also called "Prince River"; similar parallelism between "sea" and "rivers" occurs in I–J. The waters stand for anti-creation forces, chaos, but God is the God of order and rebukes the chaos, showing his dominance over it by drying up the waters.

God's appearance as avenging judge or warrior not only causes the waters (sea and rivers) to dry up but also causes fertility to "wither" away (K–L). The first colon (K) references Bashan and Carmel (which would appear to the east and west respectively of someone in central northern Israel), regions known for their fruitful vegetation but described here as withering. The NIV obscures the verbal connection between K and L, which have the same verb ('umlal), by translating the first occurrence as "wither" (K) and the second as "fade" (L). The verb occurs as the first word in K and the last word in L, bookending the contents of the verse and providing a sense of closure. The L line refers to the blossoms of Lebanon, a northern location also known for its fertility.

Next one hears of the effects of God's appearance on the mountains (M–N), which throughout the OT symbolize stability and grandeur. However, when God appears, the mountains quake (M), and the hills melt away (N), again demonstrating God's devastating power.

After describing the effects of God's power on the waters, the vegetation, and the mountains, the poem offers a climactic summary by asserting that the entire earth trembles at God's presence (O), with P not only repeating this thought but making clear that the inhabitants of the earth are also included ("all who live in it").

The bicolon Q–R has a chiastic structure in the Hebrew that binds it together and creates closure:

> Before his indignation who can stand?
> Who can rise up in the presence of his fierce anger? (my trans.)

Q begins with a prepositional phrase (*a*) followed by an interrogative and verb (*b*) with the order reversed in R (*b'–a'*). The semantic parallelism tends toward synonymity, though it is possible that modern interpreters and translators are missing subtle nuances. However, the emphasis on human inability to challenge God's anger is made clear by this pair of rhetorical questions with one obvious answer: No one can.

The following bicolon (S–T) now describes God's anger in a way that explains why no one can stand before it. His anger is poured out like fire. The verb may suggest volcano imagery, since fire is not normally poured out except in a form such as lava. God's wrathful appearance also breaks up rocks. No wonder humans cannot stand in the presence of an angry God.

Up to this point, the poet has been describing God's stance toward his enemies, but in U–V the flip side to his anger is presented. He is good (U) specifically because he is a "refuge in times of trouble" (V), with the next colon making clear for whom he is a refuge, "for those who trust in him" (W). But then the poet immediately turns back to the negative side of God's appearing—he will bring an "overwhelming flood" (X)—forming a kind of antithetical parallelism. In the final line (Y–Z), we learn that this flood is meant for God's enemies, whom he will chase into "the realm of darkness" (Z).

Under "Voice" above, I mentioned that the NIV supplies the specific reference to "Nineveh" in colon Y. The city's name is not in the Hebrew of Nah. 1:8, which instead has "those who rise up against him." By doing this, the NIV obscures an intentional feature of this poem: delayed identification. The poem that opens the book is purposefully general: God fights his enemies and provides refuge for those who trust in him. Through a series of salvation and judgment oracles that follow, the theme of this first poem is applied to Nineveh (which stands for Assyria) and to Judah. In this way, the delayed identification generates some suspense, which is then resolved by the content that follows the initial poem.

It is now easier to see how the broken, or incomplete, nature of the acrostic in this poem contributes to its meaning. In our earlier discussion of acrostics, we observed that the acrostic pattern communicates completion and order,[1] but this is true only of complete acrostics. By contrast, it stands to reason that a broken acrostic signals disorder and even chaos. Such an understanding fits well with the content of the poem in Nah. 1, which describes the disruption and breaking apart of creation itself with the appearance of the divine warrior.

Judges 5:19–27: An Epic Poem Celebrating Victory

Context and Genre

Judges 5 is a good example of epic poetry, a type of poetry that differs from lyric, didactic, and prophetic poetry. Although the lyric poetry of the psalms bears the closest relationship to epic poetry, the two differ in the amount of specific historical details they include. The psalms purposely suppress specific references to the events that motivated the writing of the poem in order to ensure that those whose situation is not identical to the psalmists can still identify with the words of the psalm. Even Ps. 77's reference to the crossing of the sea is intended not to recount the event as such but rather to offer a stirring example of a mighty divine deed to inspire others with hope that God can likewise save them when in similar serious straits. There is a handful of similar redemptive-historical, or remembrance, psalms (Pss. 78, 105, 106, 135, 136), but like Ps. 77, these psalms look back on important and illustrative

---

1. See chap. 5 under "Acrostics," where this example from Nahum is briefly discussed.

ancient events rather than describe the specific historical circumstances of the psalmist.

By contrast, an epic poem such as Judg. 5 celebrates God's acts soon after the occurrence of the event itself (Exod. 15 is another good example). Without making a claim about the historicity of the events the poem celebrates or about its time of composition, we see that the poem appears in a prose-narrative context describing events during the Judges period when Deborah was judge and Barak, the military commander, led a force from the tribes of Zebulun and Naphtali.

The poem celebrates a victory over the Canaanites and stands in the text after a prose-narrative account of that victory. The prose account (Judg. 4) is given in the typical third-person omniscient voice with which readers are familiar from our discussion of narrative prose in chapter 4 (see under "From Author to Reader"). While the prose account does not lack liveliness, the poem crackles with energy, being told in the first person (see "Voice" below), which gives it a heightened sense of intimacy. As Elaine James informs us, "One thing that poems set in narrative do is offer expansions of psychological and emotional experience and character that we do not otherwise get in biblical narrative."[2]

I am calling this poem and others like it "epic poetry" for want of a better term. The label "narrative poetry" is not satisfactory because there are other poems that are narrative but not clearly historical (e.g., Song 5:2–6:3). I am avoiding the label "historical poetry" because, for the moment, I am bracketing out the question of historicity. Epic poetry narrates heroic deeds or a national history, though in Judg. 5 the main hero is God. However, the participating tribes are also extolled, as is a woman named Jael (see below). Epic poems tend to be longer than other types of poems, and most are derived from oral traditions (an open question in the case of biblical poems).

Voice

The prose introduction to the poem (Judg. 5:1) tells readers that Deborah and Barak sang the song "on that day," presumably in the immediate aftermath of the victory narrated in chapter 4. The poem itself, though, makes clear that it is in the voice of Deborah:

> Villagers in Israel would not fight;
> they held back until I, Deborah, arose,
> until I arose, a mother in Israel. (Judg. 5:7)[3]

2. E. James, *Invitation to Biblical Poetry*, 19.
3. See also the use of first person in 5:3, 9, also associated in context with Deborah.

In terms of audience, the first explicit appeal is to "kings" and "rulers." She asks them to witness her worship of the Lord in song (5:3). Presumably there were no kings present when this song was sung in its putative historical setting because Israel had no king at that time. However, the idea is that foreign kings will hear of this divine victory and be tamed. In v. 4 Deborah directly addresses God, who departed the land of Edom as a warrior and who, as seen in the poem in Nahum discussed above, makes the mountains quake (Judg. 5:4–5).

Deborah then reminisces about the dangerous days preceding her rise to power and the divine intervention (5:6–7). In the midst of the chaos, she recruited an army, and she quotes the people who urged her to act (5:11c–12). We learn in 5:13–18 that some tribes (Ephraim, Benjamin, Issachar, Naphtali, and Zebulun) joined her and Barak, while others stayed away and are now the objects of her questioning jeers (Reuben, tribes in Gilead, Dan, and Asher).

The portion of the poem that I have selected (Judg. 5:19–27) narrates the victory itself, both the battle between the armies and the assassination of Sisera, the Canaanite commander, at the hands of Jael, a Kenite woman. Deborah, the implied poet, mostly describes the events in terse repetitive parallelism (see the next section), making the account not only vivid and memorable but also exciting so that readers get caught up in the action. At one point, however, she breaks off the description with what seems to be a charge to herself: "March on, my soul; be strong!" (5:21c). As she recounts the battle, she brings herself back to that time in her imagination and memory and prods herself to press forward. This also lends vividness to her account and she brings readers into the action.

The poem ends by shifting the scene away from the battle and toward the Canaanites waiting in Hazor. She imagines the concern of Sisera's mother, who is ignorant of the fact that the army has been beaten and her son killed. Deborah pictures Sisera's mother looking out the window and wondering what is taking her son so long to return. Her attendants encourage her by suggesting that the army is delayed because of the amount of plunder they have to divvy up. The poem's readers, knowing that the Canaanites have been defeated and that Sisera will not be returning home, recognize the irony. The intended effect is not sympathy and sadness for Sisera's mother but satisfaction and happiness that those who wanted to destroy God's people have themselves been destroyed. The poem ends expressing the hope that all God's enemies will be destroyed in this way, while all who love God will "be like the sun when it rises in its strength" (5:31).

Poetics

A "Kings came, they fought,
B   the kings of Canaan fought.
C At Taanach, by the waters of Megiddo,
D   they took no plunder of silver.
E From the heavens the stars fought,
F   from their courses they fought against Sisera.
G The river Kishon swept them away,
H   the age-old river, the river Kishon.

I   March on, my soul; be strong!

J Then thundered the horses' hooves—
K   galloping, galloping go his mighty steeds.
L 'Curse Meroz,' said the angel of the LORD.
M   'Curse its people bitterly,
N because they did not come to help the LORD,
O   to help the LORD against the mighty.'

P "Most blessed of women be Jael,
Q   the wife of Heber the Kenite,
R   most blessed of tent-dwelling women.
S He asked for water, and she gave him milk;
T   in a bowl fit for nobles she brought him curdled milk.
U Her hand reached for the tent peg,
V   her right hand for the workman's hammer.
W She struck Sisera, she crushed his head,
X   she shattered and pierced his temple.
Y At her feet he sank,
Z   he fell; there he lay.
AA At her feet he sank, he fell;
BB   where he sank, there he fell—dead." (Judg. 5:19–27)

The opening bicolon (A–B) sets the action in motion with a terse, highly repetitious statement. The same subject ("kings") and verb ("fought") appear in both cola. The progression in B comes by specifying that the kings are from Canaan. None of the kings are mentioned by name in the poem, but the account in Judg. 4 identifies the Canaanite king as Jabin, for whom Sisera fought.

The story continues in C–D by identifying Taanach as the location of the battle, a city situated by the waters of Megiddo. The prose account says that the

Israelite charge started down the slopes of Mount Tabor (4:14), which is in the same vicinity. The second colon (D) anticipates the defeat of the Canaanites by announcing that "they took no plunder of silver," which goes only to the victor.

Rather than proceeding with a description of the battling human armies, the poem speaks of the "stars" fighting from heaven (E–F). This battle is more than a human fight; the very heavens are involved. As we noted in our discussion of the Job example (see chap. 10), stars often represent angels. So God's heavenly army joined the fray and, according to the second colon (F), fought against Sisera, the commander of the Canaanite army.

Not only the stars but also the waters are involved in the fight, specifically the waters of the Kishon River. According to the prose account (4:13), this is where Sisera rallied his troops before the battle. The second colon underlines the antiquity of that river and therefore its significance, celebrating its assistance in the victory. The assertion of cola E through H is that God uses nature itself as he battles the forces of evil.

In the middle of her depiction of the battle, the poet Deborah suddenly speaks to herself (I). I understand this exclamation as a monocolon in which she imagines herself back in the battle and urges herself to persevere despite the display of power around her. She could also be simply encouraging herself to tell the story.

Deborah continues by turning to the human side of the battle. Readers should remember that the prose account describes the attack of ten thousand men led by Barak coming down the slopes of Mount Tabor (4:14). Readers don't know how many were mounted, but they can imagine and even hear in their minds the thundering warhorses as they charge (J). The K colon heightens the drama through the repetition of the verb "gallop," which produces alliteration (*middaharot daharot*).

Suddenly and unexpectedly the poet turns from an account of the battle to a curse uttered by "the angel of the Lord," a name often applied to the Lord himself. Meroz is singled out for cursing (L), but its location is unknown. In the second colon (M), the curse is intensified by specifying the inhabitants of Meroz and adding the word "bitterly."

The next bicolon (N–O) tells us why Meroz deserves to be cursed: they did not aid in the fight against the Lord's enemies. There is an interesting semantic/syntactical hook connecting N and O, with the phrase "to help the Lord" occurring at the end of N and then again at the beginning of O. The O colon sharpens N by adding "against the mighty," referring to the powerful Canaanite army faced by Deborah and Barak's forces.

Cola P through BB change the scene and recount the assassination of Sisera at the hands of a woman named Jael. Though it continues the account of the downfall of the Canaanite oppressors, the difference in setting suggests that a new stanza is needed. The prose account of these events appears in Judg. 4:16–22. As the Israelite army routed the Canaanites, Sisera fled the scene and sought refuge in the tent of Jael, the wife of Heber the Kenite. The narrator tells us of an alliance—the Hebrew uses the word *shalom*, "peace"—between Jabin king of Hazor and the family of Heber, who had moved away from the other Kenites (4:11). Because of this alliance, Sisera expected protection, which Jael seemed to extend to him. However, after lulling him into complacency, she drives a tent peg through his temple and kills him. She informs Barak of this when he comes by in pursuit of Sisera. The poem celebrates her act by recounting the event in a dramatic fashion, leading readers to see her as the one who fulfills Deborah's statement to the hesitant Barak: the honor of the victory would not be his, but "the LORD will deliver Sisera into the hands of a woman" (4:9).

In the opening poetic line of this stanza (the tricolon P, Q, and R), Deborah the poet pronounces a blessing on Jael. The line opens and closes with the verb "to bless" (*barak*). After naming the heroine Jael in P, the second colon (Q) identifies her as the wife of Heber the Kenite, and the third colon (R) blesses her again and calls her a "tent-dwelling" woman.

The prose account describes how Jael offers Sisera hospitality and refuge, concealing him "with a blanket" (4:18). Thirsty from his exertions, Sisera asks for water. The narrator then reports, "She opened a skin of milk, gave him a drink, and covered him up" (4:19). The poem, however, cuts right to the giving of the milk in a very energetic and dynamic retelling, highlighting that she goes above and beyond his request for water by giving him milk, which seems to be an act of caring but is intended to lull him to sleep. In colon S, she gives him milk after he asks for water, and colon T intensifies the quality of the gift by saying that she served the milk "in a bowl fit for nobles" and further that the milk was not ordinary milk but "curdled milk." The NIV translation of S is excellent, but the Hebrew is more concise, illustrating terseness:

> Water he asked; milk she gave.

Indeed, S–T may actually be a quadricolon of two Hebrew words each:

> Water he asked;
>> milk she gave.
> In a bowl for nobles,
>> she brought him curdled milk.

The prose account of the moment when Jael dispatches Sisera gives more detail, but again the poetic account is more dynamic and exciting in its brevity. Here
is the prose account: "But Jael, Heber's wife, picked up a tent peg and a hammer
and went quietly to him while he lay fast asleep, exhausted. She drove the peg
through his temple into the ground, and he died" (Judg. 4:21). The poem reads:

> U Her hand reached for the tent peg,
> V   her right hand for the workman's hammer.

Colon V does not repeat U but speaks of her grasping the second implement
needed to assassinate Sisera. Her hand (presumably her left) grabbed the tent
peg (readers have already been informed that Jael is a tent-dwelling woman),
and her right hand grasped the hammer.

The next bicolon (W–X) then describes the coup de grâce. Colon W tells us
that she struck Sisera's head, and then X specifies that she pierced his temple
with the tent peg. The second colon (X) both intensifies ("shattered") and
specifies ("temple" replacing the more general "head").

The dramatic conclusion to this episode and stanza (Y–BB) is achieved
through the repetition of two verbs, "sank" (*kara'*) and "fell" (*naphal*), each
occurring three times. The language evokes the picture of a slow-motion collapse, and Sisera's collapse was decisive, first communicated by the second
part of Z ("there he lay") and then by the final word of BB, "dead."

The NIV formatting of Y–BB is defensible, though a different layout could
also be presented that highlights the repetition and the definitive end of Sisera:

> At her feet, he sank, he fell;
>   there he lay.
> At her feet, he sank, he fell;
>   where he sank, there he fell—dead.

Finally, we should acknowledge a difference between the prose account and
the poetic retelling of Sisera's death. In the narrative of Judg. 4 we are told that
Sisera was in a deep sleep when Jael drove the tent peg through his head and
into the ground. The poem, however, depicts Sisera as standing upright when
he is struck and then falling to the ground. Given the other hyperbolic imagery
appearing in the poem (e.g., the stars and river waters joining in the battle),
it is possible that the difference is simply intended to heighten the dramatic
effect of Sisera's downfall, the poet's interest in literary impact outweighing
the need for historical accuracy. Whatever the explanation, I will not try to
offer a harmonization, since my interest is not referentiality but literary.

The Old Testament as Literature

In this book, we have focused on the literary nature of the OT. Beginning with theory in chapter 1, we considered the locus of meaning in light of the communication model of literature (author→text→reader). The second chapter charted the relationship between biblical and literary studies with an emphasis on the period starting in the 1970s. The early years of this period saw a move away from efforts to recover the author's intention toward a close study of the text or toward the reader as the locus of meaning. Deconstruction offered the most radical proposal by questioning whether a text had a determinate meaning at all. Admitting the impossibility of getting into an author's mind, I nevertheless reasserted the importance of ascertaining the author's intention based on a close reading of the author's writerly performance. Interestingly, much recent literary theory outside of biblical studies has returned to a focus on authorial intention and rejected deconstruction. I proposed a text-centered approach to hearing the voice of the author while also being mindful of the importance of reading in community to transcend the limitations of one's own narrow perspective.

Since access to the intention of the biblical author—or implied author, if one prefers—is gained only through a close reading of the text, we must learn to read well by being mindful of the conventions employed by Hebrew storytellers and poets. I quoted Robert Alter several times to the effect that every time period and every culture tells its stories and writes its poems in different ways. This crucial insight must undergird all proper interpretation. One must become competent in the genres as well as the narrative and poetic conventions of the time in which the books of the OT were written.

Therefore, in chapter 3, we explored the nature of genre, the literary types in which Hebrew authors wrote and which send signals to readers on how to take their writing. No two texts are exactly alike, but they bear similarities with other texts that provide a kind of literary context in which to read them. In addition, we acknowledged that a text bears different types of relationships to other texts and thus participates in more than one genre, both vertically (based on the number of features it shares with other texts) and horizontally (based on the types of features it shares with other texts).

In chapters 4 and 5 we considered two main genres of Hebrew literature—narrative prose and poetry—and their respective conventions. The chapter on prose looked at the ways in which authors use narrators to manage the presentation of characters, the dialogue between those characters, and the setting and time of the action and how narrators provide a focal point from which to tell the story. The chapter on poetry examined a variety of Hebrew poetic conventions, beginning with the pervasive categories of terseness, parallelism, and various types of figurative language. Though these conventions are not completely absent in prose, the use of parallelism and figurative language is heightened and intensified in poetry. We concluded that it is absolutely essential that interpreters know how parallelism works ("A, what's more, B"), how to unpack a variety of tropes (metaphor, simile, hyperbole, etc.), and how to identify secondary poetic devices (chiasm, acrostics, etc.).

In chapter 6 we examined the intertextual relations between biblical texts. I expressed my preference for a diachronic, author-centered approach to the relationship between texts with one major exception. A synchronic, canonical reading is possible if it is grounded in an author-centered approach based on God as the ultimate author of Scripture.

An attentive and wise reader of biblical texts pays close attention to the genre and conventions described and illustrated in chapters 3 through 6. This we attempted to do in our literary analyses in part 2 (chaps. 7–8 on prose narrative) and part 3 (chaps. 9–11 on poetic texts), using the tools gained from the previous chapters to interpret particular narratives and poems.

My hope is that this book will not only inform but also encourage us to be mindful of the literary nature and quality of the OT as we read. Responsible interpretation requires careful, slow, and close reading as we seek to draw out the profound meaning of the books included in what we call the OT. Given the literary nature of the OT, a literary approach is where interpretation should begin.

BIBLIOGRAPHY

Abrams, M. H. *A Glossary of Literary Terms.* 4th ed. New York: Holt, Rinehart & Winston, 1981.

Abrams, Roger D. "The Complex Relations of Simple Forms." *Genre* 2 (1969): 104–28.

Abbott, H. Porter. *The Cambridge Introduction to Narrative.* 2nd ed. Cambridge: Cambridge University Press, 2008.

Alter, Robert. *The Art of Biblical Narrative.* New York: Basic Books, 1981.

———. *The Art of Biblical Poetry.* 1985. Rev. ed. New York: Basic Books, 2011.

———. *The Hebrew Bible: A Translation with Commentary.* New York: Norton, 2019.

———. "How Convention Helps Us Read: The Case of the Bible's Annunciation Type-Scene." *Prooftexts* 3 (1983): 115–30.

———. "Response." *Prooftexts* 27 (2007): 365–70.

Auerbach, Erich. *Mimesis: The Representation of Reality in Western Literature.* Princeton: Princeton University Press, 1953. Reprinted, 2003.

Baden, Joel S. *The Composition of the Pentateuch: Reviewing the Documentary Hypothesis.* New Haven: Yale University Press, 2012.

Bakhtin, Mikhail M. *The Dialogic Imagination.* Edited by Michael Holquist. Austin: University of Texas Press, 1981.

Bal, Mieke. *Death and Dissymmetry: The Politics of Coherence in the Book of Judges.* Chicago: University of Chicago Press, 1988.

———. *Narratology: Introduction to the Theory of Narrative.* 4th ed. Toronto: Toronto University Press, 2017.

Barbour, Jennifer. *The Story of Israel in the Book of Qohelet: Ecclesiastes as Cultural Memory.* Oxford: Oxford University Press, 2012.

Bar-Efrat, Shimon. *Narrative Art in the Bible.* Sheffield: Almond, 1989.

Barthes, Roland. "Introduction to the Structuralist Analysis of Narrative." In *Image/Music/Text*, translated by Stephen Heath. New York: Hill & Wang, 1977. Originally published in *Communications* 8 (1957): 1–27.

Bartholomew, Craig G. *The Old Testament and God: Old Testament Origins and the Question of God*. Grand Rapids: Baker Academic, 2022.

Beal, Timothy K. *The Book of Hiding: Gender, Ethnicity, Annihilation, and Esther*. London: Routledge, 1997.

Benjamin, Mara H. "The Tacit Agenda of a Literary Approach to the Bible." *Prooftexts* 27 (2007): 254–74.

Berlin, Adele. *Poetics and Interpretation of Biblical Narrative*. Winona Lake, IN: Eisenbrauns, 1994.

Black, Max. *Models and Metaphors*. Ithaca, NY: Cornell University Press, 1962.

Boda, Mark J. "Authors and Readers (Real or Implicit) and the Unity/Disunity of Isaiah." In *Bind Up the Testimony: Explorations in the Genesis of the Book of Isaiah*, edited by Daniel Block and Richard Schultz, 255–71. Peabody, MA: Hendrickson, 2015.

Bodner, Keith. *The Artistic Dimension: Literary Explorations of the Hebrew Bible*. London: Bloomsbury, 2013.

Booth, Wayne C. *The Rhetoric of Fiction*. 1961. 2nd ed. Chicago: University of Chicago Press, 1983.

Boström, G. *Paronomasi i den äldre hebreiska maschallitteraturen: Med särskild hänsyn till proverbia*. Lund: Gleerup, 1928.

Breed, Brennan W. *Nomadic Text: A Theory of Biblical Reception*. Bloomington: Indiana University Press, 2014.

Brueggemann, W. *In Man We Trust: The Neglected Side of Biblical Faith*. Richmond, VA: John Knox, 1972.

———. *The Message of the Psalms: A Theological Commentary*. Philadelphia: Augsburg, 1984.

———. *The Psalms and the Life of Faith*. Edited by P. D. Miller. Minneapolis: Augsburg Fortress, 2013.

Bullinger, E. W. *Figures of Speech Used in the Bible: Explained and Illustrated*. 1898. Mansfield Centre, CT: Martino, 2011.

Buss, Martin J. "The Study of Forms." In *Old Testament Form Criticism*, edited by John H. Hayes, 1–56. Trinity University Monograph Series in Religion 2. San Antonio: Trinity University Press, 1974.

Buth, Randall. "The Taxonomy and Function of Hebrew Tense-Shifting in the Psalms (*qatal-yiqtol-yiqtol-qatal*, Antithetical Grammatical Parallelism)." *Selected Technical Articles Related to Translation* 15 (1986): 26–32.

Byargeon, R. W. "Structure and Significance of Proverbs 9:7–12." *Journal of the Evangelical Theological Society* 40 (1997): 367–73.

Carr, David M. *Reading the Fractures of Genesis: Historical and Literary Approaches.* Louisville: Westminster John Knox, 1996.

Chatman, Seymour. *Story and Discourse: Narrative Structure in Fiction and Film.* Ithaca, NY: Cornell University Press, 1978.

Childs, Brevard S. *Biblical Theology of the Old and New Testaments: Theological Reflection on the Christian Bible.* Minneapolis: Fortress, 1993.

———. *Introduction to the Old Testament as Scripture.* Philadelphia: Fortress, 1979.

Clines, David J. A. *Job 1–20.* Word Biblical Commentary. Dallas: Word, 1989.

———. "A World Established on Water (Psalm 24): Reader-Response, Deconstruction, and Bespoke Interpretation." In *The New Literary Criticism and the Hebrew Bible,* edited by J. C. Exum and D. J. A. Clines, 79–90. Sheffield: Sheffield Academic, 1993.

Collins, J. J. *The Bible after Babel: Historical Criticism in a Postmodern Age.* Grand Rapids: Eerdmans, 2005.

Cook, Stephen L., John T. Strong, and Steven S. Tuell. *The Prophets: Introducing Israel's Prophetic Writings.* Minneapolis: Fortress, 2022.

Creach, Jerome. *Yahweh as Refuge and the Editing of the Hebrew Psalter.* Sheffield: Sheffield Academic, 1996.

Culley, R. C. "Exploring New Directions." In *The Hebrew Bible and Its Modern Interpreters,* edited by D. A. McKnight and G. M. Tucker, 167–200. Philadelphia: Fortress; Chico, CA: Scholars Press, 1985.

Cunningham, Conor. *Darwin's Pious Idea: Why the Ultra-Darwinists and Creationists Both Get It Wrong.* Grand Rapids: Eerdmans, 2010.

Davage, David. *See* Willgren, David.

Dearman, J. Andrew. *Reading Hebrew Bible Narratives.* New York: Oxford University Press, 2019.

deClaissé-Walford, Nancy. *Reading from the Beginning: The Shaping of the Hebrew Psalter.* Macon, GA: Mercer University Press, 1997.

De Lauretis, Teresa. "Queer Theory: Lesbian and Gay Sexualities: An Introduction." *Differences: A Journal of Feminist Cultural Studies* 3 (1991): iii–xviii.

Dell, Katharine J. "Deciding the Boundaries of 'Wisdom': Applying the Concept of Family Resemblance." In *Was There a Wisdom Tradition? New Prospects in Israelite Wisdom Studies,* edited by Mark R. Sneed, 145–60. Atlanta: SBL Press, 2015.

Dell, Katharine J., and Paul M. Joyce, eds. *Biblical Interpretation and Method: Essays in Honor of John Barton.* Oxford: Oxford University Press, 2013.

Dinkler, Michal Beth. *Literary Theory and the New Testament.* New Haven: Yale University Press, 2019.

Doty, W. G. "The Concept of Genre in Literary Analysis." In Society of Biblical Literature 1972 Seminar Papers, 2:423–48. Missoula, MT: Scholars Press, 1972.

———. "Fundamental Questions about Literary Critical Methodology: A Review Article." *Journal of the American Academy of Religion* 40 (1972): 521–27.

Dube, Musa W., Andrew M. Mbuvi, and Dora R. Mbuwayesango, eds. *Postcolonial Perspectives in African Biblical Interpretations*. Atlanta: SBL Press, 2012.

Dubrow, Heather. *Genre*. Critical Idiom 42. New York: Methuen, 1982.

Eco, Umberto. *Six Walks in the Fictional Woods*. Cambridge, MA: Harvard University Press, 1994.

Elliott, Mark, Kenneth Atkinson, and Robert Rezetko, eds. *Misusing Scripture: What Are Evangelicals Doing with the Bible?* London: Routledge, 2023.

Emerton, J. M. "An Examination of Some Attempts to Defend the Unity of the Flood Narrative, Part II." *Vetus Testamentum* 38 (1988): 1–21.

Enns, Peter. *Inspiration and Incarnation*. 2nd ed. Grand Rapids: Baker Academic, 2015.

Eshkenazi, Tamara C. *In an Age of Prose: A Literary Approach to Ezra-Nehemiah*. Atlanta: Scholars Press, 1988.

Exum, Cheryl. *Fragmented Women: Feminist (Sub)versions of Biblical Narratives*. Sheffield: Sheffield Academic, 1993.

Firth, David G. *Joshua*. Evangelical Biblical Theology Commentary. Bellingham, WA: Lexham, 2021.

———. "When Samuel Met Esther: Narrative Focalization, Intertextuality, and Theology." *Southeastern Theological Review* 1 (2010): 15–28.

Firth, David G., and Brittany N. Melton. *Reading Esther Intertextually*. London: T&T Clark, 2022.

Fish, Stanley. *Is There a Text in This Class? The Authority of Interpretive Communities*. Cambridge, MA: Harvard University Press, 1980.

Fishbane, M. *Biblical Interpretation in Ancient Israel*. Oxford: Oxford University Press, 1985.

———. *Biblical Text and Texture: A Literary Reading of Selected Texts*. Oxford: Oneworld Books, 1998.

Fisher, Loren R. *The Many Voices of Job*. Eugene, OR: Cascade Books, 2009.

Fokkelmann, J. P. *Narrative Art in Genesis: Specimens of Stylistic and Structural Analysis*. Eugene, OR: Wipf & Stock, 1991.

Foster, B. R. "Epic of Creation." In *The Context of Scripture*, edited by W. W. Hallo, 1:390–402. Leiden: Brill, 1997.

Fowler, Alastair. *Kinds of Literature: An Introduction to the Theory of Genres and Modes*. Cambridge: Cambridge University Press, 1982.

Fowler, E. "Personification." In Greene et al., *Princeton Encyclopedia of Poetry and Poetics* (4th ed.), 1025–27.

Fox, Michael V. "Frame Narrative and Composition in the Book of Qohelet." *Hebrew Union College Annual* 48 (1977): 85–106.

———. *The Song of Songs and the Ancient Egyptian Love Songs*. Madison: University of Wisconsin Press, 1985.

Frei, Hans. *The Eclipse of Biblical Narrative: A Study in Eighteenth and Nineteenth Century Hermeneutics*. New Haven: Yale University Press, 1974.

Frow, John. "Character." In M. Garrett, *Cambridge Companion to Narrative*, 105–19.

———. *Genre*. 2nd ed. London: Routledge, 2015.

Garrett, Duane. *Job*. Evangelical Exegetical Commentary. Bellingham, WA: Lexham, forthcoming.

Garrett, Matthew, ed. *The Cambridge Companion to Narrative Theory*. Cambridge: Cambridge University Press, 2018.

Geller, Stephen A. *Parallelism in Early Biblical Poetry*. Ann Arbor, MI: Scholars Press, 1979.

Genette, Gérard. *Narrative Discourse: An Essay in Method*. French original, 1972. Translated by Jane E. Lewin. Ithaca, NY: Cornell University Press, 1980.

———. *Narrative Discourse Revisited*. French original, 1983. Translated by Jane E. Lewin. Ithaca, NY: Cornell University Press, 1988.

———. *Paratexts: Thresholds of Interpretation*. French original, 1987. Translated by Jane E. Lewin. Cambridge: Cambridge University Press, 1997.

Gottwald, Norman K. *The Tribes of Yahweh: A Sociology of the Religion of Liberated Israel, 1250–1050 BC*. Maryknoll, NY: Orbis Books, 1979. Reprinted, Sheffield: Sheffield Academic, 1997.

Grayson, A. K. *Babylonian Historical-Literary Texts*. Toronto: University of Toronto Press, 1975.

Greenblatt, Stephen. *Renaissance Self-Fashioning: From More to Shakespeare*. 1980. Reprinted, Chicago: University of Chicago Press, 2005.

Greene, Roland, et al., eds. *The Princeton Encyclopedia of Poetry and Poetics*. 4th ed. Princeton: Princeton University Press, 2012.

Greenstein, Edward L. *Essays on Biblical Method and Translation*. Providence: Brown University Press, 1989.

Grohmann, Marianne, and Hyun Chul Paul Kim, eds. *Second Wave Intertextuality and the Hebrew Bible*. Atlanta: SBL Press, 2019.

Guest, Deryn, et al., eds. *The Queer Bible Commentary*. London: SCM, 2015.

Gunkel, Hermann. "Nahum 1." *Zeitschrift für die alttestamentliche Wissenschaft* 13 (1893): 223–44.

———. *The Psalms: A Form-Critical Introduction*. Philadelphia: Fortress, 1967.

Halberstam, Chaya. "The Art of Biblical Law." *Prooftexts* 27 (2007): 345–67.

Hallo, W. W. "'As a Seal upon Thy Heart': Glyptic Roles in the Biblical World." *Biblical Research* 1 (1985): 20–27.

Hanson, P. D. "A Response to J. J. Collins' Methodological Issues in the Study of 1 Enoch." Society of Biblical Literature 1978 Seminar Papers, 307–9. Missoula, MT: Scholars Press, 1978.

Harshav, Benjamin. *Explorations in Poetics*. Stanford, CA: Stanford University Press, 2007.

Havea, Jione, and Peter H. W. Lau, eds. *Reading Ecclesiastes from Asia and Pasifika*. Atlanta: SBL Press, 2020.

Hayes, J. H., ed. *Old Testament Form Criticism*. Trinity University Monograph Series in Religion. San Antonio: Trinity University Press, 1974.

Hays, Richard B. *Echoes of Scripture in the Gospels*. Waco: Baylor University Press, 2016.

———. *Reading Backwards: Figural Christology and the Fourfold Gospel Witness*. Waco: Baylor University Press, 2014.

Hays, Richard B., Stefan Alkier, and Leroy A. Huizinga, eds. *Reading the Bible Intertextually*. Waco: Baylor University Press, 2008.

Heim, Knut M. *Like Grapes of Gold Set in Silver: An Interpretation of Proverbial Clusters in Proverbs 10:1–22:16*. Berlin: De Gruyter, 2001.

Hempfer, K. *Gattungstheorie*. Munich: W. Funk, 1973.

Herman, David. *Basic Elements of Narrative*. Chichester, UK: Wiley-Blackwell, 2009.

———. *Story Logic: Problems and Possibilities of Narrative*. Lincoln: University of Nebraska Press, 2002.

Herman, David, et al., eds. *Narrative Theory: Core Concepts and Critical Debates*. Columbus: Ohio State University Press, 2012.

Herman, David, Manfred Jahn, and Marie-Laure Ryan, eds. *Routledge Encyclopedia of Narrative Theory*. New York: Routledge, 2005. Paperback, 2008.

Herman, Luc, and Bart Vervaeck. "Postclassical Narratology." In D. Herman, Jahn, and Ryan, *Routledge Encyclopedia of Narrative Theory*, 450–52.

Hirsch, E. D. *Validity in Interpretation*. New Haven: Yale University Press, 1967.

Ho, Peter C. W. *The Design of the Psalter: A Macrostructural Analysis*. Eugene, OR, 2019.

———. "The Macrostructural Design and Logic of the Psalter: An Unfurling of the Davidic Covenant." In *Reading the Psalms Theologically*, edited by David M. Howard Jr. and Andrew J. Schmutzer, 36–62. Bellingham, WA: Lexham Academic Press, 2023.

Holmstedt, Robert D. "Hebrew Poetry and the Appositive Style: Parallelism, *Requiescat in pace*." *Vetus Testamentum* 69 (2019): 617–48.

Hwang, Jerry. *Contextualization and the Old Testament: Between Asian and Western Perspectives*. Carlisle, UK: Langham Global Library, 2022.

Irigaray, Luce. *Speculum of the Other Woman*. Ithaca, NY: Cornell University Press, 1985.

Iser, W. *The Act of Reading: A Theory of Aesthetic Response*. Baltimore: John Hopkins University Press, 1978.

Jahn, Manfred. "Focalization." In D. Herman, Jahn, and Ryan, *Routledge Encyclopedia of Narrative Theory*, 173–77.

Jakobson, Roman. "Grammatical Parallelism and Its Russian Facet." *Language* 42 (1966): 399–429.

James, Elaine T. *An Invitation to Biblical Poetry*. Oxford: Oxford University Press, 2022.

James, Henry. "The Art of Fiction." *Longman's Magazine* 4 (1884): 502–21. Record of a lecture, April 24, 1884. http://virgil.org/dswo/courses/novel/james-fiction.pdf.

Janowski, Bernd. *Arguing with God: A Theological Anthropology of the Psalms*. Louisville: Westminster John Knox, 2013.

Jauss, Hans-Robert. *Toward an Aesthetic of Reception*. Minneapolis: University of Minnesota Press, 1982.

Jobes, Karen H. *Esther*. NIV Application Commentary. Grand Rapids: Zondervan, 1999.

Kaiser, Walter. *Toward an Exegetical Theology: Biblical Exegesis for Preaching and Teaching*. Grand Rapids: Baker, 1998.

Kawashima, Robert S. *Biblical Narrative and the Death of the Rhapsode*. Bloomington: Indiana University Press, 2004.

———. "Comparative Literature and Biblical Studies: The Case of Allusion." *Prooftexts* 27 (2007): 324–44.

Kirk-Duggan, C. A. "Let My People Go! Threads of the Exodus in African American Narratives." In Sugirtharajah, *Voices from the Margin*, 258–78.

Koosed, Jennifer L. *(Per)mutations of Qohelet: Reading the Body in the Book*. New York: T&T Clark, 2006.

Knierim, Rolf. "Old Testament Form Criticism Reconsidered." *Interpretation* 27 (1973): 435–68.

Kraus, H.-J. *Theology of the Psalms*. Minneapolis: Augsburg, 1986.

Kristeva, Julia. *Revolution in Poetic Language*. French original, 1974. Translated by Margaret Waller. New York: Columbia University Press, 1984.

———. "Word, Dialogue, and Novel." Translated by A. Jardine, T. Gora, and L. S. Roudiez. In *The Kristeva Reader*, edited by Toril Moi, 34–61. New York: Columbia University Press, 1986.

Kugel, James. *The Idea of Biblical Poetry: Parallelism and Its History*. New Haven: Yale University Press, 1981. Reprinted, Baltimore: Johns Hopkins University Press, 1998.

———. "On the Bible and Literary Criticism." *Prooftexts* 1 (1981): 217–36.

Kynes, Will. "Intertextuality: Method and Theory in Job and Psalm 119." In *Biblical Interpretation and Method: Essays in Honour of John Barton*, edited by Katharine J. Dell and Paul M. Joyce, 201–13. Oxford: Oxford University Press, 2013.

———. *"My Psalm Has Turned into Weeping": Job's Dialogue with the Psalms*. Beihefte zur Zeitschrift für die alttestamentliche Wissenschaft 437. Berlin: De Gruyter, 2012.

———. *An Obituary for "Wisdom Literature": The Birth, Death, and Intertextual Reintegration of a Biblical Corpus*. Oxford: Oxford University Press, 2019.

Leitch, V. B. *Deconstructive Criticism: An Advanced Introduction*. New York: Columbia University Press, 1983.

LeMon, J. M., and Brent A. Strawn. "Parallelism." In *Dictionary of the Old Testament: Wisdom, Poetry and Writings*, edited by T. Longman III and P. Enns, 502–15. Downers Grove, IL: InterVarsity, 2008.

Lentricchia, F. *After the New Criticism*. Chicago: University of Chicago Press, 1980.

Letzen-Dies, F. "Methodologische Überlegungen zur Bestimmung 'literarischer Gattungen' im Neuen Testament." *Biblica* 62 (1981): 1–20.

Levenson, Jon D. *The Death and Resurrection of the Beloved Son: The Transformation of Child Sacrifice in Judaism and Christianity*. New Haven: Yale University Press, 1993.

———. *The Hebrew Bible, the Old Testament, and Historical Criticism*. Louisville: Westminster John Knox, 1993.

Lewis, C. S. *Fern-Seed and Elephants, and Other Essays on Christianity*. [London]: Colina/Fontana, 1975.

Long, V. Philips. *1 and 2 Samuel*. Tyndale Old Testament Commentaries. Downers Grove, IL: IVP Academic, 2020.

Longman, Tremper, III. *Confronting Old Testament Controversies: Pressing Questions about Evolution, Sexuality, History, and Violence*. Grand Rapids: Baker Books, 2019.

———. "A Critique of Two Metrical Systems." *Biblica* 62 (1982): 230–52.

———. *Daniel*. NIV Application Commentary. Grand Rapids: Zondervan, 1997.

———. "Determining the Historical Context of Ecclesiastes." In *The Words of the Wise Are Like Goads: Engaging Qohelet in the 21st Century*, edited by M. J. Boda, T. Longman III, and C. G. Rata, 89–102. Winona Lake, IN: Eisenbrauns, 2013.

———. *Ecclesiastes*. New International Commentary on the Old Testament. Grand Rapids: Eerdmans, 1998.

———. *The Fear of the Lord Is Wisdom: A Theological Introduction to Wisdom in Israel*. Grand Rapids: Baker Academic, 2017.

———. *Fictional Akkadian Autobiography: A Generic and Comparative Approach*. Winona Lake, IN: Eisenbrauns, 1993.

———. *Genesis*. Story of God Bible Commentary. Grand Rapids: Zondervan, 2016.

———. "History and Old Testament Interpretation." In *Hearing the Old Testament: Listening for God's Address*, edited by Crag G. Bartholomew and David J. H. Beldman, 96–121. Grand Rapids: Eerdmans, 2012.

———. "Israelite Genres in Their Ancient Near Eastern Context." In *The Changing Face of Form Criticism*, edited by Marvin A. Sweeney and Ehud Ben Zvi, 177–95. Grand Rapids: Eerdmans, 2003.

———. *Job*. Baker Commentary on the Old Testament Wisdom and Psalms. Grand Rapids: Baker Academic, 2012.

―――. *Literary Approaches to Biblical Interpretation*. Grand Rapids: Zondervan, 1987.

―――. "Nahum." In *The Minor Prophets: An Exegetical and Expository Commentary*, edited by Thomas E. McComiskey, 3:765–829. Grand Rapids: Baker, 1993.

―――. *Proverbs*. Baker Commentary on the Old Testament Wisdom and Psalms. Grand Rapids: Baker Academic, 2006.

―――. *Psalms*. Tyndale Old Testament Commentaries. Downers Grove, IL: InterVarsity Press, 2014.

―――. "Qohelet as Solomon: 'For What Can Anyone Who Comes after the King Do?' (Ecclesiastes 2:12)." In *Reading Ecclesiastes Intertextually*, edited by Katharine Dell and Will Kynes, 42–56. London: Bloomsbury T&T Clark, 2014.

―――. *Revelation through Old Testament Eyes*. Grand Rapids: Kregel, 2022.

―――. "The Scope of Wisdom Literature." In the *Cambridge Companion to Biblical Wisdom Literature*, edited by Katharine J. Dell et al., 13–33. Cambridge: Cambridge University Press, 2022.

―――. *Song of Songs*. New International Commentary on the Old Testament. Grand Rapids: Eerdmans, 2001.

―――. "To Answer or Not to Answer: Reading Text, Culture, Soul with Wisdom." *Word and World* 41 (2021): 231–38.

Longman, Tremper, III, and John H. Walton. *The Lost World of the Flood: Mythology, Theology, and the Deluge Debate*. Grand Rapids: InterVarsity, 2018.

Lowth, Robert. *Lectures on the Sacred Poetry of the Hebrews*. G. Gregory's 1787 translation of vol. 1 of *De sacra poesi Hebraeorum*. Oxford: Clarendon, 1753. Revised, 1763.

Mangum, Douglas, and Douglas Estes. *Literary Approaches to the Bible*. Bellingham, WA: Lexham, 2017.

Martin, W. "Metaphor." In Greene et al., *Princeton Encyclopedia of Poetry and Poetics* (4th ed.), 863–70.

―――. "Metonymy." In Greene et al., *Princeton Encyclopedia of Poetry and Poetics* (4th ed.), 876–78.

Mays, H. G. "Some Cosmic Connotations of *mayim rabbim*, 'Many Waters.'" *Journal of Biblical Literature* 74 (1955): 9–21.

McCann, J. Clinton. *Theological Introduction to the Book of Psalms: The Psalms as Torah*. Nashville: Abingdon, 1993.

McConnell, Walter. "Meter." In *Dictionary of the Old Testament: Wisdom, Poetry and Writings*, edited by Tremper Longman III and Peter Enns, 471–76. Downers Grove, IL: IVP Academic, 2008.

Middleton, J. Richard. *Abraham's Silence: The Binding of Isaac, the Suffering of Job, and How to Talk Back to God*. Grand Rapids: Baker Academic, 2021.

Mitchell, David C. *Message of the Psalter: An Eschatological Programme in the Book of Psalms*. Sheffield: Sheffield Academic, 1997.

Moberly, R. W. L. *The Bible, Theology, and Faith: A Study of Abraham and Jesus.* Cambridge: Cambridge University Press, 2000.

Moore, Stephen D. "History after Theory? Biblical Studies and the New Historicism." *Biblical Interpretation* 5 (1997): 289–99.

Mowinckel, Sigmund. *The Psalms in Israel's Worship.* Translated and revised by D. R. Ap-Thomas. 2 vols. New York: Abingdon, 1962.

Muilenberg, James. "Form Criticism and Beyond." *Journal of Biblical Literature* 88 (1969): 1–18.

Nazarov, Konstatin. *Focalization in the Old Testament Narratives with Specific Examples from the Book of Ruth.* Carlisle, UK: Langham Publishing, 2021.

Newman, Michael. "Mimesis." In D. Herman, Jahn, and Ryan, *Routledge Encyclopedia of Narrative Theory*, 309–10.

Noegel, Scott. *Janus Parallelism in the Book of Job.* Journal for the Study of the Old Testament Supplement Series 223. Sheffield: Sheffield Academic, 1996.

Notarius, Tania. "Poetic Discourse and the Problem of Verbal Tenses in the Oracles of Balaam." *Hebrew Studies* 49 (2008): 55–86.

O'Connor, Michael. *Hebrew Verse Structure.* Winona Lake, IN: Eisenbrauns, 1980. Reprinted, 1997.

Origen. *On First Principles (De principiis).* Translated by G. W. Buttersworth. Notre Dame, IN: Ave Maria Press, 2013.

Orsini, G. N. G. "Genres." In *The Princeton Encyclopedia of Poetry and Poetics*, edited by A. Preminger, 307–9. 1st ed. Princeton: Princeton University Press, 1965.

Partes, Ilana. *The Biography of Ancient Israel: National Narratives in the Bible.* Berkeley: University of California Press, 2002.

Paul, S. "A Lover's Garden of Verse: Literal and Metaphorical Imagery in Ancient Near Eastern Love Poetry." In *Tehillah le-Moshe: Biblical and Judaic Studies in Honor of Moshe Greenberg*, edited by M. Cogan et al., 99–110. Winona Lake, IN: Eisenbrauns, 1997.

Paytner, Helen. *Telling Terror in Judges 19: Rape and Reparation for the Levite's Wife.* London: Routledge, 2020.

Pemberton, Glenn. *After Lament: Learning to Trust God Again.* Abilene, TX: Abilene Christian University Press, 2013.

Phelan, James, and Peter J. Rabinowitz. "Narrative as Rhetoric." In D. Herman, Jahn, and Ryan, *Routledge Encyclopedia of Narrative Theory*, 3–8.

Pike, Kenneth. *Language in Relationship to a Unified Theory of Human Behavior.* The Hague: Mouton, 1967.

Pixley, G. V., and C. Boff. "A Latin American Perspective: The Option for the Poor in the Old Testament." In Sugirtharajah, *Voices from the Margin*, 207–16.

Plantinga, Alvin. *Warranted Christian Belief.* Oxford: Oxford University Press, 2000.

Polzin, Robert M. *Biblical Structuralism: Method and Subjectivity in the Study of Ancient Texts*. Semeia Supplements. Philadelphia: Fortress, 1977.

Poythress, Vern S. "Analysing a Biblical Text: Some Important Linguistic Distinctions." *Scottish Journal of Theology* 32 (1979): 113–37.

Preminger, A., ed. *The Princeton Encyclopedia of Poetry and Poetics*. 1st ed. Princeton: Princeton University Press, 1965.

Prickett, Stephen. *Words and "The Word": Language, Poetics and Biblical Interpretation*. Cambridge: Cambridge University Press, 1986.

Puckett, Kent. *Narrative Theory: A Critical Introduction*. Cambridge: Cambridge University Press, 2016.

Richards, I. A. *The Philosophy of Rhetoric*. New York: Oxford University Press, 1936.

Ryken, Leland, and Tremper Longman III, eds. *A Complete Literary Guide to the Bible*. Grand Rapids: Zondervan, 1993.

Said, Edward. *Orientalism*. New York: Pantheon Books, 1978.

Salinger, J. D. *The Catcher in the Rye*. 1945. New York: Back Bay Books, 2010.

Sandoval, Timothy J. "Prophetic and Proverbial Justice: Amos, Proverbs, and Intertextuality." In Grohmann and Kim, *Second Wave Intertextuality*, 131–51.

Saussure, Ferdinand de. *Course in General Linguistics*. Edited by Charles Bally and Albert Sechehaye. French original, 1916. Translated by Wade Baskin. New York: Philosophical Library, 1959.

Seow, C.–L. *Job 1–21: Interpretation and Commentary*. Illuminations Commentary Series. Grand Rapids: Eerdmans, 2013.

Sherwood, Yvonne. "'Not with a Bang but a Whimper': Shrunken Apocalypses of the Twentieth Century and the Book of Qohelet." In *Apocalyptic in History and Tradition*, edited by Christopher Rowland and John Barton, 229–51. Journal for the Study of the Pseudepigrapha Supplement Series 43. London: Sheffield Academic, 2002.

———. "Rocking the Boat: Jonah and the New Historicism." *Biblical Interpretation* 5 (1997): 364–402.

Skehan, Patrick. "The Seven Columns of Wisdom's House in Proverbs 1–9." *Catholic Biblical Quarterly* 29 (1967): 162–80.

Sneed, Mark R. "'Grasping after the Wind: The Elusive Attempt to Define and Delimit Wisdom." In *Was There a Wisdom Tradition? New Prospects in Israelite Wisdom Studies*, edited by Mark R. Sneed, 39–67. Atlanta: SBL Press, 2015.

Snell, Daniel C. *Twice-Told Proverbs and the Composition of the Book of Proverbs*. Winona Lake, IN: Eisenbrauns, 1993.

Sommers, Benjamin D. *A Prophet Reads Scripture: Allusion in Isaiah 40–66*. Stanford, CA: Stanford University Press, 1998.

Sternberg, Meir. *Expositional Modes and Temporal Ordering in Fiction*. Bloomington: Indiana University Press, 1978.

————. *The Poetics of Biblical Narrative: Ideological Literature and the Drama of Reading*. Bloomington: Indiana University Press, 1985.

Stewart, David Tabb. "LGBT/Queer Hermeneutics and the Hebrew Bible." *Currents in Biblical Research* 15 (2017): 289–314.

Stokes, Ryan E. *The Satan: How God's Executioner Became the Enemy*. Grand Rapids: Eerdmans, 2019.

Stovell, Beth M. "'Where Would We Put Them?': Hermeneutical Categorization and Marginalization in Biblical Studies." *Didaktikos* 5.1 (2021): 9–12.

Strawn, Brent A. "Imagery." In *Dictionary of the Old Testament: Wisdom, Poetry and Writings*, edited by T. Longman III and P. Enns, 502–15. Downers Grove, IL: InterVarsity, 2008.

Strickland, Geoffrey. *Structuralism or Criticism? Thoughts on How We Read*. Cambridge: Cambridge University Press, 1981.

Sugirtharajah, R. S., ed. V*oices from the Margin: Interpreting the Bible in the Third World*. 3rd ed. Maryknoll, NY: Orbis Books, 2006.

Sweeney, Marvin A. "The Literary-Historical Dimensions of Intertextuality in Exodus–Numbers." In Grohmann and Kim, *Second Wave Intertextuality*, 41–52.

Tilford, Nicole L. *Sensing World, Sensing Wisdom: The Cognitive Foundation of Biblical Metaphors*. Atlanta: SBL Press 2017.

Todorov, Tzvetan. *The Fantastic: A Structural Approach to a Literary Genre*. Translated by R. Howard. Ithaca, NY: Cornell University Press, 1981.

Troeltsch, Ernst. "Historiography." In *Encyclopedia of Religion and Ethics*, edited by James Hastings et al., 6:716–23. New York Scribner, 2014.

————. "Über historische und somatische Methode in der Theologie." In *Gesammelte Schriften*, 729–53. Tübingen: Mohr, 1913.

Tucker, Gene. *Form Criticism of the Old Testament*. Guides to Biblical Scholarship. Philadelphia: Fortress, 1971.

Upstone, Sara. *Literary Theory. A Complete Introduction*. London: John Murray Learning, 2017.

Uspensky, Boris. *A Poetics of Composition*. Berkeley: University of California Press, 1973.

Vanhoozer, Kevin J. *Is There a Meaning in This Text? The Bible, the Reader, and the Morality of Literary Knowledge*. Grand Rapids: Zondervan, 1998.

Wafawanaka, Robert. "'The Land Is Mine!': Biblical and Postcolonial Reflections on Land with Particular Reference to the Land Issue in Zimbabwe." In Dube, Mbuvi, and Mbuwayesango, *Postcolonial Perspectives*, 221–34.

Waltke, Bruce K. *The Book of Proverbs: Chapters 1–15*. Grand Rapids: Eerdmans, 2004.

Walton, John H. "Genesis." In *Zondervan Illustrated Bible Backgrounds Commentary*, edited by J. H. Walton, 1:2–159. Grand Rapids: Zondervan, 2009.

———. *The Lost World of Genesis One: Ancient Cosmology and the Origins Debate.* Downers Grove, IL: IVP Academic, 2009.

Walton, John H., V. Matthews, and M. Chavalas, eds. *The IVP Bible Background Commentary.* Downers Grove, IL: InterVarsity, 1997.

Warhol, Robyn. "Feminist Narratology." In D. Herman, Jahn, and Ryan, *Routledge Encyclopedia of Narrative Theory*, 161–63.

———. "Narrative Values, Aesthetic Values." In D. Herman, Jahn, and Ryan, *Routledge Encyclopedia of Narrative Theory*, 165–68.

Washington, Harold C. "Violence and the Construction of Gender in the Hebrew Bible: A New Historicist Approach." *Biblical Interpretation* 5 (1997): 324–63.

Watson, W. G. E. *Classical Hebrew Poetry: A Guide to Its Techniques.* Sheffield: Sheffield Academic, 1984.

Weiser, Artur. *The Psalms.* Old Testament Library. Philadelphia: Westminster, 1962.

Weiss, Meir. *The Bible from Within: The Method of Total Interpretation.* Jerusalem: Magnes, 1984.

Weitzman, Steven. "Before and after *The Art of Biblical Narrative*." *Prooftexts* 27 (2007): 191–210.

Wellek, René, and Austin Warren. *Theory of Literature.* New York: Harcourt Brace Jovanovich, 1965.

Wellhausen, Julius. *Prolegomena to the History of Israel.* Translated from the original 1885 German edition by J. S. Black and A. Menzies. Atlanta: Scholars Press, 1994.

Whybray, R. N. *The Book of Proverbs.* Cambridge: Cambridge University Press, 1972.

Willgren, David. *Formation of the "Book" of Psalms: Reconsidering the Transmission and Canonization of Psalmody in Light of the Material Culture and the Poetics of Anthologies.* Tübingen: Mohr Siebeck, 2016.

———. [as David Davage]. Review of *The Design of the Psalter*, by Peter C. W. Ho. *Svensk exegetisk årsbok* 85 (2020): 247–51.

Williams, Michael. *Deception in Genesis.* New York: Peter Lang, 2001.

Williams, Patrick. "Post-Colonialism and Narrative." In D. Herman, Jahn, and Ryan, *Routledge Encyclopedia of Narrative Theory*, 451–56.

Wilson, Gerald. *The Editing of the Hebrew Psalter.* Chico, CA: SBL Press, 1985.

Wimsatt, W. K., Jr., and M. Beardsley. "The Affective Fallacy." *The Sewanee Review* 57 (1949): 31–55.

———. "The Intentional Fallacy." In *The Verbal Icon: Studies in the Meaning of Poetry*, 3–18. Lexington: University of Kentucky Press, 1954. First published in *The Sewanee Review* 54 (1946): 468–88.

Woudstra, Marten H. *The Book of Joshua.* Grand Rapids: Eerdmans, 1981.

Yarchin, William. "Were the Psalms Collections at Qumran True Psalters?" *Journal of Biblical Literature* 134 (2015): 775–89.

Yoo, Philip J. *Ezra and the Second Wilderness*. Oxford: Oxford University Press, 2017.

Younger, K. Lawson. *Ancient Conquest Accounts: A Study of Ancient Near Eastern and Biblical History Writing*. JSOTSup 98. Sheffield: Sheffield Academic, 1990.

Zenger, Erich. "Das Buch der Psalmen." In *Einleitung in das Alte Testament*, edited by Erich Zenger, 348–70. Stuttgart: Kohlhammer, 1995.

———. "Der Psalter als Buch." In *Der Psalter in Judentum und Christendom*, edited by Erich Zenger and Norbert Lohfink, 1–58. Freiburg: Herder, 1998.

———. "Was wird anders bei kanonischer Psalmenauslegung." In *Ein Gott, eine Offenbarung: Beiträge zur biblischen Exegese, Theologie und Spiritualität; Festschrift für Notker Füglister*, edited by Friedrich V. Reiterer, 397–413. Würzburg: Echter, 1991.

SCRIPTURE INDEX

Old Testament

Genesis

1 170, 182, 197
1–2 90, 182, 184n8
1–3 59, 179
1–11 179, 180, 187
1:2 222
1:14–19 114
1:28 197
2 182, 183
2:4 180, 183
2:4–25 181
2:5 181
2:7 181
2:9 184
2:15–17 184
2:16–17 184
2:17 184
2:20 186
2:21–23 59
3 90 166, 179–87
3:1 166, 184
3:2 184
3:3 184
3:5 184
3:6 185
3:6–7 184
3:8 140, 184
3:9 140, 184
3:12 185
3:13 185
3:14 185
3:15 185
3:17 186
3:18 186
3:19 186
3:20 186
3:21 186
3:21–24 186
4–Rev. 20 90
4:7 186
4:25 186
5:1 180
6–9 177, 179
6:5 187
6:9 180
6:15 148
6:17 187
7:2–3 187
7:9–20 148
7:11 187
7:19 187
7:20 187
10:1 180
11:10 180
11:27 180
11:27–25:11 89
11:27–37:1 90
12–50 180
12:1 148
12:1–3 188, 191, 221
12:3 191
15 196
15:6 191
17 196
18:1 100
18:1–2 100
18:3–5 100
18:5 100
18:6 100
18:9 100
18:10 100
18:12 101
18:13 100
18:13–14 101
18:15 101
21:1 188
21:1–7 188
21:16 77, 78
21:22–23
22 89, 179, 188–96, 196n21
22:1 78, 89, 190
22:2 78, 193
22:3 190
22:5 189
22:6–8 189
22:7 190
22:8 190, 191
22:10 190
22:11 190
22:12 191
22:14 191
22:15–18 191
22:16–17 194
22:19 191
22:28 191
24 191
25:2 180
25:9 191
25:19 180
28:20–22 85
32:28 139
34 83, 102
34:2 84
34:8–12 83
34:13 84
34:21 84
34:23 84
34:25–26 84
34:30 84
34:31 84
35:1–15 85
36:1 180
36:9 180
37–50 101, 102n70
37:1–3 89
37:2 180
37:26–27 102
37:27 91
38 102, 102n70
38:15 101
38:26 91
41:25–36 101
44:18–34 102
44:30–32 91
49 61
50:20 86, 89
50:22–26 196
50:24–25 89, 196

Exodus

1 177, 196–98
1:1–5 196
1:7 197
1:8 197
1:9–10 197
1:10 197
1:11 197
1:13–14 197
1:15–16 85
1:17 85, 198
1:18 198

1:19 85, 198
1:20–21 198
1:21 85
6:16 216
6:18 216
6:21 216
12:6 99
12:18 99
14 145
14–15 222
15 54, 61, 259
15:2–3 113
17:8–16 80
17:26 201
20:8–11 205
20:16 85
24:4 1
34:6 256
34:7 256
34:27 1
38 78
38:15 78

Leviticus

16:29 98
21:13–15 206
23:5 99
23:24 98
23:26–32 98
23:33–43 98

Numbers

6:24–26 225
11:1–3 217
14:18 256
16 216
33:2 1

Deuteronomy

1:1 74
1:28 147
5:12–15 205
17:14–20 57
23:3 203
25:17 201
27:1 74
27:9 74
27:11 74
29:1–2 74
31:7 74
31:9–10 74

31:22 1
32:14 127
33:1 74
34 8

Joshua

1–2 147
1–5 77
1–12 148
3–4 145
6 76, 77
11–12 148
11:23 148
13 148
13:1–7 148
16:10 148

Judges

1 147
4 264
4:9 263
4:11 263
4:13 262
4:14 262
4:16–22 263
4:18 263
4:19 263
4:21 264
5 54, 61, 259
5:3 260
5:4 260
5:4–5 260
5:6–7 260
5:13–18 260
5:19–27 209, 258–64
5:21 260
5:31 260
12:4–6 102
14 103
14:2 103
14:3 103
14:6 122
16:9 122
16:12 122

1 Samuel

8:4–5 77
8:22 78
9:1–2 80
9:2 92
9:6–10 78
10:8 78

10:23 201
13 201
15 80, 201
16:14–23 203
16:18 203
16:18–23 200
17 177, 199–203
17:1–3 199
17:3 200
17:4–7 92, 200
17:9 202
17:11 200
17:12–15 200
17:16 200
17:17–19 201
17:20–24 201
17:25 203
17:25–27 201
17:28 201
17:29 201
17:33 201
17:37 201
17:42 199, 202
17:43 199, 202
17:47 202
17:52–53 202
17:55–56 202
17:57–58 202
22:5 103
22:20–23 104
23:1–6 103
23:6 104
24 170
24:20–22 97
25 93, 97, 98
25:1 97
25:1–2 95
25:2 94
25:3 94
25:4 95
25:14 95
25:18 97
25:20 96
25:21 94, 95
25:24 94
25:25 94
25:26 94
25:27 94
25:28 94
25:29 94
25:30 94
25:31 94
25:33 94

25:36 96
25:37 94
25:41 94
26 170

2 Samuel

5:2 201, 230
7 170
7:8 230
7:14 56, 171
7:16 57
11–12 169
11:2 92
14:25–26 92
15–17 212
16:5 80
18:10 92
18:14 92

1 Kings

3:1–28 163
4:29–34 163
6–8 98
8 163
8:1 163
8:2 163
8:14 163
8:22 163
8:55 163
8:65 163
10:1–13 163
12:25–33 79
12:26–27 79
13 79
13:1–3 78
13:2–3 79
13:11 79
13:15 205
13:17–18 205
13:18 79
13:21–22 79
14:11 127
16:4 127
17:7–24 190
21:23–24 127

2 Kings

9:10 127
9:36 127
18 95
23:15–18 78

1 Chronicles

6:31–47 223
15:16–22 223
16:7–37 212

2 Chronicles

20:19 216
22:5 189

Ezra

1–6 74, 98
1:1 98
1:2–3 98
1:5–11 98
2:1–67 98
2:68 98
3:1 98
3:4 98
3:8 98
3:10–13 98
4 98
4:1 98
4:1–5 99
4:5 98
4:6–23 99
4:7–23 99
4:24 99
5 99
5:1–2 99
6:15 99
7 74
7–10 69, 203
7:1–10 74
7:11 74
7:12–26 74
9 74
9:6–15 204
10 74

Nehemiah

1–7 70, 203
1:1 74
7:73 74
8–10 69–70, 203
8–12 207
9:17 256
11–13 70, 203
12:27 74
12:27–47 74
13 177, 199, 203–7
13:1 203

13:3 203
13:4–5 203
13:6 204
13:8 204
13:10–11 204
13:13 204
13:14 74, 204
13:21 206
13:22 74, 206
13:23 74, 206
13:24 206
13:25–27 206
13:28 206
13:31 74

Esther

1 96
1:1 82
1:3–4 82
1:5 82, 92, 93
1:6 93
1:7 93
1:9 82
1:11 77, 93
1:13–22 83
2 86
2:4 86
2:5 80
2:7 86, 93
2:10 87
2:12 86
2:14 86
2:19–23 81
2:20 87
3:1 80
3:2 80
3:6 80
4 35, 87
4:3 87
4:11 81
4:13–14 88
5:3 81
5:6 81
5:14 88
6:1–11 81
6:6 77
6:13 81
7 81
7:1–10 81
7:9–10 88
8–10 81
9:22 93

9:24 93
9:26 93

Job

3–37 54
3:1–2 72
3:3 132
3:11 132
3:16 132
4:1 72
7:17 165
7:17–21 164–66
7:18 165
28 8
31:35–37 249
38:1 249
38:2 114
38:2–7 209, 231,
 248–51
38:4–7 114–15, 250
40:8 249
42:7–17 72, 249

Psalms

1 57, 171
1–2 173, 174
1:1 110, 121
1:3–4 132–33
2 56–57, 112, 171, 174
2:1 111
2:1–2 152
2:1–3 56, 115–16
2:4–5 112
2:4–6 56, 152
2:6 112
2:7 56, 171
2:7–9 56, 152
2:10–12 56, 152
3 211, 211n2
3:4 121
3:5–6 149
6 217
7 211n2, 217
7:8–9 205
8 151, 164–66
8:1 151
8:1–4 164
8:4 165
8:9 151
9 153
10 153
14 139

14:7 138
16 52
16:5 229
18 173, 211n2
22 126–27
22:6–8 126
22:12–13 127
22:16 127
22:19–11 127
23 123, 125–26, 209,
 226–30
23:1 109, 213n4, 227
23:2–3 227
23:3–4 230
23:4 125, 140, 228,
 230
25 153
29:3 222
30 224
32 217
33 172n33
34 153, 211n2
37 153
38 217
41 171
42 216
42:1–5 151
42:4 219
42:5 151
42:6–11 151
42:11 151
43:1–5 151
44 216, 217
45 217
46 209, 212–17
46:1 217
46:1–3 213
46:2 213
46:4–6 214
46:7 214
46:8 215, 217
46:9 215
46:10 215, 216, 217
46:11 216
47 56, 216
48 213, 216
48:1–2 144n43
49 216
50 223
51 169, 211n2, 217
51:1 1
51:1–2 169
51:3–6 146

51:5–6 146, 146n44
52 211n2
54 211n2
56 211n2
57 211n2
60 211n2
62:9 151
63 211n2
66 172n33
67 172n33, 209,
    224–26
68:22 151
69:22–28 217
72 171, 173n34
72:20 173, 174
73–76 223
74:14 16
76 213
77 209, 217–24, 258
77–83 223
77:1 217
77:1–2 223
77:2 218
77:3 219
77:3–6 223
77:4 219
77:5–6 219
77:7 223
77:7–9 220, 223
77:10 220
77:11 223
77:11–12 220
77:13 223, 224
77:13–15 221
77:16–20 221–22
77:20 126
78 133, 258
78:7–8 133
78:62 133
78:65 133
78:65–72 133
78:66 133
78:70–72 126
82 212
82:2–7 212
82:7 212
82:8 212
84 216
85 216
86 172n33
86:15 256
87 216
88 216, 217

88:6 109
89 171, 172, 173n34,
    174
89:1 172
89:10 172
89:17 172
89:39 171
89:45 171
93 56
93:4 222
95 56
96 55, 56
96:1–3 55
96:10 55
96:13 55
97 56
98 53–56, 141
98:1–3 55, 141
98:4–6 54, 55
98:7–9 55, 145
98:8 54
102 172n33, 217
103:1 212
103:8 256
103:20–23 212
105 258
106 258
107:25–26 147
111 153
112 153
114 145
116:13 229
119 153, 153
121:6 152
122 172n33
124 172n33
125:4 110
130 217
131 169, 172
131:1–2 170
132 171, 172, 172n29,
    173n34, 174
133 172
135 258
136 150, 258
136:1–3 150
136:4–9 150
136:10–15 150
136:23–26 150
139:19–24 205
142 211n2
143 217
144 173

145 153
145:8 256
146–150 174

Proverbs

1–9 232, 240, 241
1:1 1, 9
1:1–7 232
1:4 241
1:5 71, 241
1:7 238
1:8–9:18 9
1:20–21 233
1:20–33 144, 234
1:22–23 233
2:1–22 232
2:15 228
3:6 228
4:11 228
5:15–20 128
6:16–19 243
8 232, 234
8:1–3 237
8:15–16 168
8:22–31 167
8:30 167
9 144, 233, 238, 240
9:1–6 144, 209, 231–38
9:3 144, 236
9:7–12 236, 238
9:10–12 238
9:13–18 209, 231–38
9:14 236
10–31 239, 240, 241
10:1 9, 241
10:1–4 116–17
10:1–22:16 239
10:2 139
10:3 117
10:4 238
10:9 228
10:17 136
10:18 243
10:20 139
11:5 228
12:1 136
12:17 243
12:19 243
12:22 243
14:1 235
14:1–7 209, 238–44
14:5–12 239

14:8–15 239
14:15–32 239
16:23 140
20:1 140
22:17 9, 233
22:17–24:34 239
24:23 9, 233
25 9
25–29 9
25:1 9, 233
25:1–29:27 239
26:4–6 140, 240
26:7 109
26:8 136
26:11 136
26:18–19 136
26:23 40
30:1 9, 233
30:1–33 239
30:20 154
31 153
31:1 9, 233
31:1–9 239
31:10 240n16
31:10–31 35, 153, 239,
    240n16

Ecclesiastes

1:1 162
1:1–11 73, 162, 245
1:2 73, 162, 245
1:3–11 162
1:9 163
1:12 162, 245
1:12–12:7 73, 130,
    162, 244, 245
1:14 163
1:16 163
2:12 163
2:24–26 244
3:12–14 244
3:22 244
4:1 163
5:8–9 163
5:18–22 244
7:27 162, 246
8:15 244
9:7–10 244
9:11 248
9:11–12 209, 231,
    244–48
9:12 248
10:20 163

12:1–5 129–30
12:4–5 73
12:8 245
12:8–14 73, 245
12:12 245
12:13–14 162, 246

Song of Songs

1:2 108
1:2–3 121–22
4:1–5:1 127–29
4:4 133–35
4:12–15 128
5:2–6:3 62
7:20 186
8:5–6 117–18

Isaiah

1:1 1
1:5–6 118–19
7:14 10–11, 13
7:15–16 11
7:16 12
8:6–8 12
8:9–10 13
8:10 13
13:10 130
17:12–13 222
27:1 16
40:3 13
40:3–5 13
51:17 229

Jeremiah

1:1 1
14:12 139
19:5 188, 193
25 161
25:11–12 17, 161
25:15–17 229
29 161
29:10 17
29:11 161
32:35 188
51:9 147
51:55 222

Lamentations

1 153
1:1 135–36, 141
1:2 142

1:8 136, 142
1:9 142
1:9–16 142
1:18 142
1:18–22 142
1:20 135
2 153
3 153, 195
3:1 143
3:7–18 143
3:20–22 154
3:21–24 143
3:21–42 154
3:25–43 143
3:28–30 195
3:40–42 143
3:43–66 143
4 153
5 153
5:19–20 136

Ezekiel

23:31–34 229
34 230
39:18 127

Daniel

7 14
7–12 59
7:1 73
7:25 59
9 17, 161
9:1 161
9:2 161
9:24 17, 161
12:1–3 190
12:7 59

Hosea

2:14–15 13
11:1 11

Amos

4:1 127
5:8 130
7:9 138, 139
7:16 138
8:9 130

Micah

7:9 140

Nahum

1:1 258
1:2 255
1:2–8 253–58
1:3 255
1:6 255
1:7 255
1:8 254, 255
1:9 254
1:10 254
1:11–14 254
1:12–13 253
1:14 253
2:1 137
2:3–10 254
2:4 136–37
3:1 131
3:2–3 131, 254
3:4–7 131
3:5–7 253

Haggai

1:1 99
1:15 99
2:10 99

Zechariah

1:1 99
1:7 99
14 14

New Testament

Matthew

1:22–23 12
1:23
2:15 11
3:3 13
3:10 13
3:11–12 14
11:3 14
24 14

Mark

1:1 57
14:36 229

Luke

1:26–38 13

John

1:1–3 237

Acts

4:25 56
13:33 57

1 Corinthians

2:11 68
10:16 229

Colossians

1:15–17 167, 237
2:3 168
2:13–15 14

2 Timothy

3:16–17 11

Hebrews

1:5 57
5:5 57
11:17–19 196
11:19 190

James

2:14–24 191
2:20–24 196
2:26 191

2 Peter

1:20–21 11

Jude

1–2 51

Revelation

12:5 57
12:9 166
13 16
16:19 229
19:15 57
20:7–10 166
21–22 90

AUTHOR INDEX

Abbott, H. Porter 61, 62n1, 96, 96n64
Abrams, M. H. 123, 123n25, 124n28
Abrams, R. D. 51, 51n17
Alter, Robert 3, 4, 20, 22, 23, 27, 28, 41, 42,
    43n75, 43n77, 44, 64, 64n8, 69n23, 96, 100,
    100n67, 107, 107n1, 112, 113n9, 122, 265
Aristotle 48, 48n2, 63, 124
Arnold, Matthew 24
Augustine 41, 123, 123n21, 156, 180, 180n3

Baden, Joel S. 44n80
Bakhtin, Mikhail M. 158, 158n3
Bal, Mieke 36, 76, 76n44
Barbour, Jennifer 162, 162n16
Bar-Efrat, Shimon 28, 28n25, 89n51, 103n72
Barthes, Roland 29, 29n29, 64
Bartholomew, Craig G. 25n15
Beal, Timothy K. 35, 35n48, 35n49, 91, 91n56
Beardsley, M. 3, 27, 27n21, 27n22, 28
Berlin, Adele 28, 28n25, 77n47, 91n57
Black, Max 126, 126n30
Bloom, Harold 19n2
Boda, Mark J. 68n22
Boff, C. 37, 37n56
Booth, Wayne C. 67, 67n19, 70n29
Bostrom, G. 239n9
Breed, Brendan 33, 33n43, 34, 34n44
Brueggemann, W. 54, 54n25, 195, 195n19, 226,
    238n8
Bullinger, W. W. 124, 124n27, 138n40
Buth, Randall 150n48
Byargeon, R. W. 238, 238n7

Carr, David M. 43, 43n79
Chatman, Seymour 62, 62n4, 89n52

Chavalas, M. 197n23
Childs, Brevard 41, 41n71, 170, 170n27
Clines, David J. A. 31, 31n35, 31n36, 32, 34
Coleridge, Samuel Taylor 58
Collins, John J. 21n7, 50n13
Cook, Stephen L. 12, 13
Culley, R. C. 29, 29n31
Cunningham, Conor 123n22

deClaisse-Walford, Nancy 172n30
Dell, Katharine J. 20n4, 51, 248n27
Derrida, Jacques 19n2, 30, 32, 43
Dickens, Charles 91
Dinkler, Michal Beth 28n26
Doty, W. G. 50, 50n13
Dube, Musa W. 38n63
Dubrow, Heather 58, 58n31

Eco, Umberto 58, 58n30
Elliott, Mark 20n5
Emerton, J. M. 43n78
Enns, Peter 190n12
Eshkenazi, Tamara C. 70n28
Exum, Cheryl 31, 31n37, 35, 36n50

Firth, David G. 76, 77n46
Fish, Stanley 33, 33n41, 34
Fishbane, Michael 159n10
Fisher, Loren R. 8
Fokkelmann, J. P. 28, 28n25
Forster, E. M. 62, 91
Foster, Benjamin R. 115n10
Fowler, Alastair 51
Fowler, E. 141, 141n41

288 AUTHOR INDEX

Fox, Michael V. 73n35, 245n24
Frow, John 90, 90n53, 95, 95n62, 126, 126n31

Garrett, Duane 119n16, 120, 120n17
Geller, Steven A. 112, 112n7, 120, 120n18
Genette, Gerald 29, 29n28, 45, 64, 67, 67n18, 68, 75, 75n37, 96, 96n65, 180n1
Gottwald, Norman K. 36, 36n53, 36n54, 37, 37n55
Grayson, A. K. 48n3
Green, Graham 68
Greenblatt, Stephen 39, 39n65, 40
Grimm, Jacob 48
Grimm, Wilhelm 49
Guest, Deryn 38n59
Gunkel, Hermann 4, 20, 21, 40, 48, 48n6, 49, 49n7, 50, 154

Hallo, W. W. 19, 119, 119n15
Harshav, Benjamin 27n20, 124n29
Hartman, Geoffrey 19, 19n2
Havea, Jione 38n62
Hays, Richard B. 160, 160n12
Heim, Knut 239, 239n11
Hempfer, K. 53n24
Herman, David 62, 62n3, 63, 63n6, 65n11, 65n12, 65n13, 66, 66n14, 66n15, 66n16, 66n17, 67, 67n20, 68, 90n54, 99, 100n66, 101, 101n69
Herman, Luc 65n10
Herodotus 82
Hirsch, E. D. 26, 26n16
Ho, Peter C. W. 170, 172, 172n31, 172n32, 173, 173n34, 173n35, 174, 174n36, 174n37, 174n38, 212
Holmstedt, Robert D. 122, 122n20
Humboldt, Wilhelm von 24
Hwang, Jerry 38n62

Irigaray, Luce 35, 35n49
Iser, Wolfgang 33, 33n39

Jahn, Manfred 76n43
Jakobson, Roman 120, 120n18
James, Henry 89, 89n52, 155, 155n55, 155n56, 259, 259n2
Janowski, Bernd 57n28
Jauss, Hans-Robert 33, 33n40
Jerome 41, 57, 156
Josephus 41, 156

Kaiser, Walter 14
Kawashima, Robert S. 42, 42n74

Kirk-Duggan, C. A. 37, 37n57, 39
Knierem, Rolf 50, 50n13
Koosed, Jennifer L. 32n3
Kraus, H.-J. 49, 49n10
Kristeva, Julia 157, 157n1, 157n2, 158, 159
Kugel, James 42, 42n73, 111, 111n4, 112, 112n5, 112n6, 113, 113n9, 116, 116n12, 122, 156, 156n57, 156n58, 242, 242n19
Kynes, Will 20n4, 51, 51n19, 51n20, 52, 52n21, 52n22, 56, 158, 165n19, 232, 232n2

Lau, Peter H. W. 38n62
Lauretis, Teresa de 37, 37n58
Leitch, V. B. 19n2
LeMon, J. M. 115n11
Lentricchia, F. 30n34
Letzen-Dies, F. 50n13
Levenson, Jon D. 21n7, 192n14
Levinas, Emmanuel 35
Lewis, C. Day 123
Lewis, C. S. 25, 25n13
Long, V. Phillips 94, 94n60, 94n61
Longman, Tremper, III 8, 9, 14, 19n1, 21n6, 48n4, 52n21, 52n23, 59n33, 100, 117n13, 117n14, 123n23, 127, 131, 136, 144n43, 146n44, 147n47, 156, 161n14, 161n15, 163n17, 165n18, 166, 168n24, 171n28, 174n39, 184n8, 187n10, 226n7, 231n1, 239n10, 240n17, 241n18, 245n22, 245n23
Lowth, Robert 24, 110, 111, 111n2, 111n3, 122

Man, Paul de 19n2, 32, 43
Martin, W. 124, 124n26, 137n38, 137n39
Matthews, V. 197n23
Mays, H. G. 222n5
Mbuvi, Andrew M. 38n63
Mbuwayesango, Dora R. 38n63
McCann, J. Clinton 172n30
McConnell, Walter 156n59
Middleton, J. Richard 192, 192n14, 192n15, 193–96, 196n21
Miller, J. Hillis 19n2
Mitchell, David C. 172n30
Moberly, R. Walter L. 192n14
Moore, Stephen D. 40n66, 44, 44n81
Mowinckel, Sigmund 49, 49n8
Muilenburg, James 22, 50, 50n12

Nazarov, Konstatin 75n40, 76, 76n42
Newman, Michael 63n7
Noegel, Scott 119, 119n16, 120
Notarius, Tania 150n49

O'Connor, Michael 122, 122n19
Origen. 123, 123n22, 156, 181, 182n5
Orisini, G. N. G. 49, 49n11

Pardes, Ilana 43n76
Paul, S. 128n33
Paytner, Helen 36, 36n52
Pemberton, Glenn 54, 54n26, 195, 195n20, 226,
    226n8
Phelan, James 65, 66, 71, 71n31
Philo 41
Pike, Kenneth 48n5, 52
Pixley, G. V. 37, 37n56
Plantinga, Alvin 32
Plato 48, 48n2, 63, 101
Polzin, Robert M. 29n32
Poythress, Vern S. 48n5
Prichett, Stephen 24, 24n9, 24n11, 24n12, 25,
    25n14, 75, 75n38, 75n39
Puckett, Kent 63, 63n5, 70n29, 76n41, 92n58

Quintilian 124

Rabinowitz, Peter J. 65, 66, 71, 71n31
Rad, Gerhard von 40
Ranke, Leopold von 40
Richards, I. A. 125, 125n29

Said, Edward 38, 38n61
Salinger, J. D. 72, 72n33, 102
Sandoval, Timothy 159, 159n7, 159n8
Saussure, Ferdinand de 28, 28n27, 29, 30,
    30n33, 66
Schwally, Friedrich 40
Seow, C.-L. 34n45
Sherwood, Yvonne 40, 41n70, 130n34
Skehan, Patrick 235n4
Sneed, Mark R. 51, 51n18
Sommers, Benjamin D. 159n10, 160n13
Sternberg, Meir 27, 28, 28n23, 69, 69n24,
    69n25, 77, 77n45, 83, 83n49
Stewart, David 38, 38n60

Stokes, Ryan E. 166n22
Strawn, Brent A. 115n11, 123, 123n24
Strickland, Geoffrey 26, 26n17, 50n14
Strong John T. 12, 13
Sweeney, Marvin A. 159n6

Todorov, Tzvetan 29, 29n30, 51n16, 64
Troeltsch, Ernst 20n6
Tuell, Steven S. 12, 13

Uspensky, Boris 77, 77n47, 78

Vanhoozer, Kevin J. 33, 33n42, 50n14
Vervaeck, Bart 65n10

Wafawanaka, Robert 38, 38n64
Waltke, Bruce K. 239n13, 239n14
Walton, John H. 71n32, 123n23, 148n47,
    166n21, 187n10, 197n23
Warhol, Robin 34, 34n46, 34n47
Warren, Austin 51, 51n15
Washington, Harold 40, 40n67, 40n68, 40n69
Watson, W. G. E. 150n50
Weiser, Arthur 49, 49n9
Weiss, Meir 25n15
Weitzman, Steven 24n10
Wellek, Rene 51, 51n15
Wellhausen, Julius 21, 21n8, 40, 43
Whybray, R. N. 235n5
Willgren, David 174n38
Williams, Michael 84n50
Williams, P. 38n61
Wilson, Gerald 170, 170n26, 172, 172n29, 174,
    174n38, 212
Wimsatt, W. K., Jr. 3, 27, 27n21, 27n22, 28
Woudstra, Marten H. 147n45

Yoo, Philip J. 70n26
Younger, K. Lawson 148n46

Zenger, Erich 172n30

SUBJECT INDEX

acrostics 152–54, 255–56
anthropomorphism 140–41, 185
author 9–14, 25–27, 67–70
authorial intention 8–14, 18, 66. *See also* location of meaning

character/characterization 89, 90–95
  evaluation of 83–88
  motivations 78–83
  physical description 92–95
  shaped by dialogue 102–3
chiasm 152

deconstruction 29–32
dialogue 99–104
discourse/story 62, 88
Documentary Hypothesis 21

ellipsis 109–10

fabula/sjuzet 62, 88
feminist interpretation 34–36
focalization 69–70, 75–88
form criticism 21, 48–50

genre 47–59
  definition 47–48, 51–52
  identification (examples) 179–82, 187–88,
    212–13, 217, 224, 226, 232–33, 240–41,
    245–46, 248–49, 253–54, 258–59
  reading strategy 57–59
  signals 50
grammatical parallelism 120–22

historical-critical method 20–22
hyperbole 145–48

ideal/implied reader 71–75
ideological interpretation 34–39
imagery. *See* poetry, conventions of
implied author 10, 67–68
inclusio 151
intertextuality 157–75

location of meaning 7–18
  author 9–14, 25–27, 67–70
  reader 15–17, 71–75
  text 8–9, 27–29

Marxist interpretation 36–37
memoir 69–70, 74–75
merism 151–52
metaphor 124–31
meter 156
metonymy 137–40
mimesis 63

narratee 71–75
narrative, conventions of
  description 61–64
  discourse/story 62, 88
  fabula/sjuzet 62, 88
  narrator 63, 67–70, 91
narratology 64–67
New Criticism 27–28, 65, 67
New Historicism 39–41
New Testament use of Old Testament 10–14

parallelism. *See* poetry, conventions of
personification 141–45
plot 88–90
Psalms, editing of 168–75
poetry, conventions of 107–56
  acrostics 152–54, 255–56
  anthropomorphism 140–41, 185
  chiasm 152
  ellipsis 109–10
  hyperbole 145–48
  imagery 122–48
    hyperbole 145–48
    metaphor 124–31
    metonymy 137–40
    personification 141–45
    simile 132–37
    synecdoche 137–40
  inclusio 151
  merism 151–52
  meter 156
  parallelism 110–22
    analysis of (examples) 213–16, 217–23,
      224–26, 227–30, 234–37, 241–44, 247–48,
      249–51, 255–58, 261–64
    grammatical 120–22
    semantic 110–20
  refrain 150–51
  sound plays 154–55
  terseness 107–10
  verbs in poetry 149–50
  voice (poetic) 155–56, 216–17, 223–24, 226,
    230, 233–34, 241, 246, 249, 254–55, 259–60
point of view. *See* focalization
postcolonial interpretation 38

poststructuralist approaches 29–32
  deconstruction 29–32
  feminist interpretation 34–36
  ideological interpretation 34–39
  Marxist interpretation 36–37
  postcolonial interpretation 38
  queer interpretation 37–38

queer interpretation 37–38

redaction criticism 21–22
reader 15–17, 71–75
reader-response interpretation 33–34
refrain 150–51
Russian Formalism 27, 62, 120

semantic parallelism 110–20
setting 95–96
simile 132–37
sjuzet 62, 88
sound plays 154–55
space 95–96
story 62, 88
structuralism 28–29, 66
synecdoche 137–40

terseness 107–10
text 8–9, 27–29
time 78, 96–99

verbs in poetry 149–50
verisimilitude 63
voice (poetic). *See* poetry, conventions of